THE DARKNESS BECKONS

MARTYN FARR

THE DARKNESS BECKONS

The History and Development of Cave Diving

Foreword by Dr Bill Stone

Diadem Books · London

Cave Books · St. Louis, Missouri

UK COPYRIGHT DETAILS

Copyright © 1991 by Martyn Farr

Published in 1991 by Diadem Books, London

Trade enquiries to Hodder and Stoughton Ltd.,
Mill Road, Dunton Green, Sevenoaks, Kent TN13 2YA

British Library and Cataloguing in Publication Data:
Farr, Martyn
   The Darkness Beckons. – 2nd ed.
   1 The History and Development of Cave Diving
   I. Title
   797.2
   ISBN 0-906371-87-2

Photoset by Vitaset, Paddock Wood

Printed and bound by Butler and Tanner, Frome

US COPYRIGHT DETAILS

Copyright © 1991 by Martyn Farr

Published in 1991 by Cave Books, St Louis, Missouri

Trade enquiries to Cave Books,
4700 Amberwood Drive, Dayton, Ohio 45424

Library of Congress Cataloguing in Publication Data:
Farr, Martyn
   The darkness beckons: the history and development of cave diving
   Martyn Farr: foreword by Bill Stone
      p. cm.
   Includes bibliographical references and index.
   ISBN 0-939748-32-0
   1. Cave-diving – Great Britain – History.   2. Cave-diving – History
I. Title
   GV200.63.F37   1991   81-4075
   796.5'25-dc20   CIP

Published in Australia in collaboration with the Cave Divers Association of Australia

PHOTOGRAPHIC CREDITS

Monochrome illustrations (*denoted by page number*): 2-3, 14 John Zumrick, 19, 20 Norbert Casteret collection, 21 Bob Leakey collection, 22 Graham Balcombe collection, 25 Siebe Gorman, 26 Chris Howes collection (left), Museum of Porrentruy (right), 29 Foundation Cousteau, 35,37,38(2) Frank Frost, 39,40,41 Hywel Murrell, 42 Jim Stark, 43,44,47,51,52,53,54,55,56 Balcombe collection, 57 Leakey collection, 58,59 Balcombe collection, 61 Phill Davies collection, 62,63 Bill Mack collection, 66,67 David Hunt, 68 Davies collection, 69 Martyn Farr, 70,71 Phill Davies, 72 David Hunt, 74 Phill Davies, 76 R. S. Howes, 79,81 Martyn Farr, 82,83 Dennis Brindle, 85 Pete Livesey, 86 Martyn Farr, 89 Ken Pearce collection, 91 Tony Morrison, 92 Pete Livesey, 94,97 Martyn Farr, 98,100,102 Clive Westlake, 104 Farr collection, 105 Clive Westlake, 109 Farr collection, 110 Leo Dickinson, 111 Chris Howes, 112(left) Leo Dickinson, 112(right) Chris Howes, 113 Rob Palmer, 114 Clive Gardener, 115 Rob Palmer, 117,118 Gavin Newman, 120,121,122,123 Martyn Farr, 124,125 Clive Westlake, 127(3) Martyn Farr, 130(2),131,133 Martyn Farr, 134 Graham Wooley, 135 Neil Robertson, 137 Martyn Farr, 138 Alf Latham, 140(2 left) Lindsay Dodd, 140(right) Martyn Farr, 146,147 Oliver Statham, 148 Ian Plant, 151(2) Clive Westlake, 154 Roland Stockham, 156 Bryan Schofield, 159 Clive Westlake, 163,166(2) Farr collection, 170(top and bottom right) Foundation Cousteau (Fradin collection), 170(bottom left) Raymond Fradin, 173,176 Jochen Hasenmayer collection, 179 Russell Carter, 180 Claude Magnin, 181 Christian Locatelli, 182 Cyrille Brandt, 184(left) Francis Le Guen collection, 184(right) Claude Touloumdjian collection, 185(top) Russell Carter, 185(b.left) Marc Debatty, 185(b.right) John Cordingley, 186 Cyrille Brandt, 188(2) Mario Luini, 189(top) Cyrille Brandt, 189 Pierre Martin, 190,191 Fabrice Coffrini, 192 Cyrille Brandt, 195 Hasenmayer collection, 199 Vladimir Kisseljov, 201(3) Gleb Semionov (Kisseljov collection), 203,204(3) Garry Salsman collection, 205 Lewis Holzendorff, 206 Sheck Exley, 207 Ken Lancaster, 208,210 Wes Skiles, 215 Leo Dickinson, 216(2) Bill Stone, 221(3), 222 Ron Simmons, 224 Martyn Farr, 226,227 George Benjamin collection, 229,230(2),231,232(left) Martyn Farr, 232(right) Bill Stone, 234(2) John Zumrick, 235(left) Gavin Newman, 235(centre and right) Bill Stone, 237 Ned DeLoach, 243(top) Hugh Morrison, 243(bottom) Ian Lewis, 244 Hugh Morrison, 247 Morrison collection, 249,250,252 Le Guen collection, 254,255,256(3),257(2) Peter Rogers, 262 Roger Ellis, 263 Charles Maxwell collection, 269(top) Wes Skiles, 269(b.left) Gavin Newman, 269(b.right) Leo Dickinson, 272 Martyn Farr.

Colour illustrations: *between pages 60 and 61* 1 Phill Davies collection, 2 Martyn Farr, 3 Davies collection, 4 Martyn Farr; *between pages 120 and 121* 5 Gavin Newman, 6 Rob Palmer, 7 Leo Dickinson, 8,9 Martyn Farr, 10 Farr archive; *between pages 180 and 181* 11,12,13 Raymond Fradin, 14 Marc Jasinski, 15 John Cordingley, 16 Francis Le Guen, 17 John Adams, 18 Francis Le Guen, 19 John Adams, 20 Cyrille Brandt, 21 Alain Vaugniaux; *between pages 216 and 217* 22 Wes Skiles, 23 Leo Dickinson, 24 Wes Skiles, 25 Leo Dickinson, 26 Gavin Newman, 27,28 Wes Skiles, 29,30,31 Gavin Newman, 32 Bill Stone, 33 Dennis Williams, 34 Rob Palmer; *between pages 228 and 229* 35 Martyn Farr, 36,37 George Benjamin collection, 38,39 Martyn Farr, 40 John Zumrick, 41,42 Ned DeLoach; *between pages 240 and 241* 43 John Zumrick, 44,45 Bill Stone, 46 Hugh Morrison, 47,48 Charles Maxwell, 49 Gerald Favre, 50 Charles Maxwell, 51 Francis Le Guen, 52 Peter Rogers, 53 Francis Le Guen; *front cover* Martyn Farr; *back cover* Gavin Newman.

CONTENTS

MAPS AND CROSS SECTIONS IN THE TEXT

INTRODUCTION

It is now eleven years since the first publication of *The Darkness Beckons*, a period that has seen tremendous advances in the sport of cave diving. The bold explorations of the world's most challenging cave systems that have taken place during this time represent a major evolution, no less momentous in our sport than the ascents of the world's highest mountains in the 1950s for mountaineering, or the expansion in ocean sailing that followed Chichester's solo voyage round the world in 1967.

I originally conceived the book as a portrayal of cave diving in the United Kingdom with a modest international chapter that served to illustrate the contrasts that existed between regions. The second edition was to be an update of the first book but it soon became apparent that this would fail to do justice to the outstanding explorations that had taken place around the world in the 1980s. During this period cave diving had become a truly international sport, with cave divers joining their counterparts from other countries to mount ambitious projects in far flung sites, and a steady exchange of techniques and information. These contacts had broken down the old national insularities and cave divers everywhere had broadened their horizons.

Thus the book, though still written from a British perspective, now has a significant international dimension notably from the key European areas and those of North America. The major technological advances that have accompanied the quest to make longer and deeper dives are also covered: the use of scooters; the tactics for moving large supplies of cylinders through underwater passages; the complex chemistry of mixed gas and the equally complex decompression involved in its use; the development of habitats and a new generation of rebreathers.

In international terms cave divers come either from the world of caving or that of open water diving and are influenced in their objectives, ideas and tactics by their parent sport. Thus while the first edition was written primarily from a caver's perspective, this new edition reflects, to a far greater degree, diving mores and attitudes.

As a result of all these disparate elements, many of which fell into focus during the final stages of design, the book has developed in a rather haphazard manner. Despite the reworking we are left with a disproportionately lengthy section on the British history with many of the original photographs returned. I make no apologies for this, preferring to take the stand that the British case study provides an exemplary profile of the caving roots of the sport typical of other inland areas where diving grew out of speleology.

By contrast much of the international section, which has a heavy emphasis on the clear water systems of Florida, Mexico, Australia and France, typifies the approach that has evolved from open-water, or diving origins.

Even with the book's greater scope, activities in many nations where there is cave diving have been omitted. In the fullness of time, and with further research, I may be able to present a more balanced portrayal of the sport world-wide, but this has proved too great a task on this occasion. Despite these omissions the book – in terms of text, photos and diagrams – is over twice as big as the first edition. I hope that this will prompt all those who have the first book to buy the second, and thereby support this ongoing chronicle of extreme behaviour. We are witnessing one of the great exploration sagas of our time, and I thus have no hesitation in commending the book to all adventure sportspeople. The events that have taken place in this extreme environment will surely strike a chord with anyone who seeks challenging recreation in the natural world.

Metric or Imperial?

In the first edition the imperial unit of measurement was adopted, whereas here, other than in the case of personal quotation, all distances and depths are given in metric measures with imperial equivalents incorporated (usually at the final extent of an exploration) to make the book more 'user friendly' for those who still prefer the imperial measure.

Acknowledgements

The second edition of the book has been a marathon effort and I would like to give a sincere vote of thanks to all those contributors who waited so patiently as the book was assembled.

Firstly there are those experts who have assisted me with research and advice for the international section notably Sheck Exley, Jochen Hasenmayer, Vladimir Kisseljov, Charles Maxwell, Hugh Morrison, Bill Stone, Pete Rogers, Tim Williams, and especially Cyrille Brandt who in every respect has been an outstanding bastion of support. For additional surveys and other invaluable data I am also indebted to Francis Le Guen, Olivier Isler, Claude Touloumdjian and Oliver Knab.

In Britain, Graham Balcombe provided much advice in the historical sphere and Jack Sheppard, and Dr John Bevan have also assisted in this respect. To give an accurate picture of modern developments I have relied heavily on advice from Geoff Yeadon and Rob Palmer and I am particularly indebted to John Cordingley who has answered every request for advice, information, surveys and photographs.

Two magazines that have been valuable sources of information are *Info Plongée* (France) and *Descent* (Britain) whose editor, Chris Howes, has given me much useful advice.

All the photographers are credited on page 4 and I thank them all for their contributions and also those who submitted photos that were not used. A number of photographers made special efforts for the book, either by allowing me to retain valuable collections of pictures for a long period or by responding to frantic last-minute requests to fill some particular gap: John Adams, Nick Baker, George Benjamin, Cyrille Brandt, Russell Carter, John Cordingley, Leo Dickinson, Raymond Fradin, Chris Howes, Francis Le Guen, Marc Jasinski, Charles Maxwell, Gavin Newman, Rob Palmer, Pete Rogers, Garry Salsman, Wes Skiles, Ron Simmons, Bill Stone, Clive Westlake and John Zumrick.

Constructive criticism has been provided by many, but in particular by Bill Stone who read the whole manuscript prior to writing his impressive and perceptive Foreword. I am humbled by his unstinting efforts.

There are many others, not mentioned above or in the photo credits who have given valuable advice or assistance including Roger Cowles, Nick Geh, Frank Loftus, Alex McCormick, Jill Neate, Hubert Odier, Norman Pace, Madame Rossignol (Foundation Cousteau), Petra Sluka, and finally my publisher, Ken Wilson, who has supported, cajoled and inspired me throughout.

MARTYN FARR
Crickhowell
South Wales, 1991

FOREWORD

Cave diving has been described by some as the most dangerous sporting pursuit known to man. In Europe the high number of accidents which occurred in the early, experimental phase of the sport has now diminished, but in the United States, despite the availability of organised training programmes, no fewer than six divers perished in the springs of northern Florida alone in the first nine months of 1990. These sobering statistics underline the sport's inherent seriousness. So the questions are: why do it, is it worthwhile and need it be so dangerous?

Those at the cutting edge of this rapidly evolving high-tech endeavour would, if asked these questions by a lay person, likely respond that it is not all that dangerous for someone who knows what they are doing and that it is the lure and challenge of exploring the black unknown, one of the last true frontiers remaining on this planet, which cause them to continue. Many of the committed cave divers are quiet and introspective in everyday life, preferring to reserve their inner feelings about the sport for discussion amongst their peers. Even then it is usually done in the form of an anecdotal exchange often laced with wry black humour: of how un-cooperative currents and poor visibility nearly got them into a fix on their last mission or how their partner, riding a high-speed underwater vehicle, hit the ceiling of a flooded subterranean tunnel and snapped the manifold connecting his high-pressure tanks like a brittle stick, dumping his entire gas supply at a point 600m from the entrance. After which they eagerly relate how they had escaped this predicament.

Such bravado is shallow, however, and reveals little more than the standard lay explanations. Those experienced enough to have had close calls know that more than luck is required to enjoy and survive long in this sport.

The subject which is never discussed is fear. The activity is haunted by the ever present possibility of mishap, equipment failure or some other unforeseen event which can lead to panic and eventual death. Good training and preparation reduces this somewhat, but are no substitute for experience. There are two pieces of sage advice which are often passed on from experienced hands to aspiring ones. The first is: you've got to be afraid to panic. The second is: there are old cave divers and bold cave divers, but there are no old, bold cave divers.

Prior to setting off on his record-setting vertical descent of 267m into Mexico's Nacimiento del Rio Mante in the spring of 1989, Sheck Exley commented that he was undertaking the dive in a state of controlled paranoia. And Exley should know. In a career spanning twenty-three years and 3000 cave dives he has had his share of serious problems. Why was he still alive while several of his contemporaries were long dead? 'I pretend that the cave is *actively* out to get me,' Exley said. 'You cannot allow your concentration to slip a second. And all the while you must be thinking: what do I do next . . . if the inconceivable were to happen right now?'

From the earliest days the cave diving community has reviewed and analysed its own incidents and accidents. From these a number of safety rules have emerged: use a continuous guideline from the entrance; reserve two-thirds of your air supply for exit; never dive below forty metres on compressed air; carry a minimum of three sources of reliable under-water lights; and employ full redundancy in all life support apparatus.

Formal cave diving courses now pass on this hard-won knowledge, teaching students to etch these rules and techniques into their procedures, with the result that, despite the rapidly expanding numbers of cave divers, there are fewer accidents. In those few cases involving trained personnel, violations of the depth rule, medical complications and poor judgement were at fault. But in some ways the new knowledge, safer procedures and techniques merely allow divers to probe further into the unknown in an environment which is as unforgiving as the cold vacuum of space. Viljelmar Steffanson, one of the last great polar explorers, once said that 'adventure is the result of incompetence'. The ever more ambitious exploratory projects, the name of the game in underwater speleology is to plan for every eventuality in an effort to prevent a fact-gathering mission from turning into 'an adventure'. Conservatism is better than boldness. Despite this there are occasions when the best laid plans go wrong.

If safety and techniques can be adequately dealt with, there is still the question of why people take up cave diving in the first place. Interestingly, there are two generally accepted reasons, and they depend upon individual background. The differences can best be illustrated by example, and my own experiences are common to many who first entered the sport in the mid-1970s.

In December 1975 I was climbing a dusty trail leading to the San Juan Plateau in Mexico, laden with 300m of rope for a descent into a deep cave called Joya de las Conchas. In front of me, setting a stiff pace, was a solid, muscular Welshman by the name of Martyn Farr. He had travelled to Mexico to visit its spectacular open air pits. When he heard that original exploration was afoot on a remote mountain, he immediately dropped his own plans and teamed up with us. Along the trail Martyn described his project to dive through a series of flooded tunnels in a place called Wookey Hole in England, hoping to reach a giant cavern he believed might exist beneath the Mendip Hills. As I listened to his descriptions of 'one metre visibility, 7°C water temperatures, and underwater constrictions', I silently nodded, smiling all the while with the supportive enthusiasm of a comrade in arms, even though I had never used a Scuba tank in my life. In the privacy of my own thoughts, however, a different opinion was forming: not only was this man insane but he also had a death

wish. The exceptional competence I later witnessed during our push to −495m in Joya de las Conchas convinced me that neither of these factors applied to Martyn. But I was still not convinced of the merits of such extreme measures and resolved never to take up cave diving. The risks seemed too great.

A year later a team of some of the best deep cave explorers in North America began work on the Huautla Plateau in southern Mexico. I was fortunate to be among them. Eventually we were stopped at a depth of −861m at a flooded tunnel, which came to be known as the San Agustin sump. The thing about these unusual features, which all cave explorers eventually come across, is that you find yourself saying, 'Surely, this cave does not end here, it's just filled with water.' A look with a diving mask and lamp did little to dissuade me of this impression, for leading off into the darkness was a cobalt underwater canyon.

Shortly after returning from the expedition I signed up for a Scuba course, intent upon seeing where this tunnel went. Perhaps I convinced myself that the world's deepest cave was waiting to be discovered beyond this obstacle. Suddenly cave diving no longer seemed an insane pursuit. It had personal meaning.

In 1976 learning to be a safe cave diver was fraught with problems. There were no accessible training programmes and self-teaching was required. If you were lucky, you might meet an experienced cave diver who might adopt you as an apprentice. In this respect I was fortunate, as Mike Boon, one of Britain's most experienced cave divers in the 1960s, happened to be passing through Texas on his way to Mexico and heard of my plans to dive the San Agustin sump. He sought me out.

Boon looked me squarely in the eye and then began to question me, a bony finger poking me in the chest.

'So, I hear you've decided to take up cave diving. Dangerous business, you know.'

He then paused, pursing his lips in a twisted grimace. 'Well,' he continued, 'you'd best get it right then.'

Whereupon he informed me that my single Scuba tank with its single regulator was woefully inadequate, that at least two sets were needed, and that I should only use half of one of them for exploration, reserving the remainder for the retreat. He inspected my lights and reel, admonished me to be careful and then left.

I subsequently dived into the San Agustin sump for thirty-five metres with my lightweight tanks, far enough to see that it was still going down into an even larger underwater canyon. I emerged a different person: cold sweat and driving adrenalin swept over me like a wave, along with knowledge – new knowledge of the frontier – of a truly alien world. I knew that I had to return and learn what lay beyond. My experience, charged with the emotion of private triumph and the boost it brings to personal confidence, was not unique. Farr was obviously driven by the same lure at Wookey Hole, as were those who followed him in later years. For me the San Agustin sump came to symbolize the quintessential test of my resolve, of my ability to succeed in life.

Does this obsession make cave diving competitive? The answer is yes, but the competition is not obvious. It is all conducted in a very private, quiet manner removed from the public eye. I believe this contributes to the mystique that surrounds the underwater speleologist. Those on the cutting edge often correspond with one another, matter-of-factly relating their latest success. Diving sites are common, but those in which original exploration may still be carried out are not. Hence a competitive secrecy is the norm.

For the most part, however, there is an unspoken agreement amongst explorers that one will help out another. It was not surprising, therefore, that in 1981, when Jochen Hasenmayer was considering a 200m deep dive in the Vaucluse, Sheck Exley, who was also trying to push the depth record, sent him a vital set of commercial helium oxygen decompression tables.

There is another tenant of the explorer's code: do not steal another's exploration project. In cave exploration circles such 'scooping' is frowned upon. When, in the early 1980s, after a string of Australian successes in Cocklebiddy Cave, Exley suggested an international expedition for the next push, he found that the Australians were not enthusiastic and he therefore shelved the project. Others did not and, while their foray was highly successful, they were regarded as 'pirates' in the international exploration community, and, as a result, the levels of secrecy were tightened a further notch.

After another attempt on San Agustin in 1980, I knew I needed more cave diving experience. I contacted Exley who had just published the results of other dives in Mexico.

When I arrived in Florida I was immediately struck by the differences in equipment. I had been using classic British sump diving equipment of side-mounted tanks and a helmet with three standard miners' electric lamps for redundancy. I felt very out of place when I followed Exley and his partner into Orange Grove Sink. They were wearing huge, steel, twin 104 cu.ft back-mounted tanks. They were dressed in dry suits and their gear – back-up lights, line reels, gap reels and the like – was stowed neatly on a special rigging system. Their mastery of buoyancy control made me feel like a novice. The water clarity amazed me. Having grown used to cold, constricted, low-visibility sumps, seeing unlimited visibility underground for the first time was breathtaking. Then Exley threw a switch on his primary light and the entire scene lit up like something from a science fiction movie. A laser-like beam punched thirty metres across the void outlining the entrance of a giant side tunnel I had not even noticed.

This introduction to Florida cave diving was a revelation which emphasised the differences between 'spring' and 'sump' divers. Sump divers are generally technical cave explorers who have taken up cave diving to further the exploration of a mostly air-filled cave in which they have run into a sump. 'Spring' divers are generally sport divers who have either grown bored with boat, wreck and lake diving or, for the lack of good weather, have been attracted to the gin-clear inland springs. Being far greater in number than their sump diving counterparts (for every sump diver there are probably 200 spring divers in the USA), it was understandable that nearly all fatalities in the 1970s and early 1980s involved open water divers making their first (and last) untrained dive into Florida springs.

Having no access problems that would limit the size and weight of their hardware, spring divers have developed distinctly different styles and techniques from those employed during the early efforts of cave diving, which involved tackling sumps in known dry caves often thousands of metres from the surface. For the most part there has been little cross-breeding of these two groups, except on special expeditions.

There are some spring divers who view cave diving as an expression of machismo. This shallow perception means that their motivation is little more than simple competition, which often ends with a close escape or in some cases death after an attempt to go one up on a more experienced diver. Initiates frequently fail to understand their limitations. It is only through continual trials by fire – from dealing with situations when something really does go wrong – that one truly becomes a cave diver. Hence the story-telling at the pub becomes an important channel for passing on hard learned lessons. Regular study of published dive accounts is also most important.

What separates those who continually pursue cave diving from improperly motivated initiates is the maintenance of respect for the seriousness of each and every dive. As Exley so clearly explained, it is important to develop a sort of rational fear or controlled paranoia so that one is constantly alert.

For those who can develop these qualities the rewards are great. There is the undeniable feeling of personal confidence which comes from being a member of a still extremely small fraternity of dynamic individuals. There is also another reward, which is difficult to explain to those who have not been there: it is the feeling of having explored territory never before seen by man. And there is more. The ability to 'fly' through an apparently endless, air clear tunnel descending into the black, unknown depths is about as close to being an astronaut as it is possible to get.

I suspect that many cave divers view themselves as space explorers born a generation too early. In many respects cave diving is much better. Only twelve space travellers have ever done any original exploration (those landing on the moon), but a serious cave diver can be exploring inner space on any weekend. On a complex exploration mission a cave diver is also likely to be dealing with a more sophisticated array of equipment than that used by spacemen. In exploring the far recesses of long, deep systems this equipment can only become more complex as computer-controlled, closed-cycle life support systems replace traditional open-circuit apparatus. Indeed, the entire brief history of cave diving has been marked by technological progress. Where equipment limitations prevent the successful completion of a project, it is not long before new apparatus or techniques are devised.

Nevertheless, though one section of cave diving endeavour is focused on ever deeper and longer dives, far simpler expeditions are still possible using conventional aqualung equipment. Such projects offer equally interesting exploratory possibilities for cave divers who for reasons of time, resources or taste preference are unable to embark on complex, high technology ventures.

Despite a rich history of human drama, cave diving is still a new pursuit, barely fifty-five years old. This brief time span is underscored by the fact that two of the earliest pioneers, Jack Sheppard and Graham Balcombe, are still around, full of vitality and keenly interested in events in the caving world. Although cave diving will surely develop and expand as a sporting pursuit, presently we are witnessing the zenith of its pioneering stage, which in years to come will be looked back on much as sailing enthusiasts today recall the voyages of Magellan or Drake.

The task of bringing up to date and assembling an interesting and rounded history of cave diving is no mean feat, as much has happened in the ten years since the publication of the now classic first edition of *The Darkness Beckons*. The sport has developed at a breathtaking pace. Even as this second edition was going to press new world records were being set which demanded pause for inclusion. In this blur of stunning accomplishments it is easy to adopt a myopic appreciation for the sophistication of today's technology. As you read of the embryonic efforts of the 1930s and 1940s, put yourself in the shoes of Lavaur, Balcombe, Cousteau and Wells. Their frontiers were just as ominous and daunting as the five-kilometre penetration or the 300m vertical descent are to us today. Should there be any doubt that true exploration is alive and well in the 1990s, read on . . .

BILL STONE
Derwood, Maryland, 1991

ORIGINS

CHAPTER ONE

THE CHALLENGE OF CAVING

A cave is a mysterious place with a compelling fascination: the darkness beckoning. Upon the surface the lie of the land is plain to see. Underground you are confronted by blackness and, without lighting, it is impossible to see even a hand within inches of your face. One becomes, effectively, blind. There is no more disquieting sensation, as any underground explorer will readily admit. There are few who have penetrated this realm and not experienced the real darkness, whether intentionally or unintentionally.

To most, this eternal darkness holds little attraction, but to a select few, the cavers, pot-holers or speleologists, it is their life blood. An innate curiosity coupled with a penchant for physical exertion, generates a challenge and it is the acceptance of this which drives the caver on.

Man has explored the Earth for many thousands of years, and this characteristic curiosity has led him into most of its corners. By land, sea and air the Earth's physical features have been assessed. The South-West Face of Everest and the Eiger North Wall have been visited, seen and conquered. The untouched areas are few in number and those remaining, like the ocean deeps, are very remote. Advances in technology will, no doubt, eventually open new frontiers and allow the exploration of, for example, outer space; but, for the present, we live on a shrinking planet, a world with little room for the pioneer spirit.

Caves, however, offer great potential for discovery. Their exploration has been partial and they have certainly not been fully assessed. Here each foot of progress has been a step into the unknown, with many such steps still to be taken. This is the challenge, the

pitting of one's wits and resources against the cave. Far from being easy, it is exacting both physically and mentally. There are times when it is nothing short of masochism, but other moments provide boundless elation. Personal qualities such as determination and dedication are vitally important, while calculation and adventure draw individuals together in great camaraderie. Thus the search for new caves, new passages, the longest or deepest goes on.

Currently the world's deepest known cave system is the Gouffre Jean Bernard in Haute Savoie, France, where, on the Lapies de Foillis near Samoens, a depth of 1558m was achieved in the early 1980s. At the beginning of 1990 this was increased to 1601m, the result of extending the system upwards, to connect with an entrance situated higher on the mountain. Elaborate surveys have confirmed this record, but the actual figure and depth may well change as time and exploration proceed. Similar explorations are currently in progress in Mexico, where the recently discovered Cueva Cheve system has a realistic depth potential of at least 2600m. So the discoveries continue, deeper and further.

The longest cave is the Mammoth, Flint Ridge system in Kentucky (USA), which boasts over 530km/331 miles of cave. Of course, this is not 530km in one direction, but rather a vast complex of superimposed, interconnecting passageways. Undoubtedly many more miles remain to be discovered and surveyed, and it appears unlikely at present that any other cave could rival it. However, with new finds and connections continually being made it would be foolish to estimate any overall length.

Furthermore, the possibilities of hitherto unexplored regions are now being realised. Here new area records, both for length and depth, are frequently being established. Mexico and South America, New

Left: Fabulous stalactite and stalagmite formations in NoHoch Nah Chich cave, Yucatan, Mexico. This is the cave diver's dream site offering clear conditions, warm water, moderate depth and breathtaking scenery.

Guinea, the Soviet Union and China, each has its contribution to make to the overall picture of world caving. Wherever cave-bearing structures are found, there will cavers be drawn. It is a world of changing people, changing attitudes and changing techniques.

Exploration is constantly being held back by obstacles – sumps, blockages or dead ends – and success is wholly dependent upon progressive attitudes and suitable equipment. The evolution of these has been slow. In consequence, cavers have always been in a minority compared to many other outdoor sportsmen, but for different reasons. It is not expense which dissuades potential explorers, but rather an abhorrence of dark, wet, muddy conditions coupled with real or imagined feelings of claustrophobia. These usually convey a poor public image. Although these factors are taken into account, those who actively follow the sport look beyond to what can be gained in terms of personal satisfaction.

As a certain amount of equipment is needed to further these ends, and because manufacturers are reluctant to produce specific articles for such a limited market, cavers have become masters of im-provisation, using equipment originally designed for other purposes.

Underground, a barrier compels a temporary halt to exploration. Encountering a rock-fall at the end of a passage, for example, often means 'the end'. But not always. If the passage gives any indication of progres-sing beyond the blockage then cavers will attempt to manufacture a route through. This may only entail shifting a boulder or two, but, on the other hand, explosives may be needed. These are increasingly being used to break up obstructions and facilitate their removal by hand.

Attitudes towards a constriction in a passage or a 'squeeze' have also changed. Defying any fear of claustrophobia, some individuals think little of a section perhaps seven to eight inches high (similar to crawling under a car), provided, of course, that there is hope of greater things beyond and that safe return can be guaranteed.

Climbs or vertical ascents have long presented pro-blems. In this case advanced rock climbing techniques may be adopted or possibly the use of scaling poles.

Pits or pitches in the floor of the cave passage have become routine. In the past rope or wire (electron) ladders have been used for such descents, but today single-rope techniques (SRT) are the preferred choice on all but the shortest of vertical sections. With the development of specialised descending (variable-friction abseiling devices) and ascending gear (jumar-type ascenders) any pitch is rendered passable.

At present the deepest shaft in the world is El Sotano in northern Mexico with a drop of 410m/1346ft from the lip (the top) to the floor. Using the SRT, one can descend safely in less than half an hour and climb out again in an hour or less. Again, the Hollenhole, an incredible underground shaft in Austria, is claimed to be an amazing 450m deep, but this is not one sheer drop, rather a multi-pitch vertical cave. Although such pits are spectacular excursions in their own right, they also allow rapid access to subterranean passage systems. Be they underground, or surface in location, a growing number of such pits are being explored as time goes by.

The further one penetrates into a cave the more obstacles one encounters. Those already described are accepted by the majority of cavers, but, when it comes to water, the problems become considerably more serious. Limestone caves are formed by water action and it is not uncommon, therefore, to have to combat wet sections of passage. To alleviate the cold, protective clothing is needed, as is special lighting equipment that cannot be easily extinguished. As regards the former, the wet suit has been universally adopted in British caving circles. This has permitted exploration of the most severe stream caves in comparative comfort and safety. Lakes which hitherto required a dinghy can now be swum, for a suit also provides buoyancy. Many European cavers use special dry suits which, with watertight seals at neck, wrists and ankles, permit greater comfort by allowing room for woollen or thermal undergarments. However, to tear one's dry suit in adverse circumstances could well be fatal, while a tear in a wet suit would only render the exposed area of body uncomfortable. Currently, therefore, it is generally accepted that, where wet caving of a high standard is required, a wet suit is better.

In wet caves efficient, reliable lighting is imperative. Waterproof electrical illumination is superior to lamps with naked flames such as a carbide light. In Britain, miners' rechargeable electric lamps, or the specialist Speleo Technics FX2, are viewed as the best all-round choices, although for long trips or expeditions to isolated areas the carbide lamp is still the most practical.

But techniques and preferences vary from place to place. For example, many Continental cavers generally use dry suits and favour the carbide lamp as the main source of illumination, although the majority also carry an electric light either as an emergency spare or for use on wet pitches. It is the cave itself which dictates the best equipment to use.

Wet caves are always the most sporting, but also the most dangerous owing to hazards such as flooding. In Britain it is flash floods resulting from a sudden downpour in summer or rapidly melting snow in winter which are the most dangerous threat. However, weather reports are available and, with prudence and foresight, trouble spots can be avoided during a period of unreasonable risk.

By following swiftly flowing torrents or descending cascades and waterfalls, one may eventually arrive at a section of passage where the gradient is greatly reduced and the flow imperceptible. Such a section is often known as a canal. Furthermore, the roof may gradually dip until there are but a few inches of air-space between rock and water. To the determined caver it is merely another challenge, for an inch or two of air-space is all one needs. Then slowly and cautiously the examination proceeds. With head tilted to one side, mouth and nose pressing lightly against the roof, the caver gropes his way forward, the helmet and lamp held out ahead. Movement is wary and deliberate: each foothold must be carefully felt and any form of turbulence avoided. It is cold and extremely unnerving, but, while any hope exists, turning back is unthinkable. With luck, only a few metres further on one can pass the obstacle.

Once the initial passage has been made, the watery section or duck no longer appears the barrier it once was. Even so, one must always be mindful of such hazards, especially in wet weather, for with a slight rise in water level whole sections can fill completely. If this happens, one has no choice but to wait patiently in a safe place until the water level subsides or until a rescue party arrives. However, if one knows that the flooded section or sump (siphon) is only a few metres long then it may be possible to take a deep breath and plunge through. This is free diving, a serious procedure fraught with potential dangers.

In terms of exploration, this risky aspect of the sport began in France with Casteret's successful passage of two sumps in Grotte de Montespan in 1922 and in Britain with Sheppard's passage of Swildon's Sump 1 in 1936. Since then many short flooded sections have been conquered in caving areas all round the world and, inevitably, once passed, there are always others keen to repeat the challenge. Thus free diving short sumps is now relatively common, but the procedure should never be undertaken lightly.

To become trapped or entangled on an underwater projection while attempting a free dive is critical. The margin of safety is slight, and comparatively few cavers are prepared to run such a risk in tackling a sump longer than about three metres. The dangers of this technique were made plain in May 1976, when a party of six cavers descended Langstroth Pot in Yorkshire. Their intention was to make a through trip, coming out via a lower cave, having free dived three sumps. Of the six, only one successfully passed the sumps, three died and two had to be rescued.

There are, of course, easy ducks which have ample air-space and are comparatively short in length, for example the Valley Entrance Duck in the Kingsdale Master Cave or the Canal in Little Neath River Cave. These are an accepted part of a sporting trip and no self-respecting caver would hesitate to plunge in, knowing full well that he ran little risk.

The element of danger is important to the caver and real enjoyment of a caving trip can only come if one has successfully equated the hazards with one's own ability to overcome them. Common sense and caution are most important, and many an accident has occurred through a rash decision or momentary lapse in concentration.

Further into the cave one turns a corner and there plainly is the 'end'. This time the roof definitely dips beneath the surface and there is no way through. One's eye catches a leaf or patch of foam rotating quietly in the lethargic current. It is a moment for reflection and a bite to eat before the journey out. Surely the cave doesn't end here? But, without knowing the length of the submerged section, there is no way to continue except for the fully equipped diver. By studying a detailed survey of the cave, one can often make an estimation of how far the cave is likely to extend. Let us say, for example, that the same river which disappears at the sump reappears a mile away at a much lower elevation. Unfortunately, at the lower end of the system the river surges from a deep pool and again it can only be explored by divers. The thing which is almost certain here is that, beyond the final obstacle in the known cave, there is likely to be a dry continuation or extension.

The first course of action is a diligent search of the cave upstream from the termination. There is always hope of finding a high-level bypass, for, as streams cut down through a limestone mass, they inevitably change their course. Thus, as a cave stream abandons one level in favour of a lower one, it leaves an old fossil passage in its wake. This may be completely dry. By following the fossil passage the caver stands a fair chance of reaching the streamway at some lower point, beyond the sump. Such a route has been established at Swildon's Hole in Somerset, and exploration in an upstream direction in Dan-yr-Ogof in South Wales has led to the bypassing of its many sumps through the discovery of routes which lead to substantial extensions.

Unfortunately, in many cases, though there is a strong possibility of a dry extension, there is simply no way of reaching it. There are instances where siphons have prevented all further progress, examples being Gavel Pot in Yorkshire, P8 (Jackpot) in Derbyshire, Swildon's in Somerset and Dan-yr-Ogof in South Wales. Cavers all over the world have cursed when their explorations have been terminated, and in the words of Norbert Casteret, an early French explorer, the sump is 'enemy number one'.

Nonetheless, it was inevitable that sooner or later new techniques would evolve and the ultimate barrier be broken. The cave diver is dedicated to this end. Names such as Graham Balcombe, Mike Boon, Mike Wooding and John Parker are indelibly associated with the major British breakthroughs in this field. The story of their adventures is dramatic, charged with courage, danger and excitement. It is a history of iron-willed individuals prepared to risk all to gain the undying reward of personal achievement. Certain caves will always be associated with them and in a hundred years' time cavers will still pay tribute to the pioneers of underwater speleology.

CHAPTER TWO

THE BEGINNINGS OF CAVE DIVING

There has always been an insatiable curiosity about caves and attempts to pass sumps extend well back to the early development of caving. In 1777 William Bray wrote of an early attempt to pass the Buxton Water rising at Peak Cavern, in Derbyshire:

At the distance of about seventy-five yards from the entrance the rock came down so close to the water that it precluded all further passage; but, as there was reason to believe from the sound that there was a cavern beyond, about four years ago a gentleman determined to try if he could not dive under the rock and rise in the cavern beyond; he plunged in, but, as was expected, struck his head against the rock, fell motionless to the bottom and was dragged out with difficulty.

Casteret's Montespan Dives

Many early attempts to free-dive sumps went unrecorded and most were doomed to failure. The first recorded success did not take place until 1922, when the twenty-five year old Frenchman Norbert Casteret made an incredibly bold free-diving assault upon the Grotte de Montespan in the Pyrenees. On his first solo trip into the cave Casteret dared to tackle an icy cold sump in complete darkness:

Neck-deep in the water as I was, I nevertheless considered the rashness of persevering alone in so hazardous an undertaking. Several possibilities came to mind. After weighing these various chances in the awful silence and loneliness, I still decided if possible to force the barrier, impregnable though it seemed.

Putting my candle on a projection of the wall, I inhaled air for an immersion of two minutes (to me a familiar procedure). Then I plunged, one hand ahead, the other touching the ceiling. I felt the bumps and contours of the ceiling with infinite care; I was blind, with finger-tips for eyes. I had not only to go ahead, but to think about getting back. Suddenly, as I was going forward in this fashion, my head emerged; I could breathe.

There was no telling where I was; the darkness was complete. Obviously I had forced a siphon, a tunnel with a submerged ceiling. I turned tail at once, and plunged in the opposite direction, for in such circumstance nothing is more dangerous than to lose one's sense of direction.

Below: Norbert Casteret in Montespan (left) and a reconstruction after his second dive through the first sump (right).

Above: Norbert Casteret with his mother and his wife.

He returned the next day, equipped with candles and matches wrapped in a bathing cap.

At the siphon I took the precaution of steering in exactly the same direction as I had before, so as to find the air pocket. I came up safely with my eyes and nose just out of water. I shook my dripping bathing cap to dry it before lighting a candle. The flickering light reached but a few yards; it showed me the ceiling parallel to the water, with only a thin air-space between . . . After a hundred yards I reached a clay bank at the entrance to a vast chamber . . . The ceiling rose to a height of ten to twelve metres, and the stream was half-buried under great blocks fallen from above. The hall was adorned with beautiful stalagmite cascades. I crossed it, and started wading again . . . Having got past an enormous pillar I was faced with a new and deadly looking siphon . . .

Repeating a manoeuvre already familiar but none the less breath-taking, I dived through this siphon as well. It seemed perceptibly longer than the first. I was now locked in the bosom of the shades by a double barrier. The loneliness was tremendous; I struggled against an uneasiness slowly turning to anguish . . .

Harried by cold and apprehension, I found I might as well go on as go back. I had to crawl for some distance in the water, in a small gallery whose low ceiling sent down a veritable shower which kept putting out my candle . . . Finally it brought me to a hall much vaster than the first.

After making a thorough examination of this second chamber to try to find a dry exit, Casteret concluded:

I had no choice but to go back the way I had come. This I accomplished with increasing exhaustion . . . I passed the worst of the two siphons only on my second attempt, having dived at too great an angle the first time . . . I came out chilled to the bone, with night upon me.

This must certainly rate as one of the most audacious explorations in caving history. Such actions would clearly be regarded as rash today, but Casteret seems to have calculated the risks and advanced to each new stage with steely judgement. A clue to his amazing motivation in this exploration is found in the introduction to his classic book *Ten Years Under the Earth*. In this he explains how caving led to an interest in pre-history, geology and subterranean hydrology. At the age of eighteen he was drafted into the Army and went to serve on the Western Front. Returning safely from the war he resumed his studies and his caving activities. 'My mind was now matured under fire, my body schooled in hardship and ready for the risks I was sure to encounter.' He also noted that he was very fit and agile as a champion runner, jumper and swimmer. Under these circumstances the risks of free diving these two sumps may not have represented too daunting a prospect for one who had survived four years of trench warfare.

Casteret had also become fascinated by archeology and, in addition, was subsequently influenced by another celebrated explorer and geologist, Edouard Alfred Martel. After these initial explorations, Casteret soon returned to examine the caves more thoroughly, making important archeological discoveries in the process. Martel later commented:

. . . he made his astonishing find by a piece of unparalleled daring: he plunged under a submerged ceiling into the shadows of an underground river, braving a tunnel whose length he could not know. As he neither drowned nor cracked his skull at the first attempt, the adventure whetted his appetite. This perilous feat is now one of his professional tools.

Leakey's Dive in Gaping Gill

In Britain the outstanding explorations of Bob Leakey must also be acknowledged. In May 1941, having gained entry to Mossdale Caverns in Yorkshire, Leakey made an amazingly bold solo exploration, passing through a series of three short sumps to reach

Above: Bob Leakey in A.G. Pot and (below) a reconstruction of his free dive in Disappointment Pot, Gaping Gill, Yorkshire.

Giant's Hall. These dives were later removed by lowering the level of the floor on the downstream side. Leakey's subsequent exploration of this system was to yield nearly nine kilometres of passage, making it, at that time, Britain's longest cave. Another notable feat was his passage of the sump terminating Disappointment Pot in January 1944. Leakey was a most exceptional individual and, like Casteret, seemingly oblivious to the cold. As at Mossdale, his approach to sump exploration was simply to strip off all clothing, take a deep breath and slide in:

I had to go in backwards and feel with my feet as to where it went, and I disappeared under the water entirely. I then found one of my toes went upwards to what seemed to be higher than my head, and I wedged myself into the hole and pushed with my feet like heck. Stones collapsed at the far end. I had to do this about two or three times just pushing at stones, between breaths, naked, and eventually managed to push the stones away and made what I felt was a big enough hole for me to get through . . .

It seemed that my toes came out at the surface; it's rather difficult to be quite sure if they came out or not. I then went through

head first and found that I could get my head out, but I only just did it . . . it was an awful struggle. I eventually managed to squeeze through the boulders and could hear the water roaring away.

Leakey's dive, and the subsequent removal of the sump, proved the key to access beyond Hensler's Passage of Gaping Gill, thus avoiding the need to rig the 110m main shaft. Few other sites would ever yield to such an approach.

The Mystery of Fontaine de Vaucluse

Not only were there multitudes of underground sumps but there were also many large, clear, inviting resurgence lakes awaiting attention. The most celebrated of these is the Fontaine de Vaucluse, near Avignon in southern France. This resurgence issues below a 300m cliff and has always aroused curiosity. Edouard Alfred Martel, the acknowledged father of modern speleology, recognised it as 'one of the most powerful springs on the surface of the globe'. A trickle flows from it all the year round until March, when it erupts in a rage of water which swells the River Sorgue to flood. Unabated, it flows for five weeks and then subsides. This phenomenon had occurred every year in recorded history, but no one knew what exactly happened to discharge the amazing flood. The simplest theory regarding such an intermittent natural fountain was that an underground siphon tapped a pool of water lying higher than the water level of the open-air pool. However, the overflow of an inner pool due to heavy rain could not explain Vaucluse, because the flow did not entirely respond to rainfall. It had to be an unusually complex system.

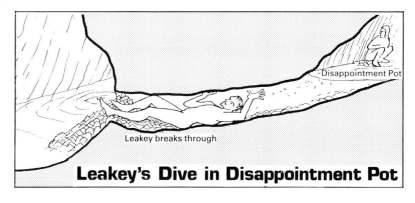

Disappointment Pot

Leakey breaks through

Leakey's Dive in Disappointment Pot

Dives Using Standard Equipment

Fontaine de Vaucluse received its first underwater exploration in March 1878. The diver was a Monsieur Nello Ottonelli, from Marseilles, who was equipped with the only form of underwater breathing apparatus then known: the heavy Standard Equipment used for deep sea diving*. Ottonelli, who was supported by the engineer Bouvier descended carefully to a depth of twenty-three metres. It was not until the 1940s that cave diving really came into vogue and then it was due to the enormous advances which were being made in the field of underwater exploration generally and in particular the advances in diving equipment generated by wartime activity. Up to that point diving (whether naval or commercial) had been backward and poorly developed. This was a worldwide phenomenon and not just true of France or even Europe. Basically, where diving with equipment was required, it was the universal Standard Equipment which was adopted. This was a completely waterproof suit surmounted by the typical globe-like brass helmet. Air was fed down to the diver from a surface pump and he was totally dependent on its reliability. The main problem was providing a steady, suitable air supply. Breathing in normal conditions requires no conscious effort, but problems arise if we alter our environment by going underwater, where the external pressure on the body becomes greater. The deeper one descends the more water one has weighing down upon the body, increasing the pressure outside it. The lungs are similar to thin elastic balloons and under this pressure they would normally collapse or suffer damage. To avoid this, the pressure inside the body must be made equal to outside conditions, and this is provided by gas pumped either from the surface or contained in a diving cylinder. Therefore, the deeper a diver goes, the higher the pressure of breathing air he requires to counteract the weight of water.

---

* This apparatus was invented in England and first used commercially by the brothers Charles and John Deane in 1829. Several manufacturers, incorporating inevitable refinements, were to appear over the next decade but the most successful company was to be that of Augustus Siebe, who commenced operations in 1840.

Left: A diver wearing the cumbersome Standard Equipment during a training dive at the Minneries Pool (Mendips) in 1935, prior to the early Wookey Hole explorations.

Pressure and volume are directly related. Under pressure, air contracts so that it is possible to contain a large quantity in a small cylinder for a diver. This is released to the lungs when required. At a shallow depth only a small amount is required to give the lungs the same pressure as the water. At twice the depth twice the amount is required, and therefore twice the amount of air is used in each breath. This is not primarily required by the body for oxygen content, but only to prevent the lungs from collapsing.

Since a greater volume of air is required at depth for each breath, then the contents of the cylinder will be used up faster, in fewer breaths. This limits the duration of a deep dive compared to one at shallow depth which can last longer with the same size cylinder.

With the Standard Equipment it was the person on the surface operating the pump who regulated the diver's flow of air. This was a critical task and failure to carry out the function correctly could easily mean the death of the partner below. Moreover, if he supplied too much air, the diver would ascend helplessly to the surface. This was known as 'ballooning' and occasioned all manner of physiological hazards, in particular the 'bends'.

Air contains three principal gases: oxygen, carbon dioxide and nitrogen. The last of these is required by the body only to dilute the others and is not readily absorbed into the bloodstream. After an extended period at depth, though, nitrogen is forced into solution in blood plasma by the added pressure. Here it remains until the diver starts rising, when, as the pressure is released, the gas comes out of solution and is breathed out. But, if the diver ascends too quickly, the nitrogen comes out of solution so fast that it forms bubbles of gas in the bloodstream. These are first felt in the joints (hence the term 'bends') and cause damage to blood vessels and particularly to the heart, possibly with fatal results. To prevent this, the diver must rise very slowly to allow the nitrogen to discharge harmlessly from the lungs.

The opposite effect to 'ballooning' was the 'squeeze', a condition caused by lack of pressure in the helmet and lungs. Problems induced by pressure changes were obviously critical and failure to handle these correctly could often result in accidents. The worst

hazard facing the deep diver was a severed air-pipe or a sudden fall. In these circumstances not only would his breathing supply cease but, should the non-return valve in his air-pipe also fail (this valve was designed to prevent any leakage back up the pipe), then his fate would be horrible. By straightforward suction through the air-pipe his underclothing and flesh would literally be stripped away to pour up the pipe. There would be little left to salvage.

Standard Equipment in the Severn Tunnel, 1880
The problems arising from delving under water were many and were clearly difficult to overcome. As developments were to show, the equipment described was invaluable to people such as salvage contractors, and in shallow water this apparatus was quite capable of doing all that was asked. In 1880 a novel situation arose which was to reveal clearly its use and limitations. The story is one of quite amazing determination and outstanding courage, and is of particular interest to cave divers. The Great Western Railway Company was in the process of constructing a tunnel under the estuary of the River Severn to shorten the journey from London to South Wales. In its day, this was the longest tunnel beneath the sea in the world. Work had been under way for nearly seven years when, on 16 October 1879, the miners intercepted a large spring draining from extensive limestone hills on the Welsh side of the river. The tunnel flooded within twenty-four hours, the costly project ground to a halt and a team of divers was called in to assist.

The conditions under which these divers were required to work were quite horrific. At a water depth of up to forty metres and in complete darkness (underwater lighting was unknown), the men were asked to block off the side gallery from which the water originated – guiding into place, by touch alone, a pair of massive oak 'shields' measuring approximately four metres by three metres, and weighing three tons apiece. Amazingly, they achieved this feat. The pumps were running the whole time and on one occasion a diver was sucked up against the inlet. It required the combined efforts of three strong men at the surface to pull him free.

Despite continual effort the water could not be

pumped out. It was not until October 1880, one year after the flood, that a solution presented itself. It seemed that the lowest level could not be pumped out unless a heavy iron door and two valves deep inside were closed. The chief engineer's plan involved a diver descending the remaining twelve metres of flooded shaft, walking 300m along the tunnel to the wall, trailing his air hose behind him. He would then climb through the door opening, pull up the steel rails (upon which the trucks ran), close the door, close the valves and then make his way out. All this would have to be done in total darkness. Few divers, even today, would relish such a prospect.

The man employed for the job was the leading diver from the Siebe Gorman Company, Alexander Lambert. Lambert was only five feet eight inches tall, but immensely strong. Wearing his 20lb diving boots, a 40lb breastplate and a 60lb helmet, he would clearly have to be strong to contemplate walking 300m dragging his air hose with him. Lambert did have two other divers to assist: one was positioned at the bottom of the shaft to guide the various tubes, while the second was to be stationed 150m further in to help drag the hose.

On 3 November 1880 Lambert made his attempt, groping his way along a tunnel that he had never seen before, negotiating all manner of obstacles and equipment which had been abandoned when the underground reservoir had been so dramatically breached. As he advanced towards the further reaches, he had to stoop to avoid the mass of supporting timbers. All the while his air-tube kept floating up against the roof, and pulling this became increasingly difficult, not to say dangerous. Eventually he reached 240m, where he was forced to admit defeat. He could go no further.

Lambert started on his way back. He now found that his air-pipe had curled up into coils, weaving, twisting and snaking around the roof timbers. Feeling around, he slowly, methodically gathered up the loops, disentangling and dragging them back along that same tortuous route. Miraculously he regained the bottom of the shaft, not so much horror-struck by his ordeal as bitterly disappointed to have failed.

The story does not end there. The engineers were becoming desperate for a solution. Within days a new idea was put to the test. Thomas Walker, the main contractor on the project, had heard of experimental apparatus belonging to Wiltshireman Henry Fleuss. Fleuss had constructed a self-contained underwater breathing apparatus. It consisted of a tightly fitting, waterproof mask over the face, which was connected by two rubber tubes to a flexible breathing bag worn on the diver's back. The bag, which was connected to a cylinder of compressed oxygen, contained a chemical which would absorb the carbon dioxide produced in breathing, so that the same oxygen could be breathed over and over again. When the oxygen in the bag was

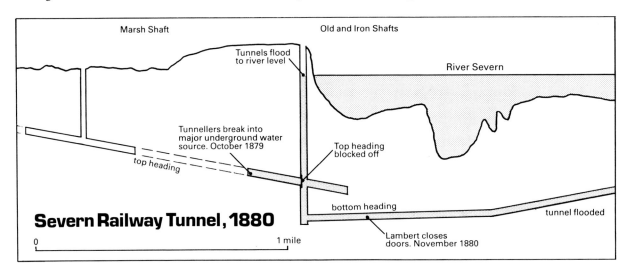

Severn Railway Tunnel, 1880

Right: A group of Siebe Gorman personnel including Alexander Lambert (in the bowler hat). Above: The Fleuss underwater breathing apparatus used by Lambert in the Severn Tunnel.

on the point of being used up, it was replenished by a fresh supply from the pressurised cylinder. As with the Standard Equipment, a heavy, waterproof brass helmet covered the head, but beneath this Fleuss had devised a simple, though effective, system for recycling the gas. Within the close-fitting mask, gas was inhaled via the nose and exhaled via the mouth back into the bag. It was quite ingenious and by this means Fleuss had devised a three-hour breathing supply. However, he had little experience of actual diving and on none of his experimental test dives had he ever been deeper than six metres.

Within days of Lambert's attempt using Standard Equipment, Walker invited Fleuss to bring his apparatus to the tunnel and persuaded him to tackle the job. As Lambert was now familiar with the situation under water, he was on hand to assist. Having familiarised themselves with the objective, Lambert descended fifty metres down the shaft to the water, then sank through the murky liquid to the pit bottom. Here he waited to guide Fleuss over the pit, constructed as a sump for the pumps, and into the first section of the tunnel.

Fleuss set off. Standing upright and without a light, it was impossible to establish any sense of direction. There was a drainage ditch on either side of the tunnel so it was difficult trying to follow the walls. The easiest way to find the route was to crawl on hands and knees between the rails. Sinking into deep mud and clambering over a fall of debris, Fleuss's nerve, understandably, soon began to falter. He finally lost his nerve completely and on exit stated quite categorically that he 'would not make another attempt for £10,000'.

Walker was still determined to close the door. He asked Fleuss to lend his apparatus to Lambert, overcoming Fleuss's initial opposition by arguing that success would be the best possible advertisement for his invention. Lambert took some persuasion, but eventually agreed. He dressed in Fleuss's apparatus and, with the inventor on hand to advise made a couple of practice dives.*

On the afternoon of 8 November 1880 Lambert commenced his dive into the tunnel. From the time

* In 1880 little was known about the effects of breathing pure oxygen for any length of time. Systematic experimentation in later years would show that it could be harmful and, at depths in excess of ten metres, could induce convulsions and sudden blackout.

Above left: The scene at Lurloch Cave, Austria, after the Trieste diver's abortive attempt to reach stricken cavers.

Above right: Standard Equipment in use at La Grotte du Creugenat, Switzerland, 1934.

he disappeared communication was impossible, and it was an extemely tense wait for all concerned. After one and a half hours he suddenly surfaced. He had travelled the 300m to the door, lifted one of the rails and closed one of the valves. He was full of confidence and was seemingly unaware of the epic pioneering achievement he had just made. In fact, he was ready to go back to complete the work with a bar, but Fleuss needed to return to London for more oxygen and carbon dioxide absorbant.

Two days later, on 10 November, Lambert set out again. One hour and twenty minutes later he returned triumphant. He had removed the rail, shut the door and closed the second valve.* All this was undertaken in total darkness with experimental apparatus and no safety back-up whatsoever. Alexander Lambert was obviously immensely strong, completely composed and totally fearless, quite an exceptional individual. Equally as clearly, luck was on his side. Had the water been a couple of metres deeper, there is little doubt the outcome would have been altogether different.

* When the shaft was eventually pumped out the contractors were able to tackle the source of the problem via a door in the oak shield. The heading was then totally blocked off with an eight-foot-thick brick wall about 450ft from the shaft. In October 1883 the spring broke through again with equally dramatic consequences. The headings flooded and Lambert's services were called upon for the second time, but on this occasion he found it impossible to reach the door in the Fleuss apparatus. The next day he completed the operation (with the assistance of other divers) in Standard Equipment. Once again the dive was undertaken in total darkness.

The unknown and insidious dangers associated with the use of oxygen were not discovered for some time. None of this, however, detracts from Lambert's achievement and from his display of qualities which cave divers worldwide would dearly love to possess.

As the reader continues through this book, Lambert's epic dives will seem to overshadow many later developments. But, as will slowly become apparent, Lambert was quite unique in the world of diving, as he assuredly would have been in any other sphere of high-risk activity.

A Cave Rescue in Austria, 1894

The usefulness or otherwise of Standard Equipment in a cave environment was dramatically demonstrated by another incident in April 1894 in Austria. At the time cave exploration in this area was becoming fiercely competitive, certainly in the city of Graz. So keen was one group of seven explorers to outdo their rivals that they entered the Lurloch Cave near the village of Demriach when weather conditions might otherwise have dictated caution. The cave flooded. As it was known that the party was probably safe in a high-level section of the complex, a massive rescue attempt was started. The following Tuesday a diver from Trieste was brought in. Great things were expected. After putting on his heavy dress, he proceeded into the icy, flood-swollen water with caution. The passage was low and he was forced to lie on his back and push himself along. But, after a few minutes, a signal of distress was received by the attendants and the diver was dragged back out. Unscrewing the glass of the eye-hole, they found the man insensible and convulsively dragging for breath. His air-tube had been bent, and his supply of air had been cut off. Even so, he soon re-entered the water in an attempt to clear the opening of tree trunks and other debris which had been washed in. But, after another few minutes of frantic effort he had to be drawn out again. The brave fellow made a few more vain attempts, but was then obliged to declare that it was utterly impossible for him to enter the narrow channel in his cumbersome diver's dress.

On Monday, 7 May, after a frantic week of intense effort – dam building, clearing and enlarging the route with explosives – the party was rescued alive. They had been trapped for 207 hours. This was one of the largest cave rescues in history. Though unsuccessful from a diving standpoint it was nevertheless the first attempt to rescue people from beyond a section of flooded passage.

Standard Equipment Used in Switzerland

Another noteworthy attempt at exploration was made in Switzerland in 1893. Using Standard Equipment, a diver named Pfund made a fifteen metre penetration into the Orbe Spring, the largest resurgence in the country. More significant, however, were a series of dives during 1934 into the sump at La Grotte du Creugenat, near Porrentruy in the Jura. Using the same bulky equipment a professional diver made a twenty-seven metre dive in early February. Two days later he returned with a longer hose and continued to a point fifty-five metres from the surface at a maximum depth of four or five metres. In early May two more professional divers, Scherrer and Spengler,

resumed the exploration. They dived together, one with a sixty-metre hose and the other with a hundred-metre hose. Supported by his friend the lead diver reached a point ninety-five metres from the surface. As it seemed the floor was rising, a further dive was made soon afterwards and this time a large air-chamber was reached. Here the water was just one metre deep, but just beyond the roof dipped once more. On this successful note the expedition was terminated.

Fontaine de Vaucluse, 1938

In September 1938 a second attempt was made on the Fontaine de Vaucluse using Standard Equipment and a Señor Negri reputedly passed his predecessor's twenty-three-metre limit and proceeded down to twenty-eight metres. The underwater passage was vast, sloping away steeply into crystal clear depths. Through a microphone installed in his helmet, Negri gave a dramatic running account of his exploration to a large crowd of onlookers stationed above. Eventually he reported that he could proceed no further because his air-pipe was dragging against a large boulder precariously balanced on a pivot. The slightest move might have toppled the rock and pinned him down. He wisely retreated.

Equipment Developments in the 1930s

It was apparent that exploring such sites as the Fontaine de Vaucluse (France), Lurloch (Austria) and Creugenat (Switzerland) using Standard Equipment was generally impractical. The objective was to evolve a self-contained diver without need to be linked to the surface and with as much control over his activities as a true amphibian. In 1933 the French Commander Yves Le Prieur designed the first mass-produced, individual diving apparatus, the dreamed of, self-contained, compressed air lung. The principle was simple: a cylinder pressurized to 150 times atmospheric pressure supplied breathing air to a full face-mask via a valve. The cylinder was strapped around the chest for easy manipulation of the hand valve. The main drawback was that the apparatus was very wasteful of air and it required constant regulation. The first completely automatic, compressed air apparatus – the

Aqualung – did not appear until 1942, a product of the combined efforts of Jacques-Yves Cousteau and Emile Gagnon. By that time rubber fins, designed by Commander Corlieu, had also come into use. Thus the 1940s saw the French take the lead in undersea exploration, emphasising that advances in recreational or sporting diving were linked to technical advances in commercial, military and scientific diving. Thus, once the new compressed air sets became readily available in France in the later 1940s and 1950s, cave diving explorations followed at a steady rate. Such equipment did not become widely adopted in Britain until the 1960s.

Cousteau's 1946 Vaucluse Attempt

The first self-contained aqualung attempt was made on a cave in August 1946. It is fitting that the site chosen was none other than Fontaine de Vaucluse, the divers being Cousteau and his colleagues of the Undersea Research Group, commanded by Captain Tailliez.

In his book *The Silent World* Cousteau described the event in some detail, noting that 'Our worst experience in five thousand dives befell us not in the sea but in an inland cave – the famous Fontaine de Vaucluse.'

The group arrived on 24 August 1946, and the mayor and half the town turned out to welcome the divers. They were overwhelmed by boys eager to help in the portage of equipment to the diving site. This included air cylinders, a portable decompression chamber, aqualungs, and diving dresses. They had come well prepared and been fully briefed on the previous attempts.

The first pair to attempt to exceed the previous depth record was Cousteau and Frederic Dumas, who had decided to rope up, mountaineering style, with a ten-metre line. A heavy weight was lowered into the deepest part of the surface pool and, while Cousteau and Dumas were kitting up, Jean Pinard made a preliminary dive, rolling this down to thirty metres' depth. Each diver was heavily laden with a three-cylinder aqualung, fins, a heavy dagger, and two large waterproof flashlights, one on the belt and one in the hand. Cousteau carried 100m of line coiled over his left arm and Dumas had an emergency micro-

aqualung on his belt, a depth-gauge and an ice-axe.

Their surface commander was Lieutenant Maurice Fargues, with whom they agreed a system of communication. This was to be via the guideline; a single tug upon the rope meant Fargues was to tighten the line to clear snags, three tugs meant that he should pay out more line, while six tugs was the emergency signal indicating that Fargues should pull them up as quickly as possible.

On submerging the pair quickly found themselves too heavy for comfort. Stones slumped away beneath their feet, and the pig-iron weight was soon roaring on down the slope in front of them, along with a multitude of disturbed rocks. Totally engrossed with the exploration of this unknown, distinctly forbidding world of darkness, and grappling with new and unusual pieces of equipment, neither diver was aware that anything was wrong, but in fact they were slowly being poisoned because their air supply was contaminated. Well beyond the range of daylight and at some considerable depth, Cousteau swam around trying to see if perhaps there was a route up, possibly to an air surface. There was not.

I was attached to something, I remembered . . . I swam to him [Dumas] and looked at his depth gauge. It read forty-five metres. The dial was flooded. We were deeper than that. We were at least sixty metres down, one hundred and twenty metres from the surface at the bottom of a crooked slanted tunnel.

We had rapture of the depths, but not the familiar drunkenness. We felt heavy and anxious, instead of exuberant . . . Dumas was passing under heavy narcosis. He thought I was the one in danger. He fumbled to release the emergency lung. As he tugged hopelessly at his belt, he scudded across the drowned shingle and abandoned the guide-line to the surface. The rope dissolved in the dark . . . My weakened brain found the power to conjure up our fate. When our air ran out we would grope along the ceiling and suffocate in dull agony. I shook off this thought and swam down to the ebbing glow of Dumas's flashlight.

He had almost lost consciousness. When I touched him, he grabbed my wrist with awful strength and hauled me towards him for a final experience of life, an embrace that would take me with him. I twisted out of his hold and backed away. I examined Dumas with the torch. I saw his protruded eyes rolling inside his mask.

Cousteau now summoned all his concentration. They had to get out and quickly. Their only hope was to find the rusty pig-iron weight which suddenly ap-

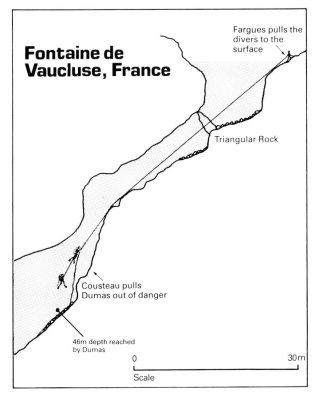

Fontaine de Vaucluse, France

Fargues pulls the divers to the surface

Triangular Rock

Cousteau pulls Dumas out of danger

46m depth reached by Dumas

0   30m

Scale

Above: Jacques-Yves Cousteau (wearing an early wet suit), the driving force behind the 1946 Fontaine de Vaucluse dives.

peared more valuable than gold. All at once, there it was, together with its guide rope which led up through the darkness to safety. With every passing moment the problems confronting them were becoming more critical. Dumas now lost his mouthpiece and swallowed a considerable quantity of water before he somehow managed to replace the grip. Cousteau realised that his companion's suit was also waterlogged, adding to the already severe overweighting, and that Dumas himself was now helpless, unable to do anything to save himself. He decided on a desperate final effort.

I would climb the rope, dragging Dumas with me. I grasped the pig-iron rope and started up, hand-over-hand, with Dumas drifting below.

What happened next added to the nightmare. Their surface controller, Fargues, who was completely unaware of the situation below, misinterpreted the jerky rhythm upon the rope. Instead of pulling them up he exacerbated the problem by letting out even more

line. Given the relatively short time that the divers had been away, Fargues was under the impression that his colleagues wished to push on further. When Cousteau, pulling upwards, found a substantial knot in his hand, and a fresh rope tied on, he realised that their communication system had failed. He therefore abandoned the rope and started to climb the rocky slope. Suddenly a section of crag proved too great a hurdle to overcome and Dumas's inert weight dragged him back down.

The shock turned my mind to the rope again and I suddenly recalled our signals: six tugs meant pull everything up. I grabbed the line and jerked it, confident that I could count to six. The line was slack and snagged on obstacles in the one hundred and twenty metres to Maurice Fargues. Fargues, do you understand my situation? I was at the end of my strength. Dumas was hanging on me.

At this moment Cousteau felt for his dagger and

seriously thought of cutting Dumas off. But, before he did so, he tried the distress signal again. Fargues was by this time becoming concerned and, despite the fact that the planned dive time had yet to expire, his intuition dictated that he should haul in the line. Cousteau suddenly experienced a ray of hope. As the rope went up he hung on tight and, with Dumas trailing behind, the pair were borne swiftly towards safety. A green glow appeared above and a minute or so later they were pulled to the surface. Cousteau was exhausted; his companion was almost unconscious. Fargues leaped into the water and dragged Dumas ashore. He lay on his stomach and vomited. It was several minutes before he was on his feet and the experiences were related.

Cousteau and Dumas had descended to over forty-five metres depth with contaminated air and had nearly died in the attempt. Another dive was made that same afternoon and their colleagues, Tailliez and Guy Morandière, had to contend with the same symptoms, but luckily escaped with less incident. Logic dictated that there had to be some reason for the extremely dangerous condition experienced by all four divers. Later they discovered that they had all been severely affected by carbon monoxide poisoning. Laboratory analysis was to show that the pollution only amounted to 1/2,000 carbon monoxide, but its toxic effect was greatly increased at depth. All the divers had been extremely lucky to regain the surface. Another lesson was learned: the team made sure that henceforth the air inlet pipe to their compressor was set well upwind from the noxious exhaust fumes.

Despite the lucky escape, the expedition of August 27, 1946 was a significant date in the history of caving, marking an audacious start to an new era of cave diving involving the compressed air aqualung.

The movement towards the exploration of deep flooded caves was understandably slow at the outset, as Cousteau and his colleagues were primarily interested in ocean-based operations. Cave diving might be challenging, but it was not their main concern. The possibilities, however, soon became apparent to cavers, and the first Frenchman to take up the gauntlet was Guy de Lavaur, who lived in Haut Quercy, near the great cave of Padirac in the Dordogne.

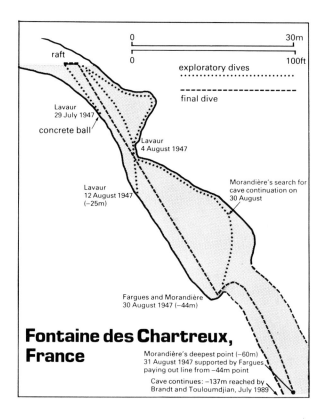

Fontaine des Chartreux, France

Chartreux Spring, 1947

In the Spring of 1947 Lavaur was asked to investigate the origins of Fontaine de Chartreux at the town of Cahors. With the financial support of an enterprising group of local businessmen, he was able to buy all the aqualung equipment that he needed. This was of the same type as that used at Vaucluse the previous year. A series of three-day operations took Lavaur to a depth of twenty-five metres, his final dive lasting for seven minutes and twenty seconds.

These dives in Chartreux showed that the site was much bigger and deeper than the team had imagined. At this point Lavaur appealed for assistance from the Undersea Research Group and two excellent divers, Fargues and Morandière, both of whom had dived at Vaucluse, arrived to assist.

On August 30 Fargues and Morandière made two dives into the resurgence. Fargues laid out fifty metres of line from his reel, terminating at what seemed to be a blank pothole at a depth of forty-three metres. An hour later, equipped with another reel of line, the search was resumed, but over the course of a fifteen-minute operation no way forward was located. The next day the pair made another dive. As before, Fargues was at the bottom of the entrance shaft, from where he was controlling his colleague as he prospected the way forward. Eventually, through a hole in the wall, Morandière found a new shaft, which he started to descend. About thirty metres of line had been reeled out when Fargues signalled that he was running short of air. Morandière rejoined him and began to ascend the first pitch. Fargues detached himself from the cable and ascended at full speed, overtaking a surprised Morandière. He reached the surface with only seconds of air left in his bottles.

Once again the objective dangers of underwater cave exploration had been emphasised. Like Vaucluse this site was to prove prohibitively deep, and at a depth of sixty metres Morandière could see no bottom to the next shaft. Sadly, two weeks after making these dives at Chartreux, First Petty Officer Fargues disappeared, just after establishing a sea diving depth record of 120m using aqualung equipment.

Fontaine de St George, 1948

In 1948 Guy de Lavaur decided to attempt another of the impressive springs of the Dordogne, namely the Fontaine de St George. Here, after a penetration of seventy metres and a depth of forty metres he reached a point where the passage seemed to have levelled off. (This was later to prove the deepest point in this first sump of the cave.) Once again the depth, the nature of the passage (constricted at the furthest point) and the limited duration of his air supply were major constraints. Another aspect of his approach also proved problematic, namely that of trailing a guideline from the surface. Although sometimes skilfully handled, this base-fed system frequently led to confusion on the part of surface controllers, which created problems for the divers.

Vitarelles Pothole

The first success in passing a sump came not at one of the great resurgence sites but at the bottom of a deep shaft, the Vitarelles Pothole, which is situated about five kilometres south-east of Gramat. About 130m

below the surface the cave intercepted a large underground river, which eventually reappeared about thirteen kilometres away to the north west at the River Ouysse, a tributary of the Dordogne. Lavaur commenced the diving here, but it fell to the Undersea Research Group to complete this operation. After a series of dives, Lieutenant Alinat reached a large above-water chamber beyond a 150m sump. Lavaur later noted:

We cannot expect speleologists, without undergoing an extensive training in diving, to achieve similar results and indeed they would be well advised not to attempt undertakings of this magnitude except with the help of a group of very experienced divers.

Accident at Lirou Cave, 1950

Diving deep or into long sections of flooded cave was clearly fraught with potential hazard. But, despite the extreme dangers presented at some of these sites, the first fatality in France was to take place at a relatively short, shallow sump at Lirou Cave.

The upstream sump in Lirou Cave, near Montpellier, had frustrated cave explorers for many years. Robert de Joly, for example, had unsuccessfully attempted to pump it out in 1938. On 22 August 1950 Henri Lombard overcame this obstacle after forty metres of swimming. He surfaced into a small air-bell, then continued through another shallow sump for a further ten metres. Beyond he was confronted by a large passage, which he followed for about fifty metres before he made his exit.

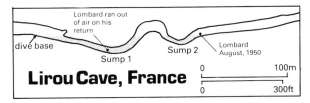

It was 8 October when he made his return, intending to follow the cave as far as possible. His surface support party expected him to be away for at least an hour. They noticed that he passed the sumps without incident; then, as expected, the line lay still. However, just twenty minutes after his departure, the pre-arranged return signal was received. Lombard was making his way back slowly. He passed the short upstream sump, then the little chamber. He had dived some metres into the longer sump when the cable to which he was attached stopped moving.

There was no relief diver in the cave and, after a long interval during which there was no further movement, the surface party determined to try and pull the lifeless diver out. They eventually recovered Lombard's body. Both bottles were found to be empty, and the air conduit had been pulled out of the valve. Neither of these were thought to have been the cause of Lombard's death and it seems very likely that these two events had occurred during the recovery operation.

It should be noted that Lombard was not a beginner; he had dived many times and this was his ninth underground operation. He knew his apparatus well and it seems unlikely he ran short of air. One possiblity is that he had encountered an atmosphere of carbon dioxide from which he was sensibly retreating. Certainly his watertight bag did not appear to have been opened and he had not used his carbide caving lamp. However, the most likely reason for the tragedy is that Lombard had little or no protection against the numbing effect of the 13°C water. It is certain, therefore, that, chilled on the outward dive, Lombard would have started his return in a state of lowered resistance and this in itself could have brought on the catastrophe.

Grotte de Deramats, 1953, and Combe Laval, 1955

Despite the tragedy at Lirou, the usefulness of the aqualung in cave exploration was beyond question. More and more operations took place in the early 1950s with a large number of sumps successfully explored in 1953. During this year the Verna group from Lyons passed the terminal sump of the Grotte des Deramats and explored about 600m of well-decorated passages beyond. By the end of 1955, for France at least, assaults on sumps had become fairly common. By this stage successes were frequent, one of the most remarkable being that by Letrone and Bonnevalle of the Tritons group of Lyons, who solved the mystery of the Cholet in the Combe Laval (Vercors) by passing a 130m-long sump.

Early Italian and Spanish Cave Diving

Despite its audacious start in the field of cave diving, France was by no means the only nation involved in early assaults on sumps. Diving in submerged caves was to develop into an acknowledged sport in many parts of the world. The Italians, for example, have a long tradition of cave exploration and were not slow to accept the challenge presented by their flooded caves. Perhaps the most noteworthy early Italian success was in 1953, when Dr Maucii and his team of seven divers achieved an exceptional feat in passing a sump in the Timavo complex, on the border between Italy and Yugoslavia. To appreciate this exploit it should be made clear that to reach the Timavo River at this point the divers had to descend to the bottom of a 329m pot in L'Abime de Trebiciano. The river at the foot of this is fast flowing and consists of glacier melt water, with visibility frequently reduced to much less than a metre. Maucii eventually made a seventy-five-metre dive here, reached a small air chamber, and was underwater for four hours. This Timavo project was subsequently advanced by the indefatigable Giorgio Cobol, the leading cave diver in Italy during the 1950s.

The approach to cave diving made by Maucii and his colleagues was significantly different from that of the French. The Italians had developed an alternative system for breathing underwater – a closed circuit, oxygen rebreathing system. This will be described in greater detail in a later section of the book.

Cave diving activities also commenced in Spain at this time. The pioneer here was Eduardo Admetlla, an exceptional diver who commenced his explorations in 1953. Using aqualung equipment, Admetlla made many deep dives in the submarine caves of the Costa Brava and Balearic Islands.

The 1950s was to witness the extension of cave diving to many countries. We shall return to analyse the most significant international explorations and trends later in the book. At this stage I propose to backtrack historically and take a more detailed look at the origins and development of the sport in Britain, the area I know best. I will then follow this through to the present day before returning to modern activities in other countries.

CAVE DIVING IN
BRITAIN AND IRELAND

CHAPTER THREE

PRE-WAR CAVE DIVING IN BRITAIN

The evolution of cave diving in Britain presents an interesting and colourful picture. It is not surprising that, as the home of British caving was the Mendip Hills, the first attempts at cave diving (using specially designed equipment) should occur here. Pioneers H. Balch and Dr E. Baker had been exploring the caves of the area since the early years of the century, and their discoveries and accounts were very impressive. One of their explorations was at Swildon's Hole, which they first entered in 1901. A wet, twelve-metre pot then held up explorations until 1914, and it was not until 1921 that the now famous Sump 1 was reached. This point, about 610m from the entrance, apparently involved a sixteen-hour round trip for its discoverers, though today it is reached in less than an hour.

Exploring the Swildon's Sumps 1 and 2, 1934-36
It was at Swildon's Hole, in 1934, that Graham Balcombe and Jack Sheppard made the first serious attempt to penetrate a water-filled passage. Their description of the floating scum and marsh gas issuing from the muddy bottom conjures up a familiar picture

Below: Sump 1 at Swildon's Hole – the site chosen for the first British cave dives in 1934. Successive blasting operations over the years have reduced the sump length from three metres to one metre and it is now free dived.

to the cave diver of today, but to these pioneers with their primitive equipment it must have held some real terrors.

An underwater respirator was constructed early in 1934 which, fitted with inlet and outlet valves, enabled the diver to inhale through a twelve-metre length of garden hose and exhale into the water. Additional equipment included a nose-clip, swimming goggles and an ordinary headband-type electric torch. This was before the invention of the wet suit and protection against the cold was nil. Initial exploration (April 1934), therefore, took place in the normal caving attire, old clothes. Balcombe subsequently described his experiences:

> My own findings were that the transition from water to liquid mud could be almost as abrupt as a light failure, that the way on was too deep for the diving contraption to work satisfactorily, and that cold water and my nervy condition quickly reduced me to a state of uncontrollable shivering.

After his attempt, Balcombe made a rapid exit from the cave to recuperate, leaving Sheppard to try his luck. His attempt nearly ended in disaster, for the hosepipe became disconnected while he was some distance under water and in the constricted space he found great difficulty in reaching air.

In retrospect it can be seen that their attempt was virtually doomed to failure before they started. The respirator took no account of depth or, more importantly, water pressure. This manifested itself as a heavy load on the intercostal muscles, for inhaling required much effort. This is a dangerous condition if suffered for any length of time, for when the muscles tire, as is inevitable, severe lack of oxygen can set in, resulting in abrupt loss of consciousness.

However, one important point was established, namely that the sump was relatively shallow and possibly short. Consequently, in June 1934, Balcombe devised a plan to blast away the roof. His first attempt took place on a weekday, when unfortunately none of his usual friends was available. Fired with enthusiasm,

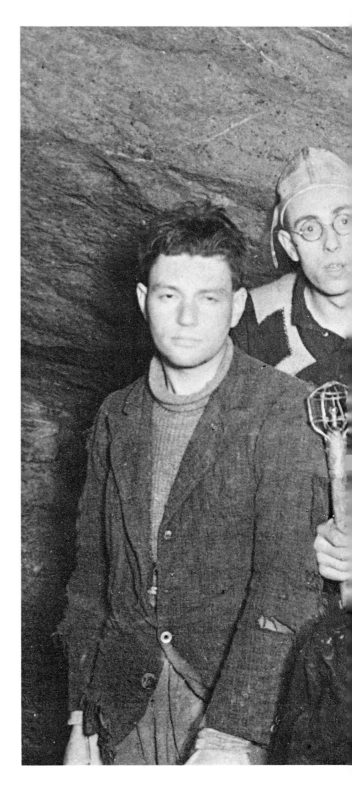

Right: The 1934 Swildon's pioneers: (left to right) Jack Sheppard, 'Jumbo' Baker, Graham Balcombe, Charles 'Digger' Harris, B. Offer, P. Brown and Bill Tucknott. Also Frank Frost who took the photograph.

he made four or possibly five trips to the bottom before the mound of equipment reached its destination. The pitches, in particular the Forty, presented special difficulties, as there was no one to untie the loads at the bottom. Balcombe relates the event:

> The jumpering did not go well either; there was little room to swing the hammer and hours of work produced a hole a mere few inches deep. Eventually I pitched camp, if that is what it might be called, on a gravelly patch not far from the sump, ate and turned in. It was weird to waken during the night to the loneliness of the cave with only the ripple and murmur of the stream and occasionally voices it seemed, but presumably only the sound of pebbles being rolled down a nearby water-chute. Next day Jack arrived and we decided to fire a small shot in the hole and to hope for the best.

In the event, the charge had little real effect, but it had given them additional experience.

On the next occasion a 10lb charge was fired, electrically detonated by means of an alarm clock,

Above: Jack Lander testing simple diving gear in Minneries Pool in the mid 30s. Others in the main picture are Paul Dolphin (working pump); Mrs Kidd, Mrs Lander and Mrs Dolphin (sitting); Frances and Geoff Tudney (standing in centre). Lander, Dolphin and Lowe made several early cave dives in South Wales in the late 40s.

which gave them time to evacuate the cave. This went off at 1.00 a.m., echoing through the peaceful night like the dull rumble of distant thunder. Balcombe continued:

> A party went down next day with ill-concealed excitement to view the wreckage. But there was none . . . a flake looked a bit loose and the mud of a tidal wave was plainly evident. Jack Sheppard, the most intrepid [member] of the advance trip attacked the flake with a crowbar and suddenly – woof! splash! The lights went out and time stood still, or nearly so, as something like the whole roof fell down before us almost scraping our knees then drenching us with the splash.
>
> A deathly silence followed, no one dared to speak until, the spell broken at last, we assured each other that we were

untouched and then lit up. About twenty tons of rock had peeled off the roof and now lay half-buried in the mud of the pool. Thus was our objective brought a little nearer.

Another trip was arranged and, loaded with 30lb of 'jelly', we wormed our way down to the pool and planted a shot in the mud in the hope that it might dislodge the supposed obstruction. Only a tidal wave resulted.

Another and larger shot was then fixed under the archway and shot off. It was evident from previous experience that it was quite safe to stay below during the fireworks and really it seemed that more disturbance was caused at the surface than below. We even managed to keep one of the many candles alight when the shot went off though the air surged violently up and down the passage in which we were ensconced. It appeared later that this shot went off during evensong (owing to a mis-setting of the clock) in the village church above our heads. Rumour has it that the hassocks jumped six inches off the floor. The congregation probably thought the Day of Judgement had indeed come and afterwards, according to the information, the vicar was heard to exceed his allotted vocabulary of 'Dear me! Tut, tut!'.

When the site was inspected later, the configuration of the final chamber was found to have been significantly modified, but the object of attack was untouched. A rethink became necessary. It was also quite plain that further activities of this type would not be looked upon favourably by the local inhabitants. Thus, with the use of explosives proving disappointing, thoughts reverted to another diving assault.

By late 1935 Sheppard had developed more equipment and had made some substantial modifications to the original respirator. A pump, originally designed as a football inflator, was now incorporated into the system. This was operated at the breathing rate of the attendant; the diver breathed at the same rate, 'in' on the downstroke and 'out' on the upstroke. The airline consisted of two twenty-three-metre lengths of ribbed garden hose. Lighting was protected behind a small perspex window inserted into a waterproof diver's helmet. It could be controlled by a switch in the side of the suit at chest level. A very significant development was the complete protection of the diver from the cold water. Fishing waders comprised the lower half of his suit, while the top half was made of rubber faced with cotton on both sides. Several thicknesses of this sheeting were used to form the helmet. A simple telephone communication system was also incorpora-

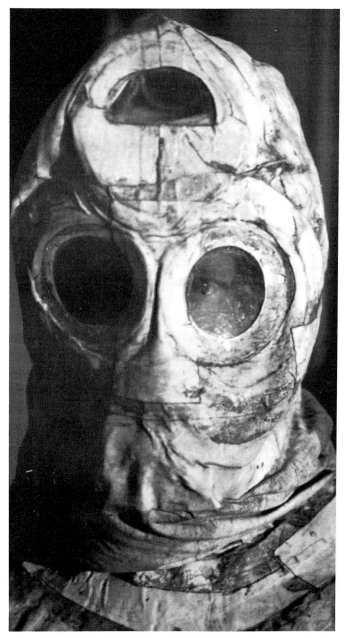

Above: Jack Sheppard in the homemade diving suit used to pass Sump 1, Swildon's Hole in 1936.

ted, consisting of an ordinary, solid back telephone transmitter and a watch-type receiver fitted into the correct positions in the helmet. The diver trailed a wire as he progressed and, via this, his support party

could maintain essential contact. With the addition of a life-line, food, torches and a complete change of clothing for the diver, the entire outfit was carried by a party of twelve. The weights were as follows:

Helmet, upper suit, telephone cable	14lbs
Lower section of suit	2lbs
Back weights, harness and belt	11lbs
Leg weights	6lbs
Pump	13lbs
Air hose	16lbs
Telephone and case	2lbs
Total	64lbs

An attempt scheduled for November 1935 had to be deferred owing to high water, but on 4 October 1936 the party reconvened for another attempt. Sheppard recalled the scene:

Above: Jack Sheppard and 'Digger' Harris before the 1936 attempt on Swildon's Sump 1.

Already I was beginning to feel somewhat apart from the others, getting some strange looks and unusual help in carrying. I had no thought of apprehension or of the danger of the dive. I had been under water three times previously and felt quite safe in my suit. At the pool GB took over complete direction of the shore party and I became even more detached from the others. This queer feeling grew as the pump, air line and telephone line assembled, and then, as the pump was started and air hissed through the suit, I drew it on and my head entered the helmet. The whole scene – cave, party, and pool – as seen through the eyepieces, became part of a film which I was viewing while staying completely detached. But then it was my show and the delay while Murrel took a flash powder photo was annoying. Then there was a job to be done and with a little guidance I entered the pool and, in stages as I went in and below water level, the shore party disappeared.

Then I was alone, in a small world of my own, limited by the light of my lamp on the rock walls of the cave. Visibility was good. The passage was soon located and entered, brilliantly illuminated. I felt warm, safe and comfortable, in striking contrast to my feeling on the previous attempt with a breathing tube. I well remember my supreme delight at being in an underwater passage, with the suit now justifying my hours of hard work and making the attempt possible.

In a short time I surfaced, removed my diving suit and looked around. There was nothing spectacular, just black rock and dripping water, but it was my cave, a completely unexplored cave never before entered. It gave me a complete feeling of the triumph of achievement, I felt like 'the monarch of all I surveyed'. The pump stopped and I pulled a torch through on a rope. I wandered happily along the passage until, after a hundred feet or so I arrived at another sump, or possibly only a duck. When I returned to the diving suit and called for the pump to be restarted, the telephone was silent. I sat down, and although I felt it was still my cave, it suddenly became an awfully lonely place, with no sound but the rushing of the stream and dripping water – no cave party, no voice on the telephone, no hissing of air, just completely cut off from the outside world. Finally, after what seemed an age, there was a voice on the telephone and the pump restarted. I slipped on the suit and began the return. The air was full of fumes from the spent acetylene and, feeling very ill indeed, I was glad to rejoin the shore party, my only thought being 'never again'.

These negative thoughts were soon replaced with a sense of triumph and curiosity about what lay ahead. The sump had only been three metres long, short enough to free dive which is exactly what Sheppard did when he returned with Balcombe two weeks later. The next sump turned out to be a duck and they then explored 300m of passages to locate Sump 2.

Below: After the successful passage of Sump 1 at Swildon's in 1936. Balcombe prepares a hot drink before the team begin their outward journey.

Above: A reconstruction of the equipment used by Balcombe and Sheppard to pass Swildon's Sump 2 in 1936.

In November Balcombe attempted this using the first completely self-contained respirator; in fact, it was nothing more than a small cylinder of compressed oxygen, instead of an air-hose, feeding the same contraption.

With this crude thing I progressed sideways, assisting this motion by working my head against the roof, one hand holding the cylinder [dangling between his knees] and the other the gas valve, opening it while breathing in and shutting it while breathing into the water. With it I reached a tiny bell-shaped chamber, then went through a frightening muddy squeeze, about five feet under water, to reach a larger chamber some twenty feet long and twenty feet high [with an air surface], where to my relief the line ran out. Following back along the forty feet of line I passed no squeeze, and in what seemed to be a few moments I was back with the party. It was as well that it was so, for, as I reached the base, the cylinder gasped its last.

A significant outcome of the passage of Sump 1 was the birth of free diving in Britain, some five years before Leakey's activities in Gaping Gill in Yorkshire. Many cavers were soon induced to share in the new discovery (up to Sump 2) and, taking a deep breath, simply plunged in.

Equipment Considerations

For cave diving the line of development evidently lay in the direction of self-contained respirators, protection from the cold, and far higher standards of safety. Buying such a set of diving equipment was out of the question. Balcombe and Sheppard had applied to the Siebe Gorman Company for the loan of Oxylithe (rebreathing) equipment, but this was refused on the grounds that it was unsuitable for use by the public. However, they were offered the loan of several sets of Standard Diving Equipment.

This equipment was of a similar type to that used by the French at the Fontaine de Vaucluse: lead-weighted boots, metal helmet and long tubes for delivery of air. The inevitable bulk and long tubes meant that the application of Standard Equipment to cave diving was limited, but, rather than turn down the offer, the cavers willingly accepted. One site in particular, Wookey Hole in Somerset, was quite capable of accommodating it.

The 1935 Wookey Hole Explorations

It was already known that the water which fed Wookey Hole had its origins high on the Mendip Hills. The distance between the disappearing surface streams, for example Swildon's, and the resurgence at Wookey was about three kilometres, but whether there was a cave in the intervening space only exploration could reveal.

Following tuition and practice on the surface, operations commenced in Chamber 3 at Wookey, some 152m from the entrance. This was the furthest dry point to which the heavy surface pump could be taken and it was from here that the diving began going upstream. The site was ideal and six divers were involved. Balcombe, the initiator of the expedition, was to be the first diver, and the second diver was to be the only woman in the group, Penelope Powell*.

---

* Her name was actually Penelope Tyndale-Powell but she recorded herself as Penelope Powell in the Log of the Wookey Hole Divers.

Scenes during the 1935 Wookey Hole explorations: Training at the Minneries Pool (top left); Balcombe being prepared for and starting the first dive (above and left); the Wookey Hole divers in Chamber 3. (left to right) Jack Sheppard, Frank Frost, Bill Bufton, 'Digger' Harris, Penelope Powell, 'Roger' and Graham Balcombe.

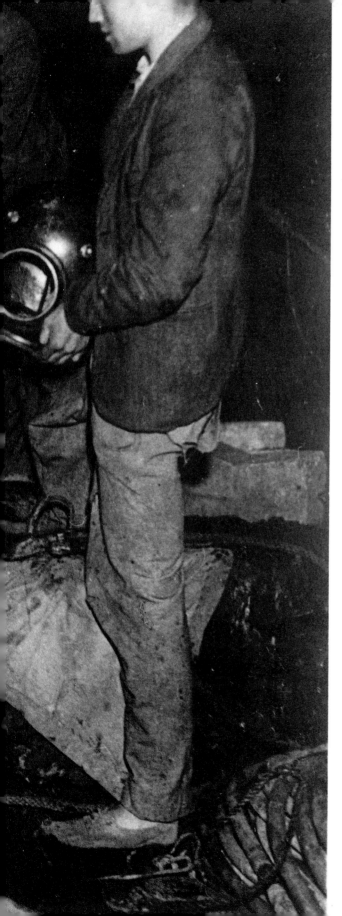

'Mossy' Powell, as she was known to her companions, was working in the Wookey shop and museum, having returned from Malaya with her two children after a failed marriage. At Wookey she had become fascinated by the archeological prospects, which had increased with the advent of the dive. Being a powerful swimmer, of an adventurous disposition and clearly having a certain charisma, she was accepted by the Wookey Hole Divers group. Balcombe recalls:

> During our training at the Minneries Pool, she undertook the invaluable role of equipment guardian, washing and storing the Siebe Gorman equipment after each weekend's training, and watching it during weekdays throughout the whole seven-week training and diving period. During this time she camped at the Minneries dump in a makeshift shelter set up between the sea chests, alone but for her dog Ting.

On the matter of her selection as the second diver, the log of the Wookey Hole Divers gives a full account. All the remaining five divers (Harris, Frost, Bufton, Tucknott and Powell – Sheppard having left) had received training at the Minneries. They had originally intended to rotate the seconding role, but it soon became clear that this was impractical and one person would have to be chosen:

> . . . in a party of volunteers, such discrimination is a difficult problem . . . It was finally decided that the best way was to give the place to the woman of the party, and royally has that choice been justified. Cool, collected, knowing no fear, she has carried out every task with an assurance and reliability that none could better.

As Balcombe and Powell entered the first sump, even with their poor lights the beauty of the underwater world was striking. The greenness of the water was all pervading and only the sound of exhausted bubbles rent the deathly silence. Powell described the scene in an evocative passage in the log:

> The first trip up the bed of the River Axe is a revelation of the beauties of this underwater world. It is almost impossible to describe the feelings as leaving the surface and the dazzling glare of the powerful lights, and slipping down from the enveloping brown atmosphere, we suddenly entered an utterly different world, a world of green, where the water was clear as

Left: Penelope Powell and Graham Balcombe preparing for a joint dive into Wookey Hole in their final push towards Chamber 7.

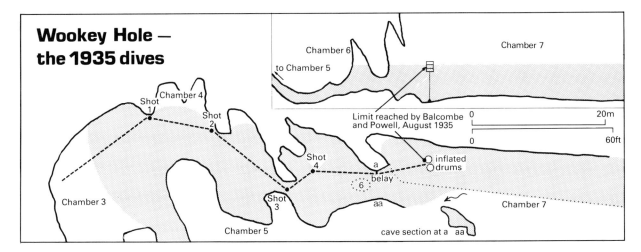

Wookey Hole — the 1935 dives

Chamber 6

to Chamber 5

Chamber 7

Chamber 4

Shot 1

Shot 2

Limit reached by Balcombe and Powell, August 1935

0   20m

0   60ft

Shot 4

a

inflated drums

belay

6

Shot 3

aa

Chamber 3

Chamber 7

Chamber 5

cave section at a   aa

crystal. Imagine a green jelly, where even the shadows cast by the pale green boulders are green but of deeper hue; as we advanced, light green mud rose knee high and then fell softly and gently into the profound greenness behind. So still, so silent, unmarked by the foot of man since the river came into being, awe-inspiring, though not terrifying, it was like being in some mighty and invisible presence, whose only indication was the saturating greenness.

This was a new world vividly beautiful on the way in, but turgid and frightening, a complete antithesis, on the return. By then the silt had become disturbed and it obscured much of the visibility, and the guideline, laid securely between weights or rocks, became their sole link with safety.

Clad in 180lb of brass and lead accoutrements, movement was slow and strenuous, exit especially so, as Powell's diary described:

His [Balcombe's] progress up the rocks, which he considered less difficult to negotiate than the awkwardly lying ladder, was an exhibition of skill and endurance not often seen and, in the intense gloom of the echoing brown cavern with its illuminated jade-green water scintillating behind, it made a truly weird picture as this awesome monster came blundering up over the slippery brown rocks. In fact a diaphanously clad spectator was so enthralled with the sight that she stood glued to the ground and clutched her skirts so frequently in her excitement that by the time he drew alongside they were well above the waistline . . . it was noticed on removing the diver's helmet that he had broken into a violent perspiration; was it *all* his woollens?

After gaining Chambers 4 and 5, which were already known as they are accessible in low water, Chamber 6

was reached. This again was a tall, dark fissure arrived at by a short dive to a depth of five metres. The main tunnel continued beneath, heading slightly deeper.

Due to the stipulations placed on the team by the cave's owners, all of these activities had to take place at night, so as not to disrupt the flow of visitors to the cave during the day. Soon all the divers were taking their turn to advance the route. Late on the night of July 20, it was Powell's turn to make a solo dive. She described this in another entry in the log:

My wrists are an awful nuisance; they are so puny I have to have rings, and rings, and rings (rubber rings used as packing or as contracting bands to prevent water getting into the suit) and they are not too comfortable then but, after fixing them in a new way and testing them in a bucket, everything seemed all right and I was soon slithering down into the water . . .

The river was not so clear as the first time I went down; it was a sort of thundery brownish foggy colour . . . and instead of enticing you like the fairy green of the week before, it kind of hated you and said, 'Get out!' as if it could not tolerate a third diver that night. Anyway, I went on, wallowing in the colossal boots like a slow-motion footballer, holding onto the shot-line with one hand and flashing the torch about with the other; everywhere was this baffling fog, the rocks only came into view when the torch nearly touched them and they glowed back with a sort of reddish-brown.

I travelled along the rocky and muddy terrace to Harris's [the previous diver that night] low archway, secured the distance-line round my right wrist, and waited a few moments for the water to clear before I inserted my cumbersome bulk into that depressing little orifice. It was the first one I had navigated and I dared not lie right down and wriggle like a lobster for fear of blowing up so I progressed very carefully, as some of the stones seemed a bit loose, on one hip and shoulder with my helmet bumping and scraping at intervals on the roof.

Flat slabs of a sort of tufa stuff kept on falling past the bull's-eye [window in the front of the brass helmet], slabs ringed with little silver bubbles, and finally I came into the new chamber. I saw a huge boss of stalagmite on the floor and went across to it to rest; the mud I'd kicked up rose above me, curling down again round my helmet like heavy smoke clouds, and finally dispersed.

On the far side of the chamber, opposite the place by which I had come in, I could see what looked like a long dark archway, low but very tempting; unfortunately, the distance-line wasn't long enough for me to get close to it, so I sat a bit longer, hitting one or two edges off the boss with the torch in true tripper style, then I rang up shore and announced my intention of returning.

Again that beastly squeeze but much less difficult the second time as it slopes up and you don't have the feeling that you might suddenly go up faster than you want to. The mud was very thick by this time; my hands were getting cold and the rubber rings making them numb but, once I'd let go of the distance line and got a grip of the shot-rope, progress was easy despite the thick fog all round me.

Suddenly I found myself pulled up tight and to take another step, however hard I tugged, was impossible. It requires a good steady pull to lug the lines along but this was no ordinary resistance; it then dawned on me that, the quintessence of bad diver-craft, I was not on the shot-rope at all! I was gaily using my own breast-rope which had somehow become hitched up good and hearty behind me and I had doubled back on it.

The telephone was just the limit; I could hear nothing they said and apparently they were deafened by my silvery voice and could get very little of what I said. It was lovely to hear the steady hahrrh-hahrrh-hahrrh of the pump and to know that, never mind how long you stayed there, or what predicament you were in, it would continue; the good old gang breathing for you! So I sat there, with a huge bank of mud looming beside me in the thick still water, waiting for it to clear a bit. After a while my hands got too numb to use my fingers and I could only do my useless best with my two wrists and one knee, lifting and gently jerking, I dared not do it too hard in case something got loose and fell on me, then waiting for the water to clear a bit to see if it had been any good. Gradually the air pipe became more tractable and, by dint of first my pulling a yard and then the crew on shore pulling a yard, it got loose; oh the joy as it slowly but surely floated past my bull's-eye!

With a little encouragement the breast-rope came too, and I shall never know what they were hooked by owing to that fearful mud. Then I 'bout turned, and slunk home . . . I crept out of the water wishing I'd never been born.

The work continued, experience was gained and a further advance was achieved. Some time later Balcombe, supported (under water) by Powell, reached Chamber 7. This was about fifty-two metres from base. The mirror-like, silvery surface was visible, but initially unattainable, high above the marooned 'bottom-walkers'. However, on a subsequent trip, a float was devised. Two five-gallon drums were rolled into the chamber and then fixed together with a bar to form a trapeze, from which an inverted Y-harness was hung and attached to a ground weight. The drums were then inflated using air leaked from the divers' sleeve and eventually the whole contraption rose to the surface with the harness rope trailing beneath to assist the divers to make an ascent.

The events of the final operation are recounted by Balcombe and Powell. Reaching the watery depths beneath Chamber 7, the pair prepared for the ascent:

There was a lot of hand tapping and signalling on bull's-eye; the receiverless No. 2 was again belayed to the rock-side and No. 1 on his way to the surface. His suit began to swell, he waved his hand, grasped the rope, and up he went, slowly and in the most dignified manner possible; the last that No. 2 saw were those fearful brass toecaps disappearing in a sulphur cloud,

Below: Powell and Balcombe set off with the five gallon drums for use in erecting the floating 'trapeze' in Chamber 7.

Passage to
Chamber 6

Above: A reconstruction of the ascent into Wookey's Chamber 7.

like a person going up to heaven. No. 2 is earthbound so more or less prepared when, with a sudden crash, down came No. 1 on her helmet!

Diver 1 then did some curious antics, whether from pleasure or from rage it was difficult to tell. Diver 2 promptly put through a request to go up also, granted by No. 1, who proceeded to de-karabine the coil of rope, spare shot-rope, so that the ascent would be less encumbered. Then up, up, went Diver No. 2, and when her head popped out and she saw Chamber Seven in all its glory. The telephone in Chamber Three echoed and re-echoed with squeals of delight as she hung, swinging and wobbling, on the iron bar of the trapeze, bathed in the orange, red, brown and gold reflections on the water.

Here was Chamber 7, winding away as far as the light could reach, towering above as far as the eye could see, two gigantic walls of clean rosy conglomerate; how could it be so many million years old? It looked as fresh and new as the day it left the Hand of its Maker. This cathedral of peace is guarded not by an angel with a flaming sword but by a huge and pointed boulder ready to destroy all who are not fit to enter and for whom it is waiting, so keen and sharp, so watchful; La Guillotine!

... When the divers were reunited on the river-bed below they executed a regular war dance, hand in hand, until their helmets crashed together and finally Diver 1 pushed his companion over which ended the performance and, sorrowful but triumphant, they wended their way home, stooping, climbing, crawling and at times shooting along face downwards as the attendants and coilers waxed more and more and more energetic and tugged with all their might.

This trip on 31 August 1935 was to mark the end of the Standard Equipment diving operations. The local villagers and the owners of the paper mill, all of whom drew a supply of water from the cave, objected to the muddy water which the explorations generated. Despite ample publicity which the divers had attracted for the show cave, permission to continue the exploration was withdrawn. The equipment itself was returned to Siebe Gorman in London, but, during the few months of activity, its advantages and disadvantages had been identified.

The task of the first diver had been particularly arduous. As with all Standard Equipment, he was required to regulate the incoming flow of air by manipulating a pressure release valve on the helmet. He also had to carry a shot-weight (over half a hundredweight) and drag the guide-rope along, besides having to haul his own air hose and telephone cable behind him. At corners and around boulders there was always a risk of the tubing or cable being caught up or damaged, and, after a certain distance, Balcombe found it physically impossible to pull all the paraphernalia behind him. Thus the assistance of the second diver was found to be essential. Equipment failures could not be ruled out and on one occasion the pump failed completely while Balcombe was beyond Chamber 6. He was only able to reach safety by breathing the air remaining in the helmet and suit – a very lucky escape requiring great presence of mind and rigid self-control. Such mishaps did not mar the overall value of this series of dives. They had been epic pioneering adventures and much had been learned, but the role of Standard Equipment was clearly at an end, and to progress further much less cumbersome, self-contained apparatus was now essential.

CHAPTER FOUR

THE OXYGEN PHASE

The need for self-contained equipment in cave diving was evident by 1936, but there was no way it could be acquired. Such apparatus simply did not exist. It was to be the demands of war that were to spur on the evolution of underwater equipment and further the cause of cave diving.

Wartime Developments

At the start of the Second World War divers and diving equipment were matters about which the general public knew little. All divers were either under the control of the Navy or were salvage contractors who, in war, worked for the Admiralty. They were Standard Equipment 'helmet divers', whose radius of activity was limited. Oxygen equipment for diving was practically unknown, except for the Davies Submarine Escape Apparatus or DSEA made by Siebe Gorman. The same firm also produced an oxygen rebreathing apparatus known as the Amphibian Mark 1, which allowed a diver to work to a depth of nine metres for up to one hour. At the time the Amphibian Mark 1 set was produced it was offered to the Admiralty, who rejected it, partly because compressed air pumps and sets were considered safer for divers, and partly because at that time it was not generally envisaged that divers would want to move about freely in water without being connected to the surface. The possibility that divers might be used as underwater combatants was discounted. Bottom-walking across a river had been tried with the Amphibian, but it was found to be too slow for tactical purposes. Consequently there was no operational requirement.

Italian underwater raids on shipping in the Mediterranean area in 1941 highlighted the shortsightedness of the British, particularly as it had been Siebe Gorman who had supplied the Italians with DSEA

equipment in the 1930s. This put the equipment in a new perspective and the Admiralty thereafter made much greater efforts to improve its underwater diving operations.

Until this time a diver had always been held in check by his surface-fed air. If it was simply the mobility that was desired then a compressed air cylinder such as the Le Prieur could be adopted. But this was undesirable, since the tell-tale trail of bubbles which reached the surface would indicate the presence of a diver to observers stationed above. The breathing apparatus, therefore, had to be closed circuit, that is, little or no gas, should be allowed to escape. This could be doubly advantageous in that detection would be extremely difficult and that, if pure oxygen were used, then the duration below water would be greatly increased.

Under the supervision of Siebe Gorman instructional staff, the first attempts were made with modifications of the DSEA. Instead of a small, front-mounted oxygen cylinder which fed a breathing bag, divers now carried two large cylinders on their backs. Soon all manner of equipment and experiments developed. Due to the cold British waters, a multiple-purpose underwater swimsuit made its appearance in 1943, the prime objective being to make man entirely amphibious. In the same year fins were obtained from the Americans. Thus the British 'frogman' made his debut, and he quickly became the best equipped in the world.

Models such as the modified DSEA, Amphibian and P Party might vary for different purposes, but the principle of operation was basically the same. Thus closed circuit equipment consists of a bag or 'counter lung' filled with oxygen, from which the diver breathes. The carbon dioxide which is the waste product of breathing is taken out of circuit by absorbent soda-lime, and the oxygen is replaced from a high-pressure cylinder. All the oxygen is used by the diver, none being breathed to waste in the water.

Equipment Uses for Cave Diving

Although closed circuit equipment proved perfectly adequate for frogmen, it had a number of shortcomings when applied to cave diving. Its assets included greater efficiency and economy, but its problems, mainly chemical and pressure related, were to prove awkward for cave divers. The most important was the constraint imposed by the old enemy, pressure. The great disadvantage of oxygen was that at depths exceeding nine metres the gas becomes toxic. Individual divers might have greater or lesser resistance, and might strengthen their tolerance through familiarity, but in general terms it was unsafe to proceed deeper than nine metres.

The cause of the hazard is complex and rooted in the law of partial pressures (Dalton's Law*). Suffice to say that the symptoms are variable but usually occur in a sequence: lip twitching, dizziness, nausea, choking sensations and convulsions resembling an epileptic fit.

Lack of oxygen could also develop with these sets and, before starting to use the apparatus, it was necessary to do a breathing drill. The purpose of this was to wash out most of the nitrogen from the lungs and the apparatus. If oxygen was then used faster than it was supplied to the breathing bag, it was easily noticeable, for the bag emptied and it became impossible to draw in a complete breath. If this initial procedure was overlooked and breathing commenced from a bag full of air, containing four-fifths nitrogen, the oxygen was used, but the nitrogen was exhaled back to the bag. After a few breaths the bag remained inflated but contained mainly nitrogen. The subject, therefore, became unconscious within a few minutes through lack of oxygen. There was no visual warning from the breathing bag, which the diver thought was still full of oxygen.

The preconditions imposed by using pure oxygen

were not the only problem, for it was also necessary to keep a watch on carbon dioxide concentration. In the first instance, the proportion of this gas could become excessive. This might occur if the rate of working was high, so that more gas was formed than could be readily absorbed by the soda-lime in the apparatus; or it could happen if the soda-lime had been used up. Breathing very shallowly, so that most of the gas in the lungs did not reach the soda-lime, also gave this effect. A proportion of five per cent CO_2 was critical and unconsciousness would result by ten per cent. The condition would clearly be difficult to diagnose considering all the other stresses which beset activity below water.

It was also possible to suffer from a lack of carbon dioxide. This was usually due to continuous deep breathing which washed out the gas from the blood. Normally respiration is controlled by carbon dioxide concentration in the blood. As the level rises, the brain detects this and triggers breathing; without this gas, the response never occurs. Thus, when carbon dioxide is removed by deep breathing, there is no desire for a new intake of breath. Such a condition might cause respiration to stop for so long that the victim went blue for lack of oxygen, gasping periodically. When the concentration rose again, breathing would return to normal. For the efficient functioning of the apparatus it was extremely important that no leakage of water should occur into the breathing bag and more especially into the soda-lime container. If this happened then the soda-lime was quickly used up, with resultant build up of carbon dioxide. A larger and more sudden incursion of water meant the diver ran the risk of a 'cocktail': inhaling caustic solution into the respiratory system, with extremely damaging consequences. Another danger apparently incorporating a psychological basis was 'shallow water blackout'. This could strike without warning. One clear necessity, therefore, was the need for close supervision of those undergoing training.

It was also essential for the diver to be constantly on the alert and capable of recognising any changes in his equipment and breathing. If regulation of his oxygen supply and mastery of this was important, so too was the need for the highest standards of physical fitness.

* Dalton's Law: In a mixture of gases, each gas exerts the pressure that it would do if it occupied the volume alone. Each constituent gas has its own partial pressure. For example oxygen becomes toxic at pressures approaching two bars in most individuals. With pure oxygen, as in a rebreathing system, this can occur by a depth of ten metres. With air containing 20% oxygen, a depth of ninety metres is attained before a partial pressure of two bars is reached.

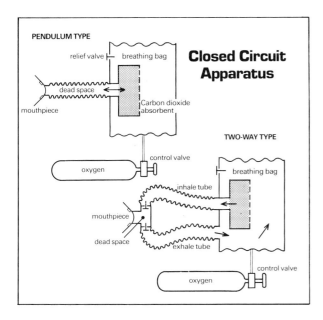

Closed Circuit Apparatus

PENDULUM TYPE

relief valve — breathing bag

dead space

mouthpiece

Carbon dioxide absorbent

control valve

oxygen

TWO-WAY TYPE

breathing bag

inhale tube

mouthpiece

dead space

exhale tube

control valve

oxygen

It soon became clear that performance whilst diving was closely related to fitness and good health, both of which were essential to combat the dangers imposed by water pressure. Very simply, with increased depth

Balcombe's closed circuit apparatus used in Keld Head in 1945.

there is increased pressure: at a depth of ten metres under water the pressure has reached twice that of the atmosphere. With depth, therefore, greater demands are made on the body, especially on the ears, sinuses and lungs, for these are all body cavities containing air which will change in volume as external pressure alters.

Increased water pressure has to be compensated for in each of these compartments, otherwise pain and physical danger ensue. A variation in pressure of a pound or two may cause great discomfort, while excessive pressures are liable to prove fatal. The ear-drum, for example, is highly sensitive to pressure differences and requires equalization immediately pain is felt. This can usually be done by swallowing, which causes the Eustachian tubes, running between the inside of the ear-drum and the back of the mouth, to open. If a diver fails to do this while moving through the water then he runs the risk of rupturing his ear-drums; this is more likely upon descent. Pressure changes in the inner ear may also lead to vertigo and disorientation. The sinuses can easily be relieved by blowing into the nose, but a cold can cause a blockage in the air-ducts. Safe diving is then rendered impossible, or at least very painful. The lungs are exceedingly vulnerable and cannot operate

Above: Balcombe demonstrates the Wookey Hole Diver's Dry Suit – known as WHODD. Left: The first Aflo or Aflolaun (apparatus for laying out line and underwater navigation) at Keld Head, 1945.

against a positive pressure of more than a pound or two. A pressure greater than two pounds will lead to a ruptured lung. On ascent it is also essential to release air from the body consistent with the decreasing water pressure otherwise a burst lung or embolism may result. Internal and external pressures have to be equalized; to hold one's breath is fatal.

Divers, therefore, had to appreciate and understand their physiology and limitations. They had to be scrupulously careful in using their equipment. For the first time they were completely self-dependent so they needed constantly to reappraise their situations while operating under water. Such divers required skill, dedication and a large amount of nerve.

Equipment Innovations

The war meant the inevitable halt of caving operations, but it also allowed Balcombe to initiate the 'self-contained' phase of cave diving. With help and advice from his Siebe Gorman contacts, he pioneered and established it as a practical caving technique. By the summer of 1944 he had assembled all the equipment that he required.

His respirator was an oxygen closed circuit-type involving a small breathing bag affixed to his chest fed by two cylinders attached to his back. Other parts of his kit, especially the suit, had also been modified. Previously the suit had been made up of a pair of trousers and a jerkin joined together with a waterproof joint. The wrists were sealed by standard moulded rubber divers' cuffs and the neck by a moderately tight rubber neckband. Dressing took a long time and, in an effort to reduce this, the tedious waist joint was eliminated. An entry hole was now inserted in a sheet of special rubber let into the chest of the suit. After entry the hole was fairly easily sealed by a metal disc, for, when unstretched, the hole was only four and a half inches in diameter. The main weakness of this kit, later known as Wookey Hole Diver's Dress,

(WHODD), was the exposure of head and neck to the cold and the use of separate goggles, which were prone to leakage, thereby impairing vision. 20-30lb of lead weights were also required and location of these on the body was another problem. Protection of the diving suit was also of paramount importance, and this necessitated the use of sturdy overalls.

The Aflo

Another innovation was a piece of equipment designed to hold the underwater light and line. Later this was known as an Aflo. It consisted of a three-and-a-half-foot rod carrying a miner's helmet lamp and its battery, together with a fifteen-inch drum of line. Held in the diver's hand, it provided a valuable increase to the range of visibility, for the rod itself could be used as a probe in the murky water. The first crude Aflo or Aflolaun (Apparatus For Laying Out Line and Underwater Navigation) can be seen in the photograph on page 52. Typically bulky were the two forty-eight-watt motor headlamps taking current from an alkali battery. Slung below the frame of the unit was a large drum with about seventy metres of line, which paid itself out as the diver progressed. Additional equipment included a compass, depth-gauge and an indicator intended to show direction of water current. The whole thing was difficult to transport and the reel had to be watched carefully to avoid malfunction. Virtually every piece of equipment and clothing, especially the navigating equipment, was clumsy and primitive.

Buoyancy Problems

It is important to realise that, unlike his counterpart the frogman (with his fins or flippers) or the open sea diver, the cave diver's method of movement at this time was to walk along the bed of the cave, a technique known as 'bottom-walking'. This was a legacy of the previous experience at Wookey Hole using Standard Equipment, but it was still the best method bearing in mind the problems that existed in attaining neutral buoyancy, which would allow the diver free movement in the water at a certain depth. If he was too light, the air contained within the suit would make him float (positive buoyancy) and, if too heavy, he would sink (negative buoyancy). In practice, neutral buoyancy was difficult to attain and the easiest solution was to make him negatively buoyant so that he walked on the bottom of the cave passage. To do this the buoyancy of the air trapped within the suit was counteracted by lead-weighted boots. The great drawback with bottom-walking was that the diver was compelled to lean forward at a steep angle to make any progress. His body was far from streamlined and offered great resistance to the water making movement very slow. Demand valves (which allowed the diver to have air when he needed it, as opposed to the continuous flow system and/or a manually operated cylinder valve, e.g. Le Prieur) and compressed air cylinders were not available; even if they had been, it would have been extremely unlikely that they would have been adopted, due to the comparatively short breathing time they afforded.

Balcombe's dives at Keld Head, 1945

Balcombe was keen to try out his new equipment, so he made a number of trips into the Yorkshire Dales from his wartime home near Leeds. Owing to an acute shortage of petrol, he was forced to travel fifty miles to the main caving areas by a tandem modified to draw a small trailer. The most promising and accessible site was Keld Head, the large rising near Ingleton.

Graham and Mavis Balcombe setting out to Keld Head.

This impressive resurgence, draining from the west side of Kingsdale, had long intrigued local cavers, and Reg Hainsworth and party had previously spent many weekends in a stout endeavour to lower the level of the water at the flooded entrance, with little success.

Between March and October 1945 the new equipment received its first field tests, and a considerable section of underwater passage was explored. At Easter Balcombe made his first acquaintance with the murky subterranean waterway. The previous night had been wild and wet, and his diary records:

... I essayed a descent, edging my way along the southern wall; the way down loomed dimly from the intense further blackness. Clutching my drum of rope I slowly groped my way downwards. Visibility quickly dropped from two feet to one foot then to about six inches from the light. Each stone on the slope seemed to be the last before the drop but after each there appeared another. The slope was very steep and the stones, about six inches in diameter, were perched precariously. When disturbed they rolled down out of sight with a queer high-pitched clink! clink! Soon the daylight disappeared, last seen as a dim orange foggy patch almost overhead; the sound of

Above: The 1945 Keld Head team (left to right) Mary and Ray O'Neill, C.R.L.D. 'Rocky' Moxon, Graham and Mavis Balcombe, and Ray Newcombe.

breathing and of the inrushing gas disappeared, a deadly silence ensued. It was disquieting and after another few feet I left my drum and climbed back with the aid of the rope anchored on the bank; the dim patch grew lighter and was daylight at last. The noise of breathing came back, and when I opened the gas valve, yes there was the rush of gas, all was well after all.

After a brief exchange with the party on the bank I went back, reached the dark and quiet by the drum, and peered down. The slope still went on. A few inches at a time I climbed down following the little patch of light. Then suddenly a level patch appeared, sand and gravel.

Here he wisely decided that nothing would be gained by pushing on in such atrocious conditions, and he made his exit. At the beginning of June a notable advance was achieved. He reached his previous limit and went on.

... after scrambling through a pile of large blocks and then on for some time I realised that I was going up. The gas-bag

Above left: Balcombe diving at Keld Head in 1945.
Above right: Balcombe and Ray O'Neill after training dives in a reservoir near Harrogate.

swelled, I blew off some gas, heard it break at a surface and the full significance broke suddenly upon me – was this the end of the sump? Excited I looked round, or groped round, for a way up; I do not remember how I did so but I reached the surface and saw a stream passage chamber, no bigger than a bus, arched as the cave passage below, with four-foot long white stalactites and a boss on the left (true) wall. I fancy I climbed a sandbank on my left to see out. The walls were everywhere overhanging.

Dropping back to the streamway and picking up the course again, still west, I went on and on over patches of sand and more fallen blocks. The drum tended to catch but this was no longer acceptable as an excuse to turn back and I soon got used to freeing it. Travelling light is delightful. When you find a gaping hole, find the bottom then lightly step in; ever so gently you sink to the bottom like an air-borne feather. However, it is not all fun and games for twice in making my way against the current, presumably in a narrower part of the cave, the current won and swung me round so I had to drop flat, pick up the route again and have another go. It is comforting when climbing over piles of loose blocks to remember that one hardly weighs anything at all.

Balcombe found a further surface beyond this and as everything was working well, he continued to the end of his reel, reaching a point fifty-five metres from base.

The return journey was specially enjoyable; after the line had corrected a few mistakes for me I began to have faith in it and soon there was a faint light patch ahead, growing bigger and brighter. Eventually the entrance slope became defined and climbing it was delightful, fine yellow stones piled up in pleasant daylight.

With further modifications to his kit, Balcombe made another dive at the beginning of August. Despite the improvements and growing confidence, however, all was destined not to go quite to plan:

I followed the line without delay and located the end. The apparatus did not seem to be going so well but I attributed that to the absorber being on its second run [this was the second dive of the day], to the breathing pipe being rather long, and to the rate of working while coming in. Thus I was breathing quite heavily while groping round for the new rope end, to be tied on to the old, when suddenly the respirator choked; the resistance shot up to an impossible figure and I knew from experience that the pipe must have kinked; rapidly I passed my hand over it, no, there was no trace of kinking. Alarmed and not knowing what the trouble could be but knowing that I could not last long in that condition I tried more gas, just in case. The working cylinder must have been very low for equalising much increased the flow; I could hear it rushing into the bag but did not realise just how much had gone in. Still the breathing bag was distended hard as ever [no relief valve at that time]; I looked up for possible escape to a surface but could see none. In desperation I tried the tube again and again but found it okay. Then suddenly the resistance dropped to normal. At the same time the bag discharged so violently it blew the gag out of my mouth and away went a bagful of gas, some five to ten litres of it, before I succeeded in cramming the mouthpiece back again. It was fortunate that it was pure water not pure sewage or something like that for I shipped quite a lot of both into me and into the absorber. It was no end of a relief to get back to normal breathing but I still did not know what to expect. Would the wetting stop the absorber action? I had vivid memory of the earlier breathing tests when my breathing became so violent that I could not retain the mouthpiece. I stood a moment, checked the line, debated whether Aflo would be help or hindrance, then taking firm command of myself, went very slowly to the bank [out]. It seems that wet soda-lime still absorbs quite well . . . I opened the equaliser once or twice on the way and when I reached the bank the attendants checked and found zero-zero, both cylinders empty, which despite accidental loss takes some explaining and gives an urgent warning.

There was no more diving that day. Awaking from a nightmare the following night, he instantly realised the cause of the trouble. Just before the dive he had fitted a mouthpiece tap and must have accidentally closed it during the dive, and later accidentally opened it again. A simple mechanical alteration had nearly cost him his life. Fortune had clearly been on his side, just as it had on a previous occasion when he had run into severe difficulties caused by shortage of oxygen – owing to omission of the breathing drill.

Alum Pot and Goyden Pot, 1945

These were the days of trial and error; learning was rapid and every mistake provided a valuable lesson. Balcombe also examined Alum Pot in June 1945, but was forced to turn back after just a few metres on discovering a deep underwater pitch at six metres' depth. It was at Goyden Pot in October 1945 that his first really satisfactory results were obtained. In a forty-minute dive he completed the short underwater traverse to the lower cave, discovered that there were no air-spaces along the route and, rather more importantly, achieved a successful performance from his respirator. On earlier dives poor reconditioning of the rebreathed atmosphere had resulted in persistent trouble from excessive carbon dioxide.

Apart from this success, Balcombe was also gaining experience in the problems which could assail an unwary diver. The lesson about function and positioning of the line was obvious. By pulling on his line in Goyden Pot, he made it slip over a tree trunk and lodge itself in a deceptively narrow spot, jamming solidly. At Swildon's Hole in November 1936 he had been lucky in similar circumstances, for then the line had pulled into a wider passage, but here, for the first time, the grave possibilities became apparent. Some anxious moments followed, but fortunately he was then working his way upstream and soon the water cleared so that he could sort things out. On reflection, other features of diving presented themselves. He found, for example, that it was extremely difficult adapting himself to such strange surroundings; one minute visibility would be good and the next atrocious; estimating distances had to be re-learnt; weighting was a novel sensation, as was the resistance posed by the water – all were strange and quite disturbing experiences.

Below: Yorkshire pioneers of the late 1940s – Bob Leakey and Reg Hainsworth.

Ogof Ffynnon Ddu, 1946

Balcombe's experiences in Goyden Pot gave a clear demonstration of the potential offered by diving and it was apparent that there would be many sites where these new techniques could lead to great discoveries. Thus, at Easter 1946, Balcombe and Sheppard visited the Swansea Valley to attempt the rising at Ffynnon Ddu. For many years cavers with an interest in the area had sought an entry to the elusive system which had to exist on the eastern side of the valley, near Abercrave. Balcombe hoped that diving would provide the key.

Balcombe and Sheppard were undoubtedly the only two people capable of performing the job adequately, and they received excellent support not only from cavers but also from the local inhabitants. In the event, they failed to enter the presumed system, but a dive of fifteen metres was made to a small, enclosed chamber above water. There was no way on and, despite several further attempts, no significant advance

Above: Bill Weaver on a training dive at Ffynnon Ddu, South Wales, 1946.

was made. It was, however from that Easter gathering that the Cave Diving Group was born.

The different approaches in France and Britain

As we have seen the first serious attempts on sumps were made in Britain and France in the 1940s. Previous dives had shown that using Standard Equipment was largely impractical, and significant progress in all underwater spheres had to await the evolution of self-contained equipment. Britain's contribution in this field had come initially with the production of the oxygen rebreathing apparatus which was demonstrated proficiently by the frogmen in World War II. As a result of this, cave diving in Britain and Italy adopted similar equipment, which was readily obtainable after the war, whereas in France, the aqualung was the favoured self-contained equipment from this time onwards.

CHAPTER FIVE

THE CAVE DIVING GROUP

The Cave Diving Group came about directly as a result of the work of Balcombe and Sheppard. It was, in Balcombe's own words, 'a product of an industrial and technical age', formed to draw together prospective cave divers from all over Great Britain and enable them to concentrate their efforts and share their knowledge. Balcombe was in every sense an innovator: 'We treat the conquest of cave obstacles primarily as technical problems and will take advantage of all technical aids to the limit of our time, ingenuity, and finance.' But it is important to note that then, as now, the Group was to exist for cavers who wished to dive, as opposed to divers who wished to cave. This was a distinct contrast to developments abroad, especially in France and the United States, where cave divers tended to be divers who turned cavers in pursuit of more challenging realms; this was prompted largely by the spacious nature of their sumps. In Britain an essential prerequisite for Group membership was that the candidate should be known to be a capable caver. The original concept still holds good today and the prime objective of the Group is 'to explore submerged caves and cave passages, and to lay down codes of diving practice for that purpose'.

The early days were heavily orientated towards the theory of cave diving, and the assembly of the optimum equipment to be used. As listed in the first letter to members, in May 1946, equipment consisted of two dresses, two respirators and certain navigating apparatus. When attention was focused on sumps, it was evident that the possibilities in all areas were legion.

The contacts in Siebe Gorman, who had been particularly helpful, were invited to join the group – a prudent move which soon paid dividends, but thereafter it became necessary to restrict membership to those with suitable qualifications. Soon the Group began to amass additional equipment, and it had five complete sets of frogman apparatus by the end of the

Below: Two early Aflo designs – the Aflo Davies (left) and the Aflo Balcombe (right), both incorporating lights and batteries, a line reel and depth gauges and a compass.

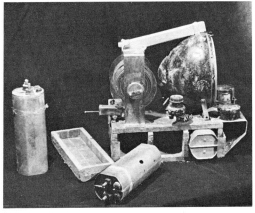

year. Training was given high priority. It was thought advisable that divers should have had at least two hours (later increased to five) under water, and a full understanding of their apparatus, before embarking on dives in dangerous places. It is interesting to note the definition of dangerous as: 'Any place where the diver goes out of control of the shore party'.

In these early days there was continuous reappraisal and modification of apparatus. The system of oxygen delivery, for example, was critical and was subjected to numerous trials. Oxygen was normally breathed without dilution, the signal for replenishment then being the mechanical collapse of the bag at the end of inhalation. There were two systems of supply, namely 'constant supply' at the maximum rate required (the surplus at lower rates of working blowing to waste), or 'supply as required' under the control of the diver. The first had the advantage of a fixed rate of use and was obviously a sound choice when the diver was in signal communication with his base. In caving this would not be practical, unless the diver carried a watch. Therefore, early ideas revolved around the second system. Another area of study was the Aflo, which was constantly modified, for it was soon realised that the first model was far too bulky for convenient use underground. With time, it became increasingly compact. Trials were undertaken with fins, but they were not popular. The technique required the diver to weight himself bow-heavy and progress with one hand on the line, using the other occasionally for fending himself off any obstacles. Control of buoyancy was vital, for the weights would not prevent floating on a full bag of oxygen, and if additional weight were used, the diver could find himself over-heavy when his bag was depleted. By November 1946 there were five divers in readiness, one of the first trainees being Donald Coase. Coase's impressions of his first cave dive, at Wookey Hole, were as follows:

The rock where Stanbury had got entangled was no distance in and I soon reached it. As I passed I found myself caught and after deliberating a second or so, I felt around and found my torch, which was hanging from a lanyard tied to my waist, had wedged between two rocks. It was soon free, and I went forward again down the boulder slope. Here the roof was rather low and

I felt my breathing bag rub against it. There was a canvas cover supplied to protect the breathing bag, but it was so stiff and unwieldy that we had decided not to use it. There and then, however, I made up my own mind that in future I would always use it, as a ripped breathing bag would not be very healthy. At last Graham [Balcombe] gave me three taps on the head, and after thinking a bit, I realised he meant me to return.

To do this I had to let go of the line to turn Aflo around, and by this time being in a cloud of sediment I had a nasty second or two before I had hold of the line again, although I knew it was only a foot to my right. I then retraced my steps and groped back along the line most of the way, owing to sediment.

In 1947 Group explorations made real progress. In Operation Janus at Wookey, for example, a ninth underwater chamber was reached, thirty metres beyond Chamber 7. In the same year Coase passed the short Sump 1 in Stoke Lane Slocker (eastern Mendip) by free diving to discover a major extension. Likewise in Derbyshire, at Peak Cavern, Operation Beta witnessed a ninety-two-metre advance in a single dive of twenty-five minutes' duration. This was the second operation by a CDG-trained diver, namely Coase; he was accompanied by Balcombe.

Operation Avanti, Wookey Hole, 1948
Success continued into 1948. As a diving site, Wookey Hole continued to dominate activities. However, despite increasing activity here after the war, much of the divers' efforts were diverted from the primary objective. The discovery of bones, for example, lying half buried in the flooded waterway, was to lead to a heavy emphasis on archaeological investigation, and many human skulls and artifacts were subsequently retrieved from areas such as the Skullery. While the finds were naturally of great interest and significance, they placed an effective dampener on the divers' efforts to push on with the exploration at the upstream limit. It was not until April 1948 and Operation Avanti that the next real progress was achieved.

The divers were Balcombe and Coase, the water conditions were perfect and for once everything went well. Firstly, they took an inflatable boat to Chamber

1. (right) Members of the Cave Diving Group training in Wookey's Chamber 3 in the 1950s. 2. (overleaf) Hepste Resurgence – a photo that conveys typical sump diving conditions, with murky water and frequent tight passages.

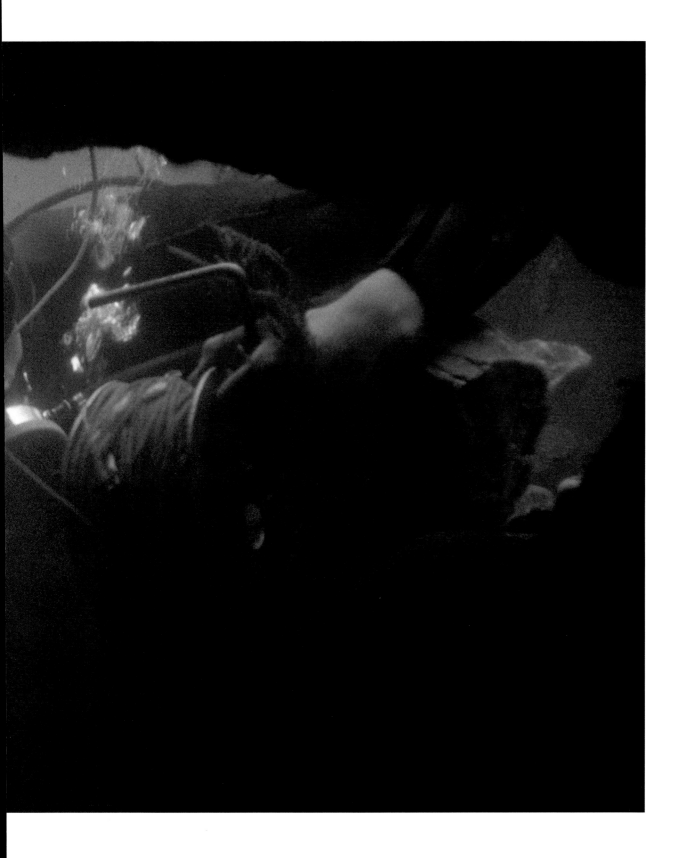

7; then, with it providing an invaluable psychological boost, they returned to base in Chamber 3 to recharge their equipment. Balcombe relates the events:

Rising up at the end of the Eighth [found the previous year] there was the mudbank to our front and right and it too led to a surface. The smooth, rounded and polished mud looked treacherous but excitement rather than caution ruled us. I signalled to Coase, 'Up!' and he promptly agreed. I fumbled with the line while tying on and at last had a belay, serviceable but doing no-one credit, and off we went. Don first, as it was his Aflo paying out the line (mine had by now jammed solid); he kept hard against the right-hand rock wall, partly for assistance from holds, partly because the mud elsewhere was so repulsive. I soon found the mud not too horrible to climb direct and made left towards the larger part of the surface and a good landing. Don was heading for some nasty rocks but as we rose so did our excitement. It was a matter of moments now. Recklessly I grabbed Don by his breathing bag and yanked him off the wall and we stood with our heads above water.

In front was a rampart of muddy pinnacles rising ten to fifteen feet from the water's edge; what was beyond we could only guess but the roof soared up to a great height and away into the darkness. As we rose out of the water, so our feet sank deeper into the mud until it was almost impossible to move.

3. *(top left) Phill Davies in action during an early attempt to pass Sump 2 of Stoke Lane Slocker, Mendips.* **4.** *(bottom left) Phil Rust fifty metres upstream from the Tradesman's Entrance of Porth yr Ogof, South Wales.*

Above: The Cave Diving Group in 1954 (left to right) D.A. Struan-Robertson, Oliver Lloyd, Oliver Wells, Phillip Davies, Graham Balcombe, Bob Davies, Derek Thorpe.

However we could just reach the bank where immediately the mud was hard and we unweighted each other; by now the excitement was displaced by all the intense irritations we experience on coming out into air. This is quite usual, it must be coupled with our inability to balance when freshly out of the all-supporting medium to which we have adapted, and we become intensely annoyed at our failures.

We parked Aflo IV at the foot of the ridge and started to climb with of all things that clumsy Aflo III. The ascent was not hard but it was exasperating and it was not until our respirators were off and lying on the summit, where the climb ended at a small platform, that I, at least, returned to normal.

Before us at a slightly lower level stretched a long expanse of sand, dipping slightly to the east. Its surface was pitted by many craters made by the drips from the roof, most about four inches deep. Beyond was the far boundary wall, rising slowly at first then steepening and shooting up to the roof, leaving one or two deeper ways on only to peter out at quite short distances. Left and right, the walls ran sheer up to the roof and up there were two huge wedged blocks, or part of the roof, waiting somewhat sinisterly I thought. The sandbank at the top of the sloping floor on the right finished at a narrow raised shelf against the wall. At its lower end it finished at a beautiful green well under the east wall . . .

Was this the Axe again or just a waterlogged hole? Surely all

Above: A scene during the 1948 Peak Cavern explorations showing (left to right) Bill Mack, Don Coase, controller, and Monty Granger (with pipe).

that sand must have come up through it? That can only mean that the main river flows along that way and is deflected round the northern boundaries to appear again at the hole we came through . . . But time was flying and the base would be anxious, worse than that, Mack [Bill Mack] the only diver there would be

duty bound to come to our rescue if we badly overshot our time. So we started back.

Respirators on, line tied off and cut, we tobogganed down the mud, a black wave advancing before us . . . We dropped down the slope to Mudball Alley into the inkiest blackness imaginable . . . Soon the way narrowed and the line led my arm into a slot only a few inches square, and there was no way on.

After a few attempts to establish the correct route the pair returned to Chamber 9. Following a brief discussion Coase, with greater reserves of gas and soda-lime, volunteered to sort out the problem. Balcombe was left to his thoughts. Time passed.

But, surely enough, such fears were quite unfounded; some few minutes later there was a pull on the line; I responded, then received 'Down!', three sharp pulls, one, two, pause then three.

The line had been buried in an undercut and, once reunited, the pair made an uneventful exit. Some thirteen years after diving first commenced in the cave they had made a creditable advance. This success gave the explorations a serious aspect. Continuing operations were envisaged for up to a kilometre. Such diving would require careful preparation, for Chamber 9 was situated about ninety-two metres from their base in Chamber 3. Consequently it was proposed that Chamber 9 be a forward base.

The actual time taken from depot to depot will be small. It is the preparations and then manoeuvring on the route which takes the time. There will have to be division of labour, divers with long duration breathing apparatus like the 'P Party', will push ahead, while other divers explore, equip, and survey the intermediate depots. The equipping will include the provision of a reliable telephone link to the main base, piling of gas and soda-lime supplies, food, spares, and first aid appliances. This in turn means much work behind the scenes, water-proof and pressure-proof carrying devices, and a host of suchlike things. Given continued access to the cave, have we the men to carry through a job like this?

Explorations in Peak Cavern, 1948

Successful operations were also being undertaken in Derbyshire, where a small group of divers had emerged, foremost of these being Bill Mack and Bill Davis. A crowning achievement here in 1948 was that at Peak Cavern, where a 110m through dive was made by Coase and Bill Davis from the Swine Hole back to the resurgence. Another notable advance was into the

Buxton Water Rising in the cave, where, in February 1949, a breakthrough was achieved, when the sump was passed to discover a major dry extension yielding well over a kilometre of particularly fine passageway. As a result of these dives the number of aspiring divers increased; of these Bob Davies proved most capable.

Coase's Experiment

Confidence was running high – confidence that was soon to be shaken. Coase had learned his lesson earlier, below Chamber 7 in Wookey. Whilst conducting an endurance experiment involving 'supply on demand', he had inadvertently encountered nitrogen excess (lack of oxygen).

> I decided to see just how long I could manage on the oxygen in the bag, after I couldn't get a full normal breath. When this happened, I started to breathe quickly and quite shallowly. This caused no obvious distress for a period of one to one and a half minutes, when I turned on the oxygen again. In fact I felt quite okay, and the shallow breathing became quite automatic. My mind became quite a pleasant void and where previously the major thoughts had been of the cold, I felt in a curiously inert or neutral state towards the temperature.

Above: The Peak Cavern team returns from the cave. Those in the picture include Trevor Ford (left), Jack Clarke (2nd from left), Don Coase (centre) and Rowland Revell (carrying two lights).

> It took an appreciable mental effort to think of turning on the oxygen again and even then there was no real desire on my part to do so. Having decided to do so, I had to think pretty hard to remember how to do this. It was more of a blind fumbling for the main cylinder valve, than putting my hand straight on it. As soon as the oxygen was turned on again, I returned almost immediately to my normal senses.

It was a foolhardy experiment and Coase was extremely lucky not to suffer a blackout.

Late in 1948 the Admiralty Experimental Diving Unit or AEDU began to show a keen interest in the activities of the CDG. 'I later discovered that they effectively infiltrated our group to find out what we were up to,' said Balcombe. The Navy divers had limited caving experience but it was thought politic to maintain harmonious relations by admitting two AEDU men to the Group (Grosvenor and Sheppard). This interest came at a time when there was a need for more equipment and divers. Balcombe summed up

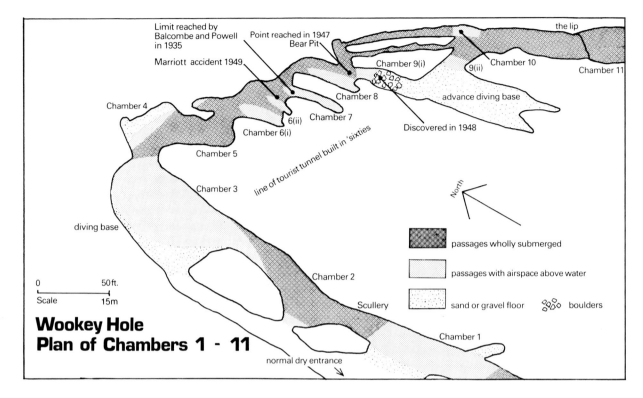

Limit reached by
Balcombe and Powell
in 1935

Point reached in 1947
Bear Pit

the lip

Marriott accident 1949

Chamber 9(i)

9(ii)

Chamber 10

Chamber 11

Chamber 4

Chamber 8

advance diving base

6(ii)   Chamber 7

Chamber 6(i)

line of tourist tunnel built in 'sixties

Discovered in 1948

Chamber 5

North

Chamber 3

diving base

passages wholly submerged

passages with airspace above water

0   50 ft.
Scale
15 m

Chamber 2

sand or gravel floor   boulders

**Wookey Hole
Plan of Chambers 1 - 11**

Scullery

Chamber 1

normal dry entrance

the position: 'What in fact has happened is that the demand for skilled and experienced divers has outstripped the supply.' A strong four-diver team was considered essential and the Group as it stood, would be hard pushed to meet such a need. There were several other aspirants to the CDG at this time among them a Butlin's Holiday Camp demonstration diver, one Gordon Marriott. Here was the classic example of a diver turned cave diver. An ex-Royal Marine, he was one of the first frogmen, having played an important role on the D-Day beaches. He exhibited exceptional skill and achievement, and held a record of some 500 hours under water. However, his only caving experience (with the CDG) was limited to one trip into Peak Cavern and another as guest attendant at a Wookey dive.

The Marriott Accident, Wookey Hole, 1949
Gordon Marriott was invited, together with Grosvenor, one of the new AEDU recruits, to take part in Operation Innominate in Wookey Hole on April 9, 1949. It was hoped to make a thorough examination of the underwater Chamber 11, which had been discovered in February. Six divers were to take part. Three experienced CDG divers, Graham Balcombe, Donald Coase and Bob Davies, would conduct the exploration in Chamber 11, while the new recruits, Marriott, Grosvenor and Lucy, would act in support. Coase, Balcombe and Davies were to use fins, which would enable them to remain high in Chamber 11, thereby reducing the risk of oxygen poisoning. The support divers were only to proceed to Chamber 9 where they would assist the exploratory divers in any way possible. Lucy and Grosvenor were to bottom-walk, but Marriott would wear fins. He was keen to join the men in Chamber 11, but was posted to Chamber 9, in accordance with CDG policy of gradual 'acclimatization'.

Before the main dive, Coase, the most experienced cave diver, took Marriott on a forty-nine-metre training dive to Chamber 6, showing him the safety platform in that location. Apart from having a light failure, Marriott handled himself well. The other newcomer, Grosvenor, was then taken by Davies on his training or acclimatization dive to Chamber 6. He experienced trouble with his face mask and withdrew from the operation. Balcombe also withdrew, but remained on hand in Chamber 3 in case of emergency.

Coase and Davies then recharged their apparatus. Marriott, however, felt no need to do so, having only used 50 atmospheres of oxygen out of a total of 130. Approaching Chamber 9, Marriott and supporter Lucy surfaced at the first available air-space, while Coase and Davies swam, via a loop passage, to the forward base at the far side of the chamber. Here, Davies corrected a leak with tools left for just such a purpose before the exploration commenced. Then they dived for over sixty metres out and beyond the cliff face in Chamber 11, which had been reached on the previous occasion. Finding nothing significant, except that the way ahead lay at a much lower level, they returned uneventfully to forward base. Here they reported back over the phone and had some food.

At about 8.30 p.m. they all started for base, Coase and Lucy via the shortest dive, while Davies and Marriott opted for the longer dive via the loop. The latter was chosen by Marriott, who was keen to see as much of the cave as possible. He was thoroughly briefed by Davies on what to expect and look out for, and appeared perfectly confident.

All went well until Chamber 8. Having chosen the correct line, Davies let Marriott go on in front. Visibility was down to zero, but the line could be felt twitching ahead, indicating that Marriott was making normal progress. When it stopped, Davies assumed that his colleague was a belay ahead and making faster progress due to the slightly better visibility in front. Only on arrival in Chamber 3, base, did he realise his error, that Marriott was in trouble and had left the guideline. He immediately returned. It was then nearly 9 p.m. Coase followed, as did Balcombe fifteen minutes later. Quite soon Davies was forced to turn to his reserve supply and Coase went ahead. Marriott was found lying face downwards along the line, pointing away from base. His bypass was opened and his cylinder and breathing bag found to be empty. The body was extricated from where it was wedged between the rocks and taken to the platform in Chamber 6, a mere three metres away.

Artificial respiration was immediately applied, but there was never any movement, pulse or reflex action. Just after 10.30 p.m. resuscitation was abandoned and Marriott pronounced dead. The body was removed.

Just what had occurred? In all probability Marriott had let go of the line when his oxygen had expired, the most likely explanation for this being that he wanted to find and operate his reserve cylinder. This was not built in to his breathing apparatus (as required by the Cave Diving Group) but was tied, by a short lanyard, to his person. The reserve was found to be missing when he was brought to Chamber 6 and, when it was found one month later, its pressure was 115 atmospheres: it was full. It appeared that he must have untied it and then dropped it. In reduced visibility finding it would be virtually impossible. Having lost his sense of direction, he located the line, but too late to reach safety.

It is interesting to reflect that in frogman training the reserve cylinder was operated by carefully projecting the valve opening under the lip of the face-mask and simply turning on the amount required. To perform this manoeuvre in nil visibility and under stress was evidently the last straw.

Afterwards certain important points came to light. One was that no personal log was kept, although Marriott's movements were recorded on the master log held by the controller[*]. The reason for this was that the group treated Marriott as a guest and expert in his own right, and therefore did not impress the normal CDG requirements upon him. Similarly, on leaving forward base, Davies was perfectly satisfied by Marriott's assurance that all was well.

The inquest returned the verdict that 'death was due to anoxemia, accidentally sustained during diving operations, when his oxygen supply became exhausted due to a fault in the test pressure gauge'. The existence of a 'fault' is doubtful and calculations made later showed that Marriott was almost guaranteed to run out of oxygen where he did. Most importantly, the inquest recommended that in future 'all divers, including guest divers, should be subjected to the same equipment tests as the members of the Cave Diving Group'.

[*] As early as 1935 it had become an accepted practice that cave divers should keep personal logs of their movements at each recordable stage of a dive. This procedure resulted from the training given by an ex-Naval instructor.

Thus passed a brilliant diver, the victim of an accident which need never have occurred. It served as a grave reminder to all other divers to weigh their preparations and actions with far greater caution than before. Applications and discipline were scrutinized and tightened but inevitably the work went on.

Operation Beta 2, Peak Cavern, 1949

In 1949 significant progress was made. Operation Beta 2 in Peak Cavern is worthy of mention, for here, during a comfortable seven-minute dive, Davis and Coase covered the sump from the resurgence to Swine Hole. They were wearing fins. Their time was excellent compared to bottom-walking rate, but there was a problem in that it would have been relatively easy for them to get lost if a false move or stop had allowed the water to become muddied and visibility to deteriorate. They had completed the dive largely without a line, for the one already laid (from the previous year) was buried and tangled. Both Davis and Coase were adamant that diving without a line was not to be recommended. Later a safety ruling completely forbade such practice. The use of fins was clearly spreading and showed several advantages over bottom-walking. There was a great increase in manoeuvrability and speed, important for long-distance work; three-dimensional movement was far easier, allowing exploration of deeps, high roofs or air surfaces, as in Wookey's Chamber 11; also swimming high above the floor stirred up less mud than walking. The disadvantages were: the technique required considerable experience; heavy or bulky objects were difficult to transport; when combating a strong current, more energy was required and therefore involved higher gas consumption; and swimmers could not follow close in line, owing to the thrashing fins. There were also positive dangers associated with the technique, for example, unpractised divers could find swimming energetic and tiring. This would lead to a greater chance of carbon dioxide excess, and

Left: Three photographs showing Phill Davies and Luke Devenish during their explorations in Tunnel Cave (Cathedral Cave) in the mid 1950s. The frogman's equipment is clearly illustrated but with lead-weighted boots for bottom-walking. The divers are wearing the oxygen rebreathing equipment that was in common use at this time.

Above: CDG members, Oliver Wells, Luke Devenish and Graham Balcombe recover after a dive in Wookey Hole in the early 1950s.

oxygen convulsions. Also, if a diver were to lose a line when slightly over-buoyant, he might float uncontrollably and lose his bearings. In bottom-walking the line could never be far away and could usually be found by groping.

The Problems of Rebreathing Apparatus

Fins might be advantageous or dangerous according to the situation, but one could never relax one's concentration whilst using rebreathing apparatus. Everything had to be checked and double checked, for a rash or erroneous decision could be fatal. The chief problem with the equipment was the way in which the early symptoms of danger could pass unnoticed. Oxygen poisoning would strike without warning,

while carbon dioxide and nitrogen excess crept on insidiously. By the time the danger had been realized it was often too late for the diver to think rationally and extricate himself. To panic or make a rapid dash for base was to invite disaster, for to deal with carbon dioxide excess in particular required the utmost self-control. Thus preparations before any dive had to satisfy all the people present, and it was essential that all the equipment be functioning correctly.

Many of the hazards were discovered during open-water dives, prompt action often saving the day. On one such occasion a diver became dazed to blackout within four minutes of executing his preparatory breathing drill. On a subsequent 'safe water' dive, attached to a rope (and therefore under the control of the shore party) he had no trouble, despite the fact that nothing had been altered in his kit. Deciding that all was now well, the diver once more unroped and proceeded. Six minutes later he was discovered by his colleague Davies, who was on a routine check, immobilised and helpless. He was very red in the face, making convulsive movements and not breathing. There was no response to tapping on the face-piece and he was immediately towed ashore. Four minutes after he had been found, he regained consciousness and was fully recovered after an hour. His symptoms had been those of oxygen excess, but, when samples of his soda-lime were analysed, they were found to be exhausted. The diver was extremely fortunate not to have incurred more severe consequences, and safety rulings were updated and reinforced.

Incident at Peak Cavern, 1952

Among the constant reminders of danger several incidents provided amusingly humorous diversions. In June 1952, for example, the BBC approached the Cave Diving Group to make a recording of an actual dive. It was considered a good opportunity for Thompson (the aforementioned diver who had lost consciousness) to give Ken Hurst his first cave dive in Peak Cavern Resurgence.

On reaching the Schoolroom, a small, above-water chamber located nine metres into the cave, telephone communication was about to be established when the lines were inadvertently dropped. Thompson had to return to the surface outside to locate them. Back in the Schoolroom group efficiency was demonstrated and, after exchanging agreed words with base, the gear was packed away. Preparations were then made for the exit. The smooth routine collapsed when the time arrived for Hurst to perform his breathing drill. When he opened his pressure reducer bypass to refill his breathing bag, there was an almighty explosion and it seemed as though the whole apparatus had blown up. Fortunately it was only a split in the pressure tubing connecting the reducer to the breathing bag. However, the equipment was now useless and Thompson was forced to leave Hurst in the Schoolroom while he obtained a replacement.

Right: Two views of Peak Cavern, Derbyshire, a magnificent passage initially reached by divers Bill Mack and Don Coase but later opened by digging activity.

Above: Graham Balcombe and Mick Glennister transporting a bulky packaged Aflo at Swildon's in 1954.

This he did, making the journey to Sheffield and back in seventy minutes.

Back at base, Thompson was ready to dive when someone prematurely threw the switch on the Aflo. Clouds of smoke were given off and the apparatus promptly plunged into the river. The battery was disconnected and, roaring with laughter, everyone saw the funny side of what might have been a serious situation. Even Hurst, informed by telephone, was amused until he realised that it was his Aflo that was smoking. With a new Aflo, the spare breathing apparatus was taken to the Schoolroom. Breathing drill completed, Hurst dived away. All went well until the telephone (in whose cable Hurst was entangled) started for base as well. Thompson grabbed the handset just in time to see the wires pull out and continue upon their journey. With a signal that Hurst

was ashore (tugs on the line), Thompson dived. Experiencing difficulties of his own, he eventually made his exit half an hour behind Hurst. Thus ended the longest first cave dive on record.

This catalogue of mishaps was amusing but it still incorporated a serious warning. The reducer bypass had to be operated gently, only a fraction of a turn being necessary to meet the need.

Communications Underwater

Another fundamental problem encountered at this time was that of communication underwater. This was never really solved, other than by primitive attempts or by laying telephone lines from base to distant air-bells. Diver-to-diver contact was difficult, being limited mainly to taps or wild gesticulations. Underwater hooters became fairly common in 1956 but their range was also limited. Purely mechanical arrangements, for example, a bicycle bell, as used by Davies at one time, could have advantages. O.C. Wells built such a device which was audible to the diver operating it, but failed to attract the attention of Balcombe, who was about ten inches away. The problem remains largely unsolved today.

Aflo Designs

Another basic problem concerning the Aflo was its size and bulk. It was unwieldy and highly susceptible to becoming entangled in guidelines. It was usually connected to the diver by a lanyard, which had to be easily disconnectable. The line reel could accidentally foul at any time and, rather than lose the whole Aflo, it was better to jettison the reel. Not only was the Aflo too expensive to lose but it also contained the lights which were essential to navigate a safe exit. Quick release devices, therefore, became quite popular at this time.

Record Dive at Clapham Beck Head, 1953

Progress in equipment design, techniques and achievements was gradual. At Clapham Beck Head in Yorkshire a record dive was made in May 1953. The divers were Davies and Buxton, who covered 117m of submerged passage until their line ran out. Their total dive, nearly 244m, took twenty-seven minutes, in a water temperature of 6.5°C. No air surfaces were observed and the passage was seen to continue spaciously at a depth of five metres.

Attempt at Swildon's Sump 3, 1954

At this time major extensions resulting from diving appeared to be restricted to the north of the country, in particular Peak Cavern, Derbyshire and Clapham Cave, Yorkshire. In the south Swildon's had remained inviolate since Balcombe had reached what was later to be known as Sump 3 in 1936. Davies, however, determined to crack the obstacle in the summer of 1954.

Preliminary trips were made on June 19 and 24 to get all the baggage to the base at Sump 2. Fifteen packs were transported on the first trip and on June 24, four 'sherpas' took down the remaining gear. Two days later Davies (who was on his first visit to the cave) and Balcombe entered at 3.50 p.m. It was three hours before they reached base, and 9.15 p.m. before

everything was tested and the logs written up. They could make no progress in Sump 3 owing to an almost complete mud fill and it was 12.30 a.m. before they gave two hoots (unheard at base), their return signal, for the 'sherpas'. They left base at 3.05 a.m. and reached surface at 9.00 a.m. The gear was recovered by a large support party later in the day.

The failure at Swildon's was disappointing, but it belied the positive progress which had been made since 1946. Cave diving had been established as a practical technique and major discoveries were sure to follow in time. Easy, short, shallow sumps were unfortunately few and far between. The potential for open passages beyond submerged sections was obvious. Lengthy dives like that at Clapham Beck Head (117m) had been proved possible, but required thorough training. This was clearly difficult in many areas as so few people had any experience of rebreathing apparatus. As it developed, tuition was restricted to the Midlands and south of the country, where expertise was to be found and where qualified divers lived. Here an active nucleus formed, intent upon the conquest of the ultimate barrier.

Below: Bob Davies and Graham Balcombe at Swildon's before their attempt on Sump 3 in 1954.

CHAPTER SIX

AQUALUNG OR MIXTURE SET

A problem which loomed large through all explorations at this time was that of oxygen poisoning, the threat of which virtually precluded all progress below a depth of nine metres. It was the great challenge of Wookey Hole which constantly drew attention to this problem. In Wookey visibility was good, preparations and kitting up were easy and access to base was pleasant. It was the home ground of the Cave Diving Group, offering not only the best conditions for training, but also the possibility of a major extension. The response to this challenge required the highest individual qualities and the very best equipment.

However, the submerged Chamber 11 was restricting all progress due to its passing below the bounds of safe diving. The roof had been examined, but it was clear that the way on lay at greater depths. In order to overcome the oxygen poisoning problem and thereby reach this elusive passage two courses of action were possible. The first was really an extension or modification of the oxygen principle: by diluting the oxygen with a proportion of nitrogen the resulting mixture was safe to greater depths than had hitherto been possible, since only pure oxygen is toxic at these depths. Siebe Gorman had run experiments along these lines during and after the war, but this refined apparatus was unavailable outside the naval sphere. The second course of action was to use a compressed air set or aqualung, as developed by the French. Despite their relative expense and limited supply, the principle was sound. Consequently, Bob Davies

Left: Charles George and Brian de Graaf who reached Oxygen Pot in Ogof Ffynnon Ddu in 1961. This photo illustrates the evolutions in old equipment in the last days before the Aqualung styles took over. Aflos were still in use and both divers are using U.B.A. (Universal Breathing Apparatus) rebreathing equipment. George's fins contrast with de Graaf's lead weighted boots.

obtained the necessary equipment and, in 1955, made several dives to ascertain its usefulness. In May at Gough's Cave, Cheddar, he made a descent of the Skeleton Pit, which he discovered attained a depth of over twenty-two metres, the limit of his belay line. The aqualung's application to deep diving in caves was thereby proven, and an assault was planned on Wookey.

The First Use of an Aqualung in Wookey, 1955
The contingency plans were complex, necessitating the co-operation of several experienced divers acting in support. On 10 December all was ready. The divers were Bob Davies, John Buxton and Oliver Wells. Basically, all three were to proceed to Chamber 9 on oxygen in normal fashion (bottom-walking). There Davies was to test his twin-cylinder aqualung and dress for swimming. Difficulties were anticipated with laying the line, owing to the possibility of it being entangled in the feet of the swimming diver. Consequently, Buxton was to lay the line as far as the lip in Chamber 11, while Davies would fin just ahead of him. Bottom-walkers Buxton and Wells would then remain at the safe limit for oxygen divers, acting as beacons. Having tied on his own line at the lip, Davies could then make a quick reconnaissance of the depths below. Under the circumstances a solo diver could be expected to do little more. Fins were necessary in this venture because a bottom-walking diver might encounter great difficulty in climbing out and, in any case, walking would be dangerously slow for the limited duration of the open-circuit aqualung. With 40 cu.ft of air in each cylinder the diver could expect to stay down for sixty to eighty minutes at a depth of less than six metres. It was agreed that, if the party became separated, the beacon divers would

Above and left: Bob Davies aided by John Buxton, sets off to test his aqualung in Skeleton Pit, Cheddar (Mendips) in 1955.

remain in place for forty-five minutes before returning and raising the alarm.

The party left Chamber 3 at 9.17 p.m. and dived on from Chamber 9 at 11.45 p.m. All went well until the lip of Chamber 11 was reached. Davies swam down and made a rapid examination, noting the way on. He then returned to his friends to tie on his line before proceeding. By this time the sediment had been disturbed and visibility was greatly reduced. In the gloom Davies failed to link the lines properly and he suddenly noticed that his Aflo was in danger of falling apart, for the container of instruments had not been securely bolted together. Anxiety and a desire to remedy his problems led to over-breathing. The fractional increase of air in the lungs in turn increased his buoyancy and he floated up against the roof, lost to his friends stationed below. Seeing him disappear in the turbid waters, they thought that he had made his way back to Chamber 9. Consequently they returned and, not surprisingly, could find no trace of him. Realizing their error, they quickly resumed their position in Chamber 11.

Davies, meanwhile, had tried locating his friends, but failed. While he was up against the roof desperately attempting to secure his Aflo, at a depth of three metres his first cylinder gave out. Immediately he equalized the pressure in his cylinders via a connecting manifold, and started on the third quarter of his total air supply.* The situation was critical and, with no communication with his friends nor a line, he had only one avenue open. To remain up against the roof was certain death, so he swam around in circles, desperately trying to locate either the divers or a guide line. Meanwhile Buxton and Wells searched the area between Chambers 9 and 11 in worsening visibility, but with negative results.

Davies Lost in Wookey Hole

At the end of his third quarter of air Davies located clear water, which meant that he was further than ever from the safety of Chamber 9 and heading upstream. Then, at a depth of fifteen metres, he noted a cross rift immediately above, and frantically set off upwards in

---

* In the system that Davies was using one cylinder was always turned off. In effect therefore half of the total capacity of the Aqualung was held in reserve at any one time. When the first cylinder was depleted the second was manually opened, allowing the equalization of pressure within both cylinders. The second was then closed, holding half of the available air reserve once more.

search of air amidst a cloud of bubbles. By an amazing stroke of luck he reached a small air-surface, in which he was able to climb out of the water. Taking off his aqualung, which was by now buoyant, he climbed up a short distance and, using one of the longest straps, pulled it up behind him. Shivering with cold and relief, he sat and reviewed the situation. It was far from healthy. The time was 12.24 a.m: he had been under water thirty-nine minutes after leaving Chamber 9.

In the vicinity of the lip Buxton and Wells had found no trace of him, and hooters elicited no response from Davies.

Eventually they decided that he was either safe in an unknown chamber or was beyond help, as he had had less than an hour's air-supply when last seen. The controller and shore party in Chamber 3 became increasingly anxious as the divers went overdue and further time elapsed. Then, at about 3 a.m., Wells and Buxton emerged to raise the alarm.

Rescue operations were commenced. Balcombe was contacted in London, so too were the naval authorities at HMS *Vernon*. Widespread facilities were made available to the divers as the seriousness of the situation was fully realized. Davies's chances were not rated highly. Back at the air-pocket, Davies explored his domain. A small passage of about a metre in

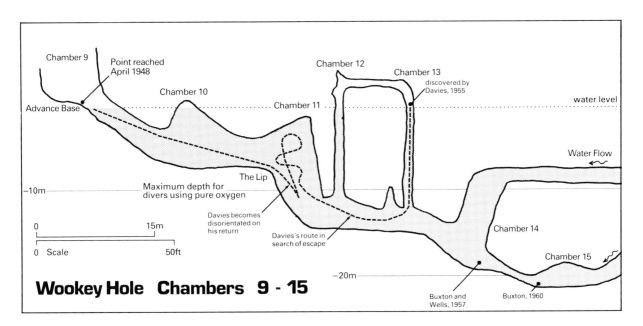

Wookey Hole   Chambers   9 - 15

Above: Bob Davies – a lucky escape from Wookey 13.

diameter led for nine metres back towards Chamber 9; it terminated at a sump pool, which he named Chamber 12. In the other direction, upstream, the passage could be seen to continue beyond his exit pool, which he now dubbed Chamber 13. With sufficient air in these chambers for several days, his immediate outlook was reasonable. But analysing his chances over a longer period left him in low spirits, for he knew that in such confinement cold and hunger would quickly weaken him. The supply in his cylinder was greatly depleted, now amounting to 35 atmospheres per cylinder, compared to 120 when full, enough, he estimated, for twelve minutes whilst swimming. But considering the distance back to Chamber 9, he felt that ten minutes would be a bare minimum, even if he achieved a straightforward uninterrupted dive. The limit was dangerously close.

Davies' Escape from Wookey

Should he, therefore, wait for rescue? This was the critical issue. For oxygen divers to descend to fifteen metres was impossible. Furthermore, they had no idea of his route, as he had left no line and they had no deep diving apparatus. For naval divers using mixtures to make the attempt would be unreasonably dangerous, because they had no cave diving experience. For the naval divers to instruct the cave divers in the use of oxygen-nitrogen apparatus, which was not yet available to civilians, could take days. They would still have to locate him, by which time his chances would be extremely slim.

Having made tentative repairs to his Aflo, Davies decided on a course of action. He would wait for about three hours, during which time he hoped the water would clear, and then attempt to exit. Laying a line would enable him to return to the sanctuary of Chamber 13 if he became short of air.

At 3.50 a.m. he set his Aflo compass in the direction which he assumed Chamber 9 to be, and dived. The upward slope to Chamber 11 verified his bearings and he continued. After taking one brief false turning, he saw the wire left by Coase in 1949. Here his first cylinder gave out. Though less than halfway back to Chamber 9, he decided to press on. In so doing he used the line to pull himself along faster. This snapped and almost simultaneously his own reel jammed solid. Quickly he removed and dropped it. Heralding the impending exhaustion of his air, his breathing became difficult. With only seconds of life left in his cylinders, he dropped his Aflo, reaching air in complete darkness. Shocked, but still thinking rationally, he located his emergency torch and re-assured himself that he was indeed in Chamber 9. The time was 4.07 a.m.

After about five minutes, he could see the glow from his Aflo at a depth of about four metres, so he swam out to retrieve it using a loop of wire. His safe exit was now almost guaranteed, for he had ample oxygen in the rebreathing set which had been left in Chamber 9.

During the difficult process of kitting up he fell over, fortunately only losing a portion of his oxygen supply. Then he made an uneventful exit to safety, reaching base with its posted observers at 5 a.m. He was tired and cold, but very happy. 'The Devil', he said, 'is a gentleman.'

The Cause of the Davies Incident

As a result of this incident opinion hardened against the use of fins and aqualungs generally. They were regarded as the exception rather than the rule and it was thought pertinent that bottom-walking divers should make a point of holding on to swimmers, particularly in poor visibility.

However, careful analysis of the cause of the affair can only lead to one logical conclusion: that far from being the aqualung which was to blame or even the mode of travel, namely finning, the fault lay in the fact that no line had been laid during reconnaissance. During this period visibility had deteriorated and Davies had become disorientated. No allowance had been made for this. Had he laid a line from Chamber 11 into the depths below, as originally planned, then the whole incident need never have occurred.

General rules were now revised. It was forbidden to dive without a completely separate bottle of gas which could be fed into the respirator in the event of an emergency. Single-cylinder aqualungs were to be avoided owing to their lack of such reserve. Overall it was thought that the special dangers inherent in diving in caves necessitated the use of closed circuit apparatus (oxygen sets), despite all their additional trouble, and a far more rigorous training schedule was required.

Mixture Sets Come into Use

Unfortunately, air could not be used on closed circuit since the flow required to prevent oxygen lack or hypoxia would be too high, resulting in the bottle emptying too quickly to be useful on a long dive.

Because of this, the obvious line of development now lay in diluting oxygen with a low percentage of nitrogen. The duration of the cylinders was not appreciably affected, as breathing was relatively constant at all depths, whereas, on open circuit, air consumption increases rapidly with depth. The main considerations, therefore, were to retain the greater duration to be achieved by the use of recirculated oxygen while preventing oxygen poisoning.

Davies and Balcombe had swiftly perceived the advantages of this system, but neither they nor any other members of the Cave Diving Group had any experience in using the more sophisticated equipment. The number of potential divers to press on with the exploration was depleted in 1956, when Davies left for America. This left Buxton and Wells actively to the fore, both obliged to play a waiting game while they became proficient with the new equipment. Practice dives took place in open water and the first cave dive on mixture occurred at Wookey in December 1956. No actual progress was made on this occasion. In April 1957, at Hurtle Pot in Yorkshire, a depth of fourteen metres was reached, at a point sixty metres from base. However, it was September before the long-awaited attempt on Wookey could be made.

Buxton and Wells in Wookey, 1957

On foot, Buxton and Wells reached the bottom of Davies's aven up to air, Chamber 13, and within a few more metres discovered a lowering of the roof. This was at a point sixty-seven metres from Chamber 9. A return was made in March 1958 and the constriction found to be awkward, but passable. Depth-gauge readings indicated that twenty metres had been reached, and this was the limit of the mixture they were using (70% oxygen, 30% nitrogen). Ahead and below, the elusive underwater Chamber 15 beckoned, its roof estimated at a depth of twenty-one metres.

Despite the cave's further rebuff, the divers were optimistic that Chamber 15 could be entered by using a weaker oxygen-nitrogen mixture, probably 50/50, which would be safe down to thirty metres. Wells reckoned that it would take twelve to eighteen months before Chamber 15 was gained, since time had to be allowed for training.

The objective dangers on dives of this nature were obviously high. The divers' reliance on their equipment was total, and there was no question whatsoever of beating a hasty retreat to an airspace should severe problems arise. It is not surprising that searching glances were exchanged at new diving sites where potential rewards in the form of dry extensions might outweigh the dangers imposed by long, deep dives.

Other Explorations by Buxton and Wells

In June 1956, for example, Buxton and Wells had passed an awkward twenty-metre sump in Threaplands Cave, Yorkshire. They had explored 180m of new passage and further openings remained to be followed. This was heralded as a major find, particularly when the length explored was later to exceed 400m. In South Wales a series of sumps had been located, those in Ogof Ffynnon Ddu being particularly promising. Consequently, in July 1958, Buxton and Wells commenced the exploration that, in 1967, would reveal the longest and deepest system in Great Britain.

Swildon's Hole, 1958

During 1958 a new assault was planned on the recently discovered Sump 4 of Swildon's, a point reached by a high-level bypass to Sumps 2 and 3, including the infamous squeeze known as Blue Pencil Passage. In September 1958 Buxton and Wells passed the constricted four-metre dive, which was quickly followed by a free diving member of the support party.

The Swildon's operation took over two weekends to execute. On September 6 twenty-eight packs were carried to the diving site and thoroughly checked for damage by the divers. The following weekend's activities were well documented. This was due largely to the success of the dive, but also to the unpleasant conditions experienced by both divers and 'sherpas'. The personal account of one of the helpers describes the scene:

The air in Paradise Regained [the passage prior to Blue Pencil – the non-diving route to Sump 4] was distinctly foul, as had been noticed the previous weekend. Lack of oxygen caused excessive panting, not made any easier by the one piece exposure suits that were worn . . . The air was so bad that in some places a candle would not burn.

Above: The streamway between Sumps 3 and 4 in Swildon's Hole, a point that can now be reached without diving by squeezing through Blue Pencil Passage.

The exploration was halted within a few metres by yet another sump – Sump 5. Carrying in the equipment had been extremely arduous, probably the worst so far encountered underground. Consequently, future dives were planned with the object of being lightweight. Wells, therefore, proceeded to modify his equipment, pruning all unnecessary weight, and in November successfully led a small party past Sump 5. The character of the passage up to Sump 5 was noted as 'unpleasant', an observation reiterated by Mike Thompson on his visit to the extension on this trip.

After a short piece of passage we were confronted with the first of the ducks, a low tunnel about thirty feet in length with an air-space varying between three inches and six inches. In turn we solemnly lay down on our backs and floated through . . . Our trial by water was by no means finished and we were now to be introduced to a duck already christened 'Buxton's Horror'! All that can be seen is a tiny triangular air-space and unless one has a snorkel-type nose it is easier to treat it as a sixth sump.

On their return, another of the explorers, L. Dawes, had a 'hair-raising experience' at this obstacle. In Dawes's own words:

> Excepting when the water is low, it is almost impossible to go through keeping one's nose in the air-space. After taking a deep breath, I dived under the duck, travelled about five or six feet and put my head up, expecting to emerge in the air-space on the far side. All I found was rock and water: no air. It flashed through my mind that the water level may have risen since we went through, so I beat a hasty retreat back again, expecting to come into the air-space I started from. But I didn't: just water and rock again. I moved forwards and backwards underneath trying to find an air-space until Mike [Thompson] saw my ankle and pulled me into the place I'd started from.

The reason for the incident was that the air-space both before and after the duck did not extend the whole width of the passage. Consequently, as it is difficult to gauge distances under water, it was all too easy to miss the relatively small sections containing air. On later dives the water-level was lowered by digging through a gravel bank (beyond Sump 5) and the hazard removed.

Moving Towards Lighter Equipment

Both the divers and the 'sherpas' on the 1958 Swildon's trip were well equipped, carrying far less gear than on previous operations and significantly free of the infamous, bulky Aflo. Lighting was obtained from ordinary cap-lamps, while much of the other equipment, for example a compass, was deemed unnecessary.

This move to lighter equipment was significant and once more a distinction could be drawn between the cave diver and the open water diver. The issue was one of objectives rather than diving for the sake of diving. The caver's aim was to discover virgin passage and he would adopt any feasible method to achieve this end. By perfecting lightweight equipment more

sites became viable and anything that reduced the sheer bulk of the apparatus was clearly welcome. In a well-planned operation there were usually many helpers, but the more numerous the helpers the more protracted and congested would be the time from surface to sump and out again. Underground the concept of larger equipment and more support did not always work out in practice. One advantage was that minimising the overall porterage not only speeded up the operation but also helped reduce the possibility of damage to the kit.

New Depth Possibilities

During this period, Buxton and Wells (by invitation of the Navy) achieved a simulated depth of sixty metres in the pressure chamber at HMS *Vernon*. French divers

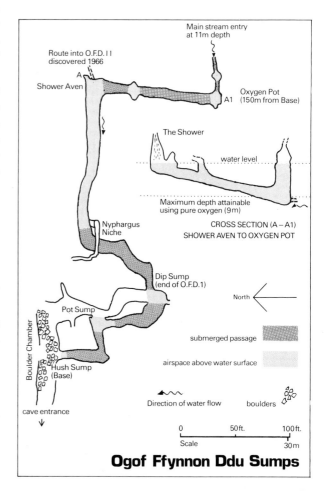

Ogof Ffynnon Ddu Sumps

had already explored to sixty metres on compressed air in the Fontaine de Vaucluse but at that depth another hazard had made its presence felt. This was the so-called 'rapture of the deep' or nitrogen narcosis, the effect of which was to blunt the diver's awareness and instil him with a false, irresponsible euphoria. Occasionally the symptoms of narcosis included depression or blackout. There is no way of preventing the hazard, but a diver is immediately cured as he ascends from depth. It is possible to build up one's narcosis tolerance by making regular dives to the depth at which the symptoms appear, but this is clearly difficult for a sporting diver.

The value of the simulated dive was immense, showing that a safe maximum depth of forty-three metres could be obtained on mixtures. With the Universal Breathing Apparatus (UBA) the Cave Diving Group possessed the equipment to operate to this depth for two hours, but the need for such dive durations was not envisaged at this time. However, explorations in many caves had now reached beyond the critical depth for pure oxygen and, as a consequence, awaited exploration on mixtures.

Ogof Ffynnon Ddu, 1960-61

One of the more important operations at this time was by Charles George and Brian de Graaf at Ogof Ffynnon Ddu. Here, during 1960 and 1961, the divers reached a point 146m from base, achieving a maximum depth of eleven metres. The final dive in a series occurred in January 1961, causing the divers great trepidation. The aim was to explore the mainstream entry to the submerged network, which involved the use of mixtures. From previous dives it was known that the way on lay at the bottom of Oxygen Pot, so called due to its location at the critical level of nine metres.

The two divers progressed on oxygen for 107m to Shower Aven, before making an underwater change to mixtures. They then walked down to Oxygen Pot and entered the fast shrinking upstream passage. The depth was by now eleven metres and they were reduced first to crawling and then to a flat-out squeeze. Trouble suddenly struck when de Graaf's reserve oxygen cylinder was accidentally turned on by rubbing against the floor. The resulting infla-

Above: The passage between Shower Aven and Oxygen Pot in Ogof Ffynnon Ddu – Paul Miles in action at a depth of six metres.

tion wedged him so firmly that he was completely immobilised until the gas had exhausted itself. On extrication, de Graaf retreated with George, viewing future diving prospects with much pessimism. However, had they but known, in September 1960 they could have gained entry to the elusive Ogof Ffynnon Ddu 2 – the master cave. On one particular dive George (using fins) had made a brief ascent to examine a small air-bell, off which he noted a small and apparently insignificant dry passage. He was unable to explore it, for de Graaf (bottom-walking) was awaiting his return below. The cavers of the area waited a frustrating six years before the divers sallied forth once more. Equipped this time with a scaling ladder, they gained the passages noted earlier, above Shower Aven. The accolade deservedly went to Charles George, whose earlier explorations had laid the basis of this success.

Chamber 15, Wookey Hole, 1960

Another significant success with mixtures was that at Wookey in December 1960. Here Buxton passed beyond the twenty-metre limit and became the first person to tread the floor of Chamber 15. This lay at a depth of twenty-three metres and proved to be the elbow or lowest point of the sump.

The Aqualung Becomes More Popular

Alongside the specialised and comparatively rare diving on mixtures, there was, at the time, a vast increase in open water diving using aqualungs. The British Sub-Aqua Club or BSAC had been formed in 1953 in response to demand from the underwater sporting fraternity. In official circles naval personnel had commenced activities on air in 1957. This was found to be eminently suitable, especially for depths of between nine and fifteen metres.

Developments in France typified the successful dives on air that were becoming commonplace abroad, and the advantages of air were proving themselves even further afield. In 1959 a depth of forty-four metres was reached in a flooded pot in Mexico, while later in the year an article in the magazine *Triton* (published by the BSAC) told of a 102m/335ft dive in the Sinoia Caves, Southern Rhodesia, to establish the bottom of the Sleeping Pool. The dive, including decompression, lasted seventy minutes.

This deep penetration was an excellent indicator of the usefulness of the equipment (aqualung and wet suit). The three people who undertook the dive were, however, under the influence of nitrogen at depth and were only able to spend a couple of seconds at the ninety-one metre level. This proved to be the practical limit on pure compressed air.

Below: Norman Brindle, wearing aqualung equipment, about to dive in New Goyden Pot, Yorkshire in 1957. Right: Brindle with his support team after the dive.

Aqualungs in the Late 50s
In caving circles at home an independent diver, Norman Brindle, experimented with an aqualung at New Goyden Pot, Yorkshire, in 1957 and discovered the inadequacies of bulky back-mounted equipment in a restricted passage. Again, in 1958, eight members of a London diving group affiliated to the BSAC made fruitful dives in Great Masson Cavern, Derbyshire, while in June 1959 Norman and Dennis Brindle passed two consecutive sumps (five metres and forty-six metres respectively) at Boreham Cave, in Yorkshire.

Why Cave Divers Preferred Rebreathing Equipment
These events took place outside the mainstream of conventional, organised cave diving, which still remained sceptical about aqualungs. Throughout the late fifties the CDG persisted with its traditional approach, although in a muted key. Oxygen and mixture diving equipment required extremely rigorous, specialised training. Facilities for recharging cylinders were limited and expensive. All this contrasted greatly with the comparatively simple training required for the aqualung. Air was also cheap, and compressors, available for use by BSAC members, were increasing in number all over the country.

Why then had the Cave Diving Group clung to methods that were generally disdained by other divers? The answer is simple. Their equipment was abundant and easy to acquire. Furthermore, conditions in British sumps, which were small and shallow with poor visibility, were radically different from the open water environment and many overseas sumps.

Continental sites are larger and often much deeper, usually with excellent visibility. They favour a 'normal' back-mounted arrangement of equipment, so in general the problems (excluding those of depth) encountered on entry to this subterranean realm were less than in Britain.

Developing from this, another major difference had isolated British divers from their overseas counterparts – that of objectives. Cave divers in Britain have always been cavers who adopted breathing apparatus to further their normal caving explorations, whereas abroad, in France and the United States, for example, open water divers have set the pace. They were often lured into spacious and accessible cave sites promoting a modified form of their sea diving techniques.

These differences were soon to be reduced, however, and by the late fifties the trend was clearly towards the aqualung. It was evident that the rebreathing apparatus so favoured by the CDG would soon be obsolete.

CHAPTER SEVEN

THE TRANSITION TO AIR

Boon's Experiments with Aqualungs

In 1962 there was a significant change, a change that was to herald a golden age for cave divers. In the van of this new approach was Mike Boon, one of Britain's most determined cavers.

With friends already active in the Cave Diving Group and the possibility of Swildon's being extended at any time Boon underwent his initial training on oxygen in 1959. However, he never got round to using the rebreathing apparatus underground. From discussions with friends in the Watford Underwater Club he soon realised the potential of compressed air equipment. Under favourable conditions the 26 cu.ft 'tadpole', which was cheap and easy to obtain, would last about twenty-six minutes. During his pool training Boon discovered that, by carefully controlling his breathing, he could virtually double this time.

Boon's early dives were made with a normal twin-hose valve of the Cousteau-Gagnan type, his cylinder being mounted conventionally on his back. Using this arrangement, he made brief cave dives in County Fermanagh, Northern Ireland, in May 1961.

However, the weakness of his technique soon became obvious. The twin-hose valve was highly susceptible to damage upon projections, as it was thin and easily severed. The positioning of the cylinder and the A-Clamp likewise made them vulnerable to knocks and abrasions. The A-Clamp occupied a blind spot at the back of the neck and, in a small passage, one had to exercise the strictest caution, for to disturb the seating of the respirator was to invite disaster.

Later the twin-hose valve was replaced by a single-hose Scubair valve of American design. This was a great improvement, for although the hose was of a smaller circumference than the twin-hose model, it was made of far thicker rubber. In consequence, it was infinitely more robust and capable of withstanding frequent abrasions in cave conditions.

In April 1962 Boon made an attempt on the sump in Hardrawkin Pot, Yorkshire, using the novel method of side-mounting his cylinder: it was slung between hip and armpit by two straps which encircled the upper part of the body. The advantages over the back-mounted set-up were clear. Firstly, the diver could at all times protect his cylinder, A-Clamp and hose by simply holding an elbow and arm over the vulnerable points. Previously there had been no way the clamp or the hose could be shielded from projections. Secondly, the diver was now far more streamlined for caving conditions. With the cylinder removed from his back, low passages proved little or no problem. The whole kit was of a thoroughly lightweight nature requiring the help of no more than two assistants on any cave portage. The main burden, the cylinder, weighed only eleven pounds; lesser items consisted of valve and face-mask, together with a knife (these being usually carried in an ex-services ammunition box), weights and line reel. From this date forward equipment underwent strict reappraisal, the main criterion being the portability of the item to the diving site. Nevertheless, the departure from established techniques was not complete and the old attitude to bottom-walking was maintained for some time.

Boon Passes Swildon's Sumps 6 and 7, 1962

In June 1962 a strong attack was mounted on Swildon's Sump 6, a site which had remained inviolate since 1958. Those involved were Boon and Mike Thompson using open-circuit equipment, and S. Wynne-Roberts and F.J. Davies using modified varieties of oxygen rebreathing equipment. Arriving at Sump 6, Boon was quickly kitted out and passed easily through the short submerged section. Transmitting a prearranged signal along the nylon line which Boon had laid, Thompson swiftly followed. However, Davies, on his attempt, found the way too low to pass as his equipment was attached to his chest and was forced to return. Wynne-Roberts found his soda-lime flooded, but, after recharging, made an uneventful passage of the sump. Together the three explored over a hundred metres to Sump 7.

Later in the month the same group returned to push home the assault on the terminal sump. Davies had now opted for the same kit as Wynne-Roberts, but both were still equipped with oxygen. On arrival at Sump 4, Thompson discovered his waterproof dry suit badly torn and was forced to retire from the main project. However, he assisted with carriage of gear to Sump 6 before making his exit. Boon's gear was then ferried over the difficult terrain to Sump 7. This proved exceptionally tight and only by pushing the cylinder ahead of him was Boon able to make any progress at all. He described the first section later as 'like squeezing through a porthole – with the ship on the bottom'.

After a short ascent he reached a small air-bell, where he was able to talk to his friend, Wynne-Roberts, via a narrow above-water fissure. Beyond this three- or four-metre mark the sump continued. The route was predictably constricted and for some unaccountable reason Boon decided to tackle this next section without a line. In his book *Down to a Sunless Sea* Boon describes the outcome of the push:

What happened next is hazy; I suppose I must have forced myself forward until the weight belt and accumulator round my waist wedged between floor and roof. I woke to the realisation that I was quite stuck; I could not move an inch in any direction. For a short while I tried to extract myself gently, then as the panic built up I started to struggle, kicking vainly against the roof and scrabbling with my hands. Still I could not move, and a black terror gripped me at the thought of wedging there until my air supply ran out and I breathed water instead of air. I remember telling myself, 'This time you've really done it' – 'You've really done it this time' over and over again, and when I dropped the gag from my mouth I wondered for a few seconds whether I should put it back or shorten the torture by drowning

Right: Mike Boon in action and at play.

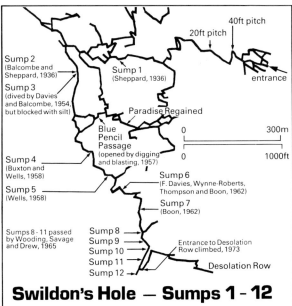

Swildon's Hole — Sumps 1 - 12

Sump 2
(Balcombe and
Sheppard, 1936)

Sump 3
(dived by Davies
and Balcombe, 1954,
but blocked with silt)

Sump 4
(Buxton and
Wells, 1958)

Sump 5
(Wells, 1958)

Sumps 8 - 11 passed
by Wooding, Savage
and Drew, 1965

Sump 1
(Sheppard, 1936)

Paradise Regained

Blue
Pencil
Passage
(opened by digging
and blasting, 1957)

40ft pitch

20ft pitch

entrance

Sump 6
(F. Davies, Wynne-Roberts,
Thompson and Boon, 1962)

Sump 7
(Boon, 1962)

Sump 8
Sump 9
Sump 10
Sump 11
Sump 12

Entrance to Desolation
Row climbed, 1973

Desolation Row

0   300m

0   1000ft

Above: Dog Leg Corner in Dan-yr-Ogof. Boon's epic fight in Swildon's Sump 7 took place in similar circumstances – less cramped but submerged in muddy water.

myself there and then. Suddenly I became aware that my left hand was flapping in an open space, a kind of low slot. I went berserk and kicked and jerked my chest half an inch at a time into it; I knew I was going away from home but I forced myself on, anxious only to be able to inflate my lungs fully. A projection from the floor snagged in my groin wedging me once more, but as I wrenched myself free I rose into the pure dark air of a cave, filled with the sound of running water. I had passed the sump into Swildon's 8.

A very relieved and chastened diver emerged. The overall length of the sump was only nine metres, but Boon had been amazingly lucky. He made a quick investigation of the on-going streamway, covering about forty metres of passage down to the next flooded section, Sump 8.

There was no question of tackling this, so Boon

anxiously began his retreat. After repositioning his battery pack on his side to make himself more streamlined in the squeezes, he summoned all his courage and re-entered the tight, murky pool. After another tense, blind (he actually lost his face-mask here) fight in Sump 7, he re-emerged tired and shaken to make his exit from the cave – lucky to be alive.

Neither of the other two could make any headway in Sump 7, because much of their equipment was firmly fixed to their bodies. Having succeeded in damaging their suits in the attempt, they retired, making an unpleasantly cold, wet trip back through the return sumps to the surface.

It was now clear from Boon's passage of Sump 7 that any type of passage was fair game: a squeeze below water could be tackled in the same way as one above. The technique was, however, an extreme measure and was not to be undertaken lightly. The consequences of getting stuck or caught up in such a squeeze were evident. Should one not gain freedom within the necessary time then air and life would rapidly fail. The water, murky and black, would gradually become calm when time ran out.

The quest for short sumps went on, catering in large measure to the interest of the cavers who hoped, one day in the future, to see for themselves just what lay beyond the now forbidden sections. It is important to note that the new aqualung equipment was of short duration, giving, in theory at least, far less time under water. In consequence, there was a degree of scepticism about the apparatus until its usefulness was proven.

The Advantages of the Aqualung

Its advantages, in practice, were soon recognised. It effectively eliminated most of the earlier physiological and chemical hazards. With air equipment one could dispense with the time-consuming and wasteful breathing drill; take advantage (with the simple mouthpiece) of any small usable airspaces to be found in the course of a dive; and revert to a more normal pattern of breathing. One was also safe from oxygen poisoning and could, therefore, expend more effort in looking for an underwater route rather than constantly having to consult a depth-gauge. The diver was now safe from excess or lack of carbon dioxide, insidious

oxygen depletion, shallow water blackout, and cocktails.

Much of the laborious training was thus unnecessary and far less stress was imposed on the diver. However, the need for training still remained, and the importance of all round caution whilst kitting up and actually diving was acute. The most vital thing the diver had to remember was that his potential time under water was short and that it was imperative to make frequent checks of his pressure gauge to ascertain the exact amount of air remaining. Another elementary, but essential, condition was to maintain regular breathing. If, for example, one held one's breath whilst on an ascent, an embolism or burst lung owing to expansion of air was quite probable. This hazard had always been present, but had never openly manifested itself since divers had been largely restricted to the floor by bottom-walking. The potential dangers became more obvious later, when the use of fins became widespread. Also, should a diver hyper-ventilate (take numerous deep breaths in succession, so as to flush out the carbon dioxide from the blood) before submerging, or endeavour to hold his breath, he ran the risk of blackout through lack of oxygen. Both of these dangers could be dismissed if the diver performed in a conventional manner. But despite these new hazards, the widespread adoption of air-breathing apparatus revitalised the cave diving scene.

It would be useful at this point to consider the number of people participating in the explorations, from the evidence of the Cave Diving Group annual reviews. In 1962 eleven different caves were explored using diving apparatus; obviously some, such as Swildon's, received numerous visits. Of the ten divers involved, all had received some training in conventional techniques based on oxygen rebreathing. Of a total of forty-eight dives, thirty were undertaken using established closed circuit equipment; the other eighteen were on air and were mostly made by Mike Boon.

Waddon's Accident in Minneries Pool

Another factor which served to hasten the transition to air was the tragedy that befell one of the leading members of the Cave Diving Group. In November 1962, due to poor weather curtailing a venue at Stoke

Lane Slocker, an impromptu training session was undertaken at the Minneries Pool on Mendip. E.J. Waddon was to try out a home-made rebreathing apparatus which was, as yet, incomplete. Consequently, certain items were borrowed and the set was made usable. In the absence of an oxygen flow-meter, the setting was adjusted by ear: the sound of the gas flow was compared to that in another valve which had been checked on a meter. Waddon wore a waterproof, lightweight submarine escape immersion suit (goon suit) to protect himself from the water, with his normal cave diving suit underneath. The whole outfit was covered by a boiler suit and nailed boots. His weight belt was an improvised haversack into which lead was placed, but it was not of a quick-release pattern. (N.B. Open water divers advocate the use of a quick-release device, so that weights can be dropped in case of an emergency, thereby allowing a rapid ascent to the surface.)

His first dive, with a companion, was cut short after about ten minutes for him to add more weights. With a total of 20lbs, he re-entered the water alone, un-attached by any form of safety-line. To the shore party all appeared normal for approximately five minutes, when a head and arms made a brief appearance above water about nine metres from the bank. Thereafter, the water became quite still with no bubbles.

Within minutes the alarm was raised, but, in the absence of a kitted diver or even functioning equip-ment, there was inevitably a delay. It was an hour and ten minutes before Boon could locate and bring Waddon ashore. Artificial respiration was immediately applied, but Waddon never recovered. He had not drowned, since water had not entered his lungs; nor had he been poisoned by caustic solution, or suffered an air embolism. Basically, his valve was faulty, giving an insufficient supply of oxygen. Anxiety, coupled with extremely bad visibility, would have led to a build up of carbon dioxide and loss of bearings. Unable to jettison his weights, he made a last futile plea for help, appear-ing above the surface, before passing out from anoxia.

It is easy to level criticism in such a case, but it should be remembered that Waddon was an ex-perienced cave diver and that his actions were not viewed as unduly rash by those on the bank. At the first sign of trouble he should have been able to remove the weights and surface in safety. It is also interesting to reflect that, if he had been diving with a line connecting him to the shore party, he could have either pulled himself ashore or had his friends tow him in.

Wet Suits Become Popular

In 1963 there was growth in activities based on air. 1963 also saw the gradual adoption of the wet suit. The principle of this suit was fundamentally different from that of the dry suit. In the latter case the main aim was to prevent any incursion of cold water. The suit itself did not provide any warmth and was always used in conjunction with woollen underclothes. The wet suit, however, consists of durable foam rubber, anything from three to seven millimetres in thickness, and is worn directly next to the skin. The more snug the fit the more efficient the insulation. The main difference, as the name implies, is that the body surface is soon wet. The minute cells in the rubber prevent any rapid exchange of water, and after the initial immersion these have the effect of partially retaining water, which is then warmed by body heat.

Buxton had used a wet suit in Wookey Hole in the preceding year, finding it quite effective in terms of warmth compared to the normal dry suit. It was clearly easier to dress in, and incorporated the important quality of non-shifting buoyancy. A dry suit contained a certain quantity of air. Under water this tended to move about the body, depending upon the angle or position of the diver at the time. The easiest way of counteracting this was to make him 'bottom heavy', so that he had to walk on the floor. A punctured dry suit, involving loss of air, was not only uncomfortable but vastly increased the weighting – critical if, for example, one were using fins. It matters relatively little if the wet suit tears as warmth is not appreciably affected by water inside. The only chilling occurs to that part of the body directly exposed by being uncovered. The buoyancy is not affected, and is at all times slightly positive. Further-more, the new suits were commercially available by 1961 and their properties were rapidly appreciated in caving circles.

Thus, at Agen Allwedd, containing one of the most isolated sumps in Great Britain, a lightweight oxygen kit was used in conjunction with a wet suit in April 1963. The dive was not without its share of incidents and one of the bottom-walking divers narrowly missed disaster when he momentarily lost his footing on the brink of a submerged pothole.

British Divers in Gouffre Berger, 1963

In August 1963 British cavers made an assault on the terminal syphon in the Gouffre Berger, France, at that time the world's deepest known system, lying 1122m/3680ft below the entrance. This ranks as one of the most ambitious undertakings ever planned, exceptional for its day, and owed its existence to the drive and enthusiasm of the Derbyshire diver Ken Pearce. In the event, Pearce was the only person to pass the sump after a sixty-one-metre dive at a maximum depth of twelve metres. His discovery was a further section of large, dry passage which unfortunately sumped after forty-six metres. He used a pair of 26 cu.ft cylinders, one mounted on each side of the body. Pressurized to 2300 p.s.i. (pounds per square inch), these gave a duration of about thirty minutes each. The wet suit was found to be very useful. This was also one of the last occasions when bottom-walking was used. A total of eleven days was spent underground by the diving and support party – one of the greatest accomplishments in world caving.

Acclaim for the new equipment and techniques was readily forthcoming, and it was thought in many quarters that the day was not far off when every serious caver would don lightweight apparatus in the same way they now carried ropes and ladders. It all appeared so easy.

An Accident at Lancaster Hole, 1964

By early 1964 the transition to air was virtually complete and the attendant surge of interest in cave diving at this time is most striking. At a conservative

Right: Ken Pearce after diving the sixty-one metre sump at the bottom of Gouffre Berger, France in 1963 – a remote and challenging enterprise lying at the foot of a 1112m cave system.

estimate, according to the Cave Diving Group's Annual Review, thirty-two sites were explored. Of the 171 dives involving at least twenty-nine different divers, only one involved oxygen. The new equipment was rapidly proving its worth and initial opposition had been completely overruled.

However, in March 1964, a tragic incident at Lancaster Hole had a sobering effect on diving activities. It was here that Boon and Alan Clegg, one of the up-and-coming northern divers, set their sights on the terminal downstream sump. After two short dives to a depth of five metres, Boon retired from the exploration, but remained kitted in the role of stand-by diver. Somehow a diving line was washed irretrievably into the sump and Clegg dived to free it. This almost routine task was to prove far from straightforward and, after an interval of eight minutes, Boon who was by then very worried, saw a stream of continuous heavy bubbles, indicating that the diver had accidentally lost his mouthpiece. The bubbles showed no signs of stopping and Boon immediately dived. Clegg was stuck in a slot in the bed of the pool and only with great difficulty was he freed. Quickly Boon pulled him to shore and applied mouth-to-mouth resuscitation, but the diver did not recover.

Thereafter, opinion hardened against the type of valve which Clegg had been using. Not only was it a fragile twin-hose, ill suited for cave conditions, but it was not designed for use on a side-mounted cylinder without a neckstrap, which was plainly unnecessary when the apparatus was back-mounted. A diver could experience grave difficulties in relocating the mouthpiece should it be torn from his grasp and, in a confined space, replacing it could well be impossible.

Throughout the various difficulties the diver might encounter, there is one factor impossible to assess – namely, panic. Using oxygen or air, it is important at all times to remain perfectly cool and in as complete control as is humanly possible. The truly phlegmatic person is undoubtedly a rarity and it is inevitable that no two people will react to a given situation in exactly the same manner. In losing his mouthpiece, Clegg undoubtedly panicked. While diving underground there is rarely a second chance and Lancaster Hole proved no exception. Alan Clegg drowned, his accident

serving as a reminder that, even with the use of air, cave diving was still an extreme technique.

For the rest of 1964 there was almost complete cessation of diving, but, when it resumed in 1965, a new generation of hardy individuals had sprung up. The pros and cons had been weighed, and the stage was set for major discoveries.

The normal apparatus used at this time consisted of wet suit (universally adopted after 1963), hood, caving helmet and standard rechargeable miner's lamp, weight-belt, cylinder, valve, pressure gauge and face-mask. Ancillary equipment included line reel, knife, depth-gauge and compass. Fins were optional and generally regarded as unnecessary in the smaller sumps. Their popularity gradually increased, however, until by 1967 they were used on virtually all exploratory dives. By this stage safety rules governing the management of air supply were beginning to be discussed. Despite his determined approach to cave exploration Boon came to advocate a normal turn-round once a quarter of the original supply had been used. This was to prove a very simple but safe guide to intending explorers. In later years it was to be the 'Third Rule' which was to be adopted by cave divers world-wide, a rule generally attributed to the American diver Sheck Exley. This involved the diver terminating his inward dive once a third of his air had been used, making his exit on the second third, leaving the last third as a safety margin. A watch is of very limited use underwater when determining how long one's air supply will last; the essential thing is to monitor one's pressure gauge frequently. Although there have been adaptations and variations in later years, this straight-forward concept still governs all cave diving activities.

Mendip Activity, 1965

In 1965 notable progress was made, especially in the Mendip Hills, by divers such as Mike Wooding, Dave Savage and Dave Drew. They had been students together at Bristol University, were highly competent cavers (Wooding and Savage had been on the successful Gouffre Berger expedition in 1963) and had naturally developed a keen interest in exploration. They quickly realised the opportunities that existed and had soon trained themselves for the task. They

Above: Dan Hasell (controller), Mike Wooding and Dave Savage at Wookey during the 1965 explorations.

styled themselves the Independent Cave Diving Group (ICDG) and, equipped with side-mounted cylinders, Scubair valves and wet suits, the trio quickly made some important advances.

The 'end' of Stoke Lane Slocker system was reached, a bypass having been found to several of the submerged sections, so that only five sumps had to be dived to reach this point. In Swildon's Hole, Sump 12, the present limit, was gained. In addition, a rewarding expedition was made to Morocco, which yielded over 1070m of new passage.

In March 1965 all three members of the ICDG joined the CDG greatly strengthening the larger organisation after a period when little seemed to have been achieved.

The CDG was also revitalised at this time by the influence of Dr Oliver Lloyd (Dr Oliver Cromwell Lloyd – OCL as he was affectionately known) who joined the group in 1965 at the age of fifty-four. He was to dominate the CDG for the next twenty years (he died in 1985) organising training sessions in Bristol, taking the role of tacklemaster, and editing and punctually distributing the CDG newsletter.

Yorkshire Activity, 1963-66

In addition to these developments in the south-west, immense potential also lay in Yorkshire and the north. Boon and Clegg had made significant discoveries at Ireby Cavern and Langstroth Cave in 1963. Savage had again discovered a major continuation at Spring Trap Cave, Wharfedale, in August 1965. A constricted sump in Danny Cave, Garsdale, led John Southworth to about 300m in October 1966. The sump at the bottom of Penyghent Gill Pot was passed after a dive of under two metres, yielding over 500m of new passage. This obstacle was later removed by blasting.

By far the most notable find due to the effort of divers was that at Langstroth Cave, Wharfedale. Over successive trips in 1966 divers, having discarded their breathing apparatus beyond three short sumps, pushed on up a series of wet pitches, using scaling poles and

Above: Bill Frakes and Neil Dyson at the camp beyond the sumps in Langstroth Cave during the notable explorations of 1966.

climbing tactics, to discover about a thousand metres of passages. With a rough knowledge of the trend of the cave, a top entrance was manufactured, allowing non-diving cavers full access to the extension down as far as the sumps. After 1973, when the underwater section was refitted with line to take full advantage of the intermediate air-bells, an increasingly popular through trip became possible, with cavers abseiling down eight pitches as far as the sumps, then free diving through the submerged sections, drawing their ropes and other equipment behind them. This was done in a downstream direction with sump lengths of two metres, three metres and just under four metres respectively. It was soon demonstrated that a proficient party could complete the traverse in two to three hours.

All of this came to an end in 1976, when the farmer banned access following a multiple accident. Out of a party of six cavers attempting the traverse only one passed the sumps, three died and two were forced to return to the foot of the abseiled pitches to await rescue.

Taken in isolation, sumps of such length should have been feasible for a well-trained party, so what happened to cause such a terrible tragedy? It was the air-bells, not the dives, which created the problem. These were small and an excessive level of carbon dioxide had developed in them, so that the atmosphere was unbreathable.* Tragically three of the cavers passed out at these resting points before they could reach safety or retreat.

Connections allowing such trips are the aim of virtually all cavers, but in every case sumps must be treated with the utmost respect.

An Amazing Free Diving Escape

One of the luckiest free diving escapes of all time occurred in July 1965 at Carlswark Cavern in Derbyshire. Whilst leading an army team on an initiative test, a youth had dived into the sump, presuming that there was an air-space within a short distance. When he did not reappear, the Cave Rescue Organisation was called. Ken Pearce made several dives, but could find no trace of the body. However, as there was a chance that the youth might have located a tight fissure with an air-space, a pump was obtained and the water-level in the submerged section of passage lowered. He was eventually found alive and well. Wearing hobnailed boots, gaiters, sweater and army battle dress the youth had covered twenty metres of sump in complete darkness. The tight fissure in which he was discovered lay to one side of the passage and it was miraculous that he should have found it under the circumstances.

The Mossdale Cavern Tragedy, 1967

Another major diving extension of great future significance was that at Dale Barn Cave, Yorkshire, where two short, but tight, sumps led to a 1000m of passage. With discoveries like this and the developments at Langstroth Cave, 1966 proved a good year for the north. 1967, however, was to be a year of tragedy.

In 1967 there occurred the worst caving disaster in British history, involving the nucleus of the new northern divers. At Mossdale Caverns in August a party of six experienced cavers comprising Bill Frakes, John Ogden and Colin Vickers, all of whom were cave divers, and David Adamson, Jeffrey Boireau and Michael Ryan were engaged in a routine non-diving exploratory trip. At about mid-day, when they were below ground, there was a cloudburst. Stream-beds which had been dry now became raging torrents, engulfing many small entrances. Unfortunately many of Mossdale's extensive network of passages flood to the roof, and the luckless cavers were caught in a long section of crawl-way. Underground the deluge would have channelled and concentrated to result in something of a tidal wave. There was no escape. Despite their futile attempts to get out of the crawls, all were overwhelmed. Some were later found wedged at the top of small avens, where they had apparently sought refuge, but such was the volume of water that there had been no sanctuary at any point. To this day even the slightest suggestion of rain makes exploration of the cave extremely hazardous.

The effect on diving in the north was immense. There had never been more than a handful of divers operating in this area at any one time. By this cruel stroke of fate to a normal caving party progress was clearly retarded and it was several years before there was again a concentrated effort to advance cave diving in the area.

Savage Reaches Chamber 18, Wookey Hole, 1966

In the late 1960s, therefore, it was in the south where the main developments took place. In 1966 Mendip yielded Chamber 18 in Wookey. This fell to Dave Savage, who was equipped with a leaking tadpole twinset (back-mounted). The bottles were coupled together by a home-made manifold with soldered joints. As a reserve set, he wore another 26 cu.ft cylinder. Single-hose valves were adopted on both sets of apparatus and movement was made by the use of fins. The new chamber proved to be the only practical air-space after leaving Chamber 9, well over 122m away. However, the apparently imminent big discoveries in Wookey still eluded divers, owing to

* The air in small air-bells naturally contains a very high proportion of carbon dioxide (2.9%). Breathing from such an enclosed space quickly leads to the percentage rising above 3%, which gives rise to discomfort. When the level exceeds 5% the situation is critical and consciousness is soon lost. There is no question of the air (oxygen) being 'used up'; what happens is that it gets poisoned with a lethal concentration of CO_2.

difficulties with the line. An excess had inadvertently been laid, and this had begun to create time-consuming problems: it hindered divers by snagging their equipment and later precluded all advance until it had been gathered and safely removed.

Explorations at Agen Allwedd and Ogof Ffynnon Ddu, 1966
South Wales was clearly lacking in any major, new, dry extension, but the situation was rectified at Agen Allwedd and Ogof Ffynnon Ddu.

At the first site Mike Wooding and John Sinclair, after three long, arduous trips (two miles/five kilometres each way) upstream to the Turkey Sump, discovered over 760m of passage. This involved three sumps of a total length of forty-three metres, and terminated at yet another sump – Sump 5.

Perhaps the most significant of all British cave discoveries, resulting from the efforts of cave divers, was at Ogof Ffynnon Ddu in the Swansea Valley. Here, in July 1966, Charles George and John Osborne finally penetrated to the amazing labyrinth of caves known as the Master System. The entry was above the so-called Shower Aven and the dry passages were gained by erecting a rigid aluminium ladder directly from the sump pool below. Many dives followed with a host of participants, all eager to explore the system which had frustrated such incredible efforts for many years.

Probably the most memorable day in the explorations beyond the sump occurred on October 8, when Charles George had a lucky escape. On their return through the new dry extension following a lengthy and tiring trip, the party of seven was making its way up through what subsequently became known as Collapse Chamber. This is a vertical chasm choked by a heap of boulders. At that time it could be passed either by a route through the middle of the boulders or by an alternative route via bedding planes which arrived near the top of the boulder heap. Rod Stewart described what happened:

The worst part of all was when I went around through the bedding planes [the alternative route] while the others went

Left: Rodney Beaumont about to dive through the eight-metre Turkey Sump 1 in Agen Allwedd, South Wales.

through to Collapse Chamber. The way up from there was through a hole in a sort of funnel of boulders. [Stewart reached the boulders.] I suddenly felt a movement in the floor I was standing on, and Charles [who was coming up through the boulders] cried out to the others to retreat while he held back a block with his foot. The next thing I was aware of was a peculiar noise – all the boulders went fluid and Charles was bobbing around with only his helmet showing. It was terrible and I could do nothing to help. I just watched as he disappeared downwards making a funny hissing noise as if all the breath was being pressed out of his body. I was certain that all the others were lost, but I waited for a while not really knowing what to do. I dared not cross the boulder floor that had all collapsed downwards, and was about to depart when they re-appeared [via the longer alternative route]. I've never been so relieved in all my life.

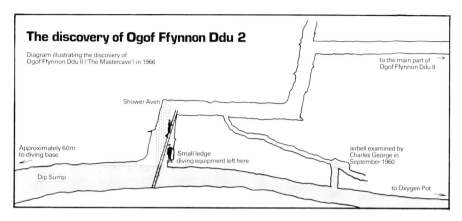

The discovery of Ogof Ffynnon Ddu 2

Diagram illustrating the discovery of Ogof Ffynnon Ddu II ('The Mastercave') in 1966

Shower Aven

Approximately 60m to diving base

Small ledge
diving equipment left here

Dip Sump

to the main part of Ogof Ffynnon Ddu II

airbell examined by Charles George in September 1960

to Oxygen Pot

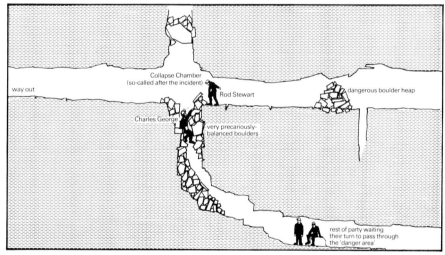

Collapse Chamber
(so-called after the incident)

way out

Rod Stewart

dangerous boulder heap

Charles George

very precariously-balanced boulders

rest of party waiting their turn to pass through the 'danger area'

Charles George also described the incident:

It is hard to imagine a more awful feeling of horror than when in the instant of being hurled down, one is struck on the head and squashed into a crouching position, unable to breathe. No sense of pain, just a ghastly realisation that one is irretrievably struck. Rod was able to climb down at great risk to himself to see that he could do nothing to help . . . Clive [Jones] saw my feet and knew he was helpless to do anything, when suddenly there was a further slip and I got thrown out.

In safety at the foot of the shaft we were convincing an incredulous John [Osborne] 'my safe way' was now gone, when with a splendid rumble the floor of Collapse Chamber vanished into the shaft blocking it utterly.

George escaped with three broken fingers on his left hand, and was severely cut and bruised about the head. A fracture of the skull was suspected, a condition

he was fortunately spared. It is interesting to note that, of the party of seven, only George was equipped with an early variety of plastic helmet, the others being clad in the old 'cardboard' miners' helmets. The latter were soon rendered pliable in a wet environment and it is evident that the more durable plastic protection saved George's life.

The accident tempered enthusiasm and it was April 8 before another dive was made. On this day a dry route, for the non-diving cavers of the area, was pioneered from the new extension into a well-known neighbouring cave, Cwm Dwr. Nearly four kilometres of new passages had already been entered, but now it was a South Wales Caving Club's field day, leading over the following few years to the mapping of the system declared Britain's longest and deepest cave.

Today, there are over thirty miles/forty-eight kilometres of passages known, with undoubtedly several more remaining to be entered. The main artery of the cave is a fine, fast-flowing streamway with sections of small cascading waterfalls. Here spacious, meandering rifts up to thirty metres high are common, while occasionally smaller streams rain from elusive passages high above. In the floor can be found an unusual feature of British caves: a multitude of swirl holes, which reach a depth of up to seven metres – a cold bath for the unwary. But the streamways form only a small part of the cave, the greater part is made up by a honeycomb of superimposed passages completely abandoned by any water and frequently well adorned with amazing formations. To the visitor it is extremely complex, a system of great beauty and sporting potential. However, in the interest of conservation the site has been designated a nature reserve and access is restricted to *bona fide* cavers by prior arrangement with the controlling club.

Little Neath River Cave, 1967

While the local divers were engaged in their mammoth task of opening up the Swansea Valley, a team of Somerset-based divers was making discreet explorations in the neighbouring Neath Valley. In January 1967, in an effort to solve the mystery of the missing drainage, Chris J. Gilmore dived the promising sump at the end of Bridge Cave. Within twenty metres he was through and into a major new streamway. The following week, accompanied by Savage and Pete Kaye, Gilmore explored over 1220m of passages.

During this trip an upstream passage was followed; its icy water clearly indicating a link with the disappearing surface river further up the valley. Reduced from stooping to crawling, they traversed the final section flat out in a fast-flowing torrent to a point where daylight was visible. The final exit was blocked by boulders, but the possibilities were realised. Having returned to the sump they turned downstream and traversed a magnificent streamway before another sump finally blocked the way.

Over the following weeks the New River Entrance (as it became known) was opened and full exploration of the passages upstream from Sump 2 was completed. It was soon apparent that far more remained to be discovered, as the known part of the cave reached less than halfway to the river's resurgence. Consequently, in March, fresh efforts were made on the terminal downstream sump – Sump 2. By July a series of sumps had been passed, leading the divers to Sump 6. Once more a whole network of dry, abandoned passages – The New World – was found. During the remainder of 1967 these were fully explored, over 1525m (230m of which were submerged) being found downstream of Sump 2.

Ogof Ffynnon Ddu, Ogof Agen Allwedd and Little Neath River Cave all testified to a golden heyday for cave divers. This magnificent series of breakthroughs was a clear reflection of the suitability of the new equipment for use underground. Closed circuit oxygen apparatus had been totally phased out after 1964 and was never again used in British cave diving circles. The transition to air was complete.

Right: Chamber 20 in Wookey Hole – discovered by John Parker during his important advance in 1970.

CHAPTER EIGHT

THE CURRENT APPROACH

Once the new techniques had become established, innumerable discoveries followed. Larger cylinders giving a greater duration of dive made their appearance after 1966 and by the 1970s the 26 cu.ft 'tadpoles' were on their way out. With time came the psychological reassurance that the breathing apparatus was basically reliable. Proficiency and practical experience in the use of a completely independent reserve set (a separate cylinder and valve mounted on the opposite side of the body to the main supply) reinforced these views.

Once the diver had accepted the limitations of the ever increasing variety of equipment, only the mental barrier remained. Training could alleviate this, but never entirely remove it. As ever, the calibre of the individual was all important. Steady personal

performance under adverse conditions could inspire confidence, and successful divers have always been those who could rely on their ability to keep their cool. It was clear that much longer sumps could now be tackled.

Chamber 22, Wookey Hole, 1970

By 1969 John Parker, a determined diver from South Wales, had made his debut, and once more Wookey Hole was to yield another major discovery. In January 1970, after a 146m dive from the last air-surface in Chamber 9, Parker reached Chamber 20. On this and subsequent dives over 820m of fresh dry passage was revealed. But the main way forward lay below water, directly under the entrance to the new extension in Chamber 20.

The challenge could not be ignored and, after several more exacting dives, Parker reached a further air-space in Chamber 22. This involved a 152m dive from Chamber 20, reaching a maximum depth of twenty-four metres in the gloom of the huge underwater Chamber 21. Less than 100m of dry passages were followed, terminating in a deep, totally enclosed lake. Here there was a real feeling of isolation: over 366m of submerged passage separated the divers from base in Chamber 3. A better impression of these dives can be gained by reference to the diagram on pages 106 and 107 from which it can be seen that the number of chambers does not always coincide with air-surfaces. The actual dives were really three in number: from Chamber 3 to Chamber 9, from Chamber 9 to Chamber 20, and from Chamber 20 to Chamber 22.

A 230m Dive in Ogof Afon Hepste, 1970

Parker, who lived at Pontypool, was naturally active in his home area, and many local sumps were also attempted. In August 1970, at a new cave (Ogof Afon Hepste) in the upper reaches of the River Neath, he made a single dive of 230m. A short section of dry passage was found, but the main way on was again sumped.

Mike Wooding's Yorkshire Dives, 1970

Another notable feat at this time was that of Mike Wooding at Keld Head, in Yorkshire. In May 1970, after a dive of fifty-one minutes' duration, he reached a point 338m from base. Fortunately, this was at a shallow depth and incorporated several small air-spaces. Later a film of Wooding's exploits at another cave in the area was made. The site in question was the famous Gaping Gill, where for many years determined cavers had been working on the connection of the system to the neighbouring Ingleborough Cave.

Left: John Parker (left) and Jeff Phillips in Ogof Rhyd Sych, South Wales. This team was involved in many notable diving explorations in the early 1970s.

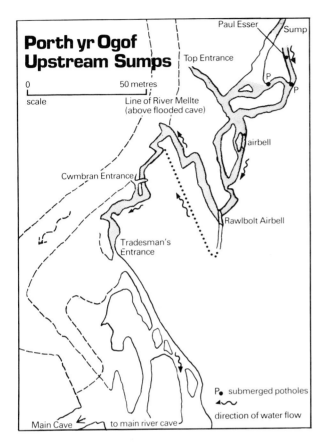

On Friday, 2 October he purchased the basic equipment, including a single cylinder (40 cu.ft) and valve. The following day witnessed his first and last cave dive. Having kitted up in the open air under the watchful eyes of his friends, he dived in, only to lose the line after about nine metres. Noticeably shaken, he made his way back to the surface through the good fortune of glimmering daylight, which permeated the area near the entrance. With his air marginally depleted, after a short rest, he re-entered the water. His movements could be felt on the line for twenty minutes, but, after thirty minutes, when he did not reappear, the Cave Rescue Organisation was called. Despite an intensive search by Wooding, Brown and others for over a week, no trace of the body was found. It was surmised that he had encountered further trouble with the line, which appeared to have been cut some distance in, but beyond this no definite conclusion could be drawn. A substantial net was laid across the mouth of the resurgence in case the body was washed out by the current, but the mystery remained unsolved. It was July 1975 before any further light was shed on the case and then, quite unexpectedly, the riddle was solved. Whilst systematically exploring the underwater complex, some divers came across Erith's remains. This was at a point 146m from the resurgence, clearly indicating that Erith had completely lost his bearings and dived further into the hillside until his air had expired. The whole affair was a serious reminder of the risks of cave diving to would-be explorers.

Esser's Accident in Porth yr Ogof, 1971

The second tragedy involved Paul Esser. He was a brilliant open-water diver, but had comparatively little experience of caving. This in no way detracted from his natural aptitude and it was thought that his potential in all spheres was immense. He had made contributions at Wookey Hole and his penultimate dive was to Sump 12 in Swildon's. On 13 February 1971 he went to Porth yr Ogof, near Ystradfellte, in South Wales, with a highly ambitious programme. Here the upstream section of this well-known cave had been extended into a veritable maze of underwater passages. In the process of exploration the complexities

However, the disappearing river in Gaping Gill terminated all progress and it fell to the diver to reveal the secrets of the unknown passages. The final connection between the two caves was to elude Wooding and his partner, Tom Brown, but their exploration signalled clearly that, under the aegis of a resourceful team, diving activities in the North had been successfully renewed following the Mossdale tragedy.

Erith's Accident in Keld Head, 1970

Following such daring undertakings in Wales, the Mendips and Yorkshire, it seemed likely that there would be a general surge in the numbers participating. This would undoubtedly have been the case, but for the untimely deaths of two divers within five months. The first accident occurred to a complete novice at Keld Head in October 1970. Alan Erith was a caver of six years' experience, but he knew little about diving.

Above: Ken Pearce and John Sinclair prepare to dive the heavily silted Sump 1 (32m) of P8/Jackpot, Derbyshire in 1965.

of the site had been increased by a great deal of unnecessary line which needed removing. Esser was to enter the system by the Tradesman's Entrance, higher up the valley, a distance under water of over 200m. Fifteen minutes after his departure from the lower entrance, three trainees also entered by the same way, aiming to cover the easy territory of about the first hundred metres. They met Esser in the air-space known as the Rawlbolt and witnessed his collection of much line. They then returned to the lower entrance, leaving him to continue alone.

Esser never reached his destination. After the pre-arranged period of time had elapsed, a rescue bid was launched with all haste. The winter cave water was icy cold, having not long been underground, and the proceedings were far from pleasant. Only after numerous dives by John Parker and others was Esser's body eventually located. Esser, like Erith, had followed the wrong line, which led not to the sanctuary of an air-surface, but upstream to no safety at all. He had undoubtedly realised his error, but by that stage had no safety margin of air left. With retreat impossible,

he was compelled to make a dash upstream in the misguided hope that the line he was following led to the Top Entrance.

In the cold and extremely hazardous conditions it was impossible to retrieve his body, but the rescuers cut off and brought out his cylinder and part of his demand valve. The equipment was completely exhausted of air, a further example of the need for abundant reserves.

These accidents emphasised that the objective dangers associated with cave diving were still very real. The growth in popularity of diving which had been anticipated failed to materialise. Instead, an attitude of suspicion on the part of its critics became increasingly prevalent. Even within the ranks of the caving fraternity, pushing divers were viewed as extremists. Consequently, in many quarters, the golden heyday was deemed to be past. No longer was there glory to be accrued as a diver's 'sherpa' and it became difficult to muster support for dives in isolated sites. Any surge in tourist diving (diving a known sump purely for experience of diving) was ruled out, as cavers saw little point in repeating any dive which had proved unfruitful.

Aquaflashes Introduced

Despite this air of scepticism which had grown around the sport, and the natural period of introspection which inevitably follows such disturbing setbacks, the mid-1970s were to witness further significant developments. The evolution of equipment and techniques both continued to gain momentum. Northern divers Geoff Yeadon and Oliver Statham were closely involved in these developments. This pair were, for example, the first to introduce Aquaflashes to the British scene. These completely sealed waterproof torches had been used by Continental divers for a number of years and were small enough to be mounted on either side of a diver's helmet. Two or more of these provided an invaluable addition to the generally poor light given by a miner's lamp, and proved a tremendous boost to a diver's confidence. A single light failure was, therefore, no longer critical.

Emphasis was now laid on sites offering enormous potential, such as the terminal downstream sump in Agen Allwedd, the distant sumps in Dan yr Ogof, P8 (Jackpot) in Derbyshire, Langcliffe in Yorkshire, and Prod's Pot in Northern Ireland. At each of these caves the potential rewards were immense, but the effort involved in the execution of such dives was also incredible. Sumps where access was comparatively easy, involving little complicated porterage, were also popular, as were places which offered a possible connection with another cave. A small hard core of divers, determined to break into new territory, continued their explorations in six main areas, which I will now describe separately.

THE MENDIP HILLS

New ground was hard to win. In the south, where caves offering virgin exploration had virtually disappeared, activity almost ceased. Training sites such as Wookey Hole or caves of easy porterage such as Swildon's were frequently visited, but little or no realistic progress was made by diving until 1976. The one major objective throughout these years had been the possibility of a connection between Swildon's Hole or St. Cuthbert's Swallet and Wookey. Both the former caves were inviolate, as their terminal sumps had precluded all progress. St. Cuthbert's

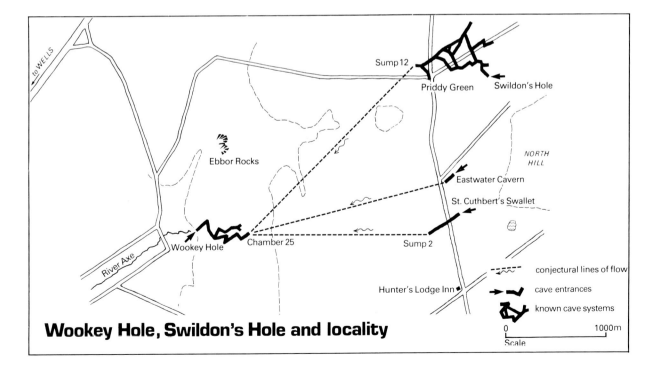

Wookey Hole, Swildon's Hole and locality

Above: Brian Hague in Sump 12 in Swildon's Hole, first reached in 1965 and dived to eighteen metres depth in 1972 by John Parker. Since then the sump and the adjacent Sump 12a have been attempted on numerous occasions but the continuation, which is very tight, has proved unpassable.

Swallet possessed a sump blocked by silt and gravel. Complicated underground dam building, siphoning and digging operations commenced here in 1967, but, despite increasingly ambitious schemes over a number of years, little advance has been achieved. At Swildon's, Sump 12 had been reached in 1965, but this also proved too constricted for safe progress. John Parker had reached a depth of eighteen metres in Sump 12 in 1972, but two awkward squeezes to reach that point made any further penetration positively dangerous. In the quest for a high-level bypass to this sump, a promising climb, Victoria Aven, was made later in the year. At a height of thirty-seven metres above the streamway, immediately prior to Sump 12, a complex series of tight passages was entered. Unfortunately there was no bypass and the extension was named Desolation Row. Thereafter hopes of a major extension and the elusive connection with Wookey appeared as distant as ever.

Wookey Extended to Chamber 24, 1976

Not until February 1976 were any significant discoveries made by diving in this area, and again they were at Wookey Hole. For over four years the 'end' (the furthest point in Chamber 22) had been virtually unassailable. It was, therefore, assumed that the way on must lie somewhere in the depths of the huge Chamber 21.

With the extension of the Show Cave by an artificial tunnel driven as far as Chamber 9 (a development of the Wookey Hole tourist attraction by the then owners, Madame Tussaud's) diving operations were made considerably easier as the chamber now made an ideal advance diving base. Forty years of exploration had culminated in a two-minute walk through a spacious passageway to the point which the oxygen divers had taken such pains to discover in 1948, the last piece of dry land that Gordon Marriott ever saw, and the most welcome sight to greet Bob Davies in 1955. All told, this is probably the most famous chamber in the history of cave diving.

This encroachment by the tourist trade made a fortuitous contribution to the further exploration of Wookey. With over seventy metres of submerged passage now bypassed, explorers could have that much more air to use for locating the way on. By this stage I had purchased several large 72 cu.ft cylinders in readiness for a major assault upon the cave. Over the winter of 1975 however, I went to North America on a three month caving trip and while I was away I loaned my bottles to Colin Edmunds who then commenced a diligent search of the further reaches. From the base in Chamber 9 a systematic exploration was made in Chamber 21, as this seemed the most likely place to advance. This met with relatively little success and on 21 February 1976 Colin moved his attention to the Chamber 22 lake that John Parker had written-off as a dead end.

As my first dive after returning home I took the role of supporter on this operation, while Colin, who had done all the groundwork, took the lead. But this was no ordinary, routine exploration, Oliver Lloyd, the person through whom CDG divers arranged all their dives in Wookey, had invited two northern divers Geoff Yeadon and Oliver Statham to conduct an exploration of their own in the cave. We in the south, more especially Colin and Richard Stevenson, who had by now conducted quite a number of dives into the zone between Chamber 20 and 22 were distinctly 'put out' by the news.

So, while we were executing our plan for the day Statham and Yeadon were quietly preparing for their own push that same afternoon. In doing this we couldn't help feeling that they were not observing the unwritten code of exploratory etiquette. Colin and Richard had proven ability and had recently discovered a new airbell chamber (subsequently named Edmunds Chamber) close to Chamber 22. I concluded that despite Lloyd's invitation this was really a response to the exploration which Roger Solari and I had made in Yorkshire two years previously, when we had inadvertently stepped on their toes and made a breakthrough in Boreham Cave. It all seems pretty trivial now, but at the time, with a major breakthrough in Wookey a distinct possibility, it seemed very important.

We reached the end uneventfully. Diving steeply to a depth of eighteen metres Colin found, and followed, a gradually ascending muddy passage for ninety metres until his line ran out. A breakthrough was imminent, as the passage gave every indication of reaching air and the depth at the furthest point was less than seven metres. As we cruised back to Chamber 9 we were in high spirits; the way on was there for the taking. We made no attempt to keep things secret, believing that the new lead was ours.

Yeadon and Statham arrived, as expected, heavily equipped with a vast array of hardware and their dry suits. They were well prepared for a long dive. That afternoon they reached Chamber 22 and presumably made a brief reconnaissance of the dry passage leading on to the lake. Having experienced the short but awkward section of above water terrain we presumed that they would decline to push our passage. We were wrong. Colin and I had planned to return in just a couple of days time but on the Monday Yeadon and Statham beat us to it. They dived once more to Chamber 22, this time using wet suits, the more practical clothing for the terrain. After laying about nine metres of additional line, they reached air in

Above: The team that made the push beyond Chamber 25, Wookey in June, 1977. Left to right: Brian Woodward, Richard Stevenson, George Bee, Colin Edmunds, Martyn Farr and Dave Morris.

what was an obvious flood overflow passage. This was numbered Chamber 23.

The divers were now confronted by a narrow, muddy rift, which terminated after forty-five metres in a small, miserable sump. Three short, shallow dives then followed in quick succession, the longest being about eighteen metres. The exit from the last sump pool was difficult, up a steep, slippery mudbank into Chamber 24.

The passage had gained in proportion, but remained muddy and dull. They fully expected another sump, but were amazed to see a huge passage disappearing into the distance.

Statham described what followed:

Panting furiously as they stripped off gear and let it fall willy-nilly to the floor, the divers started to move along a fifty by twenty foot sandy passage; then a distant growl of water made the adrenalin flow. A climb over boulders and there was a magnificent sight – the whole of the River Axe pouring down a passage forty feet high by five feet wide.

They moved along the streamway to where a swim and a subsequent section of awkward bridging led to a choice of two different routes. These again converged after about ninety metres in a beautiful blue lake. The way on was sumped. On this trip the two explorers had covered about 600m of virgin passage and, more importantly, had left the way forward wide open for further explorations.

Wookey Hole: Beyond Chamber 25

We felt the campaign by the northern divers had been particularly furtive, and Colin and I returned on 27 February annoyed and extremely determined to push on from where they had left off. From the lake in Chamber 24 I eventually made a ninety metre dive at a maximum depth of eighteen metres. At the first air-surface, in Chamber 25, the scene was muddy and

Right: The river passage leading along Chamber 24 in Wookey Hole.

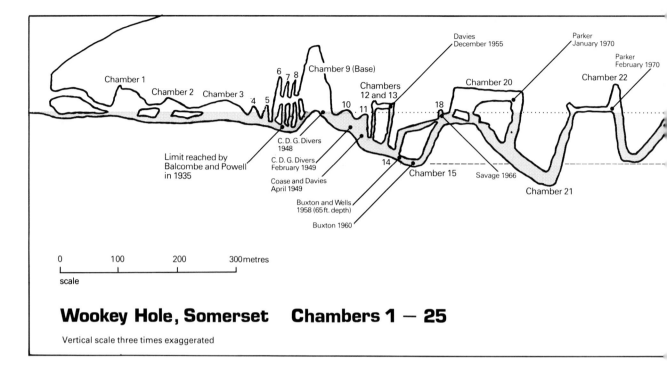

Wookey Hole, Somerset   Chambers 1 — 25

Vertical scale three times exaggerated

desolate – The Lake of Gloom. Ahead was a wall-like structure; I could just pull myself far enough up it to be able to peer into an adjoining sump pool. The sides of the lake were too steep to land, so I tied off my line to a submerged boulder and made an exit.

In April I dived to the end once more to try and find a route under the wall. If I was forced to take off kit and carry gear over this structure, it would obviously entail considerable loss of time and energy. The attempt failed, but, on full examination of Chamber 25 I found a mudbank where it was at least possible to crawl out of the water, take off kit and rest.

Owing to a spate of colds and ill health, it was July before I resumed the assault, on this occasion supported by Dave Morris and Pete Lord. Diving solo from Chamber 24, I reached Chamber 25 uneventfully and, using brute strength, hoisted myself straight over the wall fully kitted. The quest for Chamber 26 was on. I dived vertically down a well-like hole and in clear water the route was obvious. Following the junction of wall and roof gave a comfortable dive, less than a metre wide and inclined at over sixty degrees from the horizontal. To the left lay an incredible void

with no indication of a floor whatsoever. At a depth of thirty metres, and thirty metres horizontally from the well I was forced to a halt, as no further progress could safely be made. Such a deep dive was completely unexpected. Far greater reserves of air were necessary, together with an efficient suit. It was clear that future dives would be serious affairs.

Wookey Hole: The Quest for Chamber 26, 1977
For a long, deep dive such as that beyond Chamber 25 equipment had to be completely reappraised. Exploration had developed to a point where serious consideration had to be given to the afflictions normally associated with exceptionally deep dives in the sea, namely nitrogen narcosis and the problem of decompression. The complex nature of the dive profile with the cumulative problem of so many descents and rapid ascents, all of which had to be repeated on the return, complicated exploration. I resolved to make another attempt as soon as possible, but it was apparent that future exploration would need to be planned especially carefully. In an attempt to reduce the cumulative build up of nitrogen in the

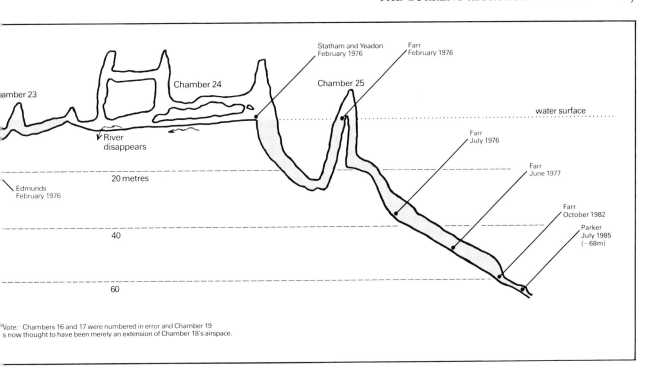

Statham and Yeadon
February 1976

Farr
February 1976

Chamber 24

Chamber 25

amber 23

water surface

River
disappears

Farr
July 1976

Farr
June 1977

20 metres

Edmunds
February 1976

Farr
October 1982

Parker
July 1985
(−68m)

40

60

Note: Chambers 16 and 17 were numbered in error and Chamber 19
s now thought to have been merely an extension of Chamber 18's airspace.

body tissue, Frank Salt devised a complex set of oxygen enriched breathing mixtures: one set for the approach sumps and a different mix for the final, solo exploration. In addition, pure oxygen was to be used for decompression purposes at depths of six metres and three metres. A strong support team would be required to transport supplies as well as much new equipment. Fortunately, financial sponsorship served to alleviate certain difficulties, but, even so, it was not until 18 June 1977 that the next advance was made. I was supported by a team of six divers on this occasion: Brian Woodward, Richard Stevenson, George Bee, Paul Atkinson, Dave Morris and Colin Edmunds, who undertook the hard work of the vital logistical build up of cylinders to Chamber 25.

Once in Chamber 25, I kitted up with an 82 cu.ft cylinder (30% oxygen mixture) and a 45 cu.ft bottle. I reached the line reel at thirty metres' depth and continued along an inclined rift over a metre wide and about ten metres high. At a depth of forty-one metres the passage showed no signs of rising; instead, I came to the lip of a sheer drop. This was only about three metres, but beyond it the passage continued to descend.

My depth gauge soon registered forty-five metres (the preset maximum depth for the operation) and all hopes of a breakthrough were dashed. That was it. I had no regrets, only thoughts of getting out as fast as possible.

Inflating the suit, I started back. Visibility was now less than a metre. Stress began to mount and suddenly a major crisis developed: I had extreme difficulty with my gas supply. Breaths were short and rapid, and I seriously wondered if I would get back to shallow water. If it was my valve at fault, I dared not swap on to the reserve supply as I felt I had no air in my lungs to last the vital seconds. I held the gag in tightly with one hand and went up. At some point positive buoyancy developed and the next thing I knew I was wedged against the roof at about thirty metres' depth. Fortunately, I was in full control of my physical reactions and immediately vented the suit, removing surplus air and restoring neutral buoyancy. Breathing, however, was still desperate and I moved on without delay. Only after I had reached eighteen metres' depth did the situation ease and it was an incredible relief just to hang on the shot line in the well.

Normality soon returned, and Dave appeared with the decompression bottle. From then on, it all went like clockwork; a series of dives, decompression stops and short sharp carries brought us back to Chamber 9 after an absence of eight hours.

There had been no breakthrough, but I had established a new British cave diving depth record of forty-five metres. The operation was also significant in that it was to the first occasion when decompression was deliberately adopted, and the first time that mixtures were used on open circuit in the British Isles.

Other projects took the limelight for a few years, but the challenge at Wookey was impossible to ignore. We knew, for example, that water only took about eleven hours to flow from St Cuthbert's Swallet in Priddy to Wookey Resurgence. A similar time had been recorded on a hydrological trace from Eastwater Swallet, while from Swildon's Hole it took twenty-five hours. If one assumes that the flow in the spacious sumps is comparatively slow, then somewhere in the mountain it has to be flowing fairly rapidly, presumably along a normal cave streamway. Detailed surveys of Cuthbert's and Wookey show that there is a height differential of at least thirty metres between the two systems. In the mile and a quarter which separates the two there must, therefore, be a reasonable gradient.

Another Wookey Attempt, 1982

Following two highly successful expeditions to the mysterious Blue Holes of the Bahamas in 1981 and 1982, the scene was set for another attempt on Wookey Hole. Long, deep dives had been commonplace in the Bahamas and, having established world records for penetrations of a submarine cave complex on both expeditions, the challenge at Wookey was suddenly a feasible prospect.

It was October 1982 when the renewed assault was mounted. The logistics of the operation were even more complex than on my previous dive and the preparations took many weeks. Once again air and oxygen had to be stockpiled deep inside the cave and on this occasion a well-provisioned, overnight camp was established at the head of Chamber 24. This was fully equipped with stove, food and sleeping bags. Owing to the severity of the decompression problem

advisors from the Royal Navy recommended that the team involved with the ongoing exploration remain at that point overnight to allow nitrogen to be safely expelled prior to return to the surface.

Four divers were involved: myself, making the solo exploration; Rob Palmer and Rob Parker supporting in Chamber 25, and Ray Stead, who assisted through the dry section of cave in Chamber 22. After leaving Chamber 9, it took us six hours to reach Chamber 25. Hot and weary once more, the moment of truth was at hand. What would the cave do beyond the 1977 limit? Would it start to ascend, hopefully to a dry cave? Would it level off and continue horizontally or would it continue to descend?

Rob Palmer shot some movie film for a short distance into the final sump; then I was on my own. I was equipped with two large 105 cu.ft cylinders of compressed air, enough to last well over three hours at shallow depths, but less than thirty minutes below forty-five metres. All went smoothly in superb visibility of rather more than six metres. It was evident that the passage was unusually large, about seven metres square. The floor continued to dip away at a steady angle, while the roof lowered rather more steeply. The least likely option had become reality and, after laying about thirty-three metres of line, I suddenly reached the magical depth of sixty metres, once again the preset maximum depth. At this point the roof closed to within one foot of the sand floor, posing an effective physical barrier. Filled with overwhelming curiosity, I pushed my head into the gap and a tantalising vision appeared. Beyond the squeeze bright blue water led the eye over speckled sandbanks down into a small, but continuing, passage. The cave was certainly negotiable, but further progress would necessitate a distinctly tricky manoeuvre. Yet again Wookey held fast to her secrets.

The ascent commenced. The first two decompression stops at twenty and fifteen metres were made in conditions of rapidly deteriorating visibility. Despite minimal movement, copious quantities of fine silt were disturbed, and an hour or so was spent in a complete blackout, during which I was unable to see any instruments at all. Cocooned in my dry suit, clinging tightly to the diving line, it was a somewhat

frightening experience. To sink from one's position could mean oxygen poisoning and blackout; to rise would entail the risk of the bends. At any moment I had to be ready to replace one exhausted supply with another. Years of training and experience proved comforting; none the less I was relieved to regain the edge of the pool some two and a quarter hours later. My two loyal supporters were shivering with cold after their long wait. There would have been no better prospect than an immediate return to Chamber 24, but the plan of operation demanded a further lengthy period of surface decompression, whereby I relaxed and continued to breathe pure oxygen for a set period.

The eventual exit was to prove far from straightforward. By now visibility was atrocious and a critical situation developed with the line. It was to take Rob Palmer three attempts before the problem was solved, three attempts before the way out could be found. With severely depleted air reserves and after losing several pieces of valuable equipment, we eventually regained Chamber 24. A warm meal, a comfortable sleeping bag and a bottle of wine proved absolute bliss.

The next morning we struggled carefully back into our sodden dry suits ready to combat the next set of

Above: Ray Stead and Martyn Farr in Chamber 9, at the start of the 1982 attempt. Below: Farr carrying out extra decompression in Chamber 25 after his dive to sixty metres.

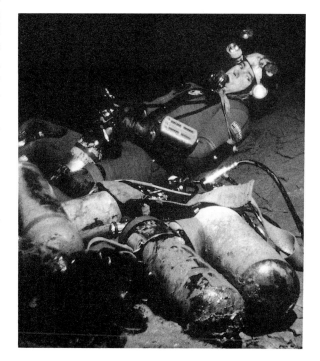

Above: Rob Parker with the helium, oxygen and nitrogen supplies which were used to make the Trimix for his 1985 record-breaking Wookey dive.

valuable insights into the problems presented by the cave. During the intervening period he had proved his outstanding abilities as both a caver and cave diver time and again. With considerable experience in the expeditionary sphere, in particular with lengthy underground camping operations and with both long and deep dives, an assault on Wookey was almost inevitable. Following his many trips to the Blue Holes, Mexico and Florida, he was certainly the most qualified diver to mount such a campaign.

From the outset Rob adopted a technological approach to the project. In order to avoid excessive accumulation of residual nitrogen he planned to camp in Chamber 24 for over a week and during this period mount, if necessary, three separate assaults on the problematic sump. Standard British cave diving equipment was deemed unsuitable for such a siege. The previous year an American expedition to the Huautla resurgence system in Mexico had pioneered the use of exceptionally lightweight, composite pressure vessels developed by Acurex Aerotherm Ltd. These had been designed specifically for space technology: 100 cu.ft cylinders with a working pressure of 333 bars. For the Wookey push these were to be adopted in the normal side-mounted fashion with the additional refinement of a flexible high-pressure linking manifold. By this method the diver had full access to both sources of gas supply in the event of a single demand valve failure.

problems. Despite failing lights, little air and both my companions' suits flooding, we made our way out. We were three hours behind schedule as we cruised back into the crowded, floodlit Showcave. For those at base the twenty-five hours of uncertainty were at an end and, clutching bottles of champagne, we enjoyed a brief moment of triumph. But after this dive I felt I had done as much as I could; it was time to step aside for a new generation.

Wookey Hole: Down to Sixty-Eight Metres, 1985

After a further lapse of three years, it was Rob Parker who took up the challenge. Rob had played a major role in the 1982 assault and, in the process, had gained

The transport of sufficient quantities of air was no problem. The most pressing issue was the reduction of nitrogen narcosis, in order to ensure complete clarity of thought and associated actions. Diving to depths in excess of sixty metres, and combating the additional stress of a constricted passage and consequent poor visibility, it was essential to give serious thought to the breathing supply. To overcome the extreme effects of narcosis anticipated at such depths, it was natural that divers should look to the advances that had been made in the sphere of commercial diving. Incorporating another inert gas, helium, into the breathing supply seemed to be the answer.

This was not a new idea as mixed gas diving had been undertaken, to a limited extent, on both sides of the Atlantic. However, even in 1985, there was considerable scepticism concerning its possible application to cave exploration. In the United States for example just four helium dives had been carried out by cave divers. Of these two had ended in tragedy, and the third team suffered from severe hypothermia during decompression, having inflated their drysuits with the same mix that they were breathing. The fourth dive took place in 1980 but despite a successful outcome the accomplishment was dismissed as the luck of a madman.

The American view was clear: in the absence of the professional facilities available to military and commercial divers, namely a warm, dry decompression chamber, it was safer to try to deal with nitrogen narcosis. This view was vindicated when, just after the successful helium diving operation in Florida, Sheck Exley continued exploration in Die Polder 2, reaching the 110m limit on air and finding the cave closed down just beyond.

In 1981 the German diver Jochen Hasenmayer made an unprecedented deep dive in the Fontaine de Vaucluse, when he reached 143m depth. In 1983 he continued to 205m. These operations were only rendered possible by the use of helium. Hasenmayer had showed the world that such diving could be done and without the advantage of professional backing.

In preparation for his Wookey push Parker undertook a series of deep dives in Florida. It was at this time, April 1985, that new opportunities quietly unveiled themselves. The training, using air, had

been set up by Bill Stone, who planned to join Parker on the English venture. In Florida they were joined by John Zumrick, the chief medical officer for the Navy Experimental Diving Unit – yet another member of the strong team which had explored the Peña Colorada resurgence, in Mexico, the previous year. Zumrick had been conducting experiments for some months using helium and it was he who hesitantly floated the practicality of using the gas for cave diving. Stone acted upon the information and came up with the gas mixture Trimix: 36% helium, 19.5% oxygen and 44.5% nitrogen. The decompression schedules were developed by Zumrick, who also suggested that the problem concerning heat loss from the body could be removed by the simple step of inflating one's dry suit from a separate cylinder of normal compressed air. This venture therefore was in every sense a scientifically

Below: Rob Parker preparing his equipment in Chamber 9, Wookey.

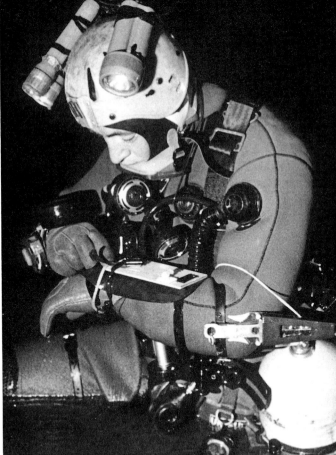

Above left: Bill Stone and Rob Parker with other support divers in Wookey's Chamber 24. Above right: Parker checks his systems and equipment prior to setting out into Wookey to make his record-breaking dive to sixty-eight metres – the furthest penetration to date in Wookey Hole.

complex operation: and in the event was extremely well planned and efficiently executed.

Despite all these careful preparations, the outcome was acutely disappointing. In July 1985, supported by Julian Walker, Bill and Pat Stone, and Ian Rolland, Parker reached a most definite 'end' less than nine metres beyond my 1982 limit. Only by squeezing down a steeply inclined gravel bank could he make any progress and at the furthest point, sixty-eight metres, the combination of extreme confinement and strong current forced an exit. On subsequent dives the early section of the sump was checked to see if there might be an alternative route forward. Nothing could be found. Fifty years of diving had yielded yet another British cave diving depth record, but sadly no connection with the feeder caves high on the plateau above.

Perhaps the most significant outcome of Parker's

dive was the set of reliable and safe procedures for using helium for cave diving. The Wookey project may not have yielded a major advance in terms of cave passage, but it was to open doors to a whole new era of deep diving, not in Britain perhaps, but certainly in the United States.

Gough's Cave, Cheddar, 1985

As the Wookey diving project drew to a close, an extremely significant development occurred near by. Cavers and divers had long sought to gain entry to the extensive system lying somewhere beneath the Cheddar Gorge: a complex of passages associated with the major tourist attraction of Gough's Cave, more commonly referred to as Cheddar Caves.

After fruitless efforts to gain entry to the submerged risings of the River Yeo, in November 1985 Richard Stevenson was lured to a small, insignificant looking sump about 200m into Gough's Cave. I had previously explored this constricted sump to a depth of ten metres in 1980. Using only one bottle and without fins, Stevenson worked his way down the sump using a feet first, downward shuffle in zero visibility, continuing past my point down the constricted shaft. He reached what appeared to be the bottom at fourteen metres, where he touched down on to a mudbank and could feel a much larger space off to one side. Unfortunately, at this point, his base-fed rope ran out, and, in any case, further progress would have been unwise until the line was firmly belayed at the bottom of the shaft, rather than risk dragging it into some tight, nasty undercut.

Stevenson returned for a second attempt a week later. Once again he dived on a single bottle and without fins. The sump was wholly uninviting, but he realised that, if it was to be thoroughly and safely explored, he would have to take a line reel. Reaching the previous deep point, he secured his line by feel to a block of lead. Provided that he didn't pull on the line, he was then reasonably confident of being able to negotiate his way back into the vertical tube which led up to safety. Amid a cloud of swirling mud, he then moved about three metres off to the side to emerge into a huge sump of crystal clear water.

Dark blue water faded into the distance. The lost river of Cheddar had been found at last. Elated, Stevenson made a jubilant exit through the constriction which was named Dire Straits.

To explore the deep subterranean river would not be easy through such a constricted approach but the vast potential offered by this system was compelling. The combined waters of the rising presented an even larger resurgence than that at Wookey Hole, and the catchment extended for many kilometres to the north. Dye tests had long established the fact that systems such as G. B. Cave, Longwood Swallet and Manor Farm Swallet, about four to five kilometres distant, all contributed water, while even more water was derived from the northern flank of North Hill, just over eleven kilometres away. Apart from the sheer extent of the system there was also a depth potential of about 300m – quite possibly, therefore, Stevenson had uncovered the key to one of the longest and deepest caves in the United Kingdom.

Right: Richard Stevenson sets up his Molephone link in Bishop's Palace, beyond Sump 1 in Gough's Cave, Cheddar.

Cheddar Explorations, 1986

Early in 1986 Stevenson and Robert Harper commenced a series of dives, extending their line further and further up the flooded tunnel. At this stage Rob Palmer was recruited, initially for his photographic skills and shortly to assist with the exploration. Luckily, the depth at which the team were operating slowly began to decrease and, on 18 March 1986, 150m from Dire Straits, Palmer and Harper surfaced in an enormous air-bell, Lloyd Hall (named in recognition of the late Dr Oliver Lloyd's contribution to British cave diving). Beyond this point the sump continued easy and shallow, and on May 2, Palmer and Stevenson surfaced into one of the largest caverns beneath the Mendip Hills, the 244m long, 24m high Bishop's Palace. At the far end of this vast, boulder-strewn chamber the river welled up from three deep, flooded shafts, the Duck Ponds.

A month later, on an exploratory dive down the main shaft into Sump 2, it became clear that further progress would be much more serious, as within a very short distance the passage reached a depth of thirty metres. Greater supplies of air would be

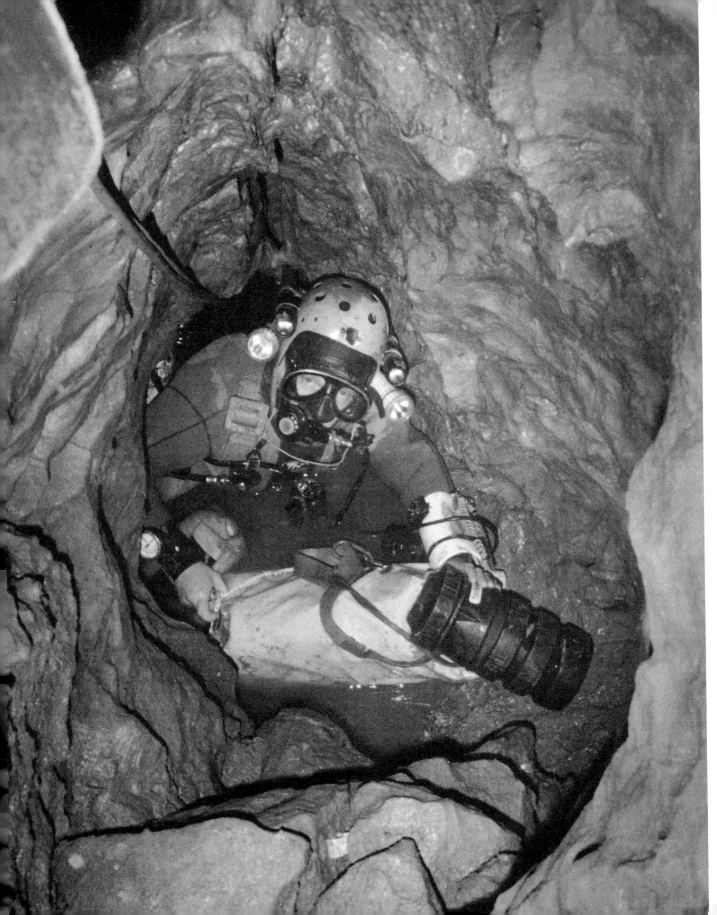

necessary, and to get these through Dire Straits presented the team with a considerable problem.

Above: Rob Palmer and Rob Harper emerge into Bishop's Palace after diving Sump 1 of Gough's Cave.

Cheddar: Progress to Sump 3

The survey which the team compiled as they progressed quickly revealed another possibility. The large, high chamber Lloyd Hall lay tantalisingly close to the neighbouring St Paul's area of Gough's Cave. A 'molephone' communication device (devised by Bob Mackin of Lancaster University, and similar to that used on the Keld Head dive in 1978 – see Yorkshire section following) was employed in August to try and establish a dry entry to Lloyd Hall. Contact was soon made, a short choke passed, and, in August 1986, the diggers working in a small passage below St Pauls were confronted with a deep shaft which echoed to

Left: Rob Palmer about to dive into the Dire Straits entry to the flooded passages of Gough's Cave. This constricted, fourteen-metre tube, first passed by Richard Stevenson in 1985, leads down to Sump 1. Subsequent surveys revealed another access route allowing this unpleasant entry to be avoided. Palmer is carrying extra equipment in a sealed bag and the molephone in a tough waterproof tube.

the sound of cheers and mighty splashes. They had discovered a new 'direct' access to the waterway twenty metres below. But the new route was dangerously loose and while it was being stabilised, diving was continued using the base at Dire Straits.

On 11 September 1986, after diving on from the Duck Ponds, at the far side of Bishop's Palace, Palmer finally passed Sump 2. Although of a similar length to the previous sumps, the increased depth involved on this dive entailed far greater air consumption. On first surfacing in Sheppard's Crook, the site which met the eye was most exciting. The river tumbled over a set of low cascades and it seemed that a major section of free flowing streamway was about to be revealed. Palmer scrambled up the greasy rocks for fifteen metres only to be confronted by the sight of a deep, black pool, from which the river welled up.

An immediate foray was made into Sump 3. Negotiating two consecutive potholes, he dropped to twenty-three-metres' depth before reaching the limit of his air-supply. Beneath his fins lay nothing but blackness. Clearly it was a long way down to the elbow of this sump.

The diving was now every bit as difficult and technical as that previously conducted at Wookey Hole. It came as a great relief to the divers when their comrades finally succeeded in establishing a safe and practical route from the environs of the Show Cave to Lloyd Hall. Just half an hour from the entrance, they now had a suitable site for an advance diving base. A platform was constructed here, which allowed the divers to kit up and enter the water with relative ease. More vitally, it allowed them to use larger bottles. The horrors of Dire Straits were thus eliminated and the assault on the lengthy sump resumed in earnest.

Cheddar: Palmer's Attempt on Sump 3, 1988

On a joint dive with Stevenson on 3 October 1987, the pair achieved a depth of forty-five metres and still they could find no sign of any bottom. The third dive was to take place in March 1988 and was to be something of an epic. Helped by Rob Harper as far as Sheppard's Crook, Palmer dived on alone to reach the base of the shaft at a depth of fifty-eight metres, a point thirty metres *below* sea-level. Wearing two 80 cu.ft bottles he was able to continue along a spacious tunnel, which gradually started to ascend. About sixty metres beyond the elbow, he reached his safe limit at a depth of forty-four metres. If this upward trend continued then there was every likelihood of reaching another air surface within a relatively short distance. The prospect was exciting, but at such a depth his supply of air was inadequate. He made a careful exit involving a further forty minutes of decompression.

By this stage problems had arisen. His dry suit had sprung a leak. He was wet and cold; and his lights were beginning to run low, so there was no question of making an immediate, fast exit through the next sump. So, Palmer was forced to sit and wait a further hour to clear some of the excess nitrogen from his bloodstream. By the time he set off to follow Rob Harper through the one-hundred-and-fifty-metre long, thirty-metre deep Sump 2, he was feeling very cold and tired, and his lighting was failing rapidly. At the deepest point, a real crisis developed. In the muddy water, he became entangled with the line and his lights faded to the point of extinction. Trying to sort out the mess was impossible and he was forced to cut himself free.

Right: On the crest of the rock pile in Bishop's Palace. The river finds a route through the boulders below.

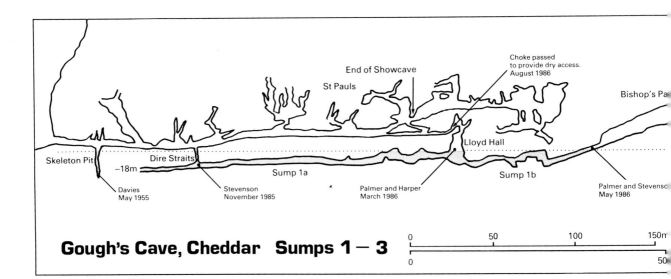

Gough's Cave, Cheddar   Sumps 1 — 3

End of Showcave

St Pauls

Choke passed to provide dry access. August 1986

Bishop's Pa

Skeleton Pit

−18m

Dire Straits

Sump 1a

Lloyd Hall

Sump 1b

Davies May 1955

Stevenson November 1985

Palmer and Harper March 1986

Palmer and Stevenso May 1986

0   50   100   150m

0   50

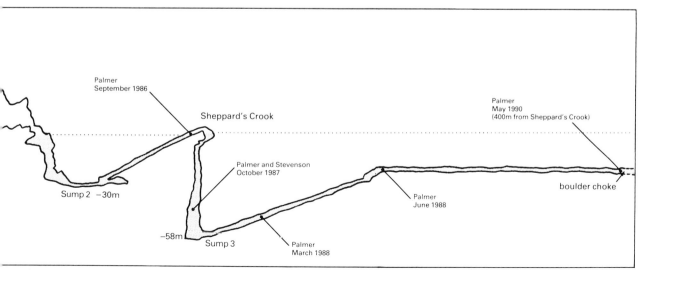

Palmer
September 1986

Sheppard's Crook

Palmer
May 1990
(400m from Sheppard's Crook)

Sump 2 −30m

Palmer and Stevenson
October 1987

boulder choke

Palmer
June 1988

−58m   Sump 3

Palmer
March 1988

Above: Looking downstream from Sheppard's Crook (named after the famous Swildon's pioneer), the last airspace before the deepest and longest sump in Gough's Cave.

As I came up the shaft in the darkness, I can remember thinking that I was becoming too old for such near misses. My girlfriend was about to give birth in a few days, and I was reflecting on the worth of risking one life so close to another's beginning. Up, up, up . . . then I became ensnared in loose line again near the top of the shaft. At such times you can only try to think how silly it would be to panic. As I sightlessly dragged in coil after coil, without finding one that pulled taut, I actually began to think for once that I might not make it out. So near to the surface, as well. Then one loop pulled taut, and I began to wonder . . . is this it? or is it just caught round a flake?

It was still some metres up to the decompression point, and in complete and utter darkness the stress level was growing unbearable. The floating coils snaked all about him, but delivery was at hand: the taut line was indeed his saviour, it was the one that led out. As he reached the oxygen bottle pre-staged at three metres' depth for decompression, he was in a state of acute stress and partially entangled yet again.

Unable to read gauges, decompression meter or tables, he was forced to wait for several minutes in complete darkness, guessing how much time had elapsed. Festooned with coils of line, he eventually rose the last few metres to the surface, fully prepared to dive back again immediately with a borrowed torch should the tables so dictate. Fortunately his guesswork was good and his meter was clear. As his friends slowly unravelled the fifteen to twenty metres of line from around his shivering body he recounted his harrowing experience.

The Second Attempt in Sump 3, Cheddar, 1988
From a close study of their surveys and of the local geology it soon became apparent that, if the ascent was maintained in Sump 3, the divers might reach air within a distance of 180-260m. As the horrors of the March dive faded, Palmer and Stevenson began planning another attempt.

It had taken ten hours to mount the previous exploration. The next assault would inevitably take longer. After several weekends of preparation the weekend of June 25, 1988 was selected for the push. A team of eight divers and some twenty cavers were involved.

The strategy involved Stevenson and Palmer making a joint exploration of Sump 3 wearing four large tanks apiece. Essential support was to be given by Rob Harper, Richard Websell and Robin Brown, who were to assist the pair up to this point. Unfortunately, events did not turn out precisely as planned.

After a series of short delays, the pair entered Sump 3 at 10 p.m. Palmer waited at forty-four metres' depth for his friend to join him, but as the minutes ticked by, there was no sign of him. He returned to the surface to discover that Stevenson, having dived to a depth of thirty-three metres, had been stricken by an acute bout of cramps and been forced to surface. Neither diver was completely happy about the plan, as it was also clear that the upper portion of the shaft would be much too constricted for two heavily equipped divers to conduct a safe decompression. A radical reappraisal was required.

The revised plan of attack involved a solo push by Palmer, who streamlined his equipment to two 94 cu.ft bottles and one hand-held 80 cu.ft stage unit. A maximum inward swim time of twenty minutes was planned. It was ten minutes after midnight when the operation recommenced.

Visibility was little more than five metres and the current was unusually strong. Palmer found swimming against it exceptionally hard. There was no possibility of using the floor to pull himself along, because this generally consisted of fine rippled mud with occasional small pebble piles in minor eddies. Beyond the elbow, the spacious passage gradually ascended and, with the stage unit dropped off, progress up the line was slightly more straightforward. A short while later, he reached the end of the old line and started into new territory. Swimming against the current, progress up the passage was not easy and the minutes ticked by on the dive computer (Aladdin) as the depth continued to decrease.

Just on twenty minutes, a significant change became apparent. From a depth of twenty-six metres the roof above him seemed to rise much more steeply and the sediment pattern changed. Suddenly, there seemed

real promise of an air-surface. But time had run out. Having now used nearly a third of his air supply, and with a decompression stop flashing on the computer, there was no choice but to cast one last look at the view ahead and retreat.

Palmer surfaced after a total dive time of two hours and three minutes. A brief message was radioed to the surface and the team settled down to try to sleep. It was mid-day on Sunday when they finally emerged to be greeted by the waiting press, cameras and a champagne reception. The 'Lost Cave Project' had not resulted in the discovery of a new air chamber, but it certainly ended on a well-deserved high note.

The 1990 Attempt in Cheddar

There was to be an interval of two years before the next attempt. Once again considerable preparation took place in advance, involving the portage of almost half a ton of equipment to the furthest air-space in Sheppard's Crook. The lead divers, Palmer and Stevenson, who had decided to dive Sump 3 together, reached the advance base at 3 p.m. on 19 May 1990. Here they took a five-hour break to shed some of the accumulated nitrogen. At 8 p.m. they prepared for the dive. Each wore four 100 cu.ft tanks. Stevenson opted to wear two side-mounted and two on his chest, while Palmer had two back-mounted and two slung from his chest. Both were equipped with powerful lights as they slowly began their descent.

Barely had they passed the deepest point and started into the upstream passage, when Stevenson suffered a massive air leak. After arresting this, he was left with insufficient air reserves to play any effective part in the exploration and was compelled to return to advance base, leaving Palmer to continue alone.

Twenty minutes and 200m into the dive, Palmer reached his previous limit. Here he retrieved his reel from beneath its two-year covering of silt and, as it was still running freely, decided to use it in preference to the one he had just carried in. About 150m later a large sand dune split the passage and, less than fifty metres beyond that, a massive boulder choke completely filled the passage, which was two metres high by six metres wide. Further progress was impossible for a diver wearing so much bulky equipment. At a depth of twenty-five metres and at a distance of 400m into Sump 3, Gough's Cave terminated.

Palmer tied off his line and retreated. Reaching the final shaft, he spent a hundred minutes decompressing, largely on nitrox mixture, before surfacing to a waiting Stevenson and Gavin Newman. A further eight hours were spent in Sheppard's Crook, eating, sleeping and taking photographs, before they left the cave early the next morning.

What the next approach will be remains to be seen, but it is abundantly clear that a system of this magnitude will not be ignored.

SOUTH WALES

The Final Sumps of Agen Allwedd

In South Wales and later in Yorkshire major discoveries were made in the 1970s and 1980s. During the early years the main activities were centred in the south, involving the exploration of those sumps which were still passable. Thus, for example, Little Neath River Cave, discovered in 1967, was explored deep into Sump 9 and the prospects of a viable through trip

Below: Dave Morris pushing his equipment along the initial crawlway of Dan yr Ogof.

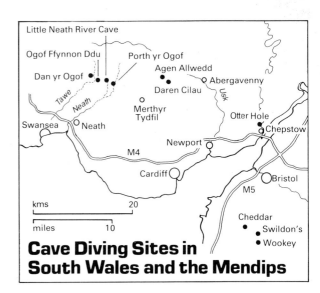

Cave Diving Sites in South Wales and the Mendips

(sink to resurgence) were seen as nil. Later, others penetrated a little further, and by 1976, nearly every submerged passage in the region had been critically examined.

One of the more exciting finds at this time was at Dan yr Ogof in the Swansea Valley. Here, in August 1972, a 119m sump was passed, after a difficult carry, to yield over two kilometres of new, dry passages. Fired by our success here, Roger Solari and I then turned to Agen Allwedd, another site of tremendous potential.

The upstream siphons or Turkey Sump had first been passed by Mike Wooding and John Sinclair in 1966, but, in 1971, John Parker and Jeff Phillips had extended this area through a fifth sump to discover nearly 600m of passages. Solari and I then pressed on through a canal of claustrophobic proportions to double the length of the new find.

However, it was at the terminal downstream sump in Agen Allwedd that the greatest rewards lay. In 1972 Parker and Phillips extended this part of the cave by nearly 450m, of which 335m were submerged. The

5. (top right) Cheddar explorers Rob Palmer and Richard Stevenson waiting in Sheppard's Crook before their push into Sump 3 of Gough's Cave in May 1990. Palmer advanced for 400m where a boulder blockage prevented further progress. **6.** *(lower right) Pete Bolt passing through Sump 1b, of Gough's Cave, Cheddar.*

7. *(top left) The camp in Chamber 24, Wookey, during the 1989 expedition.* **8.** *(lower left) The China Shop in Boreham Cave, Yorkshire –*
one of the most beautiful caving scenes in Britain. The fragility of the straws is obvious and great care is required to avoid damage.
9. *(above) Dave Morris in the long initial sump system of Boreham Cave, that gives access to the passages including that of the China Shop.*

Right: Rodney Beaumont in the fine passage beyond Turkey Sump 3, Agen Allwedd, first reached by Wooding and Sinclair in 1966.

remaining unexplored section was about two kilometres long and incorporated a vertical interval of about forty-five metres to the level of the rising. It was a tantalizing objective. However, planning and executing a dive at such an isolated point was beset with difficulties, so alternative sites were examined first.

The rising itself, Pwll y Cwm, lies directly in the bed of the River Clydach and is, as a result, choked with assorted debris transported from higher up the valley. A dive in a neighbouring cave, Elm Hole, in April 1974 confirmed a suspected connection with the main subterranean river flowing through a huge tunnel from Agen Allwedd to the west. The nature of this dive was extremely intimidating, though, as it led via several squeezes to a depth of nearly twenty-three metres. Evidently, there was no possible avenue to the missing section of cave from this access point. Thus there was almost no alternative but to accept the challenge of a long, arduous trip down Agen Allwedd.

All cavers who have visited the terminal sump (Sump 1) of Agen Allwedd will vividly recall one thing to the end of their days: the sheer, unadulterated slog down Southern Stream Passage. The notoriety of this section of cave comes from the endless succession of stoops, crawls and squeezes – in all, well over a kilometre of strenuous boredom.

In May 1974, with minimal support and diving solo, I passed through Sump 3 after 259m. The result was the discovery of a majestic 550m streamway, which in turn terminated in Sump 4. Within a week, plans were afoot for yet another push, this time in partnership with Roger Solari.

Accident in Agen Allwedd, 1974
The preparations and support were immense, and we dived optimistically with three bottles apiece and

10. (left) An airbell near the entrance of Keld Head, Yorkshire. This is one of a number of cross rifts that lie above the main Keld Head passageways. These are valuable as they can be used in emergencies. This would buy time to either regain composure and await conditions to clear or, in a dire emergency, to wait for support divers to bring in extra air supplies.

carrying an extra 427m of line. Depositing our first partially used cylinders in the air-bell between Sumps 2 and 3 (for the dive out), we continued through Sump 3 on two full cylinders each. The swim through this was uneventful and, in the passage beyond, we donned our boots for the carry down to Sump 4. As we were heavily equipped, our progress was necessarily slow and cautious, for damage to any part of the equipment would clearly be critical. Even so, the psychological isolation was thrust to one side; fatigued but hopeful, we arrived at our destination.

Hitherto we had always dived separately, waiting for one another between sumps as conditions dictated. It appeared only right that any discoveries made on this trip should be shared, so we made the ill-fated decision to dive together. Previously I had believed this sump would be short, but now for some reason we both anticipated a long dive. Depositing our boots on a mudbank, we put on our full cylinders for the exploratory stage. The ones which had been depleted

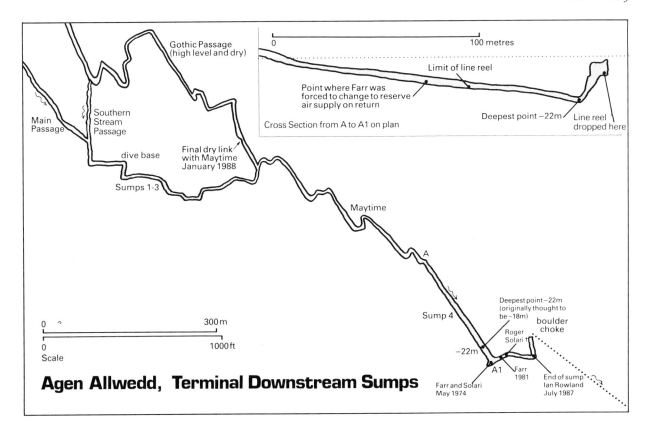

Agen Allwedd, Terminal Downstream Sumps

Gothic Passage
(high level and dry)

Southern
Stream
Passage

Main
Passage

dive base

Final dry link
with Maytime
January 1988

Sumps 1-3

Maytime

A

Sump 4

Deepest point −22m
(originally thought to
be −18m)   boulder
choke

Roger
Solari †

−22m

A1   Farr
1981   End of sump
Ian Rowland
July 1987

Farr and Solari
May 1974

0   300m

0   1000ft

Scale

Cross Section from A to A1 on plan

0   100 metres

Limit of line reel

Point where Farr was
forced to change to reserve
air supply on return

Deepest point −22m   Line reel
dropped here

during the passage of Sump 3 were in reserve. The plan and signals were clarified, but, in the final resort, each of us was to be responsible for his own welfare, he could turn back at any point with no obligation to his partner.

Roger led off, laying line from a 122m reel, while I followed, carrying a reel of 300m. Visibility was about three metres and communication was no problem. At several points it was apparent that Roger was having difficulty with his equalisation, and at the same time we were heading gradually deeper. When the first reel ran out, I consulted my pressure-gauge and, although a good third of the air had already been used (the normal point which signals a return), I decided to press on a short way further. My assumption was that Roger would now abort, because he was using

Left: The passage leading to Agen Allwedd's Terminal Sump 1, just beyond the southern and mainstream link. Right: Roger Solari.

cylinders which were slightly smaller than mine.

About thirty metres later, the passage already having levelled off, a steep gravel bank loomed up ahead. In a rash bid for air I sped up the slope, reaching a vertical wall after eighteen metres. Then, following a total vertical ascent of about fifteen metres, the unthinkable occurred – I reached a submerged roof. Along the wall a void lay to both right and left. Swimming to the right for about nine metres, I found an alcove – a hopeless situation. As I looked back, I was surprised to see Roger appearing against the roof. We were now desperate, as our air reserves were very low. I dropped the reel and, on reaching him, I signalled that we should return. His look of anguish was impossible to hide, but the predicament was of our own making. Close to panic, I dipped and started to go back. I never saw my friend again.

Within a few minutes my cylinder was almost empty and, with just under 122m to go to reach safety (Sump 4 base), I was forced to change on to my second (reserve) set. The swapping of mouthpieces successfully achieved, I waited for perhaps a minute or two before continuing. At Sump 4 base I dragged myself from the water and began an agonising wait.

Right: The Maytime river passage beyond Agen Allwedd's Terminal Sumps 1, 2 and 3. A dry passage to bypass these was discovered in 1988, allowing a direct route to the start of the daunting Sump 4 (above) where Farr waited for Solari in 1974.

Several dreadful hours passed and eventually I decided to make a quick search into the sump. On entering the water I found the line was slack. After pulling it in, I discovered it was clean cut at 131m from base. It was clear from this that Roger must have returned at least a quarter of the distance before he needed to cut the line for some reason. I was totally unable to do anything constructive, as I had very little air left and no line reel. I had no choice but to leave the cave and set in motion a later search. The first attempt, soon afterwards, was deferred because of bad visibility; while on the second, five days later, John Parker was only able to search a short distance into Sump 4. A total of 2760 man hours were spent in search attempts.

Just what had happened on that ill-fated dive? Roger had a succession of small problems, and these led to a critical situation. He had sinus trouble, was underweight and was using positively buoyant cylinders (cylinders which float when empty). On the way back to safety he must, at some stage, have had to

swap valves. Back in the early 1970s this was not an easy manoeuvre because techniques and the organisation of a diver's equipment had yet to fully develop. The spare valve was never located exactly where it should be and the neck-straps frequently obstructed the operation. In an attempt to sort this out, and given the added discomfort of rapidly mounting stress, he would have had but a few moments before his craving for air became uncontrollable. Problems may have occurred then, for on the actual exchange it would have been necessary to let go of the line for a few moments. For myself, using negatively buoyant bottles, it was simply a matter of lying on the floor on top of the line. For Roger, it would have been very different. He would have been much more buoyant and his position would have been directly under the roof, so that the only way he could possibly keep hold of the line would have been to wrap it around an arm. If the actual swap had gone off smoothly, there was always the possibility that he may have lost his sense of direction. The panic factor is impossible to assess but would obviously have been significant. Another possibility is that he may have become entangled in the line during the exchange. His troubles clearly coincided with line problems, as the cutting indicated. To infer more than this is to go beyond all known facts.

In 1981 I made a renewed assault upon Sump 4, reaching 215m from the sump base. It was a traumatic operation, with no air surface being located in the vicinity of the 1974 terminus. The cave continued beyond at 10m depth. Then, in October 1986, Ian Rolland and Julian Walker made another significant advance, and in the process located Roger's body at about 220m. Given the extremely remote nature of this sump it was felt that a recovery operation would be unsafe.

This was the first occasion on which an experienced cave diver had lost his life, and once again it was a case of human miscalculation.

Mazeways Area, Dan yr Ogof, 1978

The tragedy at Agen Allwedd had a disastrous effect upon cave diving within South Wales. Despite immense potential throughout the limestone area it was not until 1978 that another noteworthy advance was made. In partnership with Phil Rust, I resumed work beyond the sumps in the Mazeways area of Dan yr Ogof. An extremely precarious choke was eventually passed and we moved on to discover over 450m of new passage.

Subsequently, two bivouac camping operations were mounted to the end of this key section, in an attempt to siphon out and clear the obvious continuation, a boulder-choked sump. To date not much success has been achieved, but it seems highly probable that in future this area of the cave, still restricted to cave divers, will yield access to one of the longest dry systems in the British Isles, a cave in all probability extending to well over forty kilometres in length.

The Llangattock Campaign, 1984-87

It was not until 1984 that any major discoveries were made in South Wales. Significantly the next developments were to prove extremely exciting and were to dominate the British caving scene for the next five years. They involved the discovery and exploration of a huge network of passages and sumps under Llangattock Mountain.

It was 8 September 1984 when Clive Gardener, Paul Tarrant and I broke through a tight draughting choke at the end of the little-frequented Ogof Daren Cilau at Llangattock. That day we discovered over two and a half kilometres of dry passageways, strategically placed to reveal once and for all the inner secrets of Llangattock Mountain.

The following March (1985) a further breakthrough was achieved and a strong team continued on through the mountain to discover not only the largest section of passageway in the United Kingdom, the Time Machine, but also a major new streamway, which totally bypassed the terminal sumps of neighbouring Agen Allwedd. This led to a final submerged section incredibly just 500m from the main rising for the

Scenes in the Dan yr Ogof cave system, South Wales: (top right) the cascades at the head of Lake 3; (near right) at the side of Lake 11, which can only be reached by diving. The knotted sling is suspended from a dry high-level passage which was gained by a few aid moves. This allowed access to nearly four kilometres of dry passages; (far right) a passage in Mazeways 3, with tubing used in an abortive effort to drain a small sump.

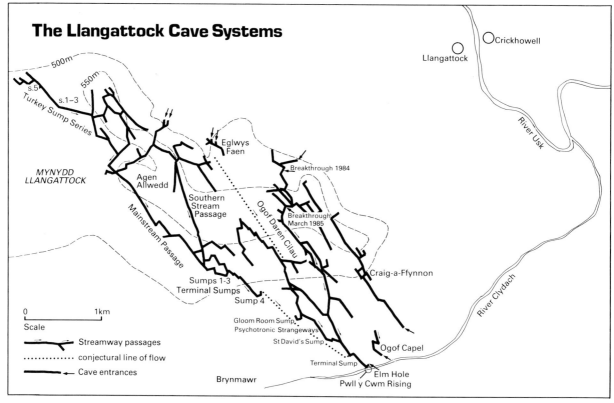

The Llangattock Cave Systems

Streamway passages

conjectural line of flow

Cave entrances

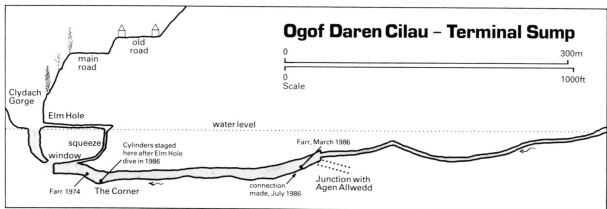

Ogof Daren Cilau – Terminal Sump

mountain, Pwll y Cwm, in the Clydach Gorge.

I realised that at long last a through trip might be feasible and all my energy was now channelled towards this project. Visibility in the Daren Sump was atrocious, never better than one metre, but after two dives I had installed 230m of line trending straight for the resurgence. I was happy with the progress, if not with the style. To ensure that nothing was missed I had to follow the wall, in and out of every small fissure and alcove. As such the line was laid through every conceivable undercut in the passage. This was extremely frustrating as in clearer conditions I could probably have progressed normally down a substantial passage.

On the third dive progress was continuing nicely, when at 310 metres I suddenly emerged at the top of a drop. Feet first I descended into the void. I could see very little, as usual, but I could 'feel' the immensity of an altogether larger passage. The floor was only three metres or so beneath at a depth of possibly fifteen metres, I sensed that this was at long last the main trunk route leading in from Agen Allwedd to the west. Somewhere to my right therefore was the passage that Roger and I had attempted to reach in 1974, the unexplored section of cave streamway downstream from Agen Allwedd's Sump 4. But that was not the objective now. My sights were set on an eventual through trip so I continued downstream using the same technique for installing the line, fixing it periodically at the junction of the floor and left wall – the 'skirting board' technique. In this manner I worked my way steadily down the murky tunnel to a point 330m from base where I tied off. This advance left a distance of only 200m from the final point of resurgence.

Rather than struggle with moving an ever increasing bulk of gear to this, the most isolated diving site in any British cave, it was decided to concentrate efforts at the small cave of Elm Hole, situated adjacent to the boulder-choked rising in the bed of the River Clydach. This site was a flood overflow route and had last been dived in 1974.

Elm Hole was an extremely daunting proposition. It was horribly tight, both above and more especially below water. But having more than halved the distance from Daren to the Clydach Gorge on March 22, I ventured into Elm Hole nine days later. My recollections of the push in 1974 were traumatic, with the result that despite the massive ongoing passage nothing had lured me back – until now. Twelve years previously I had been young and bold, game to try anything no matter what the consequences. Over the intervening period I had learned a few lessons.

I calculated that with my vastly improved equipment and refined techniques and most important a wealth of experience, I was equal to the challenge – psychologically. I was prepared to do battle. But despite the mental preparation the atmosphere of the diving site soon asserted itself. The rocks were dark, jagged and

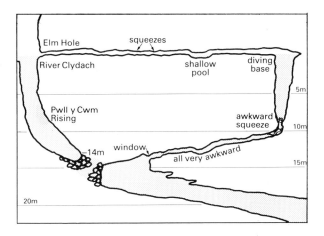

muddy, the water a stagnant peaty colour and one's breath hung in the air, as if it too felt cornered and trapped in this confined hole. This was no friendly cave like Wookey or Boreham, this emanated an almost overpowering sense of evil.

I slid cautiously down the rift stopping every couple of metres to ensure that the line was safely belayed in the widest section. Then, at ten metres depth came the squeeze. This was less than a foot wide and about three feet long, a place where you knew from experience a valve exchange would be impossible – one of those landmarks that one logs very carefully in the memory. Beyond, the route continued in a more horizontal plane, but still festooned with shelves, contortions, dips and ascents. In visibility of barely a metre I wriggled and bumped forward for about thirty metres before deciding that it was best to retreat as I was not sure that the line was properly belayed.

Were it not for the fact that I knew there was a big passage somewhere ahead I would not have returned, but, fortified by the uneventful initiation, I was back twelve days later and the real exploration began. I reached the Window and looked out onto the awesome expanse of flooded cave that I had first seen in 1974. After the claustrophobia of the Elm Hole, one had instantly to combat an equally disturbing sense of agoraphobia. There was also the sobering thought that losing the line at depths in excess of eighteen metres and in such appalling visibility would be absolutely critical. That day I advanced thirty metres beyond the Corner, my 1974 limit, and just overran thirds. Dive

Above: Murky conditions in Ogof Ffynnon Ddu's Dip Sump, similar to those in Daren Cilau's Terminal Sump, where Farr was forced to proceed with maximum caution fixing the line carefully as he progressed.

Left: Entering a tight tube in Noxon Iron Mine, South Wales. The Elm Hole is like this but tighter and more turbid.

after dive followed, of necessity with progressively larger cylinders, and on each occasion I pushed my safety margin to the limit.

Dive number six (3 July), was destined to be a tense day. Barely had I submerged than complications arose: the hand-held stage bottle was difficult to breathe, and my mask was leaking slightly. As I slid down the rift with my face pressed tightly against the rock I jammed. Taken in isolation the momentary delay was nothing but it added to the overall level of anxiety. I moved on. By the time I reached the Corner, where I had previously deposited another stage unit, all senses were on red alert. As ever there was no time to look around, no time for any delay. I ripped off the protective polythene bag, surrounding the mouthpiece, and started upon the second stage bottle. The deepest part of the dive (twenty-two metres) lay just ahead.

After a further sixty metres I dropped off the second stage bottle. Annoyingly the depth gauge now decided to work lose, and thereafter constantly threatened to fall from my arm.

At my previous limit I attached a new reel and moved quickly forward. Any second I expected to meet up with the Daren line. However, as thirty then forty metres of line was trailed out I became increasingly worried. Was I really in the right passage? Perhaps this wasn't the route to Daren at all but a parallel one leading to Agen Allwedd? Tension was mounting and with my safety margin rapidly approaching I would shortly be forced to turn back. My eyes were frantically searching that critical area at the foot of the wall, craving for deliverance.

As all hope was just about to extinguish, I arrived smack on. I'd made the link up. There was no jubilation at all, just incredible relief that I had to go no further. I tied the line off, abandoned the reel, and in visibility almost down to zero I started back.

I groped down the tunnel, collecting both stage bottles as I went. By the time I reached the Window I knew that I was almost out, yet the tension was overwhelming. No sooner had I started along the rift than a fresh set of problems developed. The line started to catch in the buckle of my fin strap. This happened twice within the first ten metres. It felt as though the cave was trying to exact some form of revenge for the success. The breathing rate went up. I reached the squeeze and as I wriggled up through I got caught yet again. By now the breathing was continuous. A surging silvery mass of bubbles mushroomed into the space around my mask, the regular muffled rumble being replaced by a thunderous roar. Thoughts of dumping the offending fin were quickly ruled out as I hadn't the room to reach down

Above: In the Psychotronic Strangeways passage of Daren Cilau, reached by Farr and Ian Rolland after a shallow, sixty-metre dive through St David's Sump.

to prise it free. With my head up in the tightest bit there was no room to exchange mouthpieces either. Other than to cut the line the only option was to try and pull forward for a metre. Mustering all my strength I heaved myself up and gained that essential room with which to manoeuvre. The line was freed.

A cold shaken diver bobbed back to the surface after forty-six minutes. After years and years of searching, three dives in Daren Cilau and six in Elm Hole a lifetime's ambition had been achieved. With the connection made, on 11 August, supported by Arthur Millett and John Cooper, I finally accomplished the through dive from Daren Cilau to the Clydach Gorge. This was filmed by HTV. In so doing this was to establish a new record for both the longest (five kilometres) and the deepest (213m) caving through trip in the British Isles.

Concurrent with explorations downstream in Daren Cilau work was also undertaken in an upstream direction. Here, just 200m from the downstream sump, a large flow of water was encountered which emerged from St David's Sump. An early dye test revealed that this water originated several miles away, in the neighbourhood of Eglwys Faen Cave.

In April 1985 I discovered over one kilometre of passage, which I called Psychotronic Strangeways, beyond a relatively easy, shallow, sixty-metre-long dive. The quest was now for a connection with Agen Allwedd itself, which lay approximately 500m to the west. The strategically placed Gloom Room Sump was continually to frustrate all attempts at exploration, but, in November 1985, Ian Rolland and Rob Parker had an amazing stroke of luck. By pushing through a dry, heavily silted side passage just short of the Gloom Room, they broke out into another section of streamway, which they named Borrowed Boots. That day they discovered another two kilometres of passage, terminating at the Seventh Hour Sump, an isolated diving site two hours' travelling time beyond St David's Sump and seven from the surface.

A strong assault upon this site early the following year made little progress at this constricted sump, but Rolland continued his work in this area and, after a bold free climb up Jacob's Ladder, was suitably rewarded by the discovery of a major, high-level series of passages, strategically placed to offer the possibility of a dry connection with Agen Allwedd. A series of epic trips were to follow, in which the explorers mounted long and arduous excursions, frequently

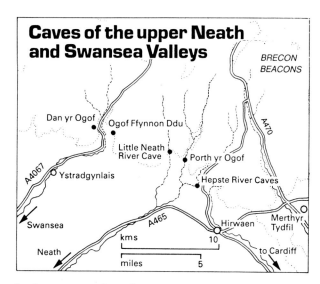

Caves of the upper Neath and Swansea Valleys

lasting twenty-three hours or more.

A dry route has now been excavated into the Borrowed Boots streamway, and non-divers are presently excavating the many leads in the Agua Colorada series. This area lies adjacent to Agen Allwedd and the long-sought connection between the two caves looks certain to be achieved in the near future.

Diving has played a major role in the discovery and the connection of the caves beneath Llangattock Mountain, opening up the possibility of many more discoveries. For example, in the summer of 1987, a loose boulder-choke was passed beyond the two short sumps in Ogof Capel. Over a kilometre of exceptionally well-decorated passage was found. But, of greater significance to divers, is the ongoing excavation at the Pwll y Cwm Rising. The successful outcome of this will eventually yield a Welsh version of Keld Head, namely access to the huge 'main drain' which I only partially explored in 1986.

Much diving remains to be undertaken right across the South Wales area, and systems such as Llygad Llwchwr in the west, Tooth Cave and Llethryd on the Gower Peninsula, and Dan yr Ogof at the head of the Swansea Valley must surely yield major discoveries in the not too distant future.

Right: The dangerous initial sump of Otter Hole which leads off the River Wye below Chepstow Racecourse in South Wales. The passage seen here is flooded at high tide but can usually be entered by cavers between tides.

NORTH WALES

The narrow band of limestone in North Wales possesses a number of caves and certainly offers considerable potential to cave divers. Within this region, there are two main caving areas: the Minera district and the Alun Valley, a few miles west of Wrexham in Clwyd.

In the Minera region access difficulties have yet to be overcome and it is abundantly evident that a number of promising sites will eventually pay dividends – when cavers and divers are allowed in. Of prime interest here is Ogof Llyn Ddu, situated in part of the active Minera quarry.

The area was extensively mined for lead in the late Eighteenth Century, and knowledge of the subterranean workings is vague today. Early miners took advantage of natural cave passages in their search for the valuable ore, and it was a diligent study of old workings which led to the 'discovery' of Ogof Llyn Ddu in 1979.

It was 1985 before dive explorations took place here. Diving in the upstream Ragman Sump, Paul Whybro made several penetrations, eventually surfacing to virgin passage after a dive of 260m. This sump is particularly nasty: visibility is atrocious, there are many twists and bends, and for much of the distance the depth is in excess of twenty metres.

In the course of two trips during the summer of 1985, Whybro made a solo exploration of an estimated 900m of dry passage, and left several significant leads, including a number of sumps, unexplored. This upstream extension occupies a prominent position and ultimately could well yield access to the neighbouring systems of Ogof Dydd Byraf and another recent discovery, Ogof Llyn Parc (over seven kilometres of passage) – two caves where access is also restricted at the moment.

In the Alun Valley there lies another major system which is rarely visited by outside groups of cavers, namely Ogof Hesp Alyn. The North Wales Caving Club made the initial discovery: over 800m of muddy crawls, loops and seven pitches to reach a sump. Thereafter, it was Cave Diving Group members, largely from the Wessex Cave Club, who have been responsible for the main explorations.

In August 1982 Chris Milne passed the sump after a low muddy dive of nine metres. He returned for his partner, Pete Moody, and together they explored a large continuation for 200m to reach two more sumps.

The following August 1983, Moody, Rich Websell and Kevin Clarke assisted Milne up to the terminal sump to resume exploration. Amazingly, just three metres later, the diver surfaced to find the cave disappearing into the distance. Within a short time the entire team had free dived through and set off to explore. However, after covering about 100m of

Left: Paul Whybro making the first dive in Powell's Lode – a natural cave exposed by lead miners 200 years ago and since flooded. After reaching a depth of 25m explorations were curtailed.

Above: Chris Milne in action in Ogof Llyn Ddu. Milne made the breakthrough in the nearby Ogof Hesp Alyn in 1982.

mixed terrain, they were confronted by a twenty-metre-deep shaft. The next day Whybro joined the men up front and a further short advance was made.

In late August, an even stronger party reached the end in record time. Whybro made a seven-metre climb to gain a draughting, boulder-strewn chamber. Beyond this lay another pitch of eight metres' depth, and about 400m of open passages, eventually terminating at chokes.

To reach the terminal boulder choke is now a strenuous affair. Route-finding is difficult and over 100m of ladder is required. The discoveries of 1984 have now established the cave as the second largest system in the North Wales area and it is evident that the draughting blockages at the end of this complex system offer considerable scope for future discoveries.

Unfortunately, drought conditions are essential for the exploration of Hesp Alyn, because, during the winter, virtually the entire cave floods to the roof and the entrance itself becomes an active resurgence.

Clearly, much exploration remains to be undertaken in North Wales, and it seems strange that so few cavers visit this interesting area.

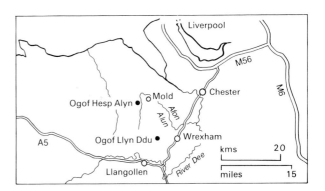

NORTHERN ENGLAND

In the early 1970s the major caving area of the Yorkshire Dales posed a significant contrast to places such as South Wales, the Mendip Hills and Derbyshire. It possessed a multitude of diving sites which had yet to be explored. Southern-based divers had often travelled to the area in the past, but it was only with the upsurge of a group of local divers that the main explorations were made. Thus the opening of the sumps in this area owed a great deal to the influence of people like Dave Yeandle, Geoff Yeadon and the late Oliver Statham.

Boreham Cave and Dub Cote, 1974

Boreham Cave in Wharfedale was one of the few sites to yield a major extension, early in 1974. The Brindle brothers of the Craven Pothole Club had passed forty-five metres of submerged passage here in 1959 to discover about 100m of passage, including a completely new streamway. Geoff Yeadon and Oliver Statham passed the next sump (96m) in 1973, and continued into a third sump for 104m including several air-bells. Early in 1974 Roger Solari and I visited the cave, completely unaware of any current activity by local divers. I added fifteen metres of line to that already installed and emerged into what was clearly a major extension, which I explored for 300m before being forced to retreat by flood conditions.

Later we phoned round, discovered who had laid the line and informed them of our find. Our northern colleagues promptly continued the exploration. The just rewards at Boreham fell to Yeadon and Statham, who explored nearly two kilometres of dry passage beyond the 260m of sumps. The formations encountered here are unrivalled in the north. In one part, pencil-like stalactites hang in dense clusters from the roof so thickly that they almost block the passage completely. These fragile 'straws' create a scene of beauty unparalleled anywhere in the British Isles.

Probably the most significant aspect of cave diving in this area in the later 1970s and 1980s was long dives. Mike Wooding set the scene in 1970 at Keld

Head, but it was Geoff Yeadon who first showed consistency in this field. To achieve greater distances, certain additions were necessary to the standard dress and equipment. Until this time the normal attire had been a single wet suit, with sometimes the additional underclothing of a neoprene vest for longer dives. Lighting usually consisted of a single miner's lamp crudely modified to exclude water. The use of depth-gauges was fairly common, but that of compasses and watches was rare. The conquest of the sumps in Dub Cote, Horton in Ribblesdale, typified this lightweight approach. After 457m of diving involving six sumps, John Parker reached a promising ongoing streamway in September 1974. However, the trip was physically and psychologically exhausting, and, after about 300m of passage had been examined, he was forced to make his exit, leaving the way on wide open. This distant extension has since yielded over two kilometres of passage heading towards Magnetometer Pot on Fountains Fell.

The long dives were to transform much of this lightweight approach and influenced the course of cave diving as a whole. For a greater duration below water, additional improved equipment was plainly necessary. Extra, thoroughly reliable lighting was essential, together with a full complement of other gear. Diving suits had to provide the necessary warmth in cold water. Yeadon's answer to this was to wear not one, but three suits. It was difficult moving along dry passages in this attire, but under water it was very beneficial.

In October 1974 a major push was made at Boreham Cave. Diving from an advance base at 244m, Yeadon penetrated a further 427m in a large, shallow passage. In May the following year a greater effort was made. The final dive was expected to be as much as 900m. Wearing three wet suits, carrying three lights and three cylinders (one of which was 80 cu.ft), Yeadon passed the terminal sump after 790m. A dry extension over 152m long was found, terminating in a six-metre pothole, which he was unable to descend.

The Kingsdale-Keld Head Exploration

A series of long dives was also made throughout 1974 in Kingsdale Master Cave at the terminal upstream

Rowten Sump. In March 1976 the 'end' was marked by tight vertical fissures at a depth of less than two metres, 637m of diving away from base.

For several years after 1970 exploration at Keld Head was neglected. This lies on the same level as the terminal downstream sump of Kingsdale Master Cave and, therefore, had limited potential in terms of dry passage. It was conjectured that in all probability a single sump of about 1500m separated the two points: an excellent project, allowing the possibility of a world record and marking a significant change in attitude. This would be diving for the sake of diving and any dry passages discovered in the course of explorations would be purely incidental.

The Dry Suit is Reintroduced

Work began at this site early in 1975. In May Oliver Statham made history when he reintroduced the dry suit to British cave diving. Great progress, in terms of design and materials, had been made with this type of suit since it had been phased out for cave use in the early 1960s. The old type of dry suit (rubberised canvas) incorporated no thermal qualities of its own and it was always necessary to wear woollen under-clothes for warmth. Furthermore, the volume of air trapped within the suit had always caused problems, including negative buoyancy at depth. In an effort to improve the design certain changes were made. Firstly, the suit was constructed of a material similar to that of the ordinary wet suit, but thicker (6mm) and more durable, so that it incorporated far more thermal qualities and could still be used with undergarments. The major improvement however, lay in the fact that the suit was 'constant volume'. To achieve this, a connection from the diver's breathing valve into the suit was established. Via this hose the normal contraction of air volume with depth could be counteracted by inflating the suit with high-pressure air from a bottle. Neutral buoyancy was thereby maintained both in shallow water and at depth. Allowances were

Left: Geoff Yeadon looks up the passage leading to the China Shop having just climbed a fifty-foot pitch up from the main Boreham streamway. The flowstone cascade has left a dammed pool at the head of the passage, and its tranquility has enabled the long straws of the China Shop to develop without disturbance.

also made for the ascent, and a pressure release valve was inserted into the front of the suit to prevent any uncontrolled ascent should positive buoyancy develop.

The main disadvantage of the new suits was the fact that they were generally unsuitable for use underground. They would plainly be susceptible to damage, which would affect buoyancy. They were also too warm for continual wear in dry passages and, being in one piece and therefore bulky were unsuitable for carrying to underground diving sites. Expense was also a major consideration. At the time, a tailor-made dry suit cost over £300, while an appropriate wet suit could be purchased for under £50.

Consequently these suits were of limited application to cave diving and could only be adopted where access was easy and risk of damage minimal. Keld Head was to meet this role perfectly, being an open water site close to a road.

The Exploration of Keld Head

The systematic exploration and survey of Keld Head started in February 1975. All concerned realised this would be a lengthy operation and, to ensure maximum safety against broken lines, it was decided to use a deliberately heavy line (5mm) from the outset; 183m of this was used, tied off to the usual lead block. Geoff Yeadon wrote:

> Earlier attempts had not been very organised, with divers swimming into the inky blackness not knowing where they were going and coming out none the wiser. Hence, when we began our survey in 1975, we realised that a very professional approach would be needed to make any significant inroads.

On 27 May 1975 Oliver Statham, equipped in his new dry suit, proceeded to add a further 152m of line to that already in place. Fortunately the main route was spacious, facilitating the use of back-mounted cylinders to supplement the normal side-mounted arrangement.

At this time it was realised that Mike Wooding had dived a completely different route to the passage

Right: Geoff Yeadon looks back at the China Shop, Boreham Cave, before exploring the rest of this lengthy high-level passage. It proved impossible to avoid water disturbance while passing through the China Shop – even small ripples threaten to snap the straws.

Keld Head pioneers Geoff Yeadon (above) and Oliver Statham (below).

Above: Derek Crossland, Oliver Statham and Geoff Yeadon (seated) at Keld Head on the day of the Erith recovery.

which had been followed in recent dives. Consequently the two routes were named according to the origin of the water they were presumed to contain. Wooding's passage now became known as the Marble Steps route, while the main passage (far larger) became the Kingsdale route.

In June 1975 Geoff Yeadon laid another forty-eight metres on to the end of the line. The total length was now 384m and the depth generally less than nine metres. Yeadon again:

To our surprise the survey showed that our first 1100ft [335m] of exploration had taken us no nearer the Kingsdale Master Cave making a connection seem even more unlikely. To make matters worse the cave was showing signs of deepening and this meant that air supply would soon become a problem.

A surprising development occurred on 4 July 1975. The body of Alan Erith, lost on 3 October 1970, was discovered. It was removed the following day. Statham commented:

The strange thing was that we were completely unmoved, but I suppose that is what we have trained ourselves to do. Geoff was affected a bit but that was because he had carried it.

Several dives took place during the remainder of the year, aimed mainly at consolidating the position so far. During these dives the search for air-bells (several were found as far in as 260m) and surveying took precedence.

On two separate dives in December 1975 and February 1976, Phil Papard advanced to 485m. Later the line was extended to 625m in a dive taking one hour and forty-five minutes. The depth was constant at nine metres and the visibility, at under two metres, atrocious. Both Yeadon and Statham used dry suits, and each was equipped with one 80 cu.ft cylinder and two 40 cu.ft cylinders of air in backpacks. Their total air consumption was 90 cu.ft per man, and it was realised that further advance was largely dependent on the use of bigger air supplies or using some form of kit depot. Air-bells were clearly advantageous in this respect, for divers could swim to them and exchange partially used cylinders for fresh ones deposited at some earlier date. To attempt such an exchange below water in poor visibility, or in a silted and constricted section would be hazardous, as visibility in the turbid waters could rapidly reduce to zero. Everything would have to be done by touch, not a reassuring thought when the diver was a long way from base.

During 1976 another group of northern divers commenced the exploration of the Marble Steps route. By 19 April all was set for a push beyond the Wooding termination at 329m. Bob Hryndyj, over two dives, then penetrated the sump for 488m, but returned when thwarted by low passages and copious quantities of mud. On the same day Geoff Yeadon extended the main Kingsdale passage to 701m.

Attempts from the Kingsdale End, 1976

Further dives up the Kingsdale Passage were clearly serious undertakings. The last air-bell to be found lay at 259m from the entrance, and so was of virtually no use for a push at the end. The logical answer was to search for a connection from the downstream sump in Kingsdale Master Cave, and activities began here in June 1976. For such dives deep underground wet suits were more appropriate than dry suits, for they could be carried virtually anywhere by assistants without too much trouble or risk of damage.

On the second dive Yeadon reached an air-bell after 305m of very mixed passage. His third dive here, on 1 July, was more eventful. Having laid an extra

ninety metres of line downstream, he commenced his exit. With ninety metres to go to reach base the valve suddenly flooded.

Having just breathed out, I quickly reached for the purge button but found none. All that was left was the rubber mouthpiece, the main body having dropped off. With lungs now demanding air with increasingly more urgent twitches I started to feel for my second valve, as the visibility was now too poor to see it. The first attempt followed up the wrong hose to the contents gauge. The second was successful, with a rush of 'Bradford' air to put out burning lungs. A minute was spent resting on the floor before carrying on.

On Yeadon's fourth dive on 10 July he reached 488m, on 24 July, 600m and another air-bell, while on 27 July he passed some tight squeezes to dump his reel at 630m. The gap between the two extensions was narrowing and he was becoming obsessed by the exploration.

Throughout these few weeks my flatmates in Harrogate had to suffer a vast survey wandering across the living-room floor. Seeing the limb of the Kingsdale Master Cave creeping towards the limit of our Keld Head explorations was totally intoxicating.

More Keld Head Attempts, 1976-77

On 5 August 1976 Oliver Statham claimed the British length record when he reached a point 838m/2750ft into Keld Head, beating the existing record of 792m established by Yeadon at Boreham Cave in October 1974. Previous dives here had reached the safe limit for air carried (two 40 cu.ft cylinders and one 80 cu.ft cylinder). On this occasion an improvised 'hypersystem' was used, consisting of two side-mounted 80 cu.ft cylinders and a twin 50 cu.ft back-mounted set. Each system was individually controlled by three demand valves. 'Herbert' (the nickname given to Statham's dry suit) was really to prove its worth on this occasion. Initially the diver was grossly overweight, carrying 160 lbs of equipment, but, on inflating the suit, equilibrium was achieved. The dive took ninety minutes and used 115 cu.ft of air. Having made a rough survey over these dives, they were now only about 275m/900ft from the point reached in Kingsdale Master Cave.

Progress was slow, but sure, and it was not until February 1977 that another push was made. This time it was Yeadon's turn and, in appalling visibility, he progressed to 925m. The European distance record was now close, but the chances of a link-up seemed to be receding. Yeadon had become doubtful:

After my dive in February our hopes faded, for although the gap was closing on my survey, the depth at the Keld Head extension had now increased to sixty feet [eighteen metres] and the two caves were getting further apart vertically. The extra depth also meant that we now had to devise ways of carrying more air.

Jochen Hasenmayer at Keld Head

News of Keld Head and the two Yorkshire divers spread abroad. In January 1978, with events drawing to a climax, Statham invited the experienced German cave diver, Jochen Hasenmayer, to join the exploration. If anyone was going to better his record set at the Rinquelle Resurgence in Switzerland, he wished to be in on the act. His ability was immediately apparent, for, on his first familiarisation dive, he swam to the end of the line. A few days later, on 5 February, a major push was planned with all three pioneers participating. It was to be an exciting day. The water was cold and visibility typically atrocious.

Hasenmayer had 270 cu.ft of air (more than Yeadon and Statham) and was to lead, since it had been decided they would dive independently at half-hour intervals. With his usual twin-set back-mounted, the German reached the end of the line. The upstream continuation was horribly tight and Hasenmayer was convinced that something had been missed. He therefore reeled in the first few metres of line and started to search for another route. He then tied on a new reel of ninety-six metres of heavy line and proceeded to lay this out. In a recent account, produced specially for the second edition of this book, Hasenmayer has given a full description of what took place:

About fifteen metres downstream from Geoff's end point I found the main continuation went through a low bedding with the only way forward, unlogically, on the left where a long slit was passable through a widening of a roof channel. On the washed out rock floor it was not possible to fix the rope in the correct way. But as this was clean rock without mud I felt sure that the others would see the problem immediately and observe the fundamental rule 'don't pull back the line of a diver who is in the sump'.

Beyond the constriction, I continued along a spacious tunnel

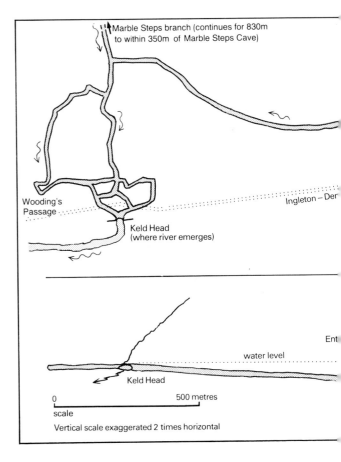

Marble Steps branch (continues for 830m to within 350m of Marble Steps Cave)

Wooding's Passage

Ingleton – Der

Keld Head (where river emerges)

Ent

water level

Keld Head

0   500 metres

scale

Vertical scale exaggerated 2 times horizontal

to 1006m – at that time a European record dive in a single sump.

By this time Statham, also wearing a back-pack, had reached the constriction and, in the disturbed water, experienced grave difficulties in attempting to continue. Eventually he manoeuvred himself into a position where he could follow, but as the line was unsecured, owing to a lack of belay points, he realised that to do so would be dangerous, as it could easily be dislodged from this the most spacious position. To continue would, therefore, put the lives of both himself and Hasenmayer in jeopardy. Mindful also of his depleted air supply, he judged it prudent to make his exit.

The Dead Man's Handshake Incident

Returning down the line Statham met Yeadon within a hundred metres or so and wrote the now immortal communication on his friend's slate:

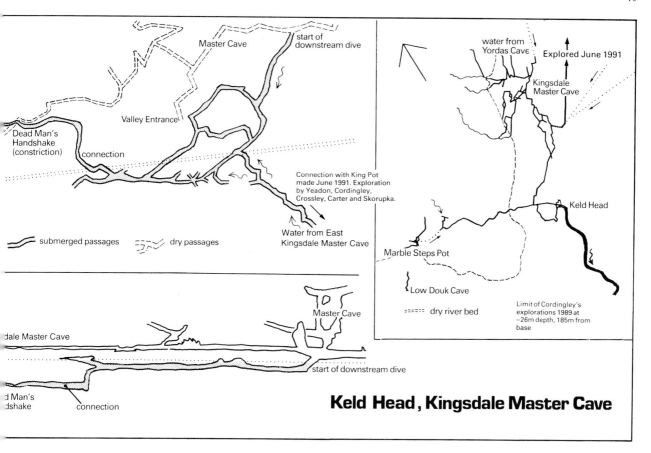

Keld Head, Kingsdale Master Cave

'3000, small with back and side, No Jochen, Trouble?'

Yeadon replied that he would go and look. Statham continued on out, leaving Yeadon to sort this one out for himself. He later described the ensuing events in an interview in *Caving International* magazine*:

He [Statham] was running short of air so he went and hid up the passage at a shallower depth of thirty feet as opposed to the sixty feet at the constriction so as to avoid going out and telling Jochen's wife that he was overdue.

At the constriction, which was a peculiar little slot . . . the line was pulled tight into the corner, because it went in and around a rock wall and then back at an angle . . . I thought, 'Christ, I'll just sit here and go down to my third margin and then I'll have to leave you'. At about that time, coming up to the third margin, I felt twitching on the rope. It was obvious that he was in some kind of trouble, so I replied with some tugs to let him know that I was there and then he came right up to me [on the other side of the narrow bedding plane] with his head on one

* No 5, October 1979.

side. . . . [then] without seeing me, went back into the bedding plane from where he had come, which left me feeling peculiar.

I then retreated to have a look at my contents gauges because all visability [at the constriction] had gone. I thought I would go over [the limit] a bit . . . I even thought of taking off my back pack and shoving it through to him because I hadn't started on that yet . . . He must have been getting low because [although he started with 270cu.ft of air] he'd been in an hour and a quarter longer than me, and probably a lot of it at sixty feet. Then he appeared at this ridiculously small hole, nowhere near where the line went. I shoved my hand into the hole and he grabbed hold of it. I thought 'I shouldn't have done this really, with the hand with my knife on!' He later said, 'You shouldn't have done that because I always carry this stainless steel wire. I could have tied you up with it and attached you to a boulder and come round the back and pinched your bottles.'

His hand was kind of shaking, and we held hands not being able to say anything, and then he stopped shaking, patted me on the hand as if to say he was going to have another go. I was trying to give him signals – telling him to go back, but there wasn't quite enough room. We were both outstretched and he didn't really get the message, though he did what I was trying to tell him eventually. I think part of the reason that he was shaking was that he had been in there so long, and also that he hadn't dived with me before. He wouldn't know if I was panicking . . . I could have been a danger to him.

Hasenmayer's recent account gives a rather different story:

When I came back the rope was tightened, so that it was pulled out of the position of the through route. It ran partly through a sand bar and partly on the left side of the main constriction and there disappeared under this impassable part of the low bedding (in the position where Yeadon and I are touching on the original diagram). As you will see, only this position of the line is compatible with the subsequent events and also with substantial parts of Geoff's account [in an earlier part of the memorandum Hasenmayer had strongly contested the position of the line drawn on the original diagram].

As the visibility had now deteriorated to one and a half metres and as I still had enough air, I decided to search systematically. I began at the extreme corner of the left hand wall, the rope tracking with me in my right hand. Just when this

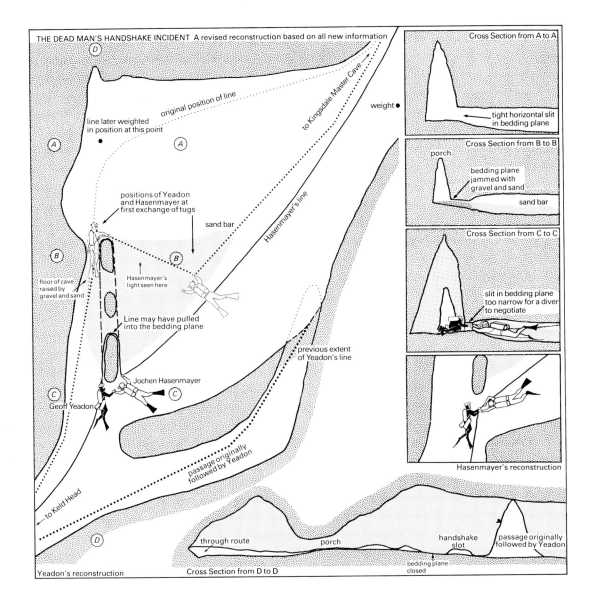

THE DEAD MAN'S HANDSHAKE INCIDENT A revised reconstruction based on all new information

was cleared I was pulled back so violently, that I could not stop until I was drawn under the shoulder of the roof where I could wedge against it. Naturally, I couldn't let go of the rope, the visibility was zero and the rope was pulling into the sand bar. In spite of all signals a tug-of-war began. I had to resist with all my force. One lamp was torn from my helmet and my right arm became longer and longer. Why was he doing this?

Suddenly he rested, I took the risk of giving up my stable position and squeezed as deep as possible into the constriction and tried to reach his hand along the rope. I succeeded, took hold of it in a very calm way, patted it. He understood my calming touches and signals and at last freed the line which was anchoring me in this impassable slit, pulling and squeezing me into the constriction. With the line slackened I could pull it back, out of the sand bar, and retreat. I knew the right direction in principle, but Yeadon had taught it to me in an unforgettable way. Now, together, each on his side, we threaded the line out of the slit back to the proven route. Eventually, when the line was in the correct 'way-out' position, the passage was again without problem.

There is a considerable difference between these two accounts and both divers are sure of their own version. In the poor visibility the situation in which they found themselves was extremely confusing. Yeadon had not dived with Hasenmayer before. His attempts to establish some form of communication may have made matters worse*. But he was very concerned about Hasenmayer's air reserves and felt certain that the German was facing an imminent crisis as he cast around (using up air) looking for a way out, hence his later comment that he was convinced he was 'shaking a dead man's hand'. Yeadon again:

He eventually came to the correct hole and I shone my light through and he popped out.

I had read all this stuff in Australian magazines about people attacking each other for air and I thought he must be low, so I retired back up the passage and into the roof to hide. I watched him come out to see what he was like, but he seemed all settled – he had regained his composure – so I came down again and asked to see his contents gauges, but he seemed to think he had plenty of air.

Hasenmayer had been stuck on the far side of the

constriction for at least ten minutes, maybe longer. Yeadon felt that he should wait to provide any support that might be necessary, but when Hasenmayer appeared through the hole he was fully composed and, despite the trauma of his entrapment, still had enough air to regain the surface without assistance from Yeadon, indeed he also transported their big reel during the way out. After a steady swim back down the line they made their exit after two and three quarter hours and two hours respectively. As Yeadon surfaced just after Hasenmayer he said to Statham 'I thought I was shaking a dead man's hand in there'. Hasenmayer's comment was no less dramatic: 'that was like something out of a horror movie'. But even at the finish there were differing views, Yeadon believed Hasenmayer had run low on air, whereas Hasenmayer now states that he had an ample surplus 'enough to dive one hour longer in the deeper regions of Keld Head'.

Hasenmayer believes that the differences between the two accounts may have developed because of media pressure. The dive had attracted the interest of the press though, to a degree, this had been courted by Statham. Hasenmayer again:

When I arrived in Yorkshire I learned that he [Statham] had his reasons for inviting me on the record push: he was interested in the publicity advantages of having me there. An 'international expedition' would be helpful and the participation of the current world record holder would increase the drama. Statham had in mind a sort of subterranean 'Race for the South Pole'. Geoff Yeadon was not very happy with this idea. He saw other priorities and he was right ... we had first of all to concern ourselves with the solution of the problem, and that called for a team approach. But then their fantasy-staging foundered on the unforeseen, insidious reefs of the constriction. What to do now? Yet wasn't the real course of events even more dramatic than the planned story? Was it not for Yeadon the shock of his life when this black hand gripped him out of the rock. Yet the shock now brought an electrifying idea which swept all the problems aside; a dead man's handshake! The show was saved, instead of reporting the European record set up by this 'bluudy German', substitute creepy entertainment and rescue action plus ... a few small corrections in the sequence of events. Only the persevering attention of Anne, Oliver's girl friend, finally ensured the troublesome record fact was at least mentioned in the public report.

Hasenmayer goes on to explain that the attentions of

---

* Subsequent observations of the slit have described the elevation that has been added to the diagram which shows the line could not have got into the position that Hasenmayer believed. It is possible that the line was pulled from its original position by Hasenmayer as he moved forward up the passage and this may have been worsened by Statham (in the manner he described) and later when Yeadon and Hasenmayer exchanged tugs. In the murky conditions Hasenmayer may have thought that the line (which was in his right hand) was passing through the handshake slit, when it seems more likely (as Yeadon firmly contends he was holding it in his left hand and it was heading towards the correct hole) to have gone forward for a distance before cutting back to Hasenmayer. Another possibility is that the handshake was through one of the holes closer to the porch, though both divers confirm the position shown. Hasenmayer's calm behaviour when he emerged from the hole, tends to confirm his claim that he was in full control of the situation.

the popular press didn't worry him too much and he was quite happy to play the supporting role in the final link up dives and also supplied new equipment. What does concern him is the perpetuation of the Dead Man's Handshake story that he thinks casts a slur over his skill as a diver. It seems clear that Yeadon's figure of speech was entirely spontaneous, though it certainly made ideal copy for the press, and has subsequently established itself in caving folklore.

It is clear that Hasenmayer's experience, skill and determination enabled him to keep steady in a potential stressful situation. If there is a lesson to be gained it must surely be that divers unfamiliar with each other's techniques and capabilities, especially when there are language difficulties, should be extremely wary when operating together.

Preparations for the Link Up

It was inevitable that the constricted section at 914m would get dubbed Dead Man's Handshake and there could not be much doubt that it constituted a real deterrent to further progress. Ever resourceful and determined to render the section safe, Yeadon

constructed an amazing side-mounted harness to hold four cylinders (two 80 cu.ft and two 50 cu.ft). Despite an acutely painful arched back, owing to all the weight being supported around the waist, a highly significant dive was made on 16 April. Depositing his two smaller cylinders at 213m and 427m respectively, Yeadon reached Dead Man's Handshake without too much trouble. The line was secured to a block of lead and in minutes the route through was proven reasonable. Continuing to Hasenmayer's limit (1006m), another thirty metres of line was reeled out. The way on was still wide open, but the depth continued at about eighteen metres.

It is interesting to note that Keld Head was not only being extended up the Kingsdale Passage but also at several other points. The underwater situation is certainly quite complex as can be appreciated from the diagram on page 143. A major find took place at this time on the 'corner' at 335m. Yeadon had discovered a large submerged inlet at this point in February 1978. Over the course of a few more dives this was extended to 823m from the entrance and was presumed to be in fact the 'true' Marble Steps Passage. More recently it has been discovered that the other major route is not an inlet at all, rather a long and devious loop which rejoins the main route near the 'corner'.

The Keld Head-Kingsdale Link

The summer of 1978 was one of intense diving activity at Keld Head. With financial support from the Royal Geographical Society, it was planned to obtain some large, 110cu.ft cylinders similar to the ones used by Hasenmayer. While their German colleague acquired these, Yeadon continued his efforts downstream in Kingsdale Master Cave. Here, on 11 June, he reached a point 732m from base, having descended a dark, gloomy pot to a depth of eighteen metres. The connection appeared imminent: the submerged passages from both ends were within sixty metres of each other and at the same depth.

Early in July Hasenmayer returned together with the long-awaited big cylinders. For the final push, on 6 July, these were pressurised to hold 160cu.ft of air apiece. Yeadon and Statham were similarly equipped, each with two 160cu.ft cylinders, together with a removable back-mounted bottle of 90cu.ft. Yeadon recalled:

Above: Bob Hryndy and Yeadon (wearing 110cu.ft cylinders) at Keld Head during preparations for the through-dive.

This time we decided to dive separately – 'Bear' (Statham) first, then me, then Jochen – each making his own push and returning to Keld Head before the other tried. 'Bear' advanced to 3600ft [1097m] and returned, but he hadn't made the connection. I couldn't believe it and thought that he must have followed the wrong passage or something, perhaps one heading towards the other side of the valley. Then it was my turn. For the now routine journey to Dead Man's Handshake I deliberately switched into 'automatic pilot', only becoming more alert as I approached the point where I would drop off my back-mounted cylinder. I chose a patch of gravel and slowly came to rest on it, like an airship coming in to its moorings. Keeping a 'tight grip' on the line with my eyes, I carefully worked off the back-pack, leaving myself 'dressed' for the constriction ahead.

The now familiar dark cleft loomed up in front instantly triggering memories of Jochen's epic. However, I was soon engrossed with the problem of passing through, turning sideways in the narrow porch, face and mask pressed uselessly against the scalloped wall as my hands worked overtime behind, feeding the cylinders through the constriction. It was essential

Above: Geoff Yeadon being assisted by supporters to assemble his heavy equipment before the through-dive to Keld Head. His equipment included side-mounted cylinders each fitted with heavy tubular battery packs to power the strong lights needed for underwater filming. He also wore a speleophone (with microphone in facemask) which enabled him to communicate with television commentators on the surface as the dive progressed.

to avoid any hurried move that might have damaged or dislodged my equipment. Moving through the bedding plane beyond was like passing through the throat of a whale and entering its stomach, only to create a certain uneasiness, wondering whether one could escape again. The next 600ft [183m] were uneventful as I followed the line. Banks of gravel and sand passed monotonously under mask, lulling me into a dream. I was like an orbiting spacecraft passing over a strange planet. Fresh-water shrimps raced across my vision like herds of stampeding zebra, the sunrise and sunset of my lamps representing perhaps the most dramatic moments in their entire

existence. The dream allowed me to keep all the dark fears of the situation gagged up inside, kept firmly into manageable proportions: the dark, deep water, the claustrophobia, the nagging fear of getting lost or being unable to get back before my air supply ran out. But my equipment was well-maintained and working without fault, and the line was laid along a known passage so in theory the situation was under control.

Nevertheless, as I came to the end of the line and started to press on into the unknown, I became tensely alert, head jerking from side to side like a night owl. Somehow I found that environment distinctly more alien than, say, that of the Moon. The loneliness gnawed at my nerves as I strained to see the Kingsdale line which I knew must be close at hand. Suddenly an orange line came into view. At first I didn't fully accept its existence but then I realised that I must have been swimming alongside it for some distance. I turned and followed it back. Then the line reel finally appeared and confirmed that the connection had been made. [Ironically it was lying very close to the spot which had been reached by Statham.] In an instant my feeling of loneliness evaporated to be replaced by bursting euphoria. I was jubilant, hardly able to restrain my delight, but a more sensible brain took over and I again switched into automatic and headed back towards Keld Head, my screams of delight restrained until my safe return. The connection had been made, yet somehow the triumph was tinged with a certain sadness that we hadn't been able to do it together.

A euphoric exit was made after two and a half hours. All the years of hard work had paid off. Hasenmayer, carrying 520cu.ft of air, made another long dive (three and three-quarter hours) the next day, but, despite an extensive search, discovered little of further significance.

The Through Trip – Kingsdale to Keld Head, 1979
All was now set for the great 1829m through trip constituting a world record dive for the shortest route between two submerged caves. At great cost, Yorkshire Television eagerly televised the event and, on 16 January 1979, Geoff Yeadon and Oliver Statham gained their due reward by linking up the two caves with a dive that took just two and a half hours. This is unquestionably the most outstanding cave diving event in the north to date, and the distance record may well be unassailable anywhere in the British Isles. All tribute is due to Statham* and Yeadon.

* On September 28, 1979 Oliver Statham committed suicide at his pottery in Sedburgh after a period of depression. A popular figure in Yorkshire caving circles, he will be greatly missed by all who knew him.

The Gaping Gill-Ingleborough Cave Connection, 1983
As the euphoria of the record dive started to subside, Yeadon and his friends began the quest for new projects. There were plenty to chose from. With an intimate knowledge of the Dales, Yeadon, like many before him, had long been intrigued by the enigma of Gaping Gill, probably the best-known cave system in the north.

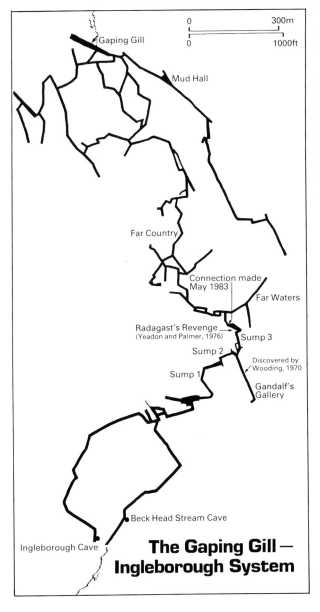

The awe-inspiring, 110m-deep shaft of Gaping Gill had first been bottomed in 1895 by the Frenchman Edouard Alfred Martel. Over the following years the cave system at its foot gained a considerable reputation as it slowly began to extend towards the large resurgence of Beck Head, a short distance above the small village of Clapham. By the late 1960s it became apparent that the greatest likelihood of a through trip would be achieved by cave divers operating from the inner reaches of Ingleborough Cave, just a short distance up the valley from the resurgence, Beck Head Stream Cave.

Bob Davies and his colleagues had made significant penetrations upstream from Beck Head Stream Cave in the early 1950s, but it was Mike Wooding who made the first 'dry' discoveries in 1970. At the end of Ingleborough Cave, Wooding passed two sumps, of ninety metres and seventy-six metres' length respectively, to reach several hundred metres of old, high-level passage, Gandalf's Gallery. Despite initial excitement, however, hopes of a connection with Gaping Gill eventually receded.

Geoff Yeadon had been closely involved in the 1970 explorations in his pre-diving days. Late in 1976, together with Rob Palmer, he passed a further sixty metre-long sump to reach what turned out to be the largest cavern in Ingleborough Cave – Radagast's Revenge. All leads in the new section of dry passage were boulder-choked, while under-water the pair quickly realised that further progress would be slow and difficult. Once more the momentum was lost, and energies were diverted to the Keld Head explorations.

Following the successful use of Bob Mackin's Mole-phone radio location device at Keld Head the apparatus was used in Ingleborough Cave in May 1982 with startling results. The two caves were found to be much closer than anyone had previously imagined. In turn this led to an accurate survey being undertaken of the further reaches of Gaping Gill. When the two surveys were drawn up to the amazement of all concerned, one passage in Gaping Gill was found to be just over three metres beneath a choke in the sump extensions of Ingleborough Cave.

On 22 January 1983 a simultaneous assault was made at both blockages. Aural contact was soon achieved and a frenzied bout of digging ensued. Late in the afternoon Geoff Crossley wormed his way down into an extremely unstable choke at the Ingleborough end, and non-diver Gerald Benn managed to shake his boot from the other side of the blockage. After 146 years of exploration the link had been found.

Unfortunately, hopes of enlarging the opening to passable, body-size, dimensions were frustrated when the sides of the hole collapsed, and it was not until 28 May that the choke was finally passed, the occasion being recorded live on film as part of a well-planned through trip. In the event, everything went smoothly. Geoff Yeadon and Geoff Crossley abseiled down the spectacular Main Shaft of Gaping Gill, while a team of eager supporters transported gear over the best part of two kilometres to the connection choke. Several hours later Jim Abbott and Julian Griffiths made their entry at Ingleborough. Rendezvous was made at Radagast's Revenge, the diving gear was exchanged and the two teams went their opposite ways.

Yeadon and Crossley emerged to a champagne reception after eleven hours, while Abbott and Griffiths

reached the surface after nine hours. By finally connecting the two caves they had made a very prestigious 'first', and established a system totalling over sixteen kilometres of passages.

The Three Counties System

All manner of other projects were now appearing throughout the Dales. The major cave systems draining to Leck Beck Head also presented a tantalising challenge. From the earliest of times a connection had been postulated between the Lancaster Hole-Easegill System under Casterton Fell to the extensive systems lying to the east. Water was known to flow from Ireby Fell at the southern edge of Gragareth, via Leck Fell, to Leck Beck Head. It seemed possible, therefore, that caves as far apart as Aygill in the west could eventually be connected to Ireby Pot in the east. Furthermore, the discovery of Rift Pot, between Ireby and Marble Steps, suggested even greater possibilities. The Rift Pot complex has two separate streams which straddle the watershed between the two valleys of Leck Beck and Kingsdale. So eventually the system

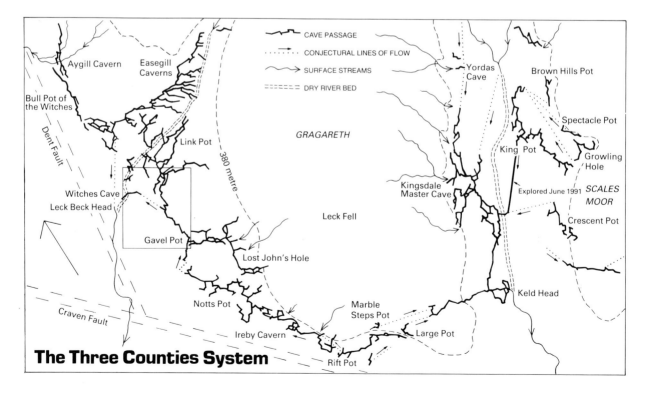

The Three Counties System

Above: The spectacular dry extension of Notts Pott, reached after a dive through a 210m sump: Barry Suddell with an elegant flowstone pillar (left) and Rick Stanton and Richard Bartrop in the main tunnel.

will extend much further east to Kingsdale and beyond. Hydrologically and geomorphologically the many fine caves in this area constitute a single entity. They straddle the county boundaries of Cumbria, Lancashire and Yorkshire, and are known collectively as the Three Counties System.

For cavers and cave divers alike the scope for connections within this massive system has been immense. In 1978 the discovery of Link Pot led to a dramatic burst of exploration. Dry connections were achieved to both Lancaster Hole and Pippikin, thereby establishing the forty-five kilometre system as the longest in Britain. Soon it was the turn of the divers.

Linking the Gavel Pot and Pippikin Systems, 1982-89
During the summer of 1982 Ian Watson mounted a series of dives into the downstream Gavel Pot-Lost John's Sump. The line was laid for 680m from Gavel base to an intimidating, low-roofed area heading directly towards the end of neighbouring Pippikin Pot. The terminal depth at the 'dark hollow' was twenty metres; to progress further was a daunting

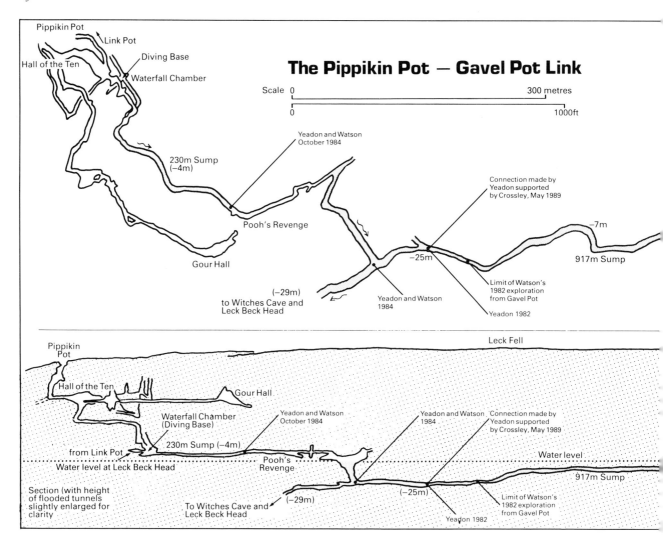

The Pippikin Pot — Gavel Pot Link

prospect. Yeadon subsequently continued for a further fifty metres before being deterred by atrocious visibility and the complex nature of the wide bedding passage.

Attention was turned to the downstream sump in Pippikin. Expecting to explore a deep sump, it was with some amazement that, in October 1984, a 200m dive gave access to a hundred-metre dry extension heading directly towards Gavel. This again fell to Yeadon, accompanied by Ian Watson.

A subsequent trip lived up to their previous expectations. A short drop soon led to a murky twenty-five-metre-deep sump, which then descended to twenty-nine metres' depth in an enormous tunnel. The distance between Gavel and Pippikin was tantalisingly short – approximately one hundred metres – but the difficulty of mustering a strong support team and the vagaries of the British weather continually thwarted the final link.

The way forward in the terminal sump was obstructed by huge silt banks and it was anticipated that several dives would be required to negotiate a route through. Good visibility was crucial. It was not until Sunday 14 May 1989 that conditions were suitable for the first attempt. An efficient team of ten porters manhandled Yeadon's two 110cu.ft bottles through the tortuous Pippikin approach, together with a set of

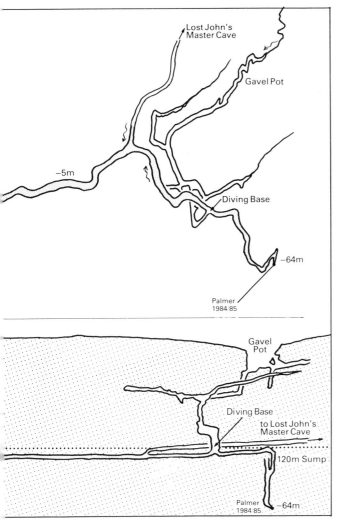

smaller bottles for his companion, Geoff Crossley. At the sump, Yeadon changed into his dry suit. As the pair slid into the water, it was confirmed that a fresh team of porters would arrive in four hours to conduct the long haul back to the surface.

After passing the first sump, the carry to the terminal sump was difficult, but, once at their objective, fortune smiled on them and their patience was rewarded. Visibility was seven or eight metres, distinctly more inviting than the normal one-metre murk to which they had become accustomed. Equipped with a full complement of gear and utilising a powerful search beam, Yeadon descended to twenty-seven

metres, feeling a lot more comfortable than hitherto. He followed the old line to the point where his compass told him that he should change direction. Here he tied on a fresh reel. Paying close attention to the roof characteristics and the vast accumulations of fine silt, he set off. Swimming over a series of 'huge whalebacks' it came as an amazing surprise when, having reeled out only forty metres of line, he suddenly intercepted the one from the other end. The connection with Gavel had at long last been achieved and, with this success, the total length of passages in the Lancaster-Easegill System was extended to over sixty kilometres. Yeadon made a slow, cautious retreat to his waiting friend and, after a thirty-minute return dive, the news was given to their enthusiastic support team.

It is worth noting at this point that the terminal limit in downstream Pippikin is only 400m from the limit of exploration set in Witches Cave, situated merely a hundred metres from Leck Beck Resurgence. In a series of dives in 1985 Rob Parker extended this cave upstream for over 400m at depths generally in excess of thirty metres.

Notts Pot-Gavel Pot Discoveries, 1984-85
The most exciting cave diving discovery to take place in the north for many years occurred at Notts Pot during the summer of 1985. Rupert Skorupka initiated the exploration here when, during an examination of a constricted 'static' sump, he discovered a sizeable continuation at nine metres' depth. Barry Suddell, Rick Stanton and Chris Danilewicz subsequently continued the project, and, following a series of operations, finally broke through to air in December 1985. The sump was 210m in length and the dry extension amounted to nearly one and a half kilometres. Further discoveries beyond and to the side of this particularly grand section of streamway – even more magnificent than the famous Lost John's Streamway – were to extend the find a further kilometre.

The new discovery was heading towards the deep, upstream terminus of Gavel Pot and the adjacent dry passages of Lost John's Hole. At least two dry connections to Lost John's seemed possible, the gap

Above: John Cordingley preparing to dive in Kingsdale Master Cave.

between the two systems being less than a hundred metres. Independently of these locally based activists, Rob Palmer was attracted to Gavel Pot in 1984. He, too, realised the great potential here and, keen to put his deep diving experience to the test, he made two notable explorations in the deep shaft at the upstream terminus of Gavel, reaching forty-five metres in 1984, then gaining the bottom of the shaft in December 1985. On the second exploration Palmer was lucky enough to obtain a couple of cylinders of Trimix, with its attendant reduction of narcosis, and thus greater clarity of thought. In 1985 the gas was unknown in British cave diving circles, but twelve composite bottles, pressurised to 5250 p.s.i., had been filled for the push at Wookey Hole in July. Given that only three of these had been used there were plenty of cylinders left over. Palmer therefore borrowed some for his Gavel push, and used the same decompression tables. Ironically, just as at Wookey, the outcome was

disappointing. Within a few metres of the bottom of the shaft he was thwarted by a constricted gravel squeeze at a depth of sixty-four metres. It would appear, therefore, that, despite a horizontal gap of approximately one hundred metres between Gavel Pot and Notts Pot, any diving connection between these two systems could still take some time to establish.

Further Possibilities from Keld Head

In terms of distance, the gaps between the various cave systems are narrowing rapidly. At Keld Head, for example, the Marble Steps Passage has been extended to just over 1219m from the entrance, with the terminal point at present less than one hundred metres from the Mohole and just 400m from connection with the sump in Large Pot. Yeadon, continuing his work in the murky depths of Keld Head, has now located the point at which water from the eastern side of the Kingsdale Valley enters the system. This link, which again is something for future generations, will take divers beneath the valley floor to link up with the hydrological network draining from King Pot and Scales Moor. Quite how extensive the Three Counties System will eventually be remains to be seen.

The Kingsdale – King Pot Link, 1991

Throughout the first half of 1991 five divers worked at the problem of finding a link from Kingsdale Master Cave to King Pot. Rupert Skorupka made a number of dives from King Pot advancing the line to 400m from base. Meanwhile John Cordingley, Geoff Yeadon, Russell Carter and Geoff Crossley, operating in various combinations, steadily explored the route from the Kingsdale end working up a main river passage with a maximum depth of thirty metres. The link-up with Skorupka's line was finally made on 7 June by Yeadon, supported by Crossley, to complete an epic exploration – perhaps the most serious project yet achieved in Britain. The through dives from King Pot to Kingsdale (about 1950m) and King Pot to Keld Head (about 3000m) are now the obvious next stage – the latter offering one of the longest through dives in the world. (This was made in August 1991 by Crossley and Yeadon.)

It is worth digressing for a moment to reflect upon the evolution of cave diving over the half century since that first successful passage of Sump 1 in Swildon's and the use of the bulky Standard Equipment at Wookey Hole. In the early years an exploration rarely took place without an associated 'epic'. Recall Graham Balcombe's trials with rebreathing apparatus at Keld Head in the early 1940s and Bob Davies's lucky escape from Wookey Hole in 1955. Equipment was often home-made and ill suited for the adverse conditions of an underwater cave. There were no manuals and few, if any, people to whom one could turn for advice. Every advance in distance, equipment and technique was made by trial and error. So it is not surprising that practitioners were few in number. Contrast this with the situation today, when major projects undertaken by experts like Yeadon and Cordingley are treated as routine events and are undertaken with relatively few incidents. This broadening of competence reflects the wide availability of proven, reliable diving equipment, and this in turn is reflected in a vastly improved safety record.

The Sumps of Chapel Le Dale

East of the Kingsdale Valley and the Keld Head hydrological system lies Chapel Le Dale. At the head of this valley is another major resurgence, namely God's Bridge. This large rising and its associated flood outlets issue water from sites such as Weathercote Cave a kilometre or more up the valley and also from other well-known caves lying beneath the hillside to the east, such as Meregill Pot and Great Douk Cave.

Serious diving began in this area in the early 1980s at Joint Hole and Hurtle Pot. Many of the valley bottom systems have now been linked. The first such connection was made between Midge Hole and Hurtle in September 1982 by Jonny Shaw and Rupert Skorupka. This entailed a dive of approximately 440m. In April 1986 Brian Smith and Brian Scofield made the connection from there to Jingle Pot; a short while later the same pair made a devious diving route to Weathercote. The total combined length of the Weathercote-Jingle-Hurtle-Midge system now amounts to over two kilometres, while the complex as a whole is one of the longest underwater systems in the country, second only to that of Keld Head.

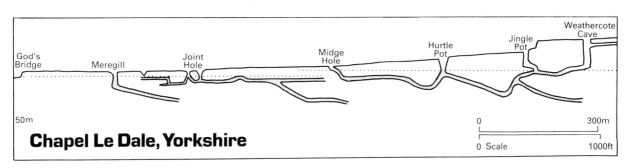

Chapel Le Dale, Yorkshire

Under optimum diving conditions (several weeks without rain), the Hurtle complex presents some of the finest cave diving in the country and is becoming increasingly popular. But, as with the majority of northern sites, at least ten dry days are required before visibility exceeds a couple of metres. In terms of safety, it is recommended that the classic Midge to Hurtle through dive be undertaken from the Hurtle end to ensure that driftwood and other flood-borne debris are not blocking the squeeze at the Hurtle end. As with Keld Head, visitors should be wary of the multitude of lines in this complex and take all necessary measures to ensure a safe exit. In addition, if they are embarking upon a through dive, they should always allow sufficient air safety margin to permit a graceful retreat if, for example, a line is found to be broken or missing. Divers should also note that, apart from typically poor visibility in the Pennine systems, water temperature is notably cold and for any lengthy immersion a dry suit is virtually essential, especially as depths exceeding twenty metres quickly take the diver into the realms of decompression.

A considerable amount of exploration still remains to be undertaken in this valley, and an obvious upstream inlet leading north-east from Hurtle still awaits conclusive examination. Geoff Crossley has explored this for over 400m at over thirty metres' depth. Likewise, it is essential to note the major contributions made by John Cordingley to the exploration and survey of places such as the 'deep route' in Joint Hole.

Few would dispute that the Yorkshire Dales area is the premier cave diving area in the British Isles and we can look forward to many more discoveries in the future.

Left: Geoff Crossley about to dive at Hurtle Pot, a photograph that illustrates the typical equipment currently in use for the more advanced British dives.

THE PEAK DISTRICT

The limestone area of the Peak District in Derbyshire may not have offered cavers quite the same potential for discoveries as that in South Wales or the Yorkshire Dales, but from the earliest years it was apparent that the area around Castleton offered many opportunities for exploration.

Castleton, a bustling small tourist centre, is the location of at least two major show caves, both of which present some interesting and challenging diving projects. These show caves, Speedwell Cavern at the foot of the Winnats Pass and the vast, extremely impressive Peak Cavern, were connected in 1970 by Tom Brown via the twenty-one-metre Treasury Sump. The overall length of the Peak-Speedwell complex then exceeded eight kilometres, and in virtually every direction submerged sections barred the route forward. Ken Pearce, John Sinclair, Tom Brown and others made tentative forays into these sumps and established considerable potential on all fronts. Disappointingly, however, after 1970 access was barred to cavers from both systems for nine years.

Attempts on P8's Sumps, 1971-87

During the intervening period the only significant diving advance into the caves of this area was made into one of the principal 'feeder' caves for the Peak Cavern, namely P8 or Jackpot, high on the moors below Rushup Edge. Over ten separate stream sinks are to be found in this locality, disappearing at the shale-limestone boundary and reappearing six kilometres to the east at the Peak-Speedwell complex. Ken Pearce had commenced diving at P8 late in 1964. The following year he was joined by Mike Wooding, Dave Drew, Dave Savage, Dave Roberts and John Sinclair. In poor visibility and complex passages, this project was tricky, but, in June 1966, three sumps had been passed: Sump 1 (32m), Sump 2 (30m) and Sump 3 (23m).

The ongoing streamway led to Sump 4 after sixty metres, but here progress was to halt for nearly five years. As in the first three sumps, copious quantities of ever-shifting silt deterred the divers and it was not

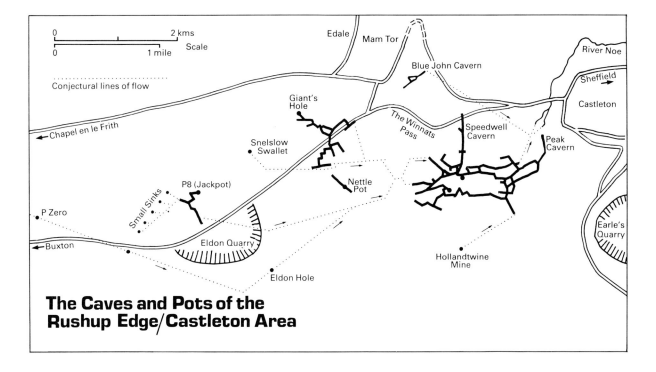

The Caves and Pots of the Rushup Edge/Castleton Area

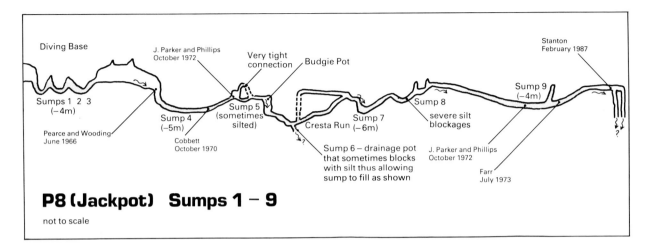

Diving Base

Sumps 1 2 3
(−4m)

Pearce and Wooding
June 1966

J. Parker and Phillips
October 1972

Sump 4
(−5m)

Cobbett
October 1970

Very tight
connection

Sump 5
(sometimes
silted)

Budgie Pot

Cresta Run

Sump 6 – drainage pot
that sometimes blocks
with silt thus allowing
sump to fill as shown

Sump 7
(−6m)

Sump 8

severe silt
blockages

J. Parker and Phillips
October 1972

Farr
July 1973

Stanton
February 1987

Sump 9
(−4m)

P8 (Jackpot)   Sumps 1 – 9

not to scale

until John Parker, supported by Jeff Phillips, visited the site in August 1971 that the next real advance was achieved. He passed the low, silted Sump 4 and continued through three further sumps – Sump 5 (10m), Sump 7 (60m) and Sump 8 (10m) – to terminate his activities 100m into Sump 9 (Sump 6 being bypassed). With support from Roger Solari and Colin Fairbairn, I extended the exploration of Sump 9 to 152m in 1973 and made several attempts to progress further during the next decade, all of which were frustrated by blockages of silt. It was not until the spring of 1987 that this sump was finally passed. A fortuitous break in the cave's normal silting tendency gave Rick Stanton the long-sought advance, and about forty metres beyond my limit the sump surfaced. However, only ninety metres further on, Stanton reached a deep pothole, which, without ladders, he was unable to descend. Unfortunately, when he returned to tackle this pot, he was unable even to reach Sump 9, as Sump 8 was completely blocked with silt. This persistent silting has proved so severe that no further progress has been possible.

Ink Sump, Peak Cavern, 1981

In 1980 diving access was regained to Peak Cavern and thus to Speedwell via Treasury Sump. Major assaults began on all fronts by the Derbyshire section of the Cave Diving Group.

Ink Sump was the prime site and the first to succumb. The divers here were Steve Tucker and

Brian Hague. Progressing from the previous limit of 122m an air-bell was gained at 180m. Just beyond lay a submerged boulder blockage, which seemed to indicate that the end of the sump was close. Explosives were to prove the key to this problem, which involved considerable work behind the scenes. On 15 February 1981 a five kilo 'bomb' was laid. Steve Tucker relates:

The dive was straightforward . . . The twenty-five thousand volt firer was connected and everyone fell to silence, so as to hear any sign of a bang. The quiet proved unnecessary, as a loud crack echoed around the chamber. It was heard as far away as Far Sump and Anniversary Aven. An instant later a vigorous surge of water rose, receded and rose again, as people clutched at gear to stop it being washed away. But the water did not rise more than about forty-six centimetres and then fell back.

On 1 March the pair returned to view the outcome. The result was not altogether satisfactory, and a quick reconnaissance revealed that the only way up was by a very tight squeeze. Removing one of his cylinders, Hague eventually wriggled through to reach the end of the sump at 192m, only to find a high aven discharging a stream. At this point Tucker was getting extremely cold standing up to his chest in water in the nearby air-bell. Feeling hard tugs on the line, he wondered if this meant he was to follow his friend through or that he was having trouble. Eventually, he set off to follow. By the time he reached the boulders visibility was down to zero and, as he felt his way into the squeeze, he met Hague's fin coming in the other direction which dislodged his mask. He guided the fin and then a leg through the boulders, and with great relief the pair returned to the air-bell. Ink Sump had been cracked.

On later visits the aven was climbed and a further impenetrable choke was encountered, which has since witnessed the most extensive digging activity undertaken beyond a sump of this length in Britain.

Peak Cavern: The Far Sump Extensions, 1981-89
Jerry Murland and Tim Nixon explored Far Sump for a hundred metres during 1980 and 1981. Then, working alone, I took up the assault. Three dives were sufficient to complete exploration in March 1981, and the passage surfaced after 385m. The dry extension beyond was promptly explored for 700m. At the end was another set of sumps but also, *en route*, there was a series of high avens, down which miners had descended over 200 years earlier in search of lead deposits.

I explored two of the easiest avens on subsequent visits, discovering another hundred metres of passages, including the largest cavern in the entire Peak-Speedwell complex. However it was John Cordingley who conducted the more thorough exploration, systematically climbing and exploring every possible extension. (In these explorations Farr and Cordingley were tackling slimy cave walls using artificial techniques, pegs, bolts, etriers, etc., and sometimes using backropes to ascend pitches of up to forty-six metres.)

Cordingley conducted many solo visits to tackle the Calcite Aven and was finally successful in April 1988:

Right: The dry passage beyond Far Sump, Peak Cavern, Derbyshire.

The prusik up the rope to the ledge thirty-three metres above the floor of the aven seemed ridiculously easy compared with the hours of work with a bolting tool and hammer needed to gain this point on previous trips. Being alone I took longer than usual to sort out my sackful of climbing equipment to make sure everything was safe and ready for the task ahead. When all was prepared I swung out over the awesome void on to the clean limestone wall and resumed the bolt route.

Two hours and seven metres of progress later a point was reached where the final section of the wall looked like it might be free climbable. As I was wearing an uncomfortable diving suit my arms were already beginning to tire from the continuous hammering. If I elected to continue on bolts the top would probably not be reached on this trip. However if I attempted to free climb whilst self-lifelining there would be no friendly face below to whom I could shout, 'Watch the rope, I'm coming off!'

I munched a little food, drank a few mouthfuls from the veneer of water running down the wall and contemplated the situation. It seemed almost absurd, perched over forty metres above the floor beyond a quarter-of-a-mile of difficult sump. Probably only a dozen or fifteen people in the country were capable of getting here at the time and if I did fall and injure myself badly it would be perhaps nine or twelve hours before any of them came looking for me. One thing was sure, there could be no certainty of being rescued alive from such a predicament.

On the other hand this was to be the last chance for several

months to finish the project and that big black space at the top of the aven looked temptingly close. So much effort had gone into getting me to this point. I thought of all my mates who had carried diving gear into the cave. It was early evening and they would be in the pub by now and perhaps wondering how I was getting on (in between important issues like whose round it was next). Another look up revealed what seemed like a couple of nut placements and that finally made up my mind; I was going to go for it.

Kicking free of the etriers and operating the self-lifelining device carefully allowed some thin moves to gain a horizontal break. A good nut runner went in here and gave confidence to make the mantelshelf move to easier ground and the top. I lay face downwards in the shallow streambed of a large unexplored passage and laughed almost uncontrollably in relief. Having risked everything to overcome the final pitch of this forty-six-metre high climb it was a strange mixture of satisfaction and elation which filled me as I set off to explore what turned out to be some of the biggest passages in the Peak Cavern System – and I made the pub before last orders – just!

This discovery was later found to connect back to chambers discovered in 1981 via a deep pitch. As the exploration became increasingly complex, Cordingley was joined by Russell Carter and Jim Davenport. Climbing and bolting continued in earnest. A series of avens was ascended above the Trunk Route, and eventually the team reached a point 164m above the Peak entrance, establishing it as the highest point in the system. In February 1989 another thirty-metre aven was scaled, which led to a complex area of low bedding passages bearing a remarkable similarity to the area known as The Flats in Nettle Pot, 1000m away. This area has yet to be fully explored and sports a number of mysterious deep shafts.

Much of what has been explored by Cordingley and his friends is part of a gigantic phreatic mineral vein cavity with a known vertical range of 130m. It is probably the finest example of this type of feature, for which the Castleton district is already famous. All the Far Sump Extension pitches are in it, and there are now eighteen separate pitches totalling 400m. Of these, no less than 180m were explored by bolting from below.

Recent extensions have brought the overall length of passages in the Peak Cavern System to twelve kilometres. There is now about 1500m (nearly a mile) of passage beyond Far Sump, and there is little doubt that further exploration in this area constitutes one of the most challenging projects in the British Isles.

Speedwell Cavern: Incident in Main Rising
Activities in Speedwell Cavern are also proving fruitful. The main advance in the terminal upstream sector has been at the impressive Main Rising, where, in the late 1980s, Cordingley and Carter conducted a typically methodical series of operations. However, with bad visibility the norm and with a complicated dive profile, this route will not provide an easy breakthrough. Diving here has not been without incident and on one occasion Cordingley found himself in a most awkward predicament:

We had previously explored this spectacular sump past an 'elbow' at thirty-six metres to gain a chamber at twenty metres of depth where the way on seemed to be rifts in the roof. I had been exploring up and down these trying to find airspace without success until gas safety margins dictated a return.

After a brief stop for routine equipment checks on the lip of the shaft back to thirty-six-metres' depth, the dive down towards base was begun. Normally I find the controlled descent of a big shaft quite exhilarating. This one, however, was destined to turn into a nightmare. After a few metres a dull ache in my left ear told me that it had failed to 'clear'. Moving back up to shallower depths ought to have solved the problem but no amount of going up and down helped and my eustachian tube remained locked solid.

Eventually I had to face the fact that [to escape] a descent to thirty-six metres would have to be made without any equalisation of the pressure behind my eardrum. Going down to twenty-five-metres depth increased the pain alarmingly and it became obvious that the only way out would probably be deliberately to rupture my eardrum whilst going back round the elbow. A glance at the contents gauges on the bottles told me that the decision to do this could not be delayed much longer.

Pausing only to remember the standard advice in all the diving manuals on burst eardrums I continued deeper into my lonely pit of agony, waiting for the inevitable loss of orientation as the cold water rushed in. I remember deciding that I would keep my right hand on the 'out' side of the guideline and wait until the dizziness wore off before continuing towards base. Despite the implications of my predicament there was absolutely no panic. My memory is only of an objective awareness of the options open to me and a cold calculating acceptance of what needed to be done to get out. I suppose this is where training and experience show their value.

The descent to the elbow caused indescribable pain. The eardrum did burst, none of the expected dizziness occurred and

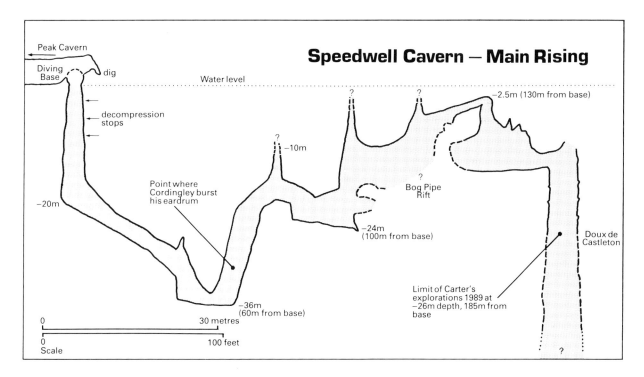

Speedwell Cavern — Main Rising

Peak Cavern

Diving Base

dig

Water level

decompression stops

−2.5m (130m from base)

?   ?

?   −10m

Point where Cordingley burst his eardrum

−20m

?

Bog Pipe Rift

−24m (100m from base)

Doux de Castleton

Limit of Carter's explorations 1989 at −26m depth, 185m from base

−36m (60m from base)

0

30 metres

0   100 feet
Scale

I was composed enough to maintain the correct ascent rate up to the oxygen bottle hanging at the first decompression stop.

Within a few weeks the ear healed up perfectly. Far worse, however, had been the damage to my left eustachian tube, the resulting scar tissue making it much harder to clear that ear even today.

We have only just begun to perform long dives with complex profiles in this country and I believe that ear clearing problems will prove to be a much bigger hazard than many people think. Since this event we have experimented with the use of plain nasal decongestant sprays (not the ones that are made to smell like cold cures). These had no effects on our tolerance to nitrogen narcosis at depths in excess of seventy metres. From now on I would recommend anyone doing dives involving complicated dive profiles, and therefore requiring re-descent on the outward journey, to use such sprays before the dive as a standard safeguard against the problem.

At the present limit in Main Rising, 185m from base, is an exceptionally deep shaft, the Doux de Castleton, estimated to reach a depth in excess of fifty metres.

Owing to access difficulties, Main Rising has yet to be conclusively explored. The site exhibits some strange hydrological characteristics: inexplicably the large stream which normally appears from Main

Rising occasionally switches course to emerge from the sump at the end of Whirlpool Rising Passage.

Cliff Cavern, Speedwell Cavern

The most significant event in Speedwell Cavern in recent years has been the ascent of the formidable Cliff Cavern close to Main Rising. Activities here have long been determined by the weather and the height of Speedwell Stream, with the result that the ascent of this impressive cavern has taken some considerable time and patience. The main climbers here were Alan Medhurst, Frank Brown and Pete O'Neill, occasionally joined by Cordingley and others. Success came in December 1987, when 200m of large passage, Cliffhanger, was explored leading westwards. The terminal sump here was later dived by Cordingley, but proved impossibly tight after forty metres.

A further ten metres of ascent above the entrance to Cliffhanger was followed by the thirty-metre Skywalk traverse, leading to Joint Effort Passage. Here, 150m of large passage led in an easterly direction, terminating once more in another sump. In January 1989 Cordingley made a solo trip to tackle this, passing the sump after twenty metres. Beyond lay the fifteen metre-high Spidros Aven, approximately thirty metres distant, and the closest point to the neighbouring Far Sump Extensions.

Explorations in the Peak-Speedwell System are evidently extremely complex. At present, for example, thirty-six sumps are known and activities are far from complete. It will probably be many years before major connections are made with other well-known caves in the area like Giant's Hole. Another deep sump terminates this system on the flank of Eldon Hill, but, as with many sites in the vicinity, visibility here is particularly poor. The Peak District has divulged a unique and intricate network of caves, which will present determined explorers with immense challenges well into the next century.

IRELAND

Geologically, almost half the entire area of Ireland consists of limestone. There are several major caving regions and many exciting diving projects have been undertaken.

The lure of the subterranean world has made little impression upon the Irish and there has been almost no motivation to pursue sump exploration. The major diving discoveries have fallen to visiting groups of British cavers. In the post-war era it was the University of Bristol Spelaeological Society who made the most significant impression upon the area, notably in County Clare on the west coast.

In the early days activities were largely restricted to Eire, away from the troublesome border. However, despite tremendous potential for the cave diver, possibly the finest in the British Isles, underwater explorations in the South were to prove extremely disappointing.

It was much later, in Northern Ireland, that the first major discoveries were made by divers. Until 1970 County Fermanagh was barely known as a caving region, because the social unrest prevalent throughout the province retarded exploration and deterred the majority of cavers.

It was the summer of 1971 when John Elliot and

Roger Solari of the Cave Projects Group (CPG) started diving in sumps which had hitherto received scant attention. The effect was to condense exploration into a brief time span, short-cutting the usual pattern of cave exploration, which normally includes intensive searches for a bypass or digging activities. Minor extensions were made on this trip, but the following year witnessed a surge of activity.

On my first visit to Ireland it was purely by chance that I was introduced to Tullyhona Cave. Almost unbelievably, an easy nine metre-long sump was passed to discover over 1219m of well-decorated passages. In 1974 non-divers found a bypass to the sump using an awkward squeeze – the Fennian Terror – and the extension was fully explored and surveyed. The sump extensions amounted to over one and half kilometres.

Explorations in Prod's Pot, 1972-74
During the summer of 1972 Solari and I joined forces for a return trip. We passed three short, constricted sumps in the Cascade Passage of Prod's Pot and explored an extension of 457m. Far more significant was the conquest of Arch Cave Sump, the upstream termination of a major resurgence system beneath Tullybrack Mountain. An eighty-metre dive, a long canal and a six-metre dive gave access to a fabulous extension running back into the mountain for another one and a half kilometres. This terminated at yet another sump, Sump 3.

The following year we returned and, unassisted, ferried our diving equipment over difficult terrain to the isolated terminal sump. This was passed after a forty-nine metre dive along a small, but comfortable, passage. However, instead of further extensions, we discovered we had connected the Arch System to Noon's Hole. This is presently the finest through trip in Ireland and now easier than hitherto, due to the successful bypass achieved to the Noon's Hole sump. Diving, though, is still essential to pass the sumps at the lower end of the system.

In 1974 the complex sump at the downstream end of Prod's Pot was finally passed and, over a series of solo operations, I was able to extend the diving 300m from base. During Easter 1976 Dave Morris and I

Above: The Refad Pot team in 1979. Left to right: Martyn Farr, J. Murphy, Dave Morris, Mark Campbell and David Woods.

passed the final dive here, and, during a six-hour exploration, discovered over a kilometre of new passage. The extension ran directly towards the resurgence in the Claddagh Glen, and in the early summer local cavers succeeded in digging a route into the system close to the divers' terminal point.

Reyfad Pot, 1978

In 1978 Irish cavers, including Hywel Ball, Mark Campbell and David Woods, made a major dry advance in Reyfad Pot, where they discovered one kilometre of streamway terminating at a sump. Supported by this group I passed this after an easy solo dive in October 1978 to discover another 400m of passage leading to Sump 2. I returned to pass this the following Easter, but was soon stopped again at the top of an eighteen-metre pitch. Things were growing serious, so I returned with a strong team, including Dave Morris, Mark Campbell and David Woods (the last two had just learned to dive). Together we explored a further 400m beyond my previous limit, but, despite taking the system as a whole to the status of the deepest in Ireland (174m), little progress could be made into a constricted, heavily silted terminal sump. A considerable distance still exists, therefore, between the end of this major system and the resurgence at Carrick Beg. This rising at the eastern edge of Tullybrack Mountain was entered for the first time in July 1976, after ten hours of digging. A 600m length of streamway led to a short sump, which was passed the following weekend. A further 396m of streamway was discovered, terminating at an extremely awkward constricted sump. Here lies the potential for one of the deepest and, in all probability, one of the longest through trips in Britain and Ireland.

The Tragedy at Pollnacrom, 1981

Local cavers persevered with the various dry leads remaining in the Reyfad-Pollnacrom complex. There seemed to be no obvious answer to the problem, so, in February 1981, David Woods decided to make another attempt to pass the terminal sump in Pollnacrom.

Apart from the possibilities of digging a dry route into the missing section of cave, there was this one strategically placed sump at the downstream terminus which had yet to be conclusively examined. I had attempted this in 1976 and had advanced for six metres before being forced to retire. The sump was distinctly nasty and, just to get started, I had had to dig my way through two horrific squeezes. The tunnel was blocked not by rocks, but, far worse, by sand. As I scooped it to one side and gouged out a channel large enough to wriggle through, I was aware that exit would be problematic, as the sand immediately filled in the channel after I had passed. Having negotiated these squeezes, I decided to call it a day. I found room to curl up and turn around, and, as expected, had to spend quite some minutes digging my way back out.

It was this sump which David Woods decided to tackle on 7 February 1981. Woods was by this stage an experienced cave diver and he had planned his assault meticulously. He decided to make his first dive with a single bottle and demand valve – hand held (as I had done in 1976). He agreed with his friend on the surface, Ed Rolston, that, if there was room enough at twenty metres, he would return for his spare set of equipment.

He dug his way through the initial squeezes, and a few minutes later a violent surge of bubbles seemed to indicate he was on his way back. However, the flow of air did not abate and Rolston quickly realised that his friend was in trouble. His valve was free flowing; precious air was venting to waste.

In the struggle to clear the squeeze it seems likely that the valve had somehow been jammed with silt and the air would have thus been used up very quickly. Rolston commented later:

> I then took a breath and went down, handicapped by buoyancy of wet suit and no visibility or mask, but eventually found Dave's hands near the entrance of the squeeze [this was less than two metres vertically beneath the surface]. I held his wrists and he held my wrists, so I knew he wanted a pull. However, pulling was ineffective, as he seemed to be solidly jammed. Then I had to get air. After two unsuccessful attempts to get

him out I went to get another bottle and attached the reserve valve. On return into the pool I could no longer find Dave's hands but instead found his bottle with the hose jammed on a corner of rock and he was no longer holding the line. I felt around with hands and feet but could find no sign of Dave to give him the bottle. At this point there seemed little hope, as he had no air, so I surfaced and strapped the bottle on to breath from myself, to look further in.

Rolston was not a diver and, despite his valiant attempts, it was soon apparent that he could do little more. He made his exit to summon help.

In the early hours of the next morning I was alerted and flown out to Belfast in an RAF Sea King helicopter, and then to the mountain itself in an army helicopter. I arrived just after dawn. By this stage Dave Drew had made a preliminary search of the sump pool, but there was no sign of the missing diver. When I entered the cave shortly after, the situation did not appear hopeful. Having kitted up, I slid slowly to the bottom of the circular funnel, where, at just under two metres' depth, the first squeeze lay. I was dreading what I would surely find. Here clearance between floor and ceiling was less than twenty centimetres, quite impossible to negotiate. I set to work scooping back the sand. I had barely started when I found David's right arm, almost completely buried just inside the squeeze. I tried and tried, but no amount of effort could free him. The body had formed an obstacle that the silt had embedded and was now solidly jammed. I did all I could, which was precious little. It was hopeless; I felt dreadful.

There was not a lot to say on the way out. I cast my mind back to those early days when he had toyed with the idea of cave diving, of his enquiries as to future prospects in the area. We had discussed this place. All those good days of talk. To think that it had come to this. All who knew him had lost a good friend.

The Pollballiny – Pollnagceim System, 1985-89

Despite the efforts of a host of activists, for many years County Clare was to present explorers with few significant breakthroughs and it was not until the 1980s that any major finds were made. The most exciting of these took place in 1985, when Brian Judd, Colin Bunce, Dave Scott and friends gained access to a new and particularly fine vertical system at the southern end of the Pollballiny depression. The cave dropped swiftly through limestone to terminate at a nasty constricted sump. This and three more were eventually passed, leading to further rapid descent along a tall, narrow rift. By the time the group reached Sump 5 at 128m underground, Pollnagceim was the deepest in the area, with the prospect of much bigger discoveries ahead.

Judd persevered with this project, contending with many difficulties and much scepticism. To the amazement of the majority of cavers, he eventually succeeded in installing a complex plumbing system, with which to siphon out the first four sumps. With these temporarily removed, diving equipment was again transported to the bottom of the cave and the assault upon Sump 5 was renewed. After several attempts upon this peaty, extremely constricted and heavily silted obstacle, Judd finally achieved much-deserved success in May 1989. After a penetration of fifty metres, he passed the sump to emerge into a huge, boulder-strewn passage, which led ever deeper into the mountain.

The breakthrough was precisely what Judd had sought. After countless years of activity, he had regained the enormous fossil passage which had been lost in a massive boulder collapse at the bottom of Pollballiny. Unfortunately, despite a hundred metres of progress, the main route was once more obstructed by boulders. This constitutes the most exciting caving discovery in Ireland for many years, and exploration is almost certain to be resumed here in due course.

The rising for the Pollballiny – Pollnagceim System, like that of Pollballyelly and Faunarooska is presently unknown. It may be under the sea, perhaps situated a short distance off the extremely rugged west coast. These major caves on Slieve Elva, which in all probability unite somewhere deep under the mountain, have a potential depth of over 240m.

The Green Holes of Doolin

Another interesting development in recent years has been the discovery of a complex network of coastal caves situated near the popular tourist village of Doolin. These completely submerged passages had been noted by open-water divers many years previously, but, in the wake of British involvement in the exploration of the Blue Holes in the West Indies, several groups of divers were lured to the west coast of Ireland to try their luck at caves which are today collectively known as the Green Holes.

Peter Glanvill and Tim Fogg were the first to examine systematically the underwater cliffs and submerged cave entrances north of Doolin, but it was locally based Brian Judd who made the first determined assaults.

These divers quickly charted the entrances of four separate caves. Close to Doolin harbour, at a depth of about eighteen metres, lie the Reef Caves. Just to the east, beneath the headland, lies the Hell Complex, and 150m to the north-east is the deeply penetrating

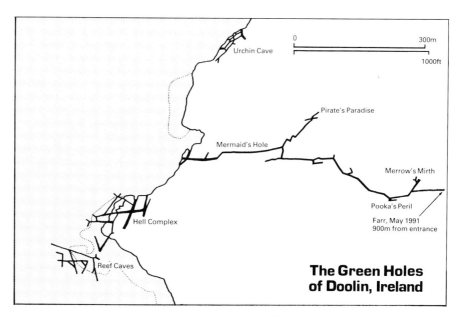

The Green Holes of Doolin, Ireland

Left: Martyn Farr preparing to set off on his 700m Pooka's Peril dive in Mermaid's Hole, Doolin, Ireland in 1987. Calm sea conditions are essential and getting back onto this awkward rocky coastline is particularly hazardous if a swell develops during the dive.
Above: Brian Judd at an airspace at 430m in the Pirate's Paradise branch of Mermaid's Hole.

Mermaid's Hole. The shallowest system is Urchin Cave, which is several hundred metres further north. Sea conditions are critical for diving in this area and there are very few days a year when exploration can be conducted safely. On this rocky coast cave divers observe a healthy respect for the elements. If the winds are anything other than easterly (rare), the swell is always rough, and the waves crash against the cliffs with the full force of the Atlantic. It is an intimidating place.

Unlike the flat, calm conditions found at the sump base of a normal cave and, indeed on the dive itself, at the Green Holes the thought of a turbulent return at the end of a dive is always a worrying prospect.

Virtually all who have dived here have colourful tales of broken or lost gear and personal injury. The problem usually centres round the extreme difficulty (with heavy cave diving equipment) of getting out of the water on to sharp and slippery rocks in what is often a significant swell. These are not satisfactory conditions in which to conduct a cave dive and they can play on the mind throughout, significantly detracting from one's normal fund of determination and resolve.

It was not until Easter 1987 that the first break-through was made. After a long winter of enforced inactivity the weather was near perfect, and the sea relatively calm. Visiting Welsh diver Steve Jones resumed exploration at Mermaid's Hole, a system heading directly back under the land and possessing a significant outflow of fresh water. A penetration of over 350m was quickly achieved. This nearly proved extremely costly: on exit from the last operation the sea conditions had worsened dramatically, and he managed to land just as his air ran out.

Following hard upon Jones's heels, another visitor, Ian Rolland, continued and after a total dive of 430m,

he broke surface into a normal section of dry cave, which was named Pirate's Paradise. Brian Judd and I subsequently completed exploration of this section of cave during the summer of 1987, and later dis-covered another major lead, called Pooka's Peril. Here I achieved a 700m penetration which gave every indication of continuing to a further section of dry cave. Weather and sea conditions frustrated further assaults on this system in 1988 and 1989, but a fortuitous visit to the area in August 1990 produced the long-awaited advance. With support from Nick Geh, Andy Whitehouse and Marco Paganuzzi, I laid another ninety metres of line from my previous limit to enter Merrow's Mirth, the largest dry chamber so far discovered in the Green Holes. This dive lasted just under three hours and we emerged to find atrocious conditions on the surface, but in this instance we managed to exit in the relative calm of the Hell complex.

This advance indicates that the Green Holes of Doolin still hold much potential and divers can expect plenty of excitement in this area.

CONCLUSION

There were significant advances in all aspects of British cave diving in the 1970s and the 1980s. Most important was the progressive attitude of the divers themselves, and nothing demonstrated this better than the distances and depths covered. These achieve-ments were made possible by the steady evolution of more suitable equipment and techniques, and by keeping a close watch on international developments. New equipment and clothing innovations are now swiftly assessed, with relevant information being rapidly disseminated among the cave diving fraternity. In this respect the role of the Cave Diving Group has been very important and virtually all British cave divers are members.

As a result of this broader basis of knowledge and better organisation more people have entered the sport. In 1975, for example, over 350 dives were made by more than seventy divers. A closer analysis reveals

that the spearhead of this advance lay in the hands of a small group of exceptionally determined individuals. Thus, during 1975, there were five people who each accomplished over twenty separate dives, which accounted for most of the progress within this period.

Ten years later the situation was only slightly different. A steady increase in the number of divers was apparent, but, of the total membership of the CDG in 1986 (approx. 195), at least half can be unofficially classified as non-divers, with respect to cave diving within the UK. Of the remainder, it is clear that no more than twenty individuals took part in original exploration.

In terms of diving and exploration, the sheer length to which sumps are now being penetrated, bearing in mind the generally hostile conditions in British sumps, is quite astounding. Dives of 300m are now routine, and even a 600m dive is not considered unduly long. This may be compared with the 1960s, when dives of 150m were considered long and even multiple dives totalling this figure were rare.

Inevitably, original exploration within the British Isles is becoming increasingly difficult, since all the easy sites have long since been explored. It is not surprising, therefore, that, along with growing affluence and improved transport, there has been a developing interest in overseas exploration. With home training in generally hostile conditions, British divers have found they are well equipped to play a significant role in overseas explorations.

Main Caving Areas of Britain and Ireland

INTERNATIONAL CAVE DIVING

The next section of the book deals with cave diving activities in various areas of the world. The enormous breadth of international activity prevents in-depth analysis. All that is possible is an overall summary, with detailed attention given to the important events in the main areas. I have endeavoured to select specific areas and specific explorations which illustrate the varying types of cave diving activity, while at the same time charting important advances in terms of length, depth and technology. This selectivity means that many worthy caving areas which have witnessed degrees of cave diving activity are not mentioned here.

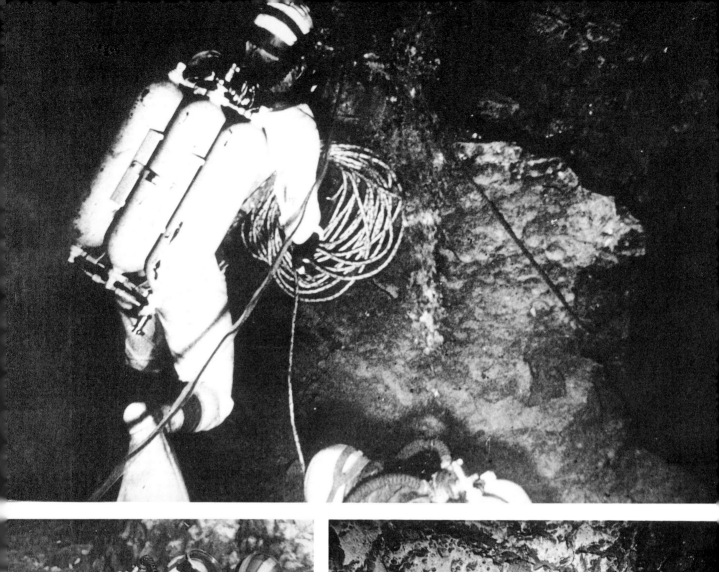

CHAPTER NINE

MAINLAND EUROPE

including the Asian part of the Soviet Union, and the Canary Islands

Europe may be regarded as the birthplace of speleology and over the past one hundred years it has remained at the forefront of caving development. In cave exploration above and below water there have been major contributions to both techniques and exploration, and European cave divers have been very active elsewhere in the world. In 1990, Europe contained nine of the twelve deepest caves in the world, it also contained more than its fair share of lengthy, dry systems and many exceptionally long diving penetrations. Of all the European countries, France, with its extensive cave systems and many experienced cavers, stands supreme.

FRANCE

Today France is one of the premier caving and cave diving areas of the world. Many caving areas exist throughout the country and about 20,000 caves are known. There are numerous diving sites, and many long, difficult explorations have been made.

The genesis of French cave diving at Fontaine de Vaucluse is described in Chapter 2. This was the first cave in the world to be examined with the cumbersome Standard Equipment (1878) and was also the first cave in the world to be explored using the aqualung (1946).

Fontaine de Vaucluse, 1955-67

Jacques Cousteau, the instigator of the 1946 attempt, mounted another expedition at Vaucluse in 1955 in company with members of the French Office of Undersea Research. On this occasion the divers

reached a depth of seventy-four metres. Once again there was no sign of any bottom to this flooded shaft, and the huge, boulder-strewn tunnel continued ever deeper at an angle of forty-five degrees.

Owing to the extreme depth of this cave there was a long interval before another advance was achieved. However, in September 1967, in an experiment again organised by the French Office of Underwater Research, Telenaut, a television-guided robot, probed the siphon to a depth of 106m. The machine had to stop when the passage narrowed, but the camera revealed that beyond this the descent continued.

Fontaine de Vaucluse, 1981 Attempts

The mystery of the Fontaine de Vaucluse appeared no nearer to a solution and, to the increasing number of highly experienced, technologically advanced divers of mainland Europe, it became more and more of a challenge. It was not until 1981, fourteen years after the 'Voyage of the Telenaut', that the next dramatic advance was achieved. After considerable effort, Claude Touloumdjian secured the necessary permission and support to mount a series of well-prepared dives. With the full technical and logistical support of the diving company Comex, preparations were well under way when the team learned of a totally unexpected development. The famous German diver Jochen Hasenmayer had made a secret exploration at the Fontaine and, during a dive lasting nearly five and a half hours, he descended to a point 143m beneath the water surface, thus establishing a new world depth record. Other than a statement regarding the depth attained, few details of this operation were ever released, but it is now clear that Hasenmayer used a rebreather, a highly technical piece of apparatus which he had designed and constructed. This is discussed

Left: Scenes during the 1955 dives in Fontaine de Vaucluse. A depth of 77m was reached, one of the deepest cave dives of its day. The two underwater photos show divers at 28m (near left) and 15m (top).

later in the description of his explorations at the Emergence du Ressel. This twist of fate led to considerable interest by the media, some of whom were intent upon heightening public awareness of the ongoing project by presenting it as a 'duel' between the French and the Germans. Despite this unsettling news, the team continued work and, on 11 October, Touloumdjian made a dive of over seven hours' duration. Descending a huge black shaft, he discovered Hasenmayer's line tied off at a depth of 143m and proceeded on to a point 153m beneath the water surface. And still there was no indication of any bottom.

Given the amazing depth, and the fact that Hasenmayer could not get official permission to dive here, one might well have imagined that it would be some time before any further advance was achieved. Undeterred, however the German returned for a second secret attempt on 9 September 1983. With his wife in

support, and their activities being conducted furtively during the hours of darkness, the result was particularly impressive. When he entered the water (12° C), his equipment weighed an astounding 400kg, comprising: nine twenty-litre cylinders of gas mixtures, an incredible array of instrumentation and, to document the event, a film camera mounted on a pole behind him. Instead of establishing stage cylinders at points on the descent, Hasenmayer's approach was one of complete autonomy. With four huge cylinders mounted on his back he towed the remaining five behind him in a specially designed 'bottle boat'.* In typically efficient manner, nothing was left to chance and Hasenmayer even took with him a specially prepared blend of food, which he carried in his helmet in a baby's bottle.

Diving with such a bulky set of apparatus, the descent was necessarily relatively slow. Hasenmayer was surprised to find Touloumdjian's line tied off at a depth somewhat less than the depth that had been reported, and well short of Hasenmayer's earlier depth.† He continued down, and forty-five minutes after leaving the diving base he reached a new and incredible depth of 205m. By the time he had regained the surface, with the prolonged decompression times involved, the entire dive lasted nine hours. The precise mixtures he used were kept secret. The dive was certainly an extreme feat of human endurance and, having been conducted with no ill effects, showed clearly that once more the frontiers of exploration had been very efficiently rolled back.

However, the exploration had failed to reach the elbow or bottom of the sump, the quest for which was now in the realms of high technology. Amazing as it may appear, just eight days after Hasenmayer's epic achievement, another team arrived at the site intent upon discovering the ultimate depth of this cave. The 'Voyage of the Telenaut' in 1967 had shown that the cave extended below sea-level. Now a new creation, the Sorgonaute – conceived by the speleological club

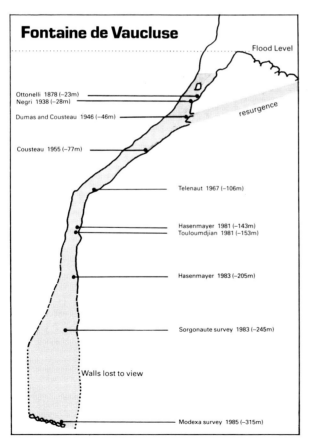

Fontaine de Vaucluse

Flood Level

Ottonelli 1878 (−23m)
Negri 1938 (−28m)
Dumas and Cousteau 1946 (−46m)

resurgence

Cousteau 1955 (−77m)

Telenaut 1967 (−106m)

Hasenmayer 1981 (−143m)
Touloumdjian 1981 (−153m)

Hasenmayer 1983 (−205m)

Sorgonaute survey 1983 (−245m)

Walls lost to view

Modexa survey 1985 (−315m)

---

* Despite his successful earlier use of rebreathers in both Ressel and Vaucluse, Hasenmayer calculated that they were not as safe as a multi-cylinder aqualung rig for his second Vaucluse dive. He thereafter used the aqualung on all his subsequent dives, which he considered still within the scope of aqualung logistics.

† It should be noted that Touloumdjian had been diving with a surface-fed mixed gas supply with a set of 'bail out' bottles for emergency use; as such he did not require a normal guide line, as this function could be supplied with the tube leading back to base. This may explain the apparent discrepancy between the two accounts.

Above: Jochen Hasenmayer before his 'clandestine' 205m dive in Fontaine de Vaucluse in 1983. He used aqualung equipment, with his own piped system for equalising the air pressure in his four-cylinder rig to maintain balance. Also of note is the plexiglass, spherical compass on his wrist, and the sealed face mask incorporating a special valve to prevent any water cooling his face or head when mouthpieces were changed.

of the major French concern Regie Renault de Cleon, and built under the direction of its promoter Jean-Pierre Viard – arrived at Vaucluse.

This new machine consisted of a small video-controlled bathyscaphe, which was directed from the surface and powered by three propulsion units. One and a half hours after leaving the surface, the Sorgonaute reached a depth of 245m. Disappointingly,

at this point, the 400m control cable ran out and the machine could go no further. However, the images it relayed to those above showed that at the furthest point lay an immense gallery, and that the final depth was therefore still a matter of conjecture.

The Bottom of Fontaine de Vaucluse

In September 1984 the group returned with a slightly modified machine and a longer cable. Sadly this mission ended in disaster. Contact with the machine was suddenly lost, and the cable was found to be severed – a catastrophic implosion had destroyed the engine.

In 1985 the bottom of the Fontaine de Vaucluse

was finally reached. At a depth of 312m the Modexa, a small, remote-controlled vehicle (ROV) owned by the Mediterranean Society of Commerce, alighted upon a cone of large boulders. To one side a sand slope led gradually deeper and, following this down, the Modexa shortly encountered a strong current. The depth at this point was 315m.

The Fontaine de Vaucluse is without doubt the deepest flooded system yet known in the world. From detailed geological and hydrological studies it has been ascertained that the resurgence takes water from a widespread area: some sinks, for example, lie as far afield as forty-five kilometres to the north-east. A great deal of scientific research remains to be done here and it will take many years of study before this fascinating complex is fully assessed.

The Gouffre Berger Sumps

Diving has been undertaken not only in the accessible resurgence sites but also in many cold, inaccessible locations. The sump at the bottom of the Gouffre Berger system, near Grenoble, was passed in 1963 and, in 1967, the system was again established as the deepest in the world at over 1135m. More recently, in July 1982, Patrick Penez furthered the exploration of this site yet again, extending the cave 170m into Sump 5 and reaching a terminal depth of 50m in the last sump. The overall depth of the system is now 1248m/ 4094ft. The final point of resurgence for the water in this system is the Cuves de Sassenage some four kilometres away, another major challenge for the future.

The Sumps of Gouffre Jean Bernard

The Gouffre Berger was the deepest known system in the world for many years, a position taken by the Pierre Saint-Martin in the 1970s. The deepest still remains in France, not in the mountains of the Pyrenees, but rather in Haute Savoie, where, on the Lapies de Foillis near Samoens, the major system of the Gouffre Jean Bernard was extended to a dramatic new depth record in the early 1980s. The bottom 140m of this depth can only be explored by divers. Sump 1, at 1400m was passed by Fred Vergier and Patrick Penez in February 1980. In icy cold water they made a forty-five metre dive at a depth of six metres. Then a dry 230m passage of awkward terrain led to an eight metre drop and Sump 2 at a depth of 1415m. Twelve months later, aided once more by a strong support team of Speleo Vulcains, another assault was mounted upon the downstream terminus of the system. The divers on this occasion were Penez and J.L. Fantoli. Sump 2 proved to be just forty metres long at a maximum depth of eight metres beyond which a further eighty-five metre section of streamway was gained and Sump 3 was reached at a depth of 1455m. Penez dived this in February 1982. It proved relatively short – thirty metres at three metres' depth, and beyond this Penez made a solo exploration of another 150m of technical passage to gain an impenetrable Sump 4 at an overall depth of 1494m/4902ft. The discovery of further passages, and a new entrance, at the upper extremity of this cave has since extended the total depth to 1601m/5251ft.

Puerta de Illamina (BU56)

French teams are highly adept at mounting dives at the bottom of these major, technically difficult systems. Another classic exploration of this nature was the one undertaken at the Puerta de Illamina (also known as BU56), close to the Spanish border in the Pyrenees. Here, in 1980 and 1981, a Franco-Spanish team made a rapid exploration of this unusually impressive system, reaching a sump at a depth of 1328m, at the time the second deepest cave in the world. Fred Vergier then passed three sumps totalling 200m of diving to reach Sump 4. The final point of resurgence for this water is nine kilometres away at the Ko-Lecia resurgence at Ste Engrace, France. This and other factors show that the geological depth potential here is 1700m/5577ft.

With caves such as these, small wonder French divers are equally at home exploring at the bottom of the world's most demanding systems and undertaking deep diving projects for their own sake. With hundreds of easily accessible, spacious sumps, it is not surprising that many long dives have also been made.

The Caves of the Dordogne

Perhaps the finest area for long dives in France, if not in Europe, is the Dordogne region. In the vicinity of

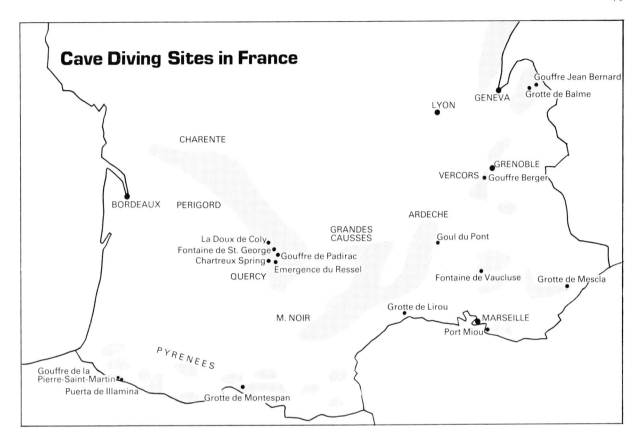

the Cele and Lot Valleys are some of the deepest and longest siphons in France, offering a wealth of fine cave diving sites perhaps only bettered in Florida or Mexico.

The water contained in these sumps in summer is amongst the clearest cave water in Europe, and with an average temperature of around 14°C, the large, flooded tunnels present superb diving conditions. This was one of the first areas of France to be seriously explored early in the century by speleologists such as Martel, de Joly and Casteret. It was here, too, that the first major diving penetrations were achieved, at places such as Padirac and the Fontaine de St George, caves long associated with Guy de Lavour, generally regarded as the true initiator of cave diving in the country, and with others including Claude Touloumdjian, Bertrand Leger and the brothers Eric and Francis Le Guen.

Many thrilling projects have been mounted here over the years. Late in 1978 Pierre Laureau made a remarkable penetration of 1180m/3871ft at Buarmes-les-Messieurs, at the time the longest dive in Europe. In August the following year a team of five divers, led by Francis Le Guen, completed the exploration of the now popular diving site Trou Madame. In total 2455m/8054ft of sump was passed, the longest single dive amounting to 1285m. The operation lasted six and a half hours.

Emergence du Ressel, Dordogne, 1978-81

The Emergence du Ressel is another classic resurgence in the bed of the Cete river near Marcilhac-sur-Cete. French divers J.L. Fantoli and Claude Touloumdjian made a lengthy penetration to a terminal depth of forty-five metres in 1978. The following year the exceptionally well-trained Swiss divers of the Group Lemanique de Plongée Souterraine (GLPS) continued the exploration at fifty metres' depth for 700m.

Above: Jochen Hasenmayer before his Emergence du Ressel dive in 1981. He is equipped with the Spelio-Twin Rebreather (STR 80) which he used in major dives in both Ressel and Vaucluse that year.

In 1980, using a scooter, the team continued at a depth of fifty-six metres to a point over 1000m from the entrance. This was an outstanding achievement in its own right, but the next advance was to prove altogether more dramatic and highly significant.

At this point Jochen Hasenmayer made his entry. For many years he had been at the forefront of developments in Europe and commanded the respect of the cave diving community worldwide. To his French and Swiss counterparts Hasenmayer was some-

thing of a mysterious character. He tended to keep very much to himself and had written comparatively little about his exploits. Working quietly from his home in southern Germany Hasenmayer strove to advance every aspect of the technical side of the sport. Time and again, this talent manifested itself in skilful design and practical ingenuity. By radical innovation and modification of existing equipment Hasenmayer not only grappled with all the problems confronting cave divers but more important, he came up with startling new and exciting solutions.

In 1980 he introduced the concept of the 'jumbo' backpack; an incredibly heavy back-mounted arrangement for using four of the massive 20 litre bottles. Each cylinder had its own regulator, but perhaps the most impressive aspect of the assembly was the integrated and patented buoyancy system which incorporated an anti-roll feature.*

This new arrangement inevitably extended the diver's range, a concept that was to be emulated by many continental divers over the next decade. But Hasenmayer's ideas ranged well beyond the conventional approach. He had been exploring submerged caves for over twenty years, and during this period had studied many aspects of human physiology relevant to deep diving. By 1980 he had succeeded in incorporating much of this knowledge into computer programmes that enabled him to calculate the complex decompres-

---

* This was an important consideration, for having established the correct trim in the water (via inflation of the drysuit) using too much air from one or other of the outside tanks ran the risk of the diver becoming lop-sided. This could be countered by frequent changes of regulators, so that all cylinders were breathed down at approximately the same rate, or possibly by transferring a lead weight to the light side. Hasenmayer's system allowed for the buoyancy of the tanks to be regulated and in such a way as to maintain the diver's trim.

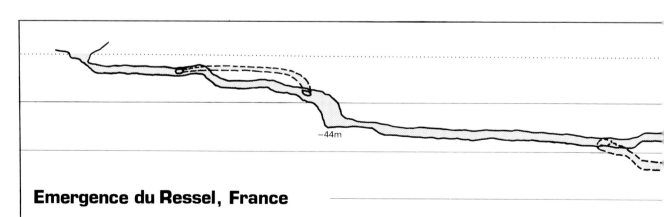

−44m

Emergence du Ressel, France

sion tactics for these increasingly daunting dives.

Altogether more futuristic, was his next project. He had become convinced that in the long term the most promising line of development lay in the field of recycling the breathing gas. This was not a new idea, rather a radical reassessment of the old wartime equipment that had been superceded by the aqualung. He therefore designed and constructed a revolutionary rebreather apparatus.

The Speleo-Twin Rebreather (STR 80) reached fruition in 1980. It had two separate rebreathers, each with a potential twenty-four hour duration, independent of depth. Each had an oxygen sensor, was computer monitored and had an optic and acoustic alarm. In case of electronic, or computer malfunction the equipment was capable of being used in a semi open circuit mode. In the unlikely event of both rebreathers becoming inoperable the apparatus was assembled to incorporate two normal open circuit respirators, each with 300 litres of mixed gas (approx. 50cu.ft). The whole outfit was back-mounted and so compact that it extended above the back to a height of just 13cms.

Hasenmayer gave this apparatus its first test dive on 9 September 1980 when he made a 600m round trip in the Source de la Loue. Its first major test took place on 25 September when he made an advance to 1240m, and 88m depth in the Emergence de Landenouze. Following this success he resolved to use it to attempt a major penetration into the Emergence du Ressel. On 22 April 1981 he swam into the unknown region beyond the Swiss limit at 1000m. That day he made a 3800m round trip reaching a point 1620m from base; of that three kilometres of the distance lay in depths between fifty-five metres and seventy metres. By using just fins his bottom time amounted to three and a half hours at an average depth of more than sixty metres, plus a further half an hour between three and fifty-five metres. According to established procedures the shortest decompression time would have been fifteen hours, but Hasenmayer decompressed in just under four hours!

At the Emergence du Ressel Hasenmayer had finally translated his theories satisfactorily into practice. On a dive conducted entirely alone, using fin power and experimental equipment, he had pushed back the frontiers in a most dramatic advance. Yet, apart from the most superficial detail, the cave diving world remained largely unaware of the full significance of this momentous event for many years.

On this operation in the Ressel Hasenmayer not only proved the worth of the rebreather, but also made sense of a very complex network of underwater passages. At his furthest point, where he had run out of line, he realised that he had missed the main route into the mountain. So, on the way out, he endeavoured to locate the main flow. At 1135m from the entrance he was successful and he noted the lead for his next visit.

Four days later he returned. On this occasion he used his jumbo rig of four large cylinders with two additional 20 litre bottles hung under an Aquazepp. He later described this penetration in a beautiful passage in his report:

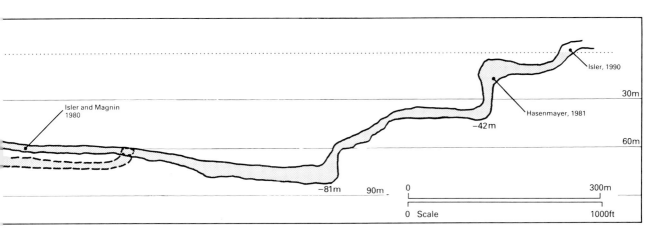

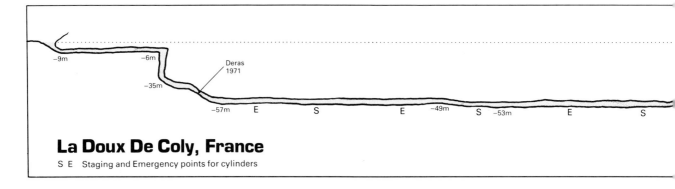

La Doux De Coly, France

S E   Staging and Emergency points for cylinders

I soared on an Aquazepp into the unknown passage in a westerly direction. The walls, more than ten metres apart, disappeared ahead into an intense blue expanse. The roof, forever flat, grew deeper until the −6om level. Five or six metres below me an eroded and undercut floor of petrified sediments flashed past. Banks of clean sand alternated with black encrustations, perforated and shaped by the deep aggressive water into weird skeleton-like structures.

At 1400m was a rise up and a good place to check on the equipment and gas reserves. At 1500m I was stopped at a cul de sac. Above was a gigantic shaft with the form and dimensions of a construction from science fiction. I rose into this like a child's balloon. Below me my thin nylon line hung in empty space. At the height of a five storey building I finally lost sight of the huge chamber below. In the beam of the 50 watt lamp on the Aquazepp a rock strewn canyon opened in front of me four metres high and two metres wide. This more recently formed passage continued to rise until the 40m level at 1650m where I parked my vehicle.

At 1700m there was a sharp bend in the passage with the continuation to the south. At 1755m I stopped at the bottom of a new shaft up, only five metres in diameter, at −20m, my limit for re-ascent having already been passed. The vertical walls rose up out of sight giving the subjective impression perhaps of an air surface. Then came the long return, finally emerging in the bed of the River Cele after a dive of 10 hours and 15 minutes. [n.b. The longer decompression time required on this second dive was due to the use of a single gas mixture, incorporating 10% helium.]

Yet again Hasenmayer had made an epic penetration. Unsupported, he had laid 620m of new line at depths touching seventy metres. Taken together, the two operations were to constitute an achievement almost without parallel. It was an incredible exploration for a solo venture; it reaffirmed Hasenmayer's status in the sport, and gave a clear indicator as to the direction of future activities in the area for the rest of the decade.

It was not until the summer of 1990 that Hasenmayer's limit was finally passed. Supported by a large team of highly experienced divers, and using a semi-closed rebreather system (RI 2000)* the Swiss diver Olivier Isler ascended the final shaft and reached air. Beyond lay a steep boulder-strewn slope leading away into the darkness. This has yet to be explored.

Isler's Record Dive at La Doux de Coly

Another inspiring and highly significant exploration in the Dordogne during the 1980s took place at La Doux de Coly, about ten kilometres from the famous cave of Lascaux. Several dives had taken place at this superb site in the 1960s, but it was not until 1971 that the cave received its first determined assault. At this time P.J. Deras made a remarkable dive of 365m/ 1197ft reaching a terminal depth of fifty-two metres.

In 1981 the Swiss GLPS team, including Jean-Jacques Bolanz, Cyrille Brandt, Claude Magnin and Olivier Isler, took up the challenge and set their mark upon the cave. Over the course of a five-day expedition they extended the line to a point 1760m from the entrance, in the final section at a relatively constant depth of fifty-six metres. Two years later another assault was mounted, which extended the cave, another 340m at a similar depth. Wearing four large bottles on his back and extending the staging technique far into the cave, Isler made a seven-hour dive to reach 2100m/

* The RI 2000 was the result of five years intensive work by the combined efforts of Alain Ronjat and Olivier Isler. Working with limited resources the pair covered virtually all development costs themselves, although Spirotechnique provided them with some basic materials. Unlike the closed circuit system developed by Bill Stone, which completely recycles the expired gas, the RI 2000 is a semi-closed circuit arrangement. This apparatus takes its supply from a cylinder of mixed gas of known characteristics, and can also be operated in the event of a total failure of the electro-mechanical system.

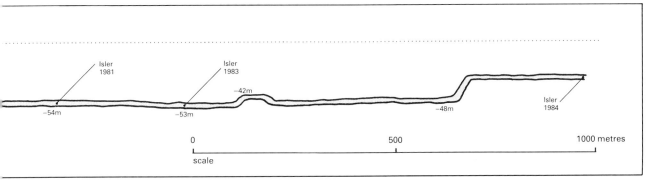

Isler
1981

Isler
1983

−42m

−54m

−53m

−48m

Isler
1984

0   500   1000 metres

scale

689oft. The exploration was not without its moments of anxiety. On the way out from his successful push, Isler accidentally fouled the guideline with his scooter's propeller. About ten metres of line ensnared the machine and the diver experienced several tense minutes before the problem was remedied.

This twelve-day venture was also filmed: *La Pointe*, a twenty-six minute video. Scooters were relied upon heavily, but several technical incidents concerning their use was one of the main reasons for the limited advance achieved.

In 1984, following a long period of preparation and training, two further explorations were made. For Europe the achievement was quite without parallel,

and there is little doubt that the approach will be regarded as a significant milestone in cave diving worldwide. Other than the use of an underwater habitat for decompression, every advanced technique was employed.

Several days' 'sherpa' diving was required to set up each dramatic advance. Dual, front-mounted stage units were deposited at 700m, 1100m and 1500m, while emergency depots were also established at 550m, 900m and 1300m. Pure oxygen, compressed air and Trimix were used on each push, while specially prepared, oxygen-enriched mixtures were used for the

Below: The resurgence pool of La Doux de Coly.

distance Isler breathed pure oxygen, transferring to compressed air for the section that took him vertically to the depths in excess of fifty metres. At a point 450m from the entrance he then mounted his pre-staged Aquazepps, which were coupled in tandem. The front-mounted, twelve-litre stage units were exchanged at the three pre-arranged depots, and at the last of these he began to breath Trimix (10% helium). His first

Above: Olivier Isler using the coupled 714T Aquazepps in La Doux de Coly in 1984. This arrangement greatly increased the diver's safety as he was able to park one in support at 2630m and continue on the other to the record-breaking distance of 3100m from the entrance.

operation extended the line to 2630m along a spacious tunnel with unrelenting depths of about fifty metres.

On the second exploration his stage units allowed him to reach at least 1900m. Here he finally swapped to his back-mounted cylinders. At the extreme point reached on the first push, 2630m, he uncoupled the propulsion units and dived on using just one machine. The tunnel here was no more than seven metres wide and scootering through the clear water at three kilometres per hour demanded the utmost concentration. The Trimix ensured a clear head, essential for monitoring gauges, adjusting buoyancy and dispensing line. So far from the surface, at such extreme depths,

outward decompression stops. But perhaps the most interesting aspect of the expedition was its heavy reliance upon Aquazepp 714T propulsion units. These were modified to yield not only a greater range but also, coupled together, to provide a much greater safety margin for the lead diver. Safety was a major consideration and all penetrations were planned to allow divers to fin back to the surface in the event of the failure of both scooters.

It fell to Olivier Isler to make the final explorations. For these dives he set off wearing four, back-mounted, twenty-litre steel bottles, each pressurised to 250 bar, which were required for the final exploratory stage of the dive. He utilised a succession of other stage bottles to take him as far as possible into the cave before his final push.

The first 300m of La Doux de Coly is shallow, generally nine metres or less in depth. Over this

11. (top right) Claude Touloumdjian preparing to dive in Fontaine de Vaucluse in 1981. 12. (near right) The Telenaut being lowered into Fontaine de Vaucluse prior to its probe to 106m depth in 1967. 13. (far right) The Modexa being moved to the pool in 1985. It reached the bottom of the sump, 315m below the surface.

14. (overleaf top) Early aqualung divers in Grotte de Han Sur Lesse, Belgium in the 1950s. 15. (overleaf bottom) Olivier Isler, using three rebreathers, about to start on his major dive in Emergence du Ressel in 1990.

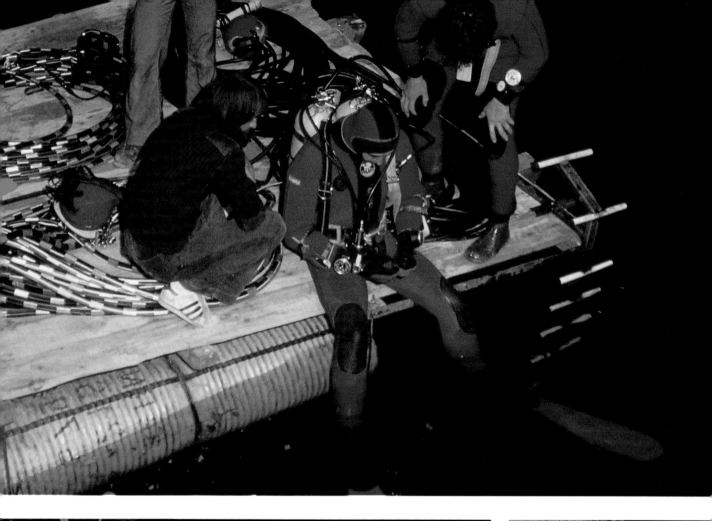

16. *(above) Eric Le Guen in Source de le Dhuit, Hte Marne, France.*

17. *(overleaf) Pat Cronin and Nick Geh head into Emergence du Ressel, Dordogne, France – at this point they are 100m from the entrance.*

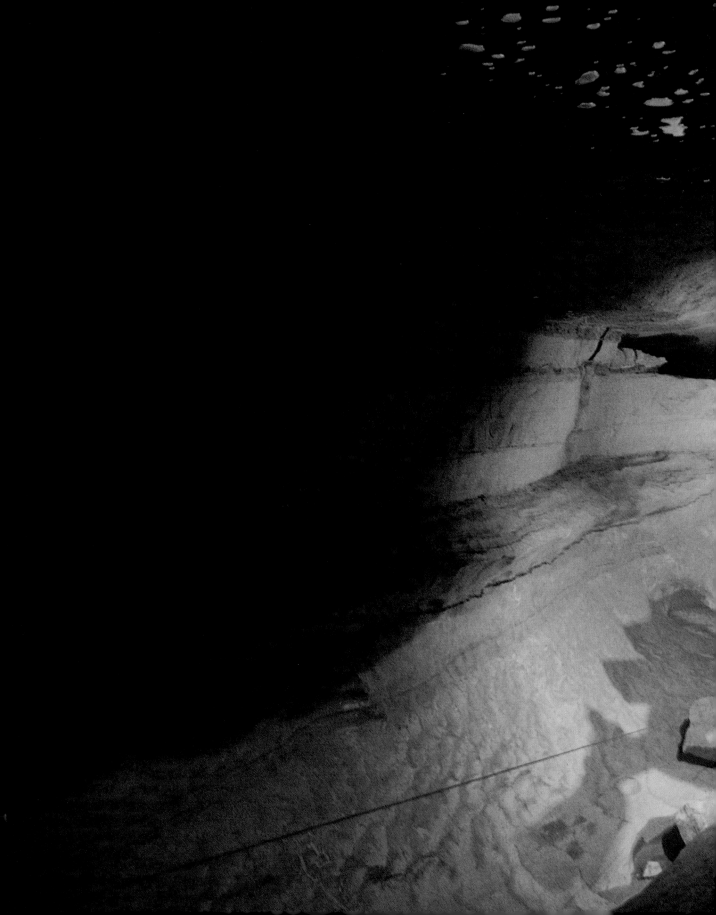

18. *(top left)* Eric Le Guen working through a narrow slit in Petit Goul de Tourne. The disadvantage of back-mounted cylinders in tight caves is obvious in this photograph. **19.** *(lower left)* Véronique and Francis Le Guen at Emergence de Finou, Dordogne, before their attempt to pass Sump 6 in 1989.

20. *(above)* Christoph Foetische at a depth of thirty metres in the entrance passage of Emergence de Bätterich, Switzerland *(see page 192).*

there was no room for the slightest error.

Just over 2700m from base, Isler reached the bottom of a ten-metre-diameter, inclined shaft, which ascended at forty-five degrees. This took the diver to a rather smaller continuation, at about thirty-two metres' depth. A tunnel resembling a metro line led horizontally from this point, the floor of which was almost uniformly covered in fine sand. It was finally at 3100m/10,170ft that his safety margins were reached and the exploration was curtailed. The smooth-bore tunnel continued on into the distance, extending an invitation for a return visit.

The record dive established by the GLPS at La Doux de Coly was to stand supreme until January 1989, when the American Sheck Exley made an equally amazing penetration. Unassisted by a scooter, Exley swam a total distance of 3183m at Chip's Cave in Florida. But, for Europe, the Doux de Coly remains by far the longest diving achievement to date.

Fontaine de St George, Gouffre de Padirac

Long and exceptionally deep dives are being made regularly in France. One of the most recent, and again one that will figure prominently in the annals of European cave diving history, is that at the Fontaine de St George, one of the principal resurgences for the famous Gouffre de Padirac. This again has been a long standing project brought one step closer to fruition by the GLPS.

The Fontaine de St George was one of the first sites ever explored by aqualung equipment. Guy de Lavour made an exploration of this impressive site in 1948, reaching a depth of thirty metres, subsequently found to be the elbow of the first sump. Sump 1 was eventually passed after a total dive of 380m. A section of dry passage, the Salle de Lavour, led quickly to a further flooded continuation.

Sump 2 was explored by Bertrand Leger in 1976. This continues at shallow depth for over 500m, but at 950m from the entrance he encountered a steep shaft, which he descended to a depth of forty-one

21. (left) Olivier Isler, heavily equipped with seven cylinders and paired Aquazepps, setting off on his 1620m probe into Atlantida Tunnel, Canary Islands, in 1986 (see page 197).

Above: Bertrand Leger, the notable French cave diving pioneer.

metres. Three years later Francis Le Guen made a determined assault upon this promising upstream lead, but was halted at seventy-one metres by an intimidating squeeze.

It was 1982 when the GLPS first took an interest in the cave. Jean-Jacques Bolanz quickly discovered a new underwater route into Sump 2, which eased the considerable problems of porterage. The next year Olivier Isler proved the worth of the new route, when he made a solo dive of six hours, reaching a final depth of seventy-six metres.

In October 1986 a major assault began. This was particularly difficult because the nature of the cave dictated that most of the outward decompression had to be made about 1000 metres from the entrance. After considerable porterage, it fell to Cyrille Brandt to make the new exploration. Passing the deepest point, a further fifty metres of diving took him to a much larger passage and, ascending a 'step-like' wall, he soon began going upwards into more shallow terrain. Passing through a succession of beautiful galleries, he was eventually halted by a huge upward chimney at a depth of just twenty metres and 320m beyond the 1983 limit. Further progress was halted owing to the additional, unexpected complications of decompression presented by this rapid reduction in depth. By the time he returned from this successful dive he had been underwater for nearly nine hours.

In July 1987 the GLPS returned to continue explora-

Above: Roland Gillet assists Olivier Isler to prepare for a dive in Fontaine de St George in 1987.

five minutes to reach his previous limit. Here he had to start a long decompression of about one and a half hours. The suspense was almost unbearable. Eventually the moment of truth arrived and Brandt rose quietly to the surface, reaching air at a point 1520m/4987ft from the entrance.

The sight which met his eyes was altogether more restful than the wild aspect of the previous deep zone. In shallow water he swam forward for 110m, passing a succession of smooth, phreatic roof-bells and finely sculpted swirl holes in the floor. At the furthest point the water was less than half a metre deep and, with his heavy equipment, it was difficult to progress. Under the circumstances removing his equipment would have been an unacceptable risk. Raising his head clear of the water he could see along the canal for at least twenty metres, beyond which was a wall that might

tion. The first two attempts to push on failed, but, on 29 July, it was Cyrille Brandt's turn to resume the lead. All went smoothly on this occasion and, equipped with four back-mounted cylinders, it took him seventy-

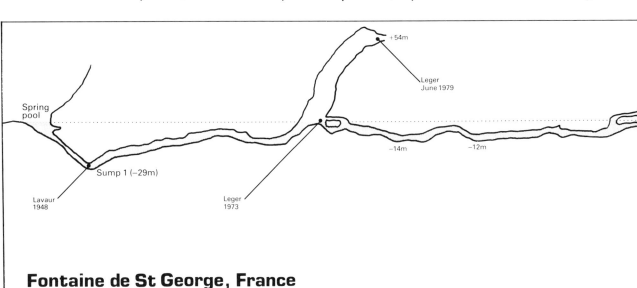

Fontaine de St George, France

indicate the beginning of another sump or merely a bend in the passage. Since little more could be achieved, Brandt began his return finally regaining the entrance after a dive of over nine hours. The successful passage of Sump 2 was another fine achievement for the GLPS and moved the project closer to a link with the eighteen-kilometre feeder system, the famous Gouffre de Padirac.

No further progress was made at the Fontaine de St George for two and a half years. Then Francis Le Guen arrived back on the scene. He knew the cave intimately from his previous explorations and, following a well-organised preparation, made his dive in January 1990. All went according to plan and Le Guen reached the end of Sump 2 and explored about 500m of dry cave to reach Sump 3. Clearly the gap between the Fontaine de St George and the Gouffre de Padirac is narrowing rapidly, and the information gained on this latest advance will be invaluable on the next exploration.

It should be noted that the Padirac itself has eight sumps; the distance from Sump 1 to Sump 8 being approximately four kilometres, and any expedition to tackle the further reaches requires a team of at least thirty members to transport the necessary equipment. The final sump here is less than five kilometres from

Sump 3 in Fontaine de St George, but forging that connection will surely remain a major challenge for some time to come.

Other Important French Dives

Many long, deep dives have been made right across the country. Francis Le Guen, his brother Eric and wife, Véronique, were to comprise the nucleus of a very formidable team throughout the 1970s and 1980s. Apart from their dives in the Fontaine de St George, this group has many fine explorations to their credit. They completed the diving at the end of the lengthy Trou Madame in 1978, and more recently have made other epic dives such as the 2250m penetration in the Grotte de Mescla in 1988 and that at Frais Puits in 1985.

It is essential to recall the amazing feats of the talented Bertrand Leger who, for well over a decade, contributed so much to cave diving explorations in France, and who tragically met his death in 1984 when he fell from a steep mountain path while portering diving equipment. It was Leger who completed most of the exploration in the Trou Madame. In February 1976, he passed a 915m sump in the Grotte de Balme to discover a 200m extension and in 1979, he dived the Bourne Sump in the Vercors for 1680m/

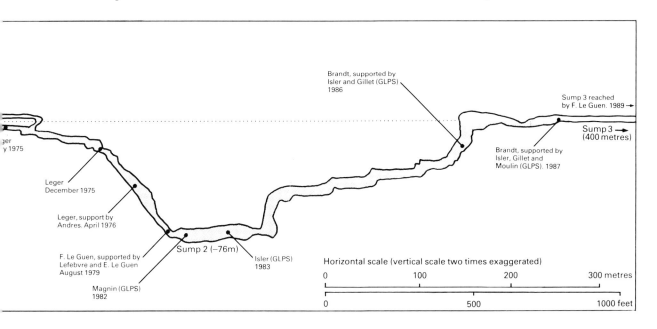

5512ft, then the longest continuous dive in the world. He was involved in countless other explorations, including long, deep penetrations at Grotte du Thais at St Nazaire-en-Royans and Grotte de Bournillon in the Vercors.

Likewise the long standing dedication of Claude Touloumdjian must also be stressed. Notable among his long penetrations was that at La Source du Bestouan in 1983 (2050m). He has also considerable expertise in the sphere of deep diving operations most notably his dive to a depth of 153m in the Fontaine de Vaucluse in October 1981. Since that time he has reached a depth of 100m at Cents Fons in 1985, 115m at Font D'estramar in 1988, and at 137m at the Fontaine des Chartreux in July 1989. In October 1990 he discovered a major lead in the Font de Lussac, part of the complex hydrological network of the Touvre Springs. This cave diving camp was, incidentally, attended by a host of other experienced divers such as Brandt and Isler, indicating the high degree of co-operation that now exists between these divers. The deepest dive on this occasion was made in the Bouillant Spring where Olivier Isler reached a depth of 148m.

Others have also made notable achievements in the deep diving sphere. In October 1985, for example,

Above: Francis Le Guen and Claude Touloumdjian, the two most prolific French cave divers of the 1980s.

Josef Schneider reached a depth of 140m at the major rising of Goul du Pont, at Bourg St Andeol, in the Ardèche area.

Spectacular caving discoveries have been made beyond many sumps in France. One interesting one took place in the early 1970s when divers from the Speleo Club de Dijon were rewarded by many kilometres of open passage beyond the 220m entrance sump of Riviere Souterraine du Neuvon. Today it is generally acknowledged that this cave, the Reseau du Verneau, is the longest system in the world to be explored beyond a series of sumps. With a length well in excess of thirty kilometres it presently rates fifth longest in France.

In June 1985 Patrick Penez made a 1080m dive in the Fontaine de Nimes to discover over three and a half kilometres of spectacular passage. There are many more examples extending throughout the country.

Near right: Claude Touloumdjian during his 2050m dive in La Source du Bestouan in 1983. The large elastic band allows stage bottles to be picked up and steamlined more easily. Top right and far right: Olivier Isler testing a dual rebreather at La Doux de Coly in 1989 which included speed trials on a modified Aquazepp 714T.

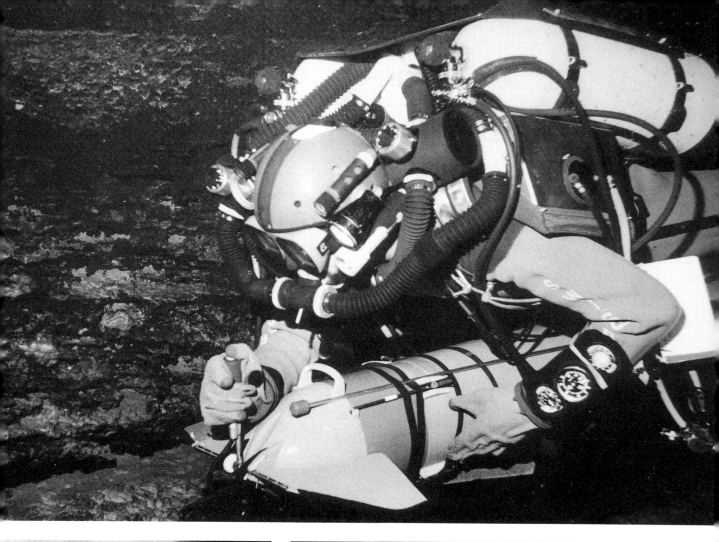

SWITZERLAND
including the French Jura.

Switzerland is a major caving country and cave diving has been undertaken here from the earliest years. As in most European nations, the first self-contained explorations into submerged caves involved the use of aqualungs, and took place in the mid-1950s. Perhaps the most significant of the early dives in this area was that at the Rinquelle Resurgence in 1959. Here, open water divers J. Marer and F. Hanschke made a one-hundred-metre penetration. It is noteworthy that much of the initial cave diving activity was made by open water divers who had trained in the Swiss lakes, where the water is often cold and turbid. Experience gained in these conditions provided a good foundation for cave diving.

It was the 1960s before real headway was achieved. Two explorations can be cited: at the Orbe resurgence and at the Chaudanne Spring. At the former, divers Protta, Sauty and Schmidt, three members of an open

Left: Francois de Charriére in the thirteen-metre shaft near the entrance of the Venoge Spring in the Jura in 1969. This cave passage was gained after an underwater dig by GLPS members. Note the single aqualung favoured by open water divers.

water association from Geneva, commenced exploration in 1961. A year later they reached a distance of 140m in a large passage at a maximum depth of twenty-three metres. In 1964, two other divers from Geneva discovered a dry extension from this sump, located just seventy metres from the entrance, which led to a major on-going cave. This was then explored by the divers and two of their friends; sadly, all other parties were excluded. The new dry cave was subsequently opened as a tourist attraction, but for cavers and cave divers little has changed and access remains difficult. The cave has now been mapped for about three kilometres and several promising sumps await thorough examination.

In the Chaudanne Spring the first dives were made in 1964 and 1965 by a few members of the Centre de Sports Sous-marins de Lausanne (CSSL): Claude Schmidt, André Piguet and Dominique d'Arman. Apart from Schmidt, they had no experience of caving. Chaudanne was narrow with ample quantities of silt. Even so the divers made a final penetration of 220m, a creditable achievement in difficult conditions.

In the late 1960s and early 1970s well trained teams began to emerge in Zurich, Geneva and Lausanne, the majority of members originating from the diving

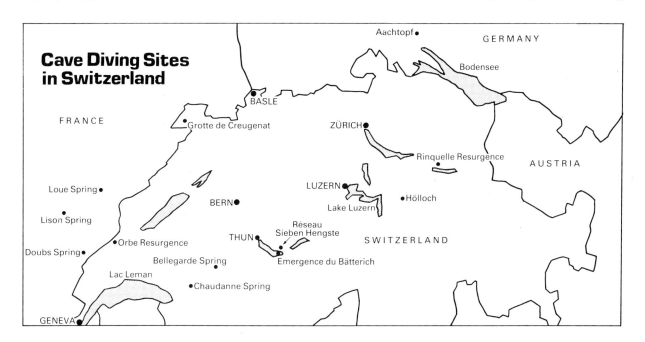

Cave Diving Sites in Switzerland

GERMANY
Aachtopf
Bodensee
FRANCE
BASLE
Grotte de Creugenat
ZÜRICH
Rinquelle Resurgence
AUSTRIA
Loue Spring
LUZERN
Hölloch
BERN
Lake Luzern
Lison Spring
Réseau Sieben Hengste
SWITZERLAND
Doubs Spring
Orbe Resurgence
THUN
Bellegarde Spring
Emergence du Bätterich
Lac Leman
Chaudanne Spring
GENEVA

sphere. It was at this time that cave diving techniques evolved and separated from those practised in the open water. The number of individuals within each group was never large and even in 1990 the total number of active divers probably did not exceed thirty.

Given the outstanding achievements of the GLPS in France, Italy and the Canary Islands, it is worth taking a brief look at the history of this group, and of the evolution of equipment and techniques. The Groupe Lemanique de Plongée Souterraine was founded in 1969 by the two speleologists Pierre Martin and Cyrille Brandt, who, at the time, were also members of the diving club (Centre de Sports Sous-marins de Lausanne, CSSL). In 1971 they were joined by Gilbert Paillex, and Mario Luini. In 1972, Gerard Domon and Olivier Isler became involved. The following year saw the addition of Claude Magnin and Philippe Schneider. Over the succeeding years four members remained very active, namely Brandt, Isler, Magnin and Schneider. Alain Vuagniaux also collaborated with their explorations in this period, and their last member, in 1981, was the equally determined, extremely capable Jean-Jacques Bolanz. The group was largely disbanded in about 1988.

From the outset their activities were centred upon the Alps and Prealps, and in the Swiss and French Jura. Notable penetrations in the early period included that at the Chaudanne, and in the Doue Spring where between 1971 and 1972 a short sump was to lead to a 350m dry extension. Also in the French Jura the Doubs Spring was penetrated for one hundred metres to a terminal depth of fifty-one metres in 1972. In 1975 a penetration of 170m, to sixty-one metres' depth, was achieved in the Bellegarde Spring (Prealps). Other dry extensions were also made at this time, namely at St Martin Cave (Alps), where a 700m discovery was achieved, and in Creugenat, where an extensive dry series nearly 1500m in length was located 150m beyond the air-bell that had been reached by the Standard Equipment divers in the 1930s.

From their inception the Swiss team were innovative and progressive, absorbing useful international techniques, and borrowing and inventing, where necessary, to advance their explorations. In 1975 constant volume dry suits were introduced, an approach copied from the Zurich cave divers. The years 1978-80 saw

Below: Gerard Domon at Doubs Spring, French Jura, during the 1972 exploration which reached a depth of fifty-one metres. Domon later became President of the Swiss Speleological Society.

the appearance of large and very large cylinders, until finally the huge, twenty-litre, back-mounted cylinders were adopted. Concurrent with this came the development of the staging technique, whereby a pair of slightly smaller bottles could be hung from the chest. In 1980 Isler, together with Magnin and Brandt, started using scooters. Cyrille Brandt commenced mixed gas diving in 1982, while at the same time he and Isler began their design of back-mounted triple, then quadruple twenty-litre sets. Perhaps the most consistent and determined member of the group, certainly in terms of inventiveness, has been Olivier Isler, who has gone on to introduce the semi-closed rebreather (RI 2000), which he developed with the help of electrical engineer Alain Ronjat.

Dives became longer and longer, and to remain at the forefront of the sport outstanding commitment is now required. What has become abundantly obvious and has been demonstrated in the recent development of the rebreather is that the time spent in technical preparation will continue to grow relative to the time spent on exploration.

Cave diving has proved extremely fruitful in Switzerland. In the first instance important caves have been connected. The best example is the connection of the

Above: Clear conditions in Blue Spring near Malbuisson, Doubs, France.

Below: Cyrille Brandt at the unassuming Chaudanne Spring which emerges at the height of 608m in the hills above Montreux. The difficulties at this important diving site are increased by the cold water conditions, the restricted 200m entry passage, and the poor visibility on exit.

Réseau Sieben Hengste-Hohgant to the Faustloch, giving a huge multi-entrance system now over 110km in length and 1020m deep. Another notable success has been achieved in the difficult terminal sump of the neighbouring Barenschacht, hydrologically also a part of the Sieben Hengste System. Here, at 565m below the entrance, access has been gained to thousands of metres of passage with the eventual hope that it will, one day, be part of a much larger system.

In a strict diving sense, long, deep sumps are relatively few, the most important exploration of this type being at the Chaudanne Spring. The GLPS mounted about twenty dives between 1984 and 1988, five of which made a significant advance. Isler and Brandt alternated the lead on these operations and the present limit here was set by Brandt in March 1988. It lies over 608m from the entrance at a terminal depth of 143m. At this point a huge shaft continues on into the

Left: Cyrille Brandt preparing his equipment in the entrance pool of Chaudanne Spring before his outstanding dive in March 1988.

Right: Brandt emerges after his epic penetration to 608m with a final depth of 140m in a cave that presents a highly technical challenge for future contenders.

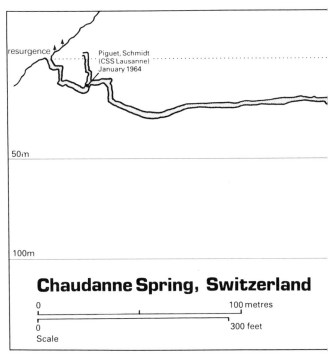

resurgence

Piguet, Schmidt
(CSS Lausanne)
January 1964

50m

100m

Chaudanne Spring, Switzerland

0	100 metres
0	300 feet

Scale

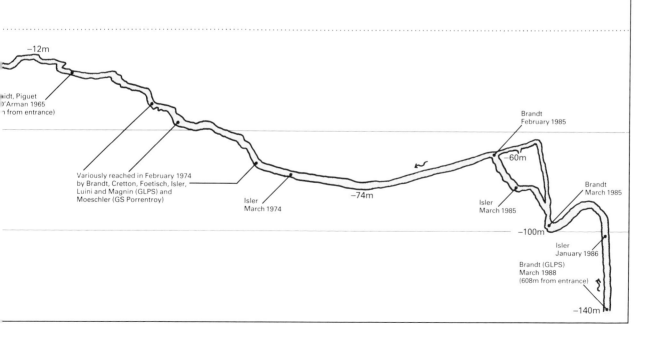

−12m

idt, Piguet
)'Arman 1965
ı from entrance)

Brandt
February 1985

−60m

Variously reached in February 1974
by Brandt, Cretton, Foetisch, Isler,
Luini and Magnin (GLPS) and
Moeschler (GS Porrentroy)

Brandt
March 1985

−74m

Isler
March 1974

Isler
March 1985

−100m

Isler
January 1986

Brandt (GLPS)
March 1988
(608m from entrance)

−140m

depths. The difficulty of mounting such a deep diving project at altitude (880m) is compounded by the narrow approach, poor visibility on exit and cold water.

A sump in the Motiers Cave has also been explored to considerable depth. The dive here is 250m in length, terminating at 103m depth, the latest penetration having been made by Jean-Jacques Bolanz in 1985.

The Rinquelle Resurgence has been the scene of the longest penetration in the country to date. The one-hundred-metre limit set in 1959 was dramatically advanced in 1973, when the German Jochen Hasenmayer reached an air surface after a 930m dive. This route, unfortunately, did not contain the main water flow, which he found later had been lost at 850m. Hasenmayer explored the correct route in

Above: Christoph Foetische at thirty metres depth in the Emergence de Bätterich (Bätterich Spring), during the 1975 GLPS explorations.

December 1975 and surfaced at 890m into an on-going passage. In 1978 he discovered Sump 2 which was later partially explored by GLPS members Magnin and Schneider. Hasenmayer continued these explorations in 1980 and 1981 and also advanced down the dead water of Sump 3 to 1080m from the entrance. Despite these efforts no continuation has been found.

Another interesting long and deep penetration has been set in the Bätterich Spring, which rises nine metres beneath the surface of Lake Thun. This complex, which is the rising for the Sieben Hengste System, has over 500m of mapped passages. The longest dive was made in 1974-75, when Brandt,

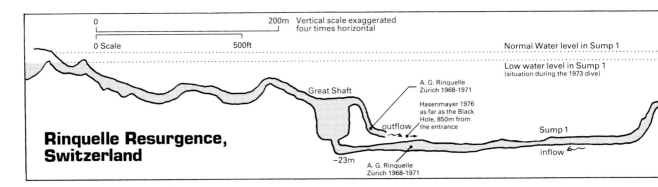

0   200m   Vertical scale exaggerated four times horizontal

0 Scale   500ft

Normal Water level in Sump 1

Low water level in Sump 1
(situation during the 1973 dive)

Great Shaft

A. G. Rinquelle
Zürich 1968-1971

Hasenmayer 1976
as far as the Black
Hole, 850m from
the entrance

Sump 1

outflow

inflow

Rinquelle Resurgence, Switzerland

−23m

A. G. Rinquelle
Zürich 1968-1971

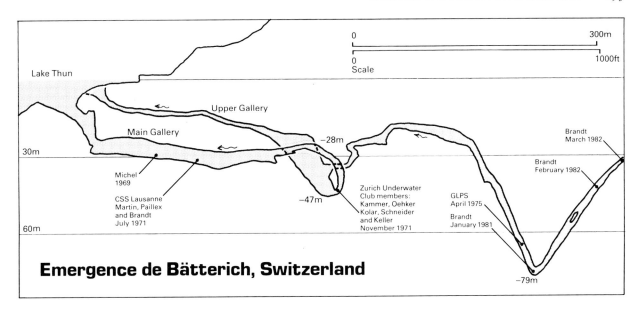

Emergence de Bätterich, Switzerland

supported by Schneider, Bolanz and others, made a 374m penetration involving a maximum depth of seventy-nine metres. Unfortunately, at the furthest point progress was halted by a boulder blockage. This dive took three hours and was made on air.

GERMANY

Cave diving in Germany has been dominated for over thirty years by Jochen Hasenmayer, who, always operating alone, has made many major discoveries. Hasenmayer became an open water diver at the age of nine. In 1958, aged fourteen, he became interested in gaining access to the Falkenstein Hölle between Stuttgart and Ulm. The water at this site is very cold

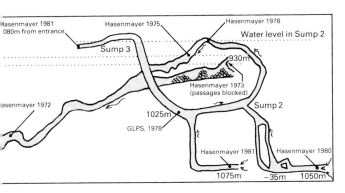

so he constructed a dry suit using rubberised bed sheets sealed with innertube repair glue. As he had no zip he had to seal himself into the suit each time he dived and cut himself out afterwards. The suit was so effective that it allowed him to wear warm woollen underwear and sweaters. The cave is guarded by small shallow sumps which he tackled by free diving, carrying an aqualung in reserve in case they proved longer than expected. In this manner he passed sumps of four metres, one and a half metres and fifty metres (much of this being a duck) at a depth of less than a metre, and thereby gained access to the main river passage. Over the following twenty years he advanced this exploration to five kilometres, overcoming twenty-six sumps. All of these were tight and heavily silted, the biggest being eighty metres long and fifty metres deep. With a total diving distance of 400m, and with the constrictions only allowing the use of small cylinders, the problem of getting sufficient air supplies to the end to make further advances is now the main obstacle to progress.

The main German cave diving sites are in the Schwäbische Alb between the Bodensee and Ulm. This is the continuation of the limestone strata that begins at Grenoble, runs as the Jura along the northern Swiss border and thence into Germany north of the Bodensee. The hydrology of the upper Danube near Tuttlingen, north-west of the Bodensee, is particularly interesting. Here the river disappears below a dry bed and enters a steep underground system which diverts it into the Bodensee, which, in turn, feeds the Rhine. After a fall of 175m, the redirected waters emerge at Aachtopf with a water-flow ranging from 10,000 to 30,000 litres per second (in spate conditions). Despite this strong current and consistent one-metre visibility, Hasenmayer has systematically explored the Aachtopf resurgence, discovering over 1000m of flooded passages and making a maximum penetration of 570m.

The Blautopf Explorations

The most notable cave in Germany is the Blautopf at Blaubeuren, west of Ulm. This is a long underwater passage with variable visibility and a water-flow ranging from 2,000 to 30,000 litres per second, the latter after storms or during a thaw. All the caverns along this passage have deep beds of silt, so visibility when returning is always bad. In 1961 Hasenmayer reached the deepest point, known as the Bunker, just over one hundred metres from the entrance and, since then, with seven more advances, has extended his penetration to reach the first air space at the stupendous Mörike Dom (Cathedral) 1250m from the entrance. This is the most impressive underground lake/cavern in Germany, measuring 125m long, 25m wide and 90m high.

Only one other group has contributed to the Blautopf exploration: in 1963 divers from the Göppinger Cave Diving Club advanced a short distance beyond the Bunker to the Lift. Sadly the Göppinger divers' activities ended in disaster four years later. When Wellhöfer and Adolf Holder were surveying the Bunker, Holder miscalculated his air supply and died. The Bunker was also the scene of another accident that befell two open water divers in 1983. As far as can be ascertained, they lost their line, became disorientated, panicked and drowned. The Göppinger accident had the effect of delaying the emergence of other groups and Hasenmayer remained the only serious cave diving activist for many years. There are now about fifteen German cave divers, the most successful of the new breed being Josef Schneider, who, in 1987, made a dive to 140m depth in Goul du Pont in France. Also of international standard is Axel Gnädinger who has been very active in Germany in multi-sumped caves.

Hasenmayer's Accident

Hasenmayer's career as one of the world's leading cave divers came to an abrupt halt in 1989, when he sustained a crippling accident while diving for TV in the Wolfgangsee, east of Salzburg. A faulty depth gauge led him to attempt decompression at twenty-five metres, rather than forty metres, and within seconds his legs were paralysed. He surfaced and was placed in a decompression chamber, where he was able to move his legs. All might have been well, but, in his subsequent treatment in two specialist hospitals further decompression errors were made and he is now permanently crippled, though he hopes to dive again. He continues his innovation and research, and is also writing his autobiography, which will surely add a wealth of fascinating detail to illuminate his amazing solo career as an underwater explorer *par excellence*.

Right: Jochen Hasenmayer with the equipment he used for a filming dive to the Mörike Dom in Blautopf in 1985.

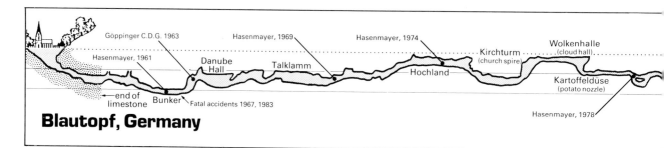

Blautopf, Germany

Göppinger C.D.G. 1963   Hasenmayer, 1969   Hasenmayer, 1974   Wolkenhalle (cloud hall)

Hasenmayer, 1961   Danube Hall   Talklamm   Kirchturm (church spire)   Hochland   Kartoffeldüse (potato nozzle)

end of limestone   Bunker   Fatal accidents 1967, 1983   Hasenmayer, 1978

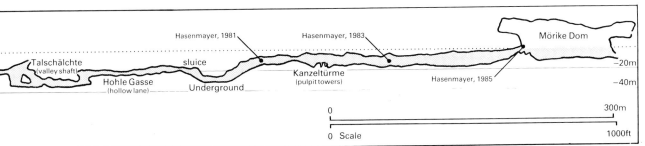

Talschälchte
(valley shaft)

Hohle Gasse
(hollow lane)

sluice

Underground

Hasenmayer, 1981

Hasenmayer, 1983

Kanzeltürme
(pulpit towers)

Hasenmayer, 1985

Mörike Dom

−20m

−40m

0

300m

0   Scale

1000ft

CANARY ISLANDS

The Exploration of the Atlantida Tunnel

While it is impractical here to give a detailed account of cave diving activities in all the major countries of Europe, I would like to conclude this section by describing the exploration of the Atlantida Tunnel. This is an intriguing subterranean passage situated on Lanzarote in the Canary Islands, off the north-west coast of Africa. Unlike the slow process of cave formation that has given rise to the limestone systems with which we are now familiar, the Atlantida Tunnel owes its origin to a sudden volcanic eruption. In this instance a flow of molten lava poured down the slope from the now dormant volcano Mont Corona. As the flow moved downhill it left in its wake a tunnel, which is over seven kilometres long, terminating at a sump when it reaches sea-level. Along the surface route there are several points where the roof has collapsed, places which today provide convenient access to the underground network. Just how far the tunnel extended out beneath the sea was impossible to establish without diving.

The exploration of this site provides an interesting and exciting story. The first recorded dive was by A. and J. M. Guerra, who reached a point 240m from base, and later 370m. In 1981 a team of Italian divers continued to 410m, followed later in the same year by a team of Spanish divers from the Club STD Madrid. Led by J. Garcia, this group pushed on to 820m and a predictably deeper terminal depth of thirty-two metres.

Two years later an extremely strong group of Americans arrived as part of a German biological expedition. The Germans were not divers, but had been studying the unique, crab-like crustaceans (*Galatheoidea*) in the terminal pool. The divers were Tom Iliffe, Rob Power, Mary van Soeren, Dennis Williams, Ken Fulghum, Clark Pitcairn and Sheck Exley. Other than the adoption of scooters, the team used all the equipment and techniques normally employed in Florida. Equipped with their normal rig of two back-mounted 100 cu.ft bottles (250 cu.ft of air), their first effective penetration reached about 810m, within sight of the Spanish limit.

The next day Exley and Pitcairn dived with four bottles apiece, intent upon pushing into uncharted territory. The passage continued, as before, along a huge black tunnel with very little silt. It was a fascinating experience, with walls frequently smooth and contoured, and displaying unique bench-like features where the fast-flowing lava had carved them away. On this dive the pair laid an additional 414m/1372ft of line, and tied off at 1278m. Here, the proverbial 'railway tunnel' continued as before, but now the depth was fifty-three metres. With this penetration Exley and Pitcairn had set a new world record penetration for marine caves, surpassing the dive made by our British team in the Bahamas in 1982.

Atlantida Tunnel: Fulghum's and Exley's Lucky Escape

For the next operation Fulghum was to be Exley's partner, while Williams and Power acted as support divers, transporting four stage bottles to the 470m mark. It appeared that another advance was virtually assured.

Initially all went according to plan. Exley and Fulghum reached the end uneventfully, tied on fresh line, and moved forward. As is normal procedure in a large passage, the pair maintained a position as close to the roof as possible to conserve their air. Even with their powerful lights the tunnel was dark, a far cry from the lighter normal cave sump. By now their depth gauges were reading over fifty-four metres, a depth at which nitrogen narcosis begins its insidious assault upon mental faculties. Suddenly, one hundred metres beyond the previous terminus, there was a crisis. One of Fulghum's regulators developed a catastrophic high pressure leak. By the time he realised something was seriously wrong and had swum on a few metres to alert Exley most of his air had vented to waste. He had about 400 p.s.i. remaining, compared to 3000 when these cylinders are full. Ironically, the dual valve manifold – which was designed to give the diver access to both bottles should either of his regulators fail – had, in this instance, emptied both bottles.

Exley now took the initiative. He insisted that they immediately start to share his (Exley's) air, keeping what little remained in Fulghum's bottles for an

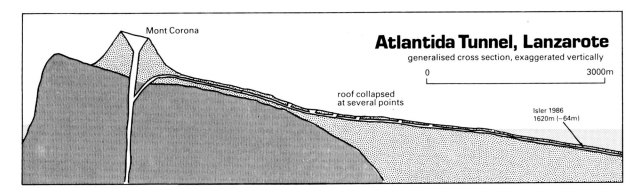

Atlantida Tunnel, Lanzarote
generalised cross section, exaggerated vertically

Mont Corona

0   3000m

roof collapsed
at several points

Isler 1986
1620m (−64m)

absolute emergency. They started on the long swim back to the surface. What followed can only be described as a nightmare. Both divers were only too aware that they were over 1200m/4000ft from safety and at a depth of over fifty metres, an awful long way in for such an unimaginable catastrophe. The stress level must have been high. Doing their best to control their breathing, both were aware that life was in the balance. How close to the edge they were became all too apparent when they began to run low on air. At this point Fulghum went back on to his own back-mounted bottles, enabling Exley to eke out his own supply a little further. Fulghum was now swimming fairly fast, possibly too energetically for optimum conservation of air. Despite all their efforts, they ran out of air completely, before reaching their first stage bottles. Fortunately they could see the supply a short way ahead and holding their breath they just made it. By now the stress was becoming overwhelming.

They had gained extra time. On and on they swam, until Fulghum ran out of air yet again. They began to share air for a second time. The situation was traumatic and Exley's incredible powers of self-discipline were put to the most severe test. Despite his iron control, the air supply was rapidly drained until the cylinder was empty. On this occasion they couldn't even see the next set of stage bottles, which were around a slight corner. Once more they held their breath, swam for their lives, and once more they were saved.

Miraculously they made it back to the decompression point. Even here their problems were not over. They were still desperately short of air. Fulghum surfaced momentarily, shouted to the other team members for emergency air, and descended again. Fortunately help was quickly at hand and both surfaced at the end of their lengthy decompression period shaken by their ordeal, but unscathed. Exley's level-headed composure and courage had delivered them both from almost certain death.

Hitherto such equipment failure had been completely unknown in cave diving and, despite the competent diving skills displayed by the pair, they could count themselves exceedingly lucky. They had established a new world record, and in all certainty had survived one of the worst traumas in the annals of cave diving.

Atlantida Tunnel Dives in 1985 and 1986
In 1985 Spanish divers from Club STD Madrid took up the challenge yet again. On a well-prepared expedition Mari Carmen Portilla and Luis Ortega Cordiente reached 1578m at sixty metres' depth.

The final stage in the exploration came in 1986 when Swiss GLPS divers, including Brandt, Schneider and Isler, joined with a Franco-Belgian group to mount the most technical expedition to date. Using a twinned Aquazepp arrangement (similar to that used at the Doux de Coly the previous year), staging techniques, gas mixtures and finally oxygen for decompression, it was predictably a very efficient and thorough preparation. Olivier Isler made the final exploration, which was terminated somewhat prematurely at 1620m/5248ft by a solid wall of rock at sixty-four metres' depth. The end of the Atlantida Tunnel, the longest marine cave in the world, and a unique volcanic tunnel in its own right, had finally been reached.

THE SOVIET UNION

It is perhaps significant that in such a brief outline of diving activities in various corners of the globe that little mention has been made thus far of the USSR both in Europe and Asia. Tremendous scope for cave exploration exists here.

The Soviet Union has some of the world's deepest caves and tremendous potential in all aspects of speleology. Over the past few years Soviet teams have made determined efforts to put a Soviet cave at the head of the depth league. In the late 1980s, for example, the Snezhnaya system, in the Caucasus, crept to second place. In 1988 this was bettered by the 1508m long Vjacheslav Pantjukhin system and it appears that a depth of 1700m is ultimately possible which, at present, would probably be sufficient to take the world depth record.

Cave diving commenced in the Soviet Union in the early 1960s concurrent with the first serious cave explorations. Divers from Moscow are credited with the earliest dive explorations in a number of resurgences in the Crimea. However, in the 1960s and 1970s few caving clubs undertook activity in this specialist area, the most notable being the Krasnojarsk club (Siberia), Sevastopol (Crimea), Perm (Urals), and Moscow.

In 1989 there were about 160 cave divers in approximately twenty clubs: Baltic States (Kaunas), Ukraine (Kiev, Dnepropetrovsk, Simferopol), Urals (Perm, Salavat, Omsk), Central Asia (Kirgizia, Turkmenia), Caucasus (Rostov, Sochi, Tbilisi), Siberia (Krasnojarsk, Tomsk), Far East (Vladivostok), Moscow, and Leningrad. To co-ordinate the activities of these widely scattered groups a cave diving commission was established by the Soviet Speleological Association in 1988. Today annual cave diving seminars are held by the Krasnojarsk cave club involving lectures and practical training sessions.

Another recent development has been the organisation of cave diving expeditions, where participation by as many clubs as possible is encouraged. The most successful of these to date has been to the West Caucasus, where, in 1986, for example, four kilometres of passages were explored and surveyed beyond a series of sumps. In January 1987 twenty cave divers from six clubs were involved and on this occasion they explored twenty new sumps totalling 830m of submerged cave with some five kilometres of passage beyond.

Soviet cave divers usually adopt two or perhaps three seven-litre cylinders, each with independent valves. Commercial or sports demand valves are not always available and divers frequently resort to models normally used for industrial purposes, equipment which often requires modification before it is suitable for use in the cave environment. Constant improvements are being made in both equipment and techniques, and during the late 1980s divers from Krasnojarsk and Rostov started to operate with a semi-open system of oxygen-air gas mixtures. Much ancillary equipment is often home-made; latex dry suits, for example, which are the most popular dress for both caving and diving, fall into this category. Diving lines are made from telephone cable, which serves not only to connect the diver with the surface, but also for communication purposes after a sump has been passed.

Cave diving is increasingly being undertaken right across the USSR, from the West Ukraine to the Far East and from the Archangel region to the southern borders. The following is a brief review of the most interesting areas and sites explored to date.

Siberia

In the Sayan region divers from Krasnojarsk have explored the Lysanskaja Resurgence Cave for a submerged distance of 400m, reaching a boulder choke 180m into the terminal sump, at a depth of eighteen metres.

Urals

Divers from the Perm club have explored numerous sumps near the Chusovaja River in the central Urals including the Blue Lake system, a resurgence which has similar characteristics to the Fontaine de Vaucluse. In the summer of 1988 they achieved a penetration of 600m to a terminal depth of fifty-six metres in this powerful resurgence. In the southern Urals a number

of difficult dives have been made in caves near the Belaja (White) River.

Central Asia

Cave divers from Gaurdak (Turkmenia) and Moscow have explored a sump in the Gissar Range of the Kugitang Mountains, passing a narrow fissure to a depth of twenty-three metres, beyond which they entered a huge chamber with a depth of over fifty-nine metres. Here the temperature of the water rose to 16°C giving clear evidence of deep thermal heating. Also in this region sump exploration has been conducted at the bottom of the major, deep cave systems of Kievskaja (−990m/3248ft) and Uralskaja (−565m/1854ft).

Caucasus

By far the most spectacular diving and the major discoveries have been made in the West Caucasus. In this region two mountain areas have proved particularly fruitful to cavers and divers alike, the

Above: A Krasnojarsk diver in the Mchishta Resurgence, West Caucasus, U.S.S.R. in 1988 – a very complex cave which has formed the focal point for prodigous efforts by Soviet cave divers in recent years.

Arabika Massif and the Bzybskij Ridge.

Major explorations on the Arabika Massif include that at the Gegskaja resurgence, where Peter Minenkow, the leading Soviet cave diver from the Krasnojarsk club, has undertaken a 220m penetration to a depth of fifty-five metres. Minenkow has also achieved many successful exploratory dives in the deep cave systems. However, the most significant discoveries to date must surely be those by Moscow divers at Vladimir Iljukhin Cave. From the first sump, situated 970m below the surface, the divers pushed through a series of three submerged sections to reach the present limit, one hundred metres into Sump 4 at twenty-two metres' depth and some 1240m below the surface.

On the Bzybskij Ridge equally determined explorations have been made. The sumps at the bottom of Napra Cave have been tackled to reach a terminal

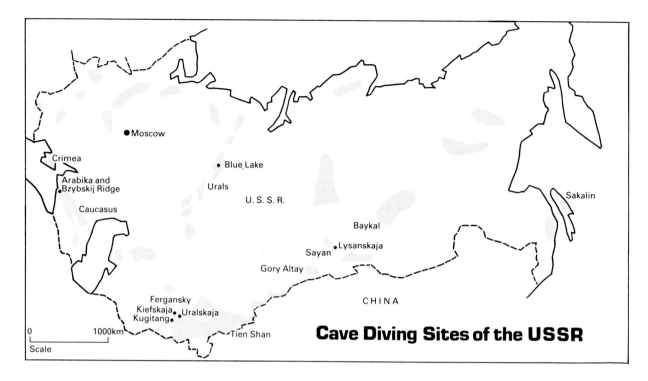

Cave Diving Sites of the USSR

depth of 920m, which, together with the neighbouring systems of Pionerskaja Shaft (800m depth) and Vesenjaja Cave (fourth sump situated at 550m depth), drain to the massive, ten-cubic-metres resurgence at Mchishta. It is not surprising that, with an overall depth potential in this system of 2345m, it has attracted highly determined efforts from many groups over the past few years.

Mchishta was dived for sixty metres in the early eighties, and, despite considerable complexity one branch was passed in August 1987, following dives of 130m (depth – twenty-two metres) and 230m (depth – forty-five metres). About one and a half kilometres of richly decorated passages were found on the first expedition, more recently extended to over three kilometres. Two further sumps are encountered at the present terminus of this system, at one of which divers from the Krasnojarsk club reached a depth of fifty-five metres in February 1988.

The complex entrance sump to Mchishta has yet to be fully explored. In 1988, for example, one of the leading French divers, Claude Touloumdjian, followed a passage to over sixty-five metres' depth – a large,

deep conduit which, according to dye tests, offers a potential continuation to the major Snezhnaya Cave, situated over ten kilometres away.

Also in West Georgia exciting discoveries have been made in the Tskhaltubo Cave system and in the one kilometre long Tsivtskala resurgence. Another impressive find, however, has been made in Sakishori Cave. Three short sumps were passed to yield about three kilometres of passage on the first expedition, while a subsequent trip extended this to over six kilometres. The longest Soviet cave surveyed beyond a dive also lies in this area, namely Khabju resurgence in the New Afon massif. Over eight kilometres of passage now lie beyond the short sump at the entrance.

Despite the limited number of activists and the evident constraints posed by lack of versatile equipment and travel difficulties, the Soviets are obviously making good progress in the field of cave diving. We can certainly expect a spate of major discoveries in the coming years.

Right: The leading Soviet cave diver Vladimir Kisseljov in action in Kungurskaja, Urals, in 1989 (near right) and after a 120m long dive in Kidobana Cave.

CHAPTER TEN

NORTH AND CENTRAL AMERICA

THE UNITED STATES OF AMERICA

The United States is a major cave diving country with tremendous potential. Aqualung diving first began here in 1951 in Florida, which, despite having generally flat, low-lying terrain, is today the foremost cave diving region in the world.

Florida has well over 1500 cave diving sites, almost all of which are totally flooded subterranean waterways mostly fed by seepage water through the surface limestone, as opposed to the sinking streams more common in Europe. The presence of such waterways is usually indicated by large surface pools or springs, which provide relatively convenient access for cave divers. The water is invariably warm, averaging 22°C, and the nature of the subterranean flow tends to create much clearer conditions than in caves fed by surface streams. Visibility often exceeds thirty metres. This remains unaffected during the severe local storms when visibility in a more typical upland cave could be reduced to zero by the rush of water passing through them. Some of the sites are very accessible, and from the outset proved popular venues for divers unable to dive in the ocean due to severe weather conditions. In terms of popularity and sheer numbers of participants the Springs of northern Florida are unequalled.

Early Exploration at Wakulla Springs
Serious cave diving exploration began in the 1950s. Without wet suits, buoyancy aids or many other items of contemporary diving equipment now taken for granted, some highly significant explorations were made. The honour of the first SCUBA dive into a cave in the United States belongs to Charles McNabb and Bill Ray at Silver Springs, but certainly the most notable exploration was that at Wakulla Springs, a huge resurgence set in the heart of swamplands thirteen miles south of Tallahassee. It was here, in 1955 and 1956, that divers Wally Jenkins, Garry Salsman, Andy Harrold, Lamarr Trott, Henry Doll and Gordon Whitney made over a hundred dives and some tremendously exciting discoveries. With an entrance twenty metres high and forty-five metres wide, this is one of the world's largest springs, with an average outflow of 390 cu.ft per minute, leading steeply and directly to a huge ongoing passage of clear water at a depth of fifty-five metres. Equipped with twin 72 cu.ft bottles, a single twin-hose demand valve apiece, and with little or no protection against the cold these divers from Florida State University eventually penetrated the massive tunnel a distance of about 150m, reaching depths of around seventy-six metres.

At the time these dives constituted both the longest and the deepest cave diving penetrations in the world. The only other comparable contemporary penetration lay at France's Port Miou, near Marseilles, on the Mediterranean coast.

Other than the achievements of length and depth, the dives were to reveal spectacular fossil remains. Large quantities of massive bones were discovered dating from the Pleistocene era, remains of animals which had been extinct in North America for well over 10,000 years. Over time the team were to recover bones of camel, deer and sloth, but certainly the most fascinating was that of a mastodon, one of the last great creatures of the Ice Age. Sufficient bones were eventually retrieved for archaeologists to be able to reconstruct one of these mammals: an animal that in life would have stood nearly three metres high at the shoulder, reached a length of five metres, weighed

Right: Garry Salsman diving in the entry pool of Wakulla in 1955.

Left: Scenes during the Wakulla dives of 1955-56. Top left: Raising a mastodon bone from the cave bed using an inflated pillow case. Top right: Garry Salsman and Wally Jenkins, the initiators of the 1955 exploration, who made the deepest penetration of the cave to a point 290m from the entrance at a depth of 73m.
Bottom: Entering the main Wakulla streamway.

Above: Sheck Exley in the 1970s wearing the typical equipment of that time including the powerful hand-held light units, essential in the large tunnels.

over ten tons, and eaten some 300lbs of leafy vegetation each day. The Wakulla mastodon is today a prime exhibit at the Museum of Florida History, Tallahassee.

The discovery of such remains is not restricted to the bottom of the entrance slope. Some bones have since been found as far as 365m into Wakulla. This and evidence derived from other sources indicates that during the last Ice Age, perhaps 20,000 years ago, the caves were dry. Animals and perhaps homo sapiens, frequented these holes in search of water, and it seems likely that many creatures were simply unable to clamber out again.

Other Early Florida Dives

Wakulla was closed to divers from the late 1950s and other sites rapidly gained in popularity. Hornsby Spring, near the town of High Springs, was the first cave in the world to witness a penetration in excess of 300m. This was achieved by John Harper, Hoyt Roberts and Larry Hylton in 1962. In December of that year, in company with Joe Fuller, Harper went on to achieve another record: a traverse of 643m at Hornsby. And so it went on. In 1969 a world record penetration of 549m/1800ft was achieved at Blue Spring, near Madison, while in June the following year Harper and Randy Hylton established another record traverse of 1430m/4693ft from Orange Grove Sink to Peacock Springs.

By 1970 another explorer had set his mark upon the American scene – Sheck Exley.* Exley was a caver, but primarily a cave diver, who has continued to make major contributions to cave diving activities throughout North America for two decades and is now regarded as one of the world's leading experts in the field – the Reinhold Messner of the cave diving world.

Exley made his first cave dive in 1965 and, when Harper retired (following the death of his friend Hylton*), led the sport to ever greater achievements.

Exley's enthusiasm was quite unique. Among his many early achievements was the establishment of a record penetration of 640m/2099ft in 1971, and he was, for example, the first explorer to achieve 1000 cave dives, closely followed by Tom Mount. He has now logged over 3000 cave dives.

Conditions and Equipment in Florida

Florida's ideal conditions are the epitome of what all cave divers would like to experience and, as a direct

---

* The unforgiving nature of the underwater world was brought home to Exley at a very early stage. In 1967 he (18) and his younger brother Edward (16) attempted to snorkel at the most impressive of Florida springs – Wakulla. Here his brother suffered a shallow water blackout, and sank to over thirty metres. By the time Sheck had sprinted to a car for an aqualung, dived and brought his brother to the surface, ten minutes had elapsed, and attempts at resuscitation proved futile.

* Randy Hylton was one of the best divers in Florida. He had routinely dived in caves to a depth of over seventy-five metres and at the time of his death (1972) had become the seventh of only eight people known to have survived a dive to 122m on air. Tragically Hylton died at a depth of forty-seven metres. It is believed he suffered a heart attack while trying to free himself from a severe line entanglement. His brother, Larry, also died (1962) while cave diving.

Above: The American dual-valve manifold based upon the successful crossover manifold designed by George Benjamin.

result of the advantageous conditions, tremendous attention has been paid to the design and evolution of optimum equipment and techniques.

Where equipment is concerned, divers have been able to reap the benefits of economy of scale. Back-mounted double cylinders (100 cu.ft each) joined by a dual-valve manifold* came to be regarded as the optimum arrangement in 1973, and this basic set up was maintained well into the 1980s. With a normal working pressure of 2400 p.s.i., experienced cave divers often fill these to 3600 p.s.i. (even 4000 for a very serious push), thereby carrying approximately 300 cu.ft of air. Sadly, the Pressed Steel Corporation,

* The dual-valve manifold is designed so that both valves provide access to the entire air supply. In the event of a malfunction to either valve the diver only has to turn off the supply to the faulty regulator, switch to the other supply and head out of the cave.

which was the sole supplier of the 104 cu.ft steel bottles in the United States, recently discontinued this line of cylinder citing liability concerns over cave divers overpumping them.

The cylinders are fitted with two single-hose regulators, one of which normally incorporates a much longer length of hose, designed for sharing air in an emergency. Today most Florida cave divers adopt a two-metre/seven-foot hose for this purpose, but some who make longer pushes utilising a scooter use a three-metre hose. These are stowed, using elastic cords, in a folded fashion behind the twin tank manifold. Illumination consists of one very bright light (generally between 125 and 150 watts) from a rechargeable belt pack, and perhaps four other supplementary or reserve units.

Constant volume dry suits are today generally regarded as essential for long or deep penetrations. Additional buoyancy compensating devices, such as BC vests (known as ABLJs in Britain) or stabilizing jackets may also be used, but considering the tremendous weight of twin hundred cylinders (approximately 125 lbs) another type of compensator is also frequently worn, namely a BC pack, more commonly referred to as 'wings'. This floatation is usually mounted directly alongside the tank assembly, the close proximity of air bladder and steel cylinders virtually eliminating the problem of instability.

The equipment list is completed by the addition of a spare mask, line reel, an emergency jump reel, depth gauge, watch, submersible decompression tables, slate and pencil, forearm knife, and compass. A prudent diver might also include a few directional line 'clips' (placed on the line at a junction to avoid any confusion with regard to the exit route) and some elementary tools.

It should be noted here that American sump divers, exploring sites similar to those encountered in Britain, are now regularly using a knot code for pointing the way to the dive base. This consists of three overhand knots in the line at ten metre intervals. Two of the knots are close together (about five centimetres) and the third is about thirty centimetres away, on the entrance side of the cluster. This can be felt even with wet suit gloves, essential in nil visibility.

As might be expected, in Florida techniques also differ substantially from methods adopted in caves with serious silting and visibility problems such as many in Britain and some in other European sites. The art of neutral buoyancy – the technique whereby the diver floats effortlessly in mid-passage in predominantly horizontal direction – has been perfected in Florida. Diving in such a manner minimizes silt disturbance and promotes good visibility on the way out. It also helps conserve the fragile environment.

Another significant contrast concerns the attitude to solo diving. In the environment of a cramped sump with a strong current it is often impossible to avoid silt disturbance. Under these conditions (the norm in Britain) diver-to-diver communication is fraught with difficulty and solo diving is generally advocated as the safest procedure. In Florida, and certainly where novices are involved, this is generally frowned upon. Many recommendations concerning cave diving in this area were originally influenced and formulated by organisations composed almost entirely of non-cavers, skin-divers who took up cave diving when the weather was too rough for sea diving. In other areas of the United States, where conditions are more akin to those of Britain, solo diving *is* the norm. For long or deep penetrations in Florida, however, the best approach would appear to be that of the three-man team, although people such as Exley frequently conduct long distance exploratory work completely alone.

Accidents and Training Programmes

As a direct result of favourable conditions and relative ease of travel the numbers of divers visiting Florida each year is substantial. In 1974 it was estimated that a minimum of 10,000 divers made at least one cave dive. The total number of dives probably exceeded a quarter of a million.

Above: Sheck Exley and Dave Cameron entering Jenny Springs, Florida. In the clear conditions of Florida caves divers often work in pairs, or even in trios.

Such participation in what is essentially an extremely dangerous pursuit for the uninitiated has inevitably led to a significant number of fatalities: in the twenty years from 1960 to the beginning of 1980, for example, 194 divers perished while attempting a cave diving experience. An additional twelve people died while cave diving in the remainder of the country during the same period. The worst year was unquestionably 1974, when no fewer than twenty-six people died. Since that time, the number of deaths has fallen sharply, despite increasing participants, thanks to the educational efforts of the various bodies associated with both diving and caving.

By the mid-1970s cave diving had come of age, and today organisations such as the Cave Diving Section of the National Speleological Society (NSS) and the National Association of Cave Diving (NACD) are respected worldwide for promoting safe cave diving.

Strong emphasis is laid upon training programmes under qualified instructors, progressive courses designed to acclimatise a qualified open water diver in the special skills and techniques of a submerged cave environment. Divers, therefore, progress from a basic

Above: A warning sign near the entrance of Little River Spring. These drastic measures have been prompted by the high level of fatalities to open water divers entering caves without adequate cave diving knowledge or training.

the uninitiated, the NSS and NACD have installed underwater signs a short distance into heavily travelled springs. These give clear warning to divers that they should be trained in cave diving or go no further. It should be noted that at least forty-six divers have died at the Peacock Springs system alone since 1968. Nearly all violated some basic tenant of safe cave diving, the most common error being continuing into the cave without a line.

Cavern Diver Course – duration approximately two days – to more advanced certification. As a measure of diver training in the area it should be noted that over 7,000 people have now passed through NSS training courses alone.

Sites such as Ginnie Springs, near High Springs, have been developed along commercial lines. Here, and at other inland dive centres, there are stores that hire and sell gear, places which cater specifically for divers intent upon a 'cave diving experience'.

Slogans such as 'never dive alone' are promoted, principles that contain obvious merit in such a favourable environment. The guidelines for a 'cavern diver' are quite specific: divers should not progress beyond the daylight zone, beyond a linear distance of forty metres, to a depth in excess of twenty-one metres, or beyond any constriction too small for two divers to pass through together. They must be connected by a line to the surface and never exceed 'no decompression' limits.

Since the early 1980's, in a further effort to deter

Tactics for Long Dives

An advanced procedure that has been well developed in this area is 'stage diving'. This consists of carrying extra aqualungs into the cave in addition to the normally adopted apparatus. Extra units may be carried in and recovered on the same dive, or they may be staged at predetermined locations on previous dives, and recovered on a later dive. In terms of weight, drag and pure bulk of equipment, this method is highly advantageous. By these means far longer dive durations are achieved.

There are, of course, problems which have to be borne in mind. The technique requires each and every member of the dive team to be thoroughly trained and confident in his ability to endure the stress of a long pushing dive. Practice in open water is essential, so that all divers pay the utmost care and attention to where and how the staging takes place. It is, of course, imperative to locate one's stage cylinders on the exit, so the whole operation must be well planned and executed. The most experienced explorers now adopt a 'staging-on-the-fly' technique for exchanging bottles underwater. While approaching the spot where a depleted stage bottle is to be deposited the diver turns off the cylinder valve and unclips this bottle from his harness before he reaches the drop zone. Then, with one hand motion, and without stopping forward movement, he clips off the bottle to the guideline. A short distance ahead, he picks up the next stage bottle 'on-the-fly', clips it to his harness and still swimming, opens the valve and then makes the switch.

Other Long Florida Dives in the 1970s

Using such equipment and methods, Exley, Paul DeLoach, Dr John Zumrick, and Mary Ellen Eckhoff continued to advance into uncharted waterways. In May 1975 Exley, Court Smith and Holtzendorff achieved a record penetration at Manatee Springs. Diving at around twenty-six metres' depth, they progressed from the previous limit of 1206m to 1253m. Again, in March 1978, Exley, accompanied this time by Dale Sweet, furthered the exploration of the Hole in the Wall Spring to 1380m/4527ft from the entrance. This operation involved a total of four hours' diving and decompression time.

Exley, Turner, Smith and Holtzendorff also made a record traverse in July 1973. Diving between the Orange Grove Sink entrance to the Waterhole entrance of Peacock Springs, the team established a line distance of 2152m/7060ft at the time the longest underwater traverse in the world. In the process, establishing this fine system as the longest known (and mapped) underwater cave system in North America. By 1979 over 5791m of passage had been surveyed. This record is today held by the Cathedral Canyon System, with over 11,000m of passage.

Diver Propulsion Vehicles

By the late 1970s the quest for ever longer penetrations was to witness another exciting development in Florida, namely the popularisation of Diver Propulsion Vehicles (DPVs) or scooters, as they are nicknamed by cave divers. Hasenmayer had used a German manufactured Aquazepp as early as 1973 at the Rinquelle Resurgence in Switzerland, while earlier still the Canadian cave diver George Benjamin had used a Farallon machine to assist his explorations in the Blue Holes of the Bahamas. In Florida scooters were first used by Tex Chalkley and Bob Goodman, when they furthered the exploration of River Sink (also known as

the Emerald or Sullivan System) in the mid-1970s.

DPVs came into play in very distinct phases in Florida. From 1973 to 1982 the Farallon Mark VII was the only available machine and this was used to considerable benefit well into the 1980s. Using these, a significant milestone at this time was the 1700m penetration set in Big Dismal Sink in 1980, by Exley's team. The Farallon DPVs continued to be used even after the Tekna machines first became available in 1980. The original problem with the Tekna was that its shell could not tolerate pressures much below forty metres, which rendered it near useless in most of the springs then being explored. People like Bill Gavin developed a novel means of converting these, usually with a small pony bottle of nitrogen strapped to the side of the scooter and a pressure balanced second stage regulator and overpressure check-valve attached to the front lens of the vehicle. In such a way the interior and exterior pressure differential never ex-

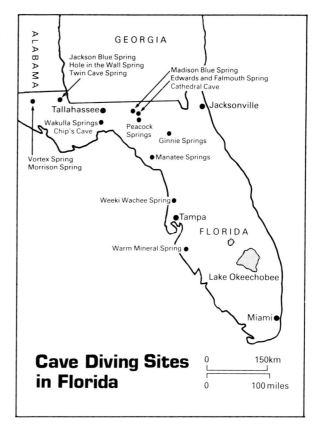

Cave Diving Sites in Florida

ceeded half a p.s.i. The powerful Aquazepps really started to arrive in the spring of 1987, and saw their first extensive use at Wakulla. These are now the norm for major pushes; Teknas are still the choice for intermediate range because of their smaller size.

Exley and colleagues soon found scooters invaluable. Their range of exploration was greatly increased. Due to the drag imposed on the diver by the addition of stage bottles divers seemingly could not get more than three knots out of the Aquazepp in top gear – half the speed quoted for normal use. But by relaxing and carefully controlling one's breathing, it was possible to double the distance which might be covered by normal swimming methods. The implications were far reaching. By the mid-1980s, used in conjunction with accepted staging techniques, phenomenal distances were being covered by divers using scooters. So important are these machines in advanced exploration, that despite their cost (Aquazepp $6000, Tekna $2000), an estimated five per cent of cave divers in Florida now possess a DPV.

Safety Considerations and Decompression

Considerable skill is required to operate a DPV in a cave and a similar amount of forethought must be given to the question of safety. An incident in June 1987 illustrates one problem that could have disastrous consequences. Three leading Florida divers, Wes Skiles, Lamar Hires and Woody Jasper had set off on a one stage pushing trip to Hart Springs. All three had Tekna scooters. Having dropped their stage units at

Left: Liz Wight using an Aquazepp in Jackson Blue Spring, Florida.

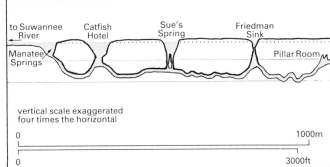

about 700m the three then continued into the upstream tunnel which had lowered into bedding passages. Suddenly, at about 1000m Jasper, who was following his friends through a narrow section in reduced visibility, hit a protruding roof pendant. This sheared one of his crossover taps. However, seconds later a second glancing blow unseated his valve, breaking the sealing rubber O-ring in the process. Despite the fact that his friends were quickly on hand Jasper lost all his air in just a couple of minutes. Amazingly the air formed an instant air-bell into which the divers surfaced to discuss their predicament. Remaining cool, Skiles and Hires pulled out their spare 3-metre hoses and proceeded to 'buddy-breathe' Jasper back to the stage bottles.

Divers must also be prepared for scooter failure. Should one's source of propulsion fail deep in a cave while diving on the normal Third Rule, the situation would immediately become critical. For this reason it is clear that a 'fourth' or 'fifth rule' is a more sensible precaution.

Time spent at depth further complicates the issue. In many cases the depth exceeds thirty metres, and the trend to greater depths is evident. In search of virgin passage, divers are being lured ever deeper, often to depths in excess of seventy-six metres. Lengthy periods of decompression are therefore becoming commonplace, involving complex calculations, which should be made before the dive begins. Although automatic decompression meters have appeared on the market in recent years, these have often proved unreliable. The most common practice is still to rely on naval tables and make manual computations of

decompression times, which can then be written on the diver's slate. More complex diving projects are now generating their own specialist decompression tables, produced by experts in the field of hyperbaric physiology. To guard against mishap the prudent diver would carry two sets of these calculations, and usually two depth gauges. Given that divers require a lengthy stay at shallow depth to decompress, additional cylinders often need to be deposited on the guideline for the return. For short excursions to depth, decompression may be undertaken using normal compressed air, but lengthy dives present an altogether more serious problem, for which the use of pure oxygen in specially marked cylinders, is now the norm.

Long Dives in Manatee Springs, 1981 and Chip's Cave, 1989

In his quest for the longest Exley again set his sights upon Manatee Springs in the late 1970s. Diving upstream from Friedman Sink, the highest known entrance, he reached 1623m from base in 1979, but two years later a major assault was undertaken. On three well-prepared, multi-stage dives the limit was extended first to 1803m, then 2094m, and finally to 2337m/7667ft on 23 August 1981. At the furthest point he and his partner, Clark Pitcairn, reached an impenetrable constriction. The dive took four hours, with a further six hours for decompression.

Bill Stone helped to recover some of the equipment used on this venture. His account gives a good description of the environment and a fair indication of the work that goes into such projects.

I have several vivid memories from this. First, the entrance is via Friedman Sink, which is a nice sounding name for a

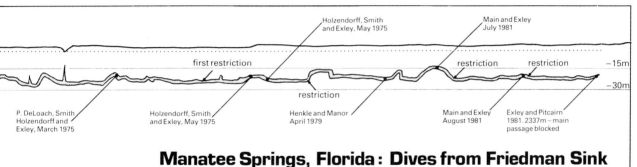

Holzendorff, Smith and Exley, May 1975

Main and Exley July 1981

first restriction

restriction   restriction

−15m

−30m

restriction

P. DeLoach, Smith Holzendorff and Exley, March 1975

Holzendorff, Smith and Exley, May 1975

Henkle and Manor April 1979

Main and Exley August 1981

Exley and Pitcairn 1981. 2337m – main passage blocked

Manatee Springs, Florida : Dives from Friedman Sink

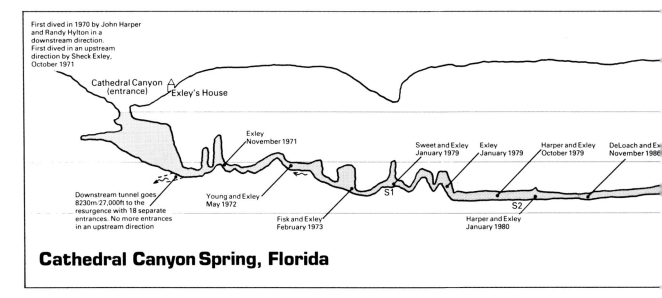

First dived in 1970 by John Harper and Randy Hylton in a downstream direction. First dived in an upstream direction by Sheck Exley, October 1971

Cathedral Canyon (entrance)

Exley's House

Exley November 1971

Sweet and Exley January 1979

Exley January 1979

Harper and Exley October 1979

DeLoach and Ex November 198(

Downstream tunnel goes 8230m/27,000ft to the resurgence with 18 separate entrances. No more entrances in an upstream direction

Young and Exley May 1972

Fisk and Exley February 1973

S1

S2

Harper and Exley January 1980

Cathedral Canyon Spring, Florida

manhole sized pothole obscurely located some sixty metres from Campground 92 at Manatee Park, hidden among the palmetos and live oak trees with a clean, oak leaf covering on the ground. You have to hang your stage bottles below you during the descent, otherwise you don't fit. It's like sliding down a vertical 1.3m diameter pipe – carved through that pitted white Floridan limestone. And down you go for over fifteen metres before suddenly breaking out into a 13m diameter underground river tunnel – and that river flows! At first you are mesmerized at the transition, and the fact that you are hovering twelve metres off the floor of a gin clear tunnel. The second thing to hit you is usually the ceiling as you are swept downstream by the incredibly forceful flow. Exley had warned me to deflate completely upon reaching the tunnel and his words now came back. I regathered my senses on the floor. We had 600m to go upstream to where spent bottles were waiting for us. From that point on we crawled. Fins were used for pushing off and most of the speed came when you could grab a boulder and pull yourself forward. My fingers were soon raw strips of flesh and the exertion of fighting that current, combined with the thirty-metre depth was sending the CO_2 through the roof. My head pounded.

With some relief the first glint of the cylinder stack came to view. I was amazed at the variety and age of the hardware. Each tank had a regulator and they were coated with a thin film of silt. I took four of these, Exley six. When we picked up our own stage bottles at 400m on the way out we were really nothing but humans riding uncontrollable bundles of tanks down this wild subterranean river. Most of the time it was dreamlike. You just loaded your buoyancy compensator so that you and the mass of tanks were neutral and the current did the rest . . . until the

passage took a sharp turn . . . and there were many. There despite the strongest finning, and mental willing, you still unceremoniously smashed into the wall and rolled sideways, the current spinning you along, until river shot you back into the main stream where you had a little manœuvering room. Once we reached the Friedman entrance, which looked like a ridiculously tiny soda straw leading out of the roof, we had another problem, which was how to get the tanks, and us back up through that. There happened to be a number of small crevices going off the pipe and we slid tanks into these left and right, like racking bottles of fine wine. As we decompressed, every ten feet would find Exley passing tanks up to me one at a time until we found more shelves and crevices. Despite the constricted quarters – it was so tight that Exley always was one stop deeper than me – our little tube had a benign and friendly ambience about it, giving plenty of pleasant time to reflect on a most unusual journey.

This American record (at the time also a world record for a continuous penetration) was to stand for over seven years. Exley made a scooter-assisted penetration of 2088m/6850ft in October 1987 at Cathedral Canyon, but it was not until the extension of Chip's Cave that the Manatee distance was bettered. In Chip's Cave, following a long, difficult project dating from September 1988, Exley undertook a marathon fourteen-hour diving operation on 28 January 1989. Some sixteen tanks were staged in the cave in addition to his back-mounted hundreds.

The dive was complicated by a jagged two-foot-

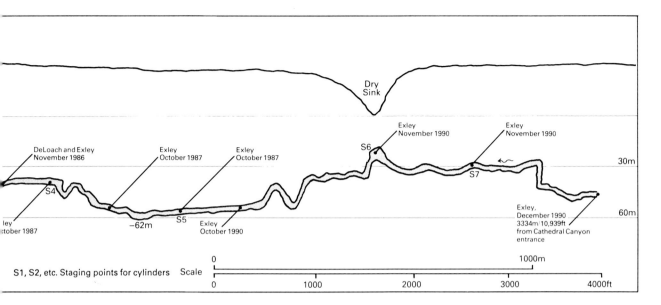

Dry
Sink

Exley
November 1990

Exley
November 1990

S6

DeLoach and Exley
November 1986

Exley
October 1987

Exley
October 1987

30m

S4

Exley,
December 1990
3334m/10,939ft
from Cathedral Canyon
entrance

60m

ley
:tober 1987

−62m   S5   Exley
October 1990

S1, S2, etc. Staging points for cylinders   Scale

0

0   1000   2000   3000   4000ft

1000m

diameter hole, near the entrance, which precluded the use of a scooter and a very strong current flowing into the ground. The first difficulty meant that he had to fin the entire distance, while the second gave him the distinctly unenviable situation of having to fight the current on his outward journey. This also gave difficulty in working out his air rules. Exit was in fact achieved by eliminating buoyancy and crawling for much of the way. The penetration took a total of six hours, twenty-four minutes, with an average depth of thirty-five metres and a maximum depth of forty-one metres. In terms of diving away from base this operation effectively bettered that of Swiss diver Olivier Isler at La Doux de Coly (3100m/10168ft) by eighty-four metres, thereby establishing not only a new American distance record but also a new world record. A dive such as this at Chip's Cave, achieved entirely by human effort, might be regarded as the diving equivalent of climbing Everest without oxygen.

A World Record at Cathedral Canyon, 1990
For some years Exley had realised that Cathedral Canyon* was a likely place for a world record distance penetration, indeed he was so interested in this site that he actually purchased the whole area and moved

his home to a house near the spring and was thus able to work unimpeded out of his own back yard.

Despite its potential and large passages this site presented two major difficulties, namely depth and poor visibility. Having made a 2088m penetration here in 1987, Exley set about his preparations for a major push in September 1990. This was not an easy project. To enable him to scooter through two sections, where the visibility was less than a metre, he had to completely reline them. Bearing in mind that the average depth was about fifty metres and the maximum (in the roof) fifty-eight metres, he also had to place a total of fourteen stage bottles, together with a long range Aquazepp which he staged at 975m – with the intention of riding a second machine up to this point. By Florida standards, the conditions were far from perfect and Exley himself had grave doubts that using an Aquazepp would be feasible. However, with the advantage of an intimate knowledge of the route gained on the preparatory dives, the exploration was made in mid-December. As on many of his operations the push was made solo.

All went to plan. Diving through spacious passages, in visibility that never exceeded eight metres, Exley eventually reached a point 3334m from the entrance.

Exley had chosen to wear a wet suit for this dive, not only for its preferable quality of streamlining, but

* The original name for the cave was Ghoul's Sink. Realising its potential, Exley changed this to the more appealing Cathedral Canyon.

also for a more basic reason – comfort. After a bottom time of three and a half hours he regained the entrance area and began a lengthy decompression. Here, using a twenty-five metre long garden hose, he piped down warm water, from a boiler in his back yard, to pump around the inside of his wet suit. Thus fortified during eight hours of decompression, the final stop being in an airbell at just under four metres' depth, he finally surfaced eleven and a half hours after entry with yet another amazing and well deserved world record to his credit.

The exploration of Cathedral Canyon was also to witness another new record. The overall length of the Falmouth-Cathedral system was further extended, to over 12,190m/40,000ft – thereby reaffirming its status as the longest underwater system in the world.

Deep Diving Problems

Deep cave diving requires considerably greater preparation and nerve than the more typical shallow dive. Below forty metres one enters the realm of nitrogen narcosis, which gets progressively worse the deeper one descends. Below sixty metres the judgement of the majority of divers is significantly impaired and by ninety metres the partial pressure of oxygen in the air has reached its safe limit.

To penetrate beyond a depth of ninety metres is to risk convulsions and sudden blackout. There is a need therefore to reduce or dilute the oxygen content of the breathing supply. To increase the proportion of nitrogen is no real solution owing to the problem of narcosis. The solution has been found by substituting part of the nitrogen with helium, thereby creating Trimix.* The greater the proportion of helium in the supply the more clear headed the diver becomes. However, the very act of including helium creates additional problems. A major one is high thermal conductivity (the diver looses his body heat more quickly than if he were using nitrogen). One solution to this has been found by equalising or inflating the

dry suit from a completely separate, small cylinder of Argon, or 75% Argon – 25% CO_2 (a readily available welding gas). The use of Argon not only prevents the loss of heat; it has less than 50% the heat conductivity of air.

The second problem is more crucial. Incorporating helium in the supply *can* complicate the decompression process. What usually happens, however, is that because of the long decompression times associated with the depths where these gases are required, people naturally look for ways to reduce the time spent on decompression. One does this by switching to Nitrox as deep as possible with the maximum tolerable safe oxygen content. (Together, isobaric counterdiffusion and a high partial pressure of oxygen radically shorten decompression time.) By this approach one should decompress using a series of Nitrox mixes beginning as deep as sixty metres and ultimately change to pure oxygen at six metres.

The main reason for adopting this multi-mix approach is that it allows some of the more serious explorations to take place: Without them decompression times would quite possibly be of the order of twenty hours, rather than ten to twelve hours. In the absence of a habitat such an extended decompression time could easily lead to a serious hypothermia problem. For relatively short excursions to depth, it is possible to transfer from Trimix directly to oxygen, as witnessed by Rob Parker's exploration of Wookey Hole in 1985, but in the majority of instances – certainly where porterage of cylinders is not too great a problem – the decompression stops are more prudently undertaken using the multi-mix approach.

To push back the frontiers in the major systems of Florida now entails very long dives often at considerable depth. Vast quantities of gas need to be carried and when, for example, one considers that at ninety metres' depth one breathes an incredible ten times the volume of gas as at the surface, the pressure gauge falls at an alarming rate.

Long decompression times are boring. At first divers eased the tedium by reading magazines or books under water, but more recently they have established decompression 'habitats'. These suspended capsules provide a viable air-space, capable of accommodating

---

* Early experiments involving Trimix for cave diving in the United States were far from successful. Of the four 'mix' dives undertaken in the States prior to 1985, two ended in tragedy: the third brought the team to a dangerous state of hypothermia, only the last, by Dale Sweet in Die Polder 2, to 110m in 1981, was fully successful and that was written off as the luck of a madman. From the time of the Louis Holtzendorff tragedy in 1975, opinion was very strongly opposed to the use of Trimix. It was the initial experiments undertaken for the 1985 push in Wookey Hole, which broke the psychological barrier in this field. Subsequently, Exley began to use it in preparation for his deep dives at Nacimiento del Rio Mante, slowly mixed-gas diving gained acceptance.

extreme depths in such a vast passage it was clear that only an exceptionally well-planned expedition would achieve any significant advance. This would surely be the ultimate challenge in Florida.

In 1986 the State of Florida purchased the property, thus allowing the resumption of explorations begun over thirty years earlier. Very little was known about this site. Where was its source? Was its water being gradually polluted by urban development in nearby Tallahassee? Under the capable and highly experienced leadership of Dr Bill Stone, the Wakulla Springs Project was formulated with the object of finding answers to these and many other questions.

With a budget of over $300,000, the team of more than a dozen divers, with a series of scientific programmes formulated by a variety of state agencies and universities, began their diving in October 1987.

Technology had come a long way since the 1950s, but even so the sphere of activity was extreme in every sense and the final success of the expedition depended upon five conditions being met:

1. That the helium-oxygen breathing mixtures would eliminate narcosis and that heat loss would be tolerable for several hours;
2. That the custom decompression tables generated for the project worked;
3. That the high-speed German Aquazepp diver propulsion vehicles, imported specially for the project, proved reliable;
4. That the purpose-built habitat and its variable-depth feature worked;
5. That the team could prepare itself psychologically for the stress of repeated diving to depths of up to ninety-two metres, where productive exploration would be limited to a few minutes on any given mission.

In the event all the conditions were met. Central to the overall success was the unique habitat designed by Stone. In view of the lengthy periods of decompression (extending to twenty-four hours), it was essential that divers be able to spend much of this time out of water. The habitat was essentially a three-metre-diameter hemispherical 'bubble' based on a framework of tubular aluminium and made with a flexible, inflatable composite shell. This was fabricated from special high-strength ballistics nylon cloth, pressure-laminated with neoprene rubber. The whole structure would be suspended in the water by heavy lead weights. Significantly the calculated 18,000lbs/8181kg of lead

Above: Bill Stone, leader of the 1987 Wakulla Project, wearing the MK-2R rebreather at Jackson Blue Spring, Florida, 1989.

two or three divers. Initially these were fairly makeshift devices, such as inverted cattle troughs which, despite obvious limitations, none the less allowed divers to get their heads and shoulders free of the water, enabling them to talk, eat and drink.

The Wakulla Explorations

Throughout the 1980s there was one site above all others which captured the imagination of divers – Wakulla Springs. The explorations conducted here late in 1987 were outstanding. Not only were dramatic distances and depths achieved but the project also indicated the direction of many possible technological developments.

Diving was prohibited at Wakulla in the late 1950s and, apart from a few clandestine visits, American explorers could only wish and wonder as to the extent of this incredible network of underwater passages. One of the largest resurgences in the world, Wakulla is the principal drainage outlet for the extensive Woodville karst plain south-east of Tallahassee, in effect a massive underground river. To dive at

Above: Paul DeLoach and Sheck Exley assembling the frame of the decompression habitat prior to its being lowered into Wakulla Spring (right).

required to hold this structure in place had to be increased to some 20,500lbs/9318kg on the site. The habitat could hold up to six divers returning from two simultaneous missions, but it was generally used for a single three-person team. Heavy structures such as this had been successfully employed in ocean diving, where powerful ship's cranes could lower them steadily to their operating depth. In the restricted conditions at Wakulla it was not possible to use a crane, so the habitat had to be set up manually. The team lost valuable time when two of the 3000lb weighting drums fell to the bottom of the entry pool and had to be raised using inflated lifting bags. This proved to be an exercise fraught with risk as the lifting bags were highly unpredictable, on one occasion hitting the roof of the cave, dropping the weight and dislodging rocks on to the fleeing divers below and on another occasion sending a weight racing back to the surface with frightening speed. The whole exercise was recorded in a spectacular television film, *Wakulla*, made by Leo and Mandy Dickinson.

After many vicissitudes the habitat was erected and tested, and, as expected, it provided a valuable diving base. Dives were made using Aquazepps of between forty and eighty minutes, at average depths of ninety metres. Decompression began at sixty metres' depth and from there it would take two to three hours to ascend to the habitat moored at the twenty-one-metre level. A total of twenty-one decompression stops, with a total time of eighteen hours, were required before the divers who had made the longest trips regained the surface.

The mixtures adopted by the majority of the team, and by all members in the later stages of the project, consisted of 14% oxygen/86% helium, which completely eliminated the problem of narcosis. With this mixture diving at below ninety-eight metres was like diving at nine metres, apart from the fact that the breathing supply was being used ten times faster. A normal 80 cu.ft cylinder, for example, would only have

22. *(right) An early habitat being tested in Peacock Springs, Florida. Tom Morris is using the 60cms of usable air space of this upturned cattle trough for safer and more comfortable decompression. With a diameter of two and a half metres there is enough room for three divers to wait here. 'Habitrofs' have been used successfully in several of the main Florida cave systems.*

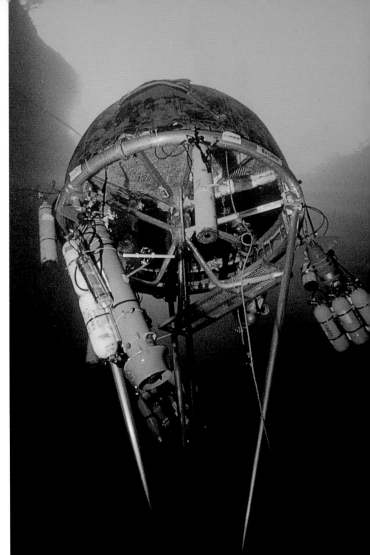

Three views of the Wakulla habitat: **23.** *(top left) Sheck Exley, Brad Percel and Wes Skiles guide a 2000lb stabilizing weight into position;* **24.** *(above left) the habitat in use, with two Aquazepps tethered outside;* **26.** *(near left) Rob Parker, Skiles and Percel relaxing inside the habitat during decompression. The block and tackle, linked to an anchor on the cave bed, enabled the divers to adjust the depth.*

25. *(far left) Bill Stone reading a novel underwater to stave off boredom during his twenty-four hour rebreather test in Wakulla.*

27. *(above) Mark Long at twenty metres depth in Little Devil's Cave moving along a typical, well-formed phreatic passage.*

28. *Mark Long and Lamar Hires using Teckna scooters in Peacock Springs, Florida on the 680m traverse from the entrance to waterhole sink.*

29. *Geoff Crossley near the entrance of Devil's Eye Spring, Florida.*

30. (left) The entry pool to Peacock Springs.

31. (bottom left) Pete Scoones in the 'gin clear' water of Sally Ward Spring, Florida.

32. (right) A huge vertical passage in Stargate Blue Hole, Andros, West Indies. Using rebreathers, Rob Parker and Stuart Clough reached a depth of ninety-eight metres here in 1987 (see page 231).

given thirty breathes at this depth. As a direct result of this rapid gas consumption, the volume of gas able to be carried by each diver soon became the controlling factor. A novel 'sledge' was devised which hung beneath the DPV, allowing each diver to carry eight cylinders of Heliox, amounting in total to about 1200 cu.ft – the equivalent of at least eleven standard 80 cu.ft diving cylinders.

Apart from the Heliox 'working' gas, the divers also used a 30% Nitrox mixture for decompression from forty metres until entering the habitat at twenty-one metres, compressed air from there to nine metres, and finally pure oxygen up to the surface.

During the ten-week project over three kilometres of tunnels were surveyed in Wakulla, the vast majority of which lay at depths in excess of eighty-seven metres. Exploration revealed that there was one primary tunnel measuring over thirty-seven metres wide by eighteen metres high (120ft × 60ft) fed by a number of branching side passages. The side leads were typically up to thirteen metres deeper than the main passage and, in view of the reduced visibility in the trunk route, the main emphasis lay upon side leads, which offered excellent visibility throughout. B Tunnel the first of the side leads, which began at 366m from the entrance, saw the longest penetration and the greatest depth (110m). In an epic eighty-minute operation, Wes Skiles, Paul Heinerth, and Tom Morris travelled up this passage for 1273m/4176ft, reaching a depth of 98m/320ft. This was an amazing journey, passing through the vast cavern, the Monolith Room, a chamber over seventy-six metres long, sixty metres wide and thirty-six metres high. This chamber is so large that, even in totally clear conditions and using high-powered primary light units, it is difficult to see the walls. The situation at the end of B Tunnel was so remote that a scooter failure would almost certainly have resulted in a fatality.

33. (top left) *Exploring the extensively decorated Lucayan Caverns, Grand Bahama (see page 230) – one of the largest flooded tunnel systems in the world.*

34. (left) *Sarah Cunliffe carefully examines the gorgeous stal formations of Sagittarius Blue Hole, Grand Bahama.*

A Close Escape from D Tunnel, Wakulla

A serious incident did, in fact, occur deep in D Tunnel and Sheck Exley, assisted by his partner, Paul DeLoach, experienced a stressful exit. Their personal accounts of this incident are particularly interesting, highlighting not only the extreme nature of the exploration but also the exceptional qualities of discipline required by the entire team. The dive, on Thanksgiving Day, 26 November, had started well. Exley recounts:

We added 406ft of line, beginning in the small silty passage where we discovered two huge breakdown rooms near the end of the line. We could not find a way on past the terminal breakdown room, so Paul tied off [at 1042m/3420ft] and we left with me surveying. In the next to last room [3300ft] I spotted an apparent balcony near the ceiling of a high dome, which was reminiscent of similar formations in Indian Springs and in Sally Ward Spring, where tunnels lead out of the ceiling. So I scootered up to investigate the dome. I discovered that it was fifty feet high, but unfortunately the balcony did not go. I started back down and suddenly there was a loud 'thunk' as my batteries broke loose from the retaining mechanism and shifted towards the scooter nose. This made the DPV want to pitch forward. The switch would not come on. I tilted it back, whereupon the batteries returned to their original position and the scooter righted itself, but it still would not power up. So I gave it to Paul to take out while I finished surveying what we had installed [the line] on this dive.

We were not very concerned at this point, because we had turned the dive early [the American term for 'commenced the exit'] and had very large reserves of gas, plus there were additional stage bottles in the cave. When I finished the survey Paul handed me the scooter. I mounted it and grabbed his T-bar for a tow after he insisted. I wanted him to motor out without me while I just swam along behind. However, he insisted, so I went ahead and got on it. We motored out successfully to Room 3 [a distance of approx 200 metres] then the compass on my right wrist was sucked into the prop of his scooter. This, in turn, caused the bungy cord around it to jam the scooter prop and pin my right wrist. I cut it loose with a forearm knife, inadvertently dropping the compass and knife, and finally cut enough of the bungy away to free the prop. We started back out. However, uncertain of his prop's sea-worthiness I elected to leave my scooter and come back to get it on a later dive. Paul towed me back to our emergency stage bottles at 1500ft.

At this point Exley firmly believed he had sufficent gas at his disposal to be able to swim the rest of the

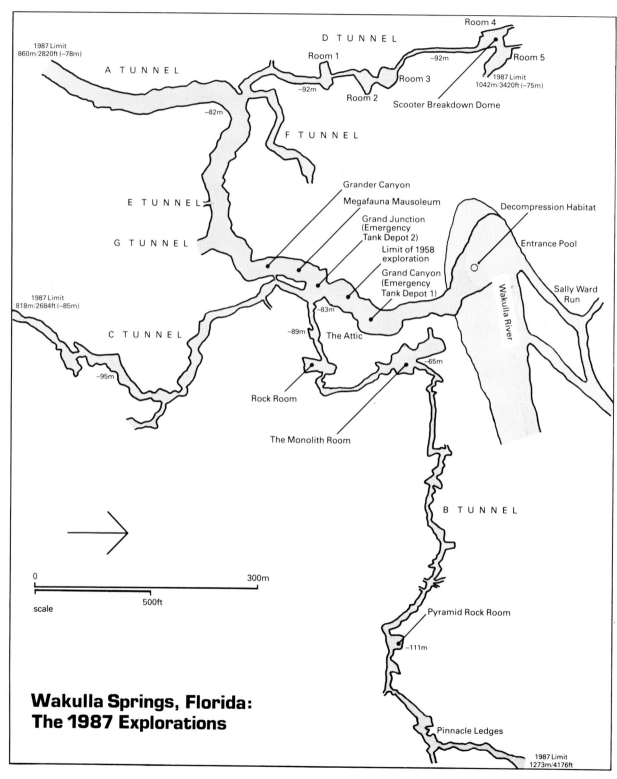

1987 Limit
860m/2820ft (−78m)

A TUNNEL

−82m

D TUNNEL

Room 1

−92m

Room 2

Room 3

−92m

Room 4

Room 5

1987 Limit
1042m/3420ft (−75m)

Scooter Breakdown Dome

F TUNNEL

E TUNNEL

G TUNNEL

Grander Canyon

Megafauna Mausoleum

Grand Junction
(Emergency
Tank Depot 2)

Limit of 1958
exploration

Grand Canyon
(Emergency
Tank Depot 1)

Decompression Habitat

Entrance Pool

Sally Ward
Run

Wakulla River

1987 Limit
818m/2684ft (−85m)

C TUNNEL

−95m

−89m

−83m

The Attic

−65m

Rock Room

The Monolith Room

B TUNNEL

Pyramid Rock Room

−111m

0   300m

500ft

scale

Pinnacle Ledges

1987 Limit
1273m/4176ft

**Wakulla Springs, Florida:
The 1987 Explorations**

way back to the entrance. A tow would undoubtedly have been preferable, but by this point additional, possibly more worrying, complications had arisen and Exley realised it was in both their interests that he should make his own way out. DeLoach explained:

After Sheck cut loose the bungy from my prop we proceeded for several hundred feet before I began to have irregular breathing patterns. It was like my chest was having palpitations. Hard as I tried, I could not seem to control my breathing, and it was extemely difficult to obtain a complete breath. Within 200ft I began to get a twitching in my eye and nose. These symptoms [indicative of the onset of oxygen poisoning] continued to build until I began to fade in and out of consciousness. Sheck realised my condition at the 1500ft depot and motioned for me to go on [alone]. I was in no place, and no condition at that time to argue with him. The twitching seemed to get longer, and breathing was more of a problem as I continued up Grander Canyon. I switched to my safety bottle, hoping that it would breathe easier, but it proved to be worse so I went back to my hundreds. I arrived at the 190ft stop and these symptoms continued until I had moved up to about 175ft. At that point I began to get some relief.

Deep inside the cave, Exley's disciplined approach was being put to the test. Exley again:

The heavy drag of my three stages and my Viking suit made exertion necessary to make any progress. On a high PO₂ [partial pressure of oxygen] for over an hour it was difficult and my breathing was ineffient. My final stage bottle, for which I had borrowed a regulator that morning, still indiciated 1500 p.s.i. when I got to Grand Junction [where B Tunnel and C Tunnel led off into the east wall] but I was out of gas in that particular tank. I picked up one of the emergency depot bottles at Grand Junction, but the regulator was bad. The other one breathed hard, but I was still able to get some gas out of it and exchanged it for one of my empties. Given the additional exertion required to swim, I was again short on air by the time I reached the three 80s at the Grand Canyon emergency depot [approximately eighty metres further on]. At this point I set my survey slate down and grabbed one of these bottles while dumping two of my empties. My primary light went out just before this so I switched on my 50 watt secondary. This completed I met up with Paul at the entrance [who having recovered slightly had motored back to assist].

Despite the stress induced by this catalogue of incidents, both divers obviously performed flawlessly in their execution of emergency procedures. As the narrative indicates, the outcome would have been altogether different were it not for the presence of three emergency gas depots.

Analysing the D Tunnel Incident, Wakulla

As with many other dives conducted at Wakulla, lessons were learned. When calculations were made the following morning it was determined that De-Loach's disturbing symptoms, could be attributed to the gas supply being used. Unlike the majority of the team, both Exley and DeLoach had been using Trimix, a gas supply which they mixed on site. This had been used successfully on previous dives and at the exceptionally deep Mexican resurgence of Nacimiento del Rio Mante the previous June. Calculations revealed that the partial pressure of oxygen was approximately 2.0 atmospheres at ninety metres' depth, the critical level at which oxygen poisoning can result. Although Exley and DeLoach had a demonstrable tolerance to this concentration for periods of up to fifty minutes on several occasions, an eight-minute exposure, combined with DeLoach's increased labour – he was steering the DPV with a substantial off-centre load under stressful conditions – apparently triggered the onset symptoms of CNS (central nervous system) oxygen toxicity. Following this incident, all team members were instructed to use Heliox-14 for deep work at Wakulla.

Scientific Discoveries at Wakulla

More than 400 dives were safely conducted during the course of the expedition. A wealth of scientific data was obtained: research in the fields of stratigraphy and lithography; sediments were obtained and studies undertaken into water quality; and, utilizing uranium isotope sampling, invaluable information was gained on the actual origins of the various tunnels. It was found, for example, that some of the water rising at Wakulla originates as much as twenty-seven kilometres away, and several other passages were hypothetically linked with neighbouring cave systems. In the biological field extremely important finds were made: several blind, albino (fully trogloditic) crawfish were collected at distances up to 1200m from the cave entrance, which are believed to be a new species. Equally interesting non-trogloditic catfish were also sighted in the same areas.

Rebreather Design at Wakulla

The various studies made at Wakulla have proved invaluable. From the exploratory point of view the achievements were to realise several important points. Even allowing for the use of scooters, staging techniques, high pressure composite diving cylinders and the most advanced gas mixtures, the limits of open circuit diving apparatus have been reached. The stage is rapidly approaching where it is physically impossible to carry sufficient quantities of gas to progress further.

The most economical way to use mixed gas is with a rebreather, whereby the inert gases are recycled with oxygen added as required to maintain a safe, breathable mixture. Bill Stone had long realised the problem and undertaken considerable research in this area. Several types of rebreather had been produced over the preceding years, for example the Rexnord CCR-1000, which is used by the American and Israeli navies. An adaptation of this had been given a field trial the previous summer on the Andros Project, namely the Carmellan Rebreather. This unit is essentially a standard Rexnord MK-155 (or CCR-155) in which the oxygen setpoint has been increased to 1.3 bar (atmospheres), compared to the 0.7 atmosphere used by the US Navy. For cave diving these units have severe limitations. A simple tear in the breathing hose, or even letting the mouthpiece slip from one's lips would be sufficient to flood the carbon dioxide 'scrubber'. Underground a situation like this would be critical. For cave diving therefore the Carmellan Rebreather needs to be backed up with an emergency bail-out system, basically a conventional open circuit cylinder of gas, from which the diver can never stray far.

In view of the remote, extreme nature of the cave diving environment there is a need for what advanced American divers term 'redundancy' – or fail-safe systems to cope with multiple equipment failure. From December 1984 Stone made a close analysis of the Rexnord Rebreather. He found that despite its admirable design for clandestine warfare in open water, the technology of the unit belonged to the seventies and early eighties. From the cave diving standpoint Stone was extremely concerned and spent a considerable length of time looking into all aspects of such equipment. With the resulting sober insight

he set about designing and constructing his own highly advanced rebreather. He designed this on the clear assumption that if one component or even several components were to fail, the user would still be left with a functional system.* This rebreathing unit received its first severe tests at Wakulla.

The Wakulla Project will perhaps not be remembered so much for the tremendous exploration which it achieved as for the series of test dives undertaken with Stone's new Cis-Lunar MK-1 rebreather. Stone's unit contained, for example, four onboard computers and sufficient gas supply to last for two days. Comparing the gas consumption rates to those observed during the exploration of Wakulla, it was calculated that the rebreather would have used between 800-1000 times less gas for the same mission. Using this sophisticated apparatus, Stone was eventually to conduct a dive of twenty-four hours on 3-4 December, 1987.

It is anticipated that the Cis Lunar MK-2R will be commercially available within the next few years. The initial cost will be about $20,000, but it is hoped to halve this cost by mass production.

Coldwater Cave, Iowa / Scott Hollow, West Virginia

With this wealth of technological equipment, the remainder of the United States offers immense potential for cavers and divers alike. It is estimated that there are over 30,000 cave systems in the whole country, with tremendous diversity of types. Outside Florida, the earliest major success in the cave diving sphere was that at Iowa's Coldwater Cave in the autumn of 1967. Here David Jagnow and Steve Barnett traversed 400m of low swim-ways and short sumps to break through into an extensive dry system. They were able to make an exploration and survey of a large part of the system – a revelation which they kept secret for over two years.

In 1972 the State of Iowa sank a dry shaft into the extension. Explorations are still continuing here. In

---

* A truly 'redundant' system would be one in which any component or sub-system, no matter how critical, can fail yet still leave the system as a whole in a functional state.

Sump divers in the USA. Near right: John Schweyen in Sump 2 of McFail's Cave, New York state and (above) Schweyen and Jim Brown organise equipment after passing the Sump 2. Far right: Brown after a dive in Scott Hollow, West Virginia.

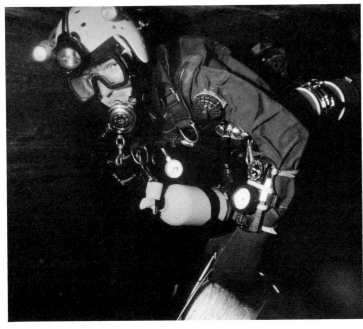

Above: Roberta Swicegood in a duck in Cutlip Cave, West Virginia.

June 1987, for example, Iowa Grotto members dived four upstream sumps, in the process discovering about 900m of new passage. The total length of the cave now exceeds seventeen kilometres, much of which is beautifully decorated.

Another, equally exciting discovery has been made in Scott Hollow Cave, in West Virginia. Discovered via a surface dig, this cave was first entered in October 1984. Within a month Michael Dore and friends had revealed a spectacular system well over three kilometres long sporting a huge river passage that they titled Mystic River. Activity here was rapid. A bolt climb successfully bypassed the first downstream sump and led to another 800m of passage and Sump 2. This lay over three kilometres from the entrance, and just under five kilometres before the eventual resurgence at the Greenbrier River. It was during a drought in November 1987 that John Schweyen passed this obstacle to continue the exploration of the missing section of cave. The sump is typical of diving sites in Britain, 213m long and normally 18m deep. Schweyen, Jim Brown and Roberta Swicegood commenced the serious task of surveying the major extension the following spring. Tragically, Swicegood's contribution here was limited: just six days after her second trip she drowned at Arch Cave Spring.

In June 1989 the divers realised that the most effective way to complete the investigation of this extension was to camp. Joined by Ron Simmons the three mounted an intensive, very technical, week's activity beyond Sump 2 making significant advances. The current terminus (excluding side leads) lies at Sump 5, nearly two-and-a-half kilometres downstream from Sump 2. By March 1990 this and other ongoing explorations in the Scott Hollow system had yielded over twenty-seven kilometres of passages.

Unlike the main Florida impetus, discoveries such as that at Coldwater and Scott Hollow are clearly influenced more by caving motives than those of pure diving. Today sump exploration is increasingly being adopted to further the exploration of caves and many long penetrations and significant extensions have been achieved.

Sullivan Sink Explorations, 1988

Using this full range of advanced techniques, the explorations conducted in North Florida in the late 1980s were quite unique. The area south of Tallahassee is perhaps the most challenging in the state, and it was there that a world record cave diving traverse was achieved in the Sullivan system during the summer of 1988. After some five months of intense activity, Bill Main, Bill Gavin, Parker Turner and Lamar English established a through trip of 2591m/8500ft on 19 June 1988. They entered at Sullivan Sink with the assistance of scooters and a strong flow of water. They made a fifty-five-minute ride, touching a maximum depth of seventy-three metres, to emerge at Cheryl Sink. The budget exceeded US $10,000 with heavy costs for Trimix, Nitrox, oxygen, experimental computer-generated decompression tables, O_2 analysers, galvanised cattle troughs for decompression habitats, many bottles, regulators and modified scooters for deep diving.

Such major ventures demonstrate that American cave divers, certainly those operating in Florida, are possibly the best trained in the world with ability derived from a number of interlinking factors: rigorous programmes of training and certification implemented on a regular basis; specialist cave diving equipment which is widely available; safety procedures which are rigidly observed; and a limitless number of cave systems for both training and exploration.

Accidents at Little Dismal Cave and Arch Cave Spring
Despite these precautions and an impeccable safety record, through most of the 1980s, it is perhaps significant that the United States lost two of its most highly experienced, certified cave divers during the summer of 1988, one in Florida, the other in Pennsylvania.

The Florida accident took place in Little Dismal Cave, Leon County, a site of major exploratory and survey projects during the previous months. Bill McFaden had undertaken nearly forty dives in this system, fifteen of which had been to depths of over sixty-six metres. With the survey almost complete, he, Bill Main and Bill Gavin set off on 15 May 1988 for some final exploration. For such an accomplished, highly experienced group the objective was fairly routine. At the outset it was decided that the party would split into two separate teams: Bill Gavin was to scooter to the extreme, downstream terminus while Main and McFaden were to swim part way along the same route and then set off into an upstream tunnel which had known depths of sixty-six metres.

Accurate surveying is a slow task and, as the tunnel was low in places, visibility soon deteriorated owing to disturbed sediment. Eventually Main 'called the dive' (signalled to commence the exit), passed his companion, and slowly made his way back to the chamber where the downstream tunnel led off. For much of this distance visibility was zero.

Main began a long wait. Just as he was about to re-enter the muddy upstream tunnel in search of McFaden he noticed Bill Gavin's light. Gavin had completed his task and was on his way out. Still there was no sign of McFaden. The two divers communicated their concern and Gavin swam into the muddy tunnel, while Main resumed the anxious wait. Within minutes McFaden was located. He had lost the line, was obviously stressed, but otherwise appeared all right.

By the time the pair reached Main in the chamber, however, McFaden had run out of air and was breathing from Gavin's spare regulator. Clearly McFaden was now deeply stressed. Gavin hooked them up to

his scooter and, with McFaden in tow, the trio began a hasty exit. Unfortunately further problems developed and just before reaching the final, awkward constriction the unthinkable occurred. Gavin also ran out of air. Two of the three-man team were now totally out of air and owing to the unforseen delay, Bill Main's supply was also running low.

The stress level was now acute. In the process of swapping on to Bill Main's supply McFaden blacked out. By this stage Main had little air left himself and Gavin was so short of air as to be virtually helpless to do anything to aid himself. A mouthpiece was thrust into Gavin's mouth, but, although breathing, all his energy was now spent. Main then courageously dragged his friend through the constriction and, finning hard, succeeded in reaching the decompression bottles. McFaden was dead but thanks to Main's coolness under stress, he and Gavin survived.

The Loss of Roberta Swicegood
The Little Dismal tragedy was to mark the end of an untarnished safety record spanning almost eight years, a period over which it has been calculated that nearly 200,000 safe dives had taken place, involving over 2000 cave divers. Sadly the US cave diving community were to lose another of their rank just over one month later.

Roberta Swicegood, one of the leading inland sump divers, had been systematically exploring and charting the extensive Arch Cave Spring in Pennsylvania. This rising has poor visibility (one metre) and cold water (approx 10°C/50°F), a far cry from the favourable conditions of Florida. It appears that things went wrong on her inward dive. Wearing a membrane dry suit and two independently-valved, back-mounted, 95 cu.ft bottles, it is possible that her suit began to leak. For whatever reason, Swicegood was retreating from a point 300m or more into Sump 2 along a passage which dropped to a depth of thirty metres at one point. A severe line entanglement occurred and she was forced to cut herself free, presumably in atrocious visibility. The line was very thin and it is possible that, during such a stressful incident, she may have lost it. It seems that she eventually located the exit route, but ran out of air about 200m from safety.

America may possess the longest cave in the world –
Mammoth Cave, with a length of over 530km/330
miles – but, for the deepest systems in the western
hemisphere and certainly for some of the most
challenging cave diving, countries in and around the
Caribbean are unrivalled. Some of the warmest and
most fabulous cave diving in the world is to be found
in this area.

The Bahamas: Exploring the Blue Holes

It was the Bahamas, a small chain of islands over
200kms south-east of Florida, which were the first to
reveal extensive submarine systems, caves that were
not only long and deep but which also possessed
other, more interesting features. Canadian diver and
photographer George Benjamin initiated activities in
this area and subsequently devoted many years of his
life to the exploration of these fabulous systems,
places which today are better known as the Blue Holes.

From the late 1950s Benjamin explored and surveyed
scores of these blue holes, but it was the eastern
Andros area which became his principal interest.
Tremendous tidal currents sweep through many of
the oceanic holes, indicating an extensive labyrinth of
tunnels beneath, but at the same time creating
potentially hazardous conditions for the explorer. At
certain sites it is physically impossible to swim against
the out-flow, while, on the reversal, any diving would
involve dire consequences. In such an environment
diving operations must be precisely timed and undertaken with great caution.

The fabulous nature of blue hole diving is exquisitely
portrayed in an extract from Rob Palmer's book *Deep
into Blue Holes*. Here he describes the setting of one
such hole situated adjacent to the tiny island of Rat
Cay, one to two kilometres off the north-east shore
of Andros.

A deeper blue tints the sea on the northern shore of the islet.
There, beneath the waves, a deep cleft splits the sea floor, a dark
opening in the azure sands. Rich and colourful corals surround
it, long waving hydroids fringe its walls, streaming to and fro in

Left: At the entrance to Conch Blue Hole, Andros, Bahamas.

Above: George Benjamin with his son, George Jnr., before an Andros dive in 1971.

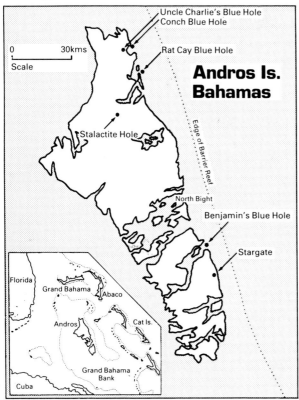

the strong currents that flow, sometimes in, sometimes out of its depths. When the waters are calm, the cleft is a peaceful scene of tranquillity, where shoals of fish float in studied laziness in the shadowed waters. Grunts and snappers inhabit the small maze of tunnels at the base of the cleft, multicoloured parrotfish chew enthusiastically at the coral, and the islet's resident barracuda casts a watchful eye over its domain. Occasionally a shark scatters the assembly, finning smoothly in to bask in the cool waters of the outflowing current.

With such a wondrous underwater world to discover it is hardly surprising that Benjamin became totally infatuated with blue hole exploration. After years of conventional sea diving along the length of Andros, in 1966 he commenced operations in the caves of the South Bight, but it was Christmas 1967 when his most significant find was made, blue hole SB4, today better known as Benjamin's Blue Hole. Benjamin recalls the initial dives here:

> . . . as soon as we entered this cave, we realised that it was much larger than anything we had seen before. We proceeded cautiously, step by step. Sixty feet [18m] down, the sloping shaft gave way to a vertical chasm. The view down below was horrifying – the cave disappeared into an immense void, beyond the range of our spotlights. We belayed the vital lifeline and proceeded downwards. It took three nerve-racking attempts to reach the bottom, at 210ft [63m]. There, the cave had only just begun.

By September 1970, Benjamin's team had been joined by two expert cave divers from Miami, Tom Mount and Dick Williams, and had penetrated 300m in a southward trending passage at a maximum depth of eighty metres. Some of the pits they passed across were much deeper, the bottoms out of sight and well beyond the range of their torches. After discovering this cave system, all the team's energies were devoted to its exploration, which slowly but surely became more and more complex. It was also to provide invaluable scientific data. The further reaches of the cave, for example, were well decorated with flowstone formations – stalactites and stalagmites. This indicated that the caves had been completely dry at some stage in their long history as calcite structures can only develop in an air-filled environment. Advanced dating techniques have shown that during the Ice Age the level of the ocean here was considerably lower than it is today, possibly by 100 or 150m.

Over two kilometres of line was installed, the longest single passage being the one trending south which was advanced to 600m/2000ft. Until this time all activities had been calculated and had progressed cautiously with no accidents. To allow for longer penetrations Benjamin, for example, had designed the 'Benjamin Crossover'* which is a linking manifold that connected two back-mounted air tanks together, and allowed two breathing regulators to be worn. This was a unique valve system which allowed each regulator to access the air in both tanks, but if one regulator failed, it could be isolated without compromising the other system. This improved diving safety considerably and was a great improvement on existing techniques. In Florida, for example, divers had simply been using a small extra tank with an extra regulator attached to the main tank.

But now, despite this innovation, the cave was reasonably long and the penetration had reached the

* The Benjamin Crossover Valve was subsequently marketed commercially and became the US standard for cave diving.

Above: Benjamin's diving party exploring the stalagmite and stalactite caverns of Benjamin's Blue Hole in 1970.

safe limits for air diving. To progress further would require special mixtures of helium and oxygen, and at such great depths, Benjamin's team decided that the risks were unacceptable.

By the early 1970s the cave had achieved a certain reputation and despite its isolated location interest in the system began to increase. Jacques Cousteau made a film of it during Christmas 1970.

On 27 August 1971 the exemplary record of safe diving ended. Benjamin's team was about to dive when another boat arrived. On board were the experienced cave diver, Jim Lockwood, and John Carcelle, a novice. Benjamin had stressed many times the need of considerable experience before embarking on any penetration into the tunnel at the foot of the deep entrance shaft. When he surfaced later that afternoon his words rang all too true. Lockwood reported that at fifty-five metre's depth Carcelle had

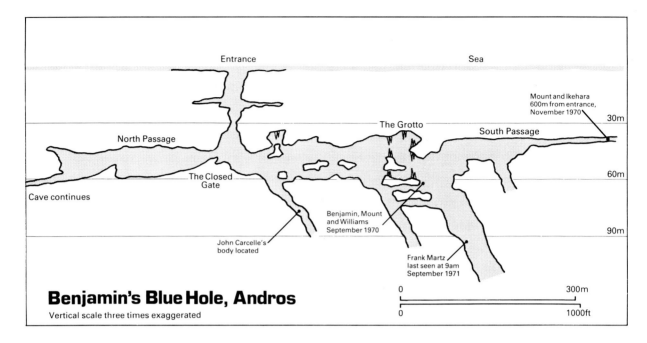

Benjamin's Blue Hole, Andros

Vertical scale three times exaggerated

(Diagram labels:)

Entrance

Sea

Mount and Ikehara
600m from entrance,
November 1970

The Grotto

North Passage

South Passage

The Closed
Gate

Cave continues

Benjamin, Mount
and Williams
September 1970

John Carcelle's
body located

Frank Martz
last seen at 9am
September 1971

30m

60m

90m

0   300m

0   1000ft

panicked, grabbed hold of the cave wall and despite all efforts refused to be moved. Early the next morning Tom Mount accompanied Lockwood back into the cave to recover the body. They found it, not at fifty-five metres, but at seventy-eight metres. Carcelle was off-line, his tanks were, effectively, empty, his bottles and mask were off, and he had removed his buoyancy vest. Tragically a combination of narcosis, panic and inexperience had proved overwhelming; the cave had claimed its first life.

But worse was to follow. Later that week the highly experienced Frank Martz joined the group. Martz was keen to explore an exceptionally deep pit over 300m into the cave. In so doing he planned to push the very limits of compressed air diving. His companion for this attempt would be Jim Lockwood. Initially all went to plan and they reached the 300m point, attached a new line and started down the shaft. At eighty-four metres depth Martz carefully negotiated a constriction, then continued down to ninety metres. At this point he tied off the line and in so doing stirred up a lot of silt. In thick cloud the divers became separated and in the ensuing confusion Lockwood believed that Martz had started up. Visibility was atrocious and Lockwood began his exit. He never saw

his friend again. Lockwood had lost two diving partners within the space of ten days. No trace was ever found of Martz's body. Precisely what happened we shall never know, but when an accident befalls such an experienced diver it inevitably leads to a period of introspection.

Deep diving is unquestionably dangerous, but under the optimum conditions experienced in this area, divers were seemingly lured on to ever greater challenge. Clearly people such as Martz were influenced by the record open water penetrations that had been undertaken off Andros in the early 1960s. In 1961, for example, Betty Singer set a world record for women when she descended to ninety-three metres (310ft). In 1962 Dick Birch and Roger Hutchins went down to 139m/462ft, establishing an outright world record. Despite the understood limitations of compressed air and the likelihood of sudden blackout due to oxygen poisoning, divers were clearly prepared to run the risk.

35. (top right) The entrance of Rat Cay Blue Hole, Andros.

36. (near right) Frank Martz and Jim Lockwood before the fateful dive into Benjamin's Blue Hole in September 1971, when Martz disappeared diving below ninety metres. *37. (far right) Benjamin's team exploring Benjamin's Blue Hole.*

38. (top) *The entry to Uncle Charlie's Blue Hole, explored by Martyn Farr and Rob Palmer in 1981.*   **39.** (above) *In Rat Cay Blue Hole.*

40. (right) *In one of the superbly decorated passages of Sistema Sac Actun, Tulum, Yucatan, Mexico. This multi-entranced cave system, first explored by Jim Coke, is typical of the shallow, warm water 'cenotes' (water-filled passages) of the Yucatan peninsular.*

In 1971, Archie Forfar, a close friend of Benjamin, planned to make a world record attempt, in partnership with Anne Gunderson, offshore from Stafford Creek. They hoped to dive to a depth of 150m. On this occasion considerable attention was given to safety, and an inflation system had been arranged whereby if anything went seriously wrong the divers could be brought back to the surface without difficulty.

Sheck Exley, who had a known tolerance to oxygen poisoning, was assigned the task of support diver. As he watched he suddenly realised that the safety measures were ineffectual, that the pair had lost consciousness and were sinking uncontrollably. In attempting to reach them he too blacked out, but fortunately not before hitting his emergency inflation device. Miraculously Exley regained consciousness on the way up, deep enough to halt his ascent and decompress before succumbing to the bends. The attempt ended in disaster, the bodies of Forfar and his girlfriend were never recovered.

It was not until 1981 that the next phase of exploration took place in the Blue Holes of Andros Island. In August Rob Palmer and I took a small team of cave divers for a month's expedition. Constrained by financial limitations and lack of knowledge of the advanced techniques developed in Florida, ours was essentially a modified British approach – improvised and lightweight.

Luck was with us. Despite a worrying set of introductory dives – falling foul of the currents and discovering the body of an unknown, totally ill-equipped diver in Uncle Charlie's Blue Hole, we went on to make a spate of interesting discoveries. Rat Cay was extended from Benjamin's limit of forty-five metres through a constricted bedding passage to reveal over 450m of passages in fabulously clear water, possessing rich and varied marine life throughout. But the most significant series of dives took place in

Above: The body of an unknown diver found in Uncle Charlie's Blue Hole by Farr and Palmer during their 1981 exploration.

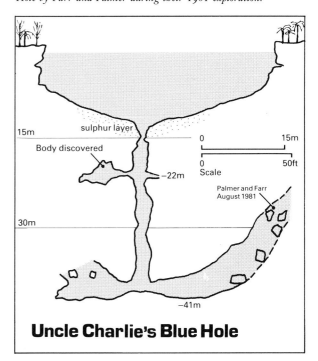

Uncle Charlie's Blue Hole

41. 42. (left) Angel Soto Porrua and Sergio Zambrano diving in Nacimiento del Rio Mante in April 1988 to support Sheck Exley. On this occasion Exley reached 238-242m, a dive which required him to spend ten hour's of carefully staged decompression (inset). In March 1989 he made another dive, reaching a record depth of 267m.

Above: Rob Palmer passing through the constricted entrance to Rat Cay Blue Hole and (right) examining a turtle shell further into the cave.

Conch Blue Hole. By the end of the expedition we had reached a point 700m from the entrance. The following year this site was extended to 1153m, at the time the longest undersea penetration in the world.

On neighbouring Grand Bahama Island another extremely lengthy system was in the process of being mapped at this time. Over a period of years locally-based Dennis Williams and friends explored and surveyed Lucayan Caverns, a confusing maze-like network of tunnels extending for a staggering ten

kilometres. Not only is this one of the longest submerged caves in the world, it is also a firm contender for the status of the most beautiful. It is profusely decorated for most of its length and, with conservation very much in mind, weaving one's way in and out of a veritable forest of stal structures is a real nightmare.

In the later 1980s perhaps the most significant exploration to date was undertaken in the blue holes of eastern Andros. Rob Palmer has played a major role here and over a number of expeditions has continued with a series of scientific projects. In 1987, for example, the first exploratory dive was made with

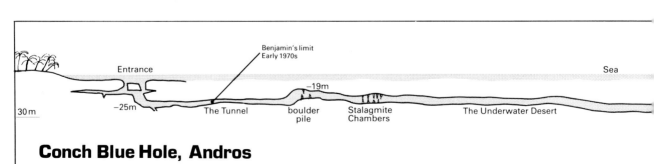

Conch Blue Hole, Andros

the Carmellan Rebreather. Two years later Palmer and Stuart Clough used this apparatus again, bettering the depth of −98m at Stargate Blue Hole when they reached −100m in Great North Road Blue Hole, Grand Bahama.

The Andros Project of 1987 was also to witness the first extensive use of Heliox in open circuit apparatus for deep cave diving. Over a dozen sites were explored and mapped to a maximum depth of ninety-seven metres. The direct beneficiary of this successful series of dives was the expedition to Wakulla Springs just two months later.

Blue Hole diving is a fabulous and amazing experi-

Above: Rob Parker ferrying bottles through a stalagmite cavern in Conch Blue Hole.

ence. Here, for example, the normally tedious time spent on decompression is full of interest. I remember vividly the few hours circling the entrance shaft of Conch Blue Hole following the record penetration in August 1982. It was just like being in an aquarium and for once you had the time to absorb the true splendour of the underwater world. There were glorious arrays of tube fans, arrow crabs, and pink and white banded coral shrimps. Each had its niche, its territory, its home, bounded by seemingly invisible borders. Beautiful

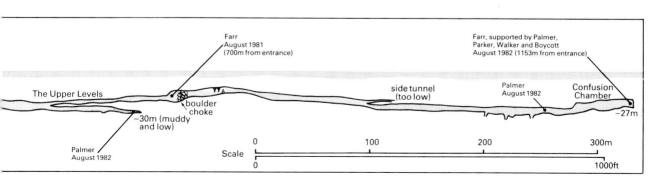

Farr
August 1981
(700m from entrance)

Farr, supported by Palmer,
Parker, Walker and Boycott
August 1982 (1153m from entrance)

The Upper Levels

boulder choke

−30m (muddy and low)

side tunnel
(too low)

Palmer
August 1982

Confusion Chamber

−27m

Palmer
August 1982

Scale

0   100   200   300m

0   1000ft

little damsel fish defended their patches of ledge against creatures altogether larger. Anything that moved too close stimulated little acts of aggression: with a thud a hermit crab, perhaps three or four times the size of the fish, would be knocked over and driven away. With a diver the brave little fish would resort to a head-on confrontation with the face mask; recurrent butts relating the clear message 'please leave me alone'. What an experience! Why explore lifeless tunnels deep underground when wonders such as these exist?

Inland, the more obvious life forms are often missing but the diving even from the tourist point of view, is often just as fantastic. Stalactite Blue Hole is a classic case in point. This site is difficult to find. Hidden in scrubland about twenty-four kilometres from the coast, at the end of a virtually non existent track. Were it anywhere else but on Andros Island it would be deluged by eager sight-seers and photographers. At the surface the site is just like all the other blue holes, a huge circular pool of placid water. However, down at twenty-two metres' depth the walls recede to yield a vast cavern, the bottom of which is lost in a void of seemingly unfathomable gloom. Here the diver checks his steady free-fall descent and floats back under the ceiling. Behind him lies the reassuring blue haze of daylight; ahead a spectacular array of massive stalactites. Some are ten metres in length and to swim amidst these is like weaving a course between enormous pillars or massive tree trunks. I suspect that this is a quite unique site in its own right: if there were 'seven wonders' in the diving world Stalactite Blue Hole would certainly feature on the list.

Blue holes are present in vast numbers right across the Bahamas and many of the sites have yet to receive even a cursory exploration. The diving presents some of the most enjoyable and challenging cave exploration anywhere in the world and, as with Florida, we can certainly expect to hear of some exciting developments in this area.

MEXICO

The Yucatan Coast

On the other side of the Caribbean pioneering work has been undertaken on the Yucatan coast of southern Mexico. Here, in the area of the Tulum and Akumal, home of the Mayan people, are numerous flooded systems known locally as 'cenotes'.

Diving in the clear, tropical waters of the Caribbean has been extremely popular for many years and, understandably, the lure of diving beneath a rocky roof in a comparatively inhospitable jungle environ-ment was initially distinctly unappealing. Thus the sport of cave diving is still in its infancy here, but none the less, incredible discoveries have already been made.

It was 1979 when Ned DeLoach persuaded Sheck Exley to visit the Yucatan area for the first time. Both were impressed by the clarity of the water, the extent of the shallow flooded passageways and the obvious potential for archaeological discoveries. Surprisingly, it was not until 1984 that any significant explorations were undertaken, when Americans John Zumrick, Noel Sloan, Gary Storrick and others of the Peña Colorada Expedition made a further reconnaissance of the area's fabulous potential.

Zumrick subsequently developed a keen interest in the Yucatan and was largely responsible for the establishment, and training, of an active exploration group here. In the late 1980s major contributions were made by people such as Parker Turner, Steve Gerrard, locally based divers such as Jim Coke and Mike Madden and many others.

Names such as Carwash – just five steps from a gravel road, Temple of Doom, Mayan Blue, and Naharon are today celebrated by visiting divers. Situated about five kilometres from the coast, the temperature of the fresh water in the flooded tunnels is 25°C (a good deal warmer in the surface pool). These complex systems are usually shallow, averaging fifteen metres deep, and are lavishly decorated.

In the late 1980s exploration increased. In February 1987, Mike Madden and Johanna Degroot connected Mayan Blue to Naharon, when, after a double-stage dive over one kilometre, they discovered a reel

deposited by Turner the previous day in downstream Naharon. Interesting archaeological finds are also being made. One example was in Carwash, known locally as Cenote Crystal, where a 200m penetration in a downstream direction led to a sizeable chamber at thirty metres' depth. Here the explorers discovered a pyramid-shaped rock which contains a carved out hollow filled with what appears to be charcoal. It is presumed this was an altar or ceremonial site left by the ancient Mayans over 15,000 years ago, when water levels were much lower than today.

Since their discovery, these caves have witnessed amazingly rapid exploration. The Naharon-Mayan Blue System was explored to nearly five kilometres in 1988, while the longest submerged system, Cueva Quebrada, on nearby Cozumel Island, also measured nearly five kilometres. Dennis Williams, Jeff Bozanic and Parker Turner have been the key figures in the latter, exploring this phenomenal length of passage in just two years.

NoHoch Nah Chich (Giant Birdhouse)

Another exciting cave discovery in the mainland area was that made by Madden and Coke in November 1987. Using pack mules to carry gear two kilometres over a rugged jungle trail the pair made the first dive in the locally named site NoHoch Nah Chich (Mayan for 'Giant Birdhouse').

In March the following year, Madden was joined by Steve Gerrard and Juan Jose Tucat for a major exploration beyond the previous limit. The system

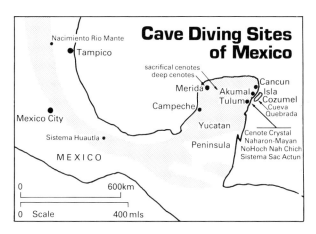

Above: Passing through the fabulous passages of NoHoch Nah Chich (Giant Birdhouse), Yucatan, Mexico, first explored by Mike Madden and Jim Coke in 1987.

Left: Approaching the Sacs Room in Naharon, a cave with dark rock that, despite crystal clear water, lends it a forboding atmosphere.

possessed an average depth of just five metres up to the furthest point (1372m from the entrance) and the trio came well equipped with the normal back-mounted 104 cu.ft bottles and two stage cylinders apiece. They also carried seven reels of line to add to that already in place. The exploration was expected to last six hours.

Diving along the fabulously decorated tunnel (one section is now called Heaven's Gate) the water was crystal clear. The first-stage bottles were dropped at 762m, and the second cylinders beneath a jungle skylight at 1189m. They reached the end of the previously installed line at 1372m/4500ft. The dive continued just as they had hoped. The depth remained shallow and the route was 'awesomely pretty' throughout. Madden later reported: 'Formations are brilliant white, in every shape, size and dimension with mountains of ivory white silt that call up thoughts of sparkling snow drifts.'

The exploration was terminated half-way through the sixth reel. They had laid an amazing 1250m/4100ft of new line – for one dive a new world record.

By the time they returned to the entrance they had been diving for five hours and forty minutes, and had swum a total distance of 2621m. A highly significant achievement, establishing the system as one of the longest underwater caves in Mexico. The overall length of the cave extended to over 9145m/30,000ft in 1990 – in terms of international ranking, second only to Cathedral Canyon in Florida. With many side passages still to be explored, it begs the obvious question: could NoHoch Nah Chich be the longest underwater system in the world?

Sheck Exley's Dives at Nacimiento del Rio Mante
Mexico not only has much fabulous shallow diving, it also offers some of the most challenging deep diving anywhere in the world. In this sphere American divers have pioneered the way, in particular Sheck Exley.

Several major risings at the foot of the Sierra Madre Oriental have considerable depth, in particular the Nacimiento del Rio Mante. This is a site which may prove to be deeper than the Fontaine de Vaucluse. Lying in the same strata of rock in which the famous shaft Golondrinas is formed, and almost certainly discharging water from the central plateau of Mexico (100km to the west of the spring), this is a firm contender for the deepest submerged cave in the world. Geologically, this site has a depth potential of 300m to 500m. Here Exley mounted a series of major operations, slowly but surely penetrating to almost unbelievable depth. In March 1979 he and Paul De-Loach reached 101m, in strong flowing, 27°C water. The narrow shaft continued into the crystal depths.

Exley had more than enough work in his local Florida springs, but Hasenmayer's dramatic penetration to 205m at the Fontaine de Vaucluse in 1983 once more served to heighten Exley's interest in the deep rising at Mante. Following the successful use of helium Trimix during the training exercises for the 1985 Wookey Hole project, he also began to experiment with mixed gas diving. Consequently, on a typically well-prepared dive operation at Rio Mante in May 1987, Exley made a bold descent to 159m. This set a depth record for the Americas and also illustrated the extreme dangers of such depths. Somewhere near the bottom Exley lost his watch, which resulted in the taxing requirement of having to count down the decompression schedule. This concentrated effort began at fifty metres. Fortunately, he had left a spare watch at the twenty-metre level, otherwise he would have had to continue for the total decompression time, which was more than ten hours.

Two months later Exley returned. With the hot summer it was hoped that the resurgence would be in an optimum state for an even deeper dive. Unfortunately,

Below: Rio Mante pioneers Sheck Exley (left), Mary Ellen Eckhoff and Paul DeLoach. Exley was supported in later dives by Ned DeLoach and the Mexicans Angel Sota Porrua and Sergio Zambrano.

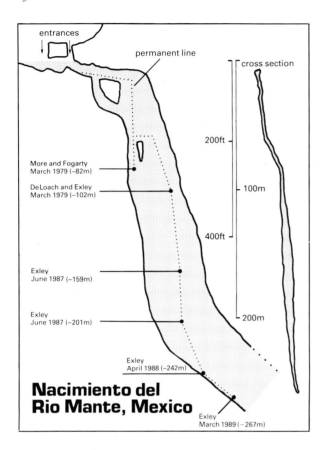

entrances

permanent line

cross section

200ft

100m

More and Fogarty
March 1979 (−82m)

DeLoach and Exley
March 1979 (−102m)

400ft

Exley
June 1987 (−159m)

Exley
June 1987 (−201m)

200m

Exley
April 1988 (−242m)

**Nacimiento del
Rio Mante, Mexico**

Exley
March 1989 (−267m)

this was not the case. Visibility was only five metres and the current flow stronger than before.

Undeterred by this, preparations went ahead. On 23 June, on a solo dive, Mary Ellen Eckhoff (Exley's wife) established a women's world depth record when she made a descent to 122m, extending her own seven-year world record of ninety-five metres. In so doing, she also became the fifth person ever to reach such an extreme depth.

Two days later Exley was ready for his own attempt on the ultimate record. Quite apart from relatively poor water conditions, the trip was destined not to go as smoothly as planned. At a depth of eighty-two metres a demand valve on one of his Trimix bottles failed. This forced him to breath compressed air on down to 100m, a point far below the normal maximum safe depth for the gas. At this point the unforseen failure had a knock-on effect and, at one hundred metres' depth, he changed on to a pre-staged bottle

left there for the ascent, using it instead for descent. Coolly Exley weighed the odds and continued on down. Eventually he reached a point where the shaft narrowed to only one and a half metres and where the current was uncomfortably strong. By now he had also overstayed his planned maximum descent time by four minutes. He quickly tied off and slowly started upon the ascent. By counting the knots on the line he had just laid he soon discovered that his terminal depth had been 201m/660ft.

Some thirty-nine decompression stops, six different gas mixtures, and eleven hours and thirteen minutes later the jubilant explorer reached the surface. Exley had used fifteen cylinders on the dive (excluding safety tanks, which were not used) and had made the longest recorded dive in caving history. The decompression schedule, based upon linear extrapolation of the Oceaneering commercial diving decompression tables, proved successful and Exley experienced few post-dive problems, only a temporary case of skin bends.

Down to 242m/795ft in Rio Mante
In passing the 200m level, Exley had almost equalled the depth reached by Jochen Hasenmayer in the Fontaine de Vaucluse. There was now little doubt that given favourable conditions he could go even deeper. Within a short while he planned another attempt.

In April 1988 Exley and supporters Ned DeLoach, Sergio Zambrano and Angel Soto Porrua, returned yet again. After several set-up dives, the push took place on 5 April, when forty-three metres of line were laid to a depth of at least 238m, possibly even as deep as 242m/795ft. The reason for the inaccuracy is that he was unable to locate an accurate 300m depth gauge, and as his line was slightly inclined near the bottom, he had to estimate the angle of the shaft. On this occasion most of his equipment worked perfectly, but, even so, the rigours of this depth were such that one demand valve failed, a pressure gauge needle stuck and one of his battery packs again imploded. The latter caused concussion which Exley described

Right: Sheck Exley embarks on his record-breaking Rio Mante dive to 238-242m in 1988 – the deepest point ever reached in a flooded cave. Descents to this depth pose daunting pressure and physiological problems. In 1989 Exley reached 267m in this cave.

as 'shaking the cave'. Such a sequence of events would surely have triggered high stress in a less experienced diver, so the total control exhibited by Exley was all the more impressive. He took just twenty-four minutes to reach this extreme depth, but the ascent time was over ten hours. On this occasion Dr R. W.(Bill) Hamilton, probably the world's greatest authority on the physiology of deep diving, had formulated the gas mixtures (eleven different types) and calculated the fifty-two decompression stops.

A Depth Record of 267m/875ft

The remarkable depth achieved at Mante put Exley in a league of his own. It did not, however, satisfy the needs or the potential of this exceptional explorer. Having regained the world length record in January 1989 at Chip's Cave in Florida, plans were formulated for an even deeper dive at Mante. Comparatively few divers worldwide had penetrated below a depth of one hundred metres in a cave, while apart from himself only Jochen Hasenmayer had reached 200m. The target Exley now set himself was 300m, over sixty metres deeper than the existing record. Even with Hamilton's support, the risks posed by this project were immense. The operation was experimental and far from any safety controls. Mixtures and timing had to be precise; any equipment failures would be critical. There is can be little doubt that the stress imposed at every stage of this dive was without parallel.

The dive took place on 28 March 1989. Exley's rig of cylinders on this occasion consisted of three 104 cu.ft tanks (pressurized to 4000 p.s.i.) linked together with two 105 cu.ft composite cylinders, which nested behind them, all constituting a substantial five-tank back-pack. In addition, he carried two 80 cu.ft stage bottles on his front. These seven cylinders constituted only his descent supply of gas; the decompression schedule required another eighteen cylinders staged for his return, the lowest at a depth of 130m.

Reaching his previous limit, everything seemed to be going to plan. He tied on and continued to descend. However, despite the use of the most efficient deep diving regulators, trouble soon developed. Basically, his breathing became increasingly laboured due to the density of the gas supply and, twenty-two metres deeper than his April 1988 limit, the situation was deemed 'extremely difficult'. The line was tied off at 267m/875ft and the long ascent commenced, involving fourteen hours of decompression.

Once more Exley had set an indelible mark on the sport. By pushing so far beyond the realm of rational diving, he had proved yet again that, given determination, good teamwork and technical efficiency, the frontiers were in no way insurmountable. The 300m barrier will surely be attained soon.

It should be noted that, quite apart from being an outstanding world depth record for a cave diving penetration, Exley's dive to 267m also constitutes by far the deepest dive attained by any amateur diver. Deeper dives have been made in the sea, but always in a supported situation. Divers working in the oil industry operate at depths of up to 400m, but only when in the proximity of a diving bell, which provides their breathing gas through an umbilical tube. They operate for limited periods and the lengthy decompression is then carried out in the warmth and comfort of a dry hyperbaric chamber, carefully monitored and controlled at all times. The situation of the solo diver, embarking from a line of prearranged decompression points, is infinitely more committing.

The greatest depth yet achieved in the sea is 531m established by divers of the oil support company Comex, on the experimental operation named Hydra VIII. Such projects are not only highly expensive but also very time-consuming. The six divers involved were compressed for five days before commencing their underwater tasks. Five days were spent at extreme depth with the divers working in the water for no longer than four hours a day. Their subsequent decompression period lasted eighteen days.

Mexican Cave Systems in the Mountains

Apart from the challenging nature of pure diving projects, Mexico is also a land of high, arid, rugged mountains and here potential is such that there may well be a contender for the world's deepest cave system. The Sierra Madre Oriental is a vast chain of karst mountains still only partially explored. Relatively close to Mante, for example, lie the awesome free fall shafts of El Sotano (Sotano del Barro) and

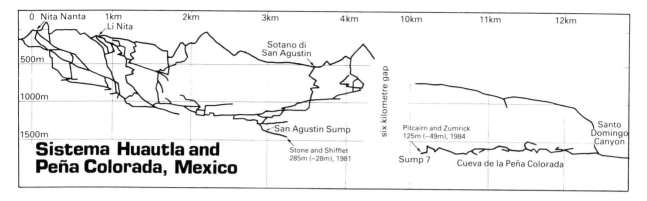

Sistema Huautla and
Peña Colorada, Mexico

0 Nita Nanta 1km 2km 3km 4km 10km 11km 12km

500m

1000m

1500m

six kilometre gap

Sotano di
San Agustin

San Agustin Sump

Stone and Shifflet
285m (−28m), 1981

Pitcairn and Zumrick
125m (−49m), 1984

Sump 7

Cueva de la Peña Colorada

Santo
Domingo
Canyon

Golondrinas. In 1978 Sistema Purificacion on the western edge of Tamaulipas was established as the deepest through trip in the world: a subterranean traverse of 868m/2848ft in a system extending, by 1990, for a total of over seventy-two kilometres. The potential of this fabulous caving region is immense.

San Agustin Sump, Huautla System

The most exciting such exploration has been at the Sistema Huautla, an amazingly intricate cave network set on a 2000m plateau in southern Mexico. This system is now over fifty-two kilometres long, terminating at a sump at 1252m depth in San Agustin.

American cavers were quick to realise the huge potential of the plateau and, in 1979, as part of the major ongoing Huautla project, Bill Stone made a tentative exploration of the final sump using small 'pony' (15 cu.ft) tanks. The submerged passage rapidly descended to over twenty metres, but this was a depth too great for any significant advance with such modest equipment.

A careful reconnaissance revealed the resurgence for the many sinks on the plateau, which lay 1600m/5249ft below and ten kilometres away. While his Huautla colleagues continued with a multitude of dry explorations, Stone conceived the idea of mounting a major diving assault on the bottom of San Agustin. The transport of conventional cylinders to the terminal sump would be almost impossible, but knowledge and contacts in the space industry led to a completely radical, innovative development. A quantity of high pressure, experimental composite fibreglass-aluminium cylinders was obtained from Acurex Aerotherm Corporation; these were exceptionally lightweight bottles with a working pressure of 5500 p.s.i. These had a

capacity of 105 cu.ft at that pressure. They weighed 19lbs when empty, 25lbs when full.

Trials with the new bottles and other equipment necessary for a deep diving cave assault took place in Florida in late 1980. The following April, after a marathon carry*, Stone made a solo dive at the downstream sump. Flood conditions had only recently abated, so visibility was far from perfect, nevertheless a penetration of 285m was achieved, reaching a terminal depth of twenty-eight metres.

The Peña Colorada Explorations

Attention turned to the presumed resurgence of the Sistema Huautla waters, an extremely isolated spring known as Peña Colorada, in the Santo Domingo valley, which had been located in 1981. A reconnaissance dive was undertaken here by Stone, John Zumrick and Pat Weideman in April 1982, again using the lightweight prototype equipment. They quickly passed a 524m sump to discover nearly a kilometre of large passage, heading directly towards San Agustin.

Two years later, in February 1984, Stone returned in force with his international Peña Colorada Expedition, comprising eleven veteran cave explorers, all thoroughly trained in the advanced equipment. Some seven tons of gear was transported in from the United States for a planned three-month expedition. Once more, Sherwood Selpac and Acurex Aerotherm rallied to the challenge and, on this occasion, supplied the team with seventy-two sets of equipment, with cylinders weighing 20lbs capable of being pressurised

* In 1981, eight men were engrossed for six weeks on the San Agustin dive. Six were 'sherpas': Alan Warild, Neil Hickson, Tony White, Ron Simmons, Chris Kerr, and Bob Jeffreys; the two divers were Stone and Tommy Shifflet. The operation involved a ten-day stay at Camp 3 (120m above the sump).

to 6000 p.s.i. giving well over an hours' duration at twenty metres' depth.

The team contained experts in every field of cave exploration: co-leader Bob Jefferys was probably America's best subterranean climber; Clark Pitcairn held the American dive penetration record (along with Exley) of 2337m/7667ft at Manatee Springs; Rob Parker was one of the most versatile cave explorers in the United Kingdom; while Sergio Zambrano and Angel Soto Porrua were the leading cave divers from Mexico. Medical and paramedical expertise came in the form of Dr Noel Sloan, Dr John Zumrick and Stone's wife, Pat Wiedeman. The core team was completed by Gary Storrick and John Evans.

With methodically efficient logistics, the team slowly but surely overcame a series of sumps, severe technical climbs and routine sections of dry cave, penetrating ever further in the direction of San Agustin. Sump 2 (14m) and Sump 3 (190m) led to extensive galleries, which necessitated an advance camp. From here Sump 4 (55m) was tackled, followed by Sump 5 (140m). Beyond this Clark Pitcairn, on his initial solo exploration, was halted by yet another steep climbing shaft. Parker and Jefferys soon overcame this 200m ascent, and 180m further on reached a long swim. Sump 6 was bypassed, but beyond was another gruelling section of over 400m involving three difficult pitches. This terminated at Sump 7. The Peña Colorada had developed into the most technical cave exploration ever attempted.

With various options eliminated, the team's efforts eventually focused on Sump 7. This operation required immense preparation, with virtually a full complement of manpower, and the establishment of a second camp over four kilometres from the entrance. Owing to lack of ledges at water-level the assault on Sump 7 was particularly awkward. Kitting up had to be undertaken at the head of a fifty-seven-metre, free-fall shaft, down which the diver had to abseil fully equipped to dive.

At Sump 7 the nature of the diving also became serious. Stone forged the initial route between boulders down to a depth of forty metres. During a ten-day push later on, Pitcairn and Zumrick continued for a further 125m to forty-nine metres' depth at the roof of a huge, ongoing tunnel. A further assault was out of the question. They had reached their logistical limit.

When the survey was complete, it showed an overall cave length of nearly eight kilometres. They had extended the resurgence system about a third of the distance towards the Sotano de San Agustin. Despite the novel difficulties the camps had presented, they were evidently an essential element in the expedition's success. Some twenty-three days were spent working beyond Camp 1, and Camp 2, sited beyond five sumps, was occupied for six days.

The story does not end here. In March 1987 Jim Smith finally connected San Agustin to neighbouring Nita Nanta by passing another short dive. The connection with this upper plateau system has increased the overall depth of the Huautla System to 1353m/4437ft. In the process Sistema Huautla took third place on the list of the world's deepest caves. The system has now fallen to sixth place (January 1991) owing to discoveries in Spain and the Soviet Union. However, a final connection with the Peña Colorada resurgence and the appreciable increase in depth which this would yield (1639m total), would certainly be sufficient to take the world depth record.

The Cueva Cheve System

Despite optimism over the long-term depth potential of the Huautla System, it is relatively limited. Recent developments have thrown another contender into the arena. To the south of Huautla the major discovery of 1989 was Cueva Cheve, a system already surveyed to a depth of 1340m/4395ft where it terminates at a sump. This is another exhilarating prospect with its limit set at a point well over ten kilometres from the entrance. The possibilities here are considerable with a further 1260m to go vertically before reaching the level of the active springs, fifteen kilometres to the south. The depth potential here is therefore 2600m – at present the deepest in the world.

43. *(top right) In Sistema Sac Actun, Mexico (see plate 40 caption).*

44. *(right) Rob Parker portering the very light Acurax/composite cylinders through a twenty-metre sump during the 1984 Peña Colorada explorations. The consignment is so light it has been lead weighted for neutral buoyancy.* 45. *(far right) Descending a 20m flowstone wall between Sumps 3 and 4 in Peña Colorada, Mexico.*

46. (above) Rex Starling and Ian Bamford manoeuvre the cylinder sledge used on the 1979 Australian Cocklebiddy expedition.

47. (top right) The South African team that explored the Dragon's Breath Hole, Namibia in 1987: (front row – left to right) Paul Williams, Dave Roux, Charles Maxwell and Phil Church; (back row) Sandy Mazzotti, Dick Howell, Sean French, Andrew Penney, Keith Pickersgill, Vince Calder and Brandon Page. **48.** (near right) The surface lake of Bushmansgat. **49. 50.** (far right) In the Dragon's Breath Hole – an overall view of the cavern and two divers returning, winding in the line reel after a survey (see page 264).

CHAPTER ELEVEN

SOUTHERN HEMISPHERE

AUSTRALIA

In comparison with the United States or Europe, cave diving in Australasia has been very much a minority pursuit. To some extent this can be explained by the vastness of the area involved and its comparative lack of cave bearing rock. Despite its relatively small population, the geographical isolation of the continent, and the remoteness of caving areas, some exciting and extremely significant explorations have taken place here.

Diving into submerged caves first occurred in the early 1950s. Sport divers took advantage of crystal clear waters in the Mount Gambier sinkholes, an area conveniently sited mid-way between Adelaide and Melbourne, while cavers from Sydney University Speleological Society were the first to tackle sumps in the Jenolan area of the Blue Mountains.

Under the leadership of Dennis Burke, the Sydney team began their exploration with air-pumps and hoses, although normal, self-contained, compressed air equipment was adopted later in the 1950s. Short sumps were successfully passed, and well over 600m of passages were discovered beyond. Further work took place in this system after 1979, when Ron Allum and colleagues made further extensions amounting to 400m. Connections between the various caves here offer scope for a system in excess of twelve kilometres, but difficulties of distance, cold water, constrictions and silt render exploration difficult and sporadic.

By the beginning of the 1960s there was an improvement in the availability of diving equipment in

Australia. Tasmania, one of the more important caving regions, was the first area to witness a major cave diving penetration. In 1961 an epic 500m dive in cold murky water was achieved in the Kubla Khan System. This record penetration stood until 1976, when exploration commenced beneath the arid Nullarbor Plain of South Australia.

The Nullarbor Plain

The Nullarbor Plain is one of the world's largest continuous areas of limestone. Covering an expanse of over 200,000 sq. km, this vast area stretches inland from the Great Australian Bight for over 300km to the Great Victoria Desert. Lying generally between eighty and a hundred metres above sea-level, the semi-desert landscape is monotonously flat with no surface streams or even dry valleys. However, isolated dolines or collapse craters indicate the subterranean cave systems which today enjoy worldwide renown.

Over 200 caves have now been explored in this area,

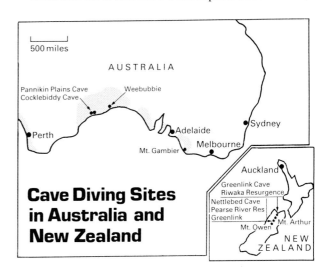

Cave Diving Sites in Australia and New Zealand

51. (bottom left) Eric Le Guen speeds through Cocklebiddy Cave on his Aquazepp. 52. (left) Members of the successful 1983 Australian Cocklebiddy team with their equipment sledges during the passage of Sump 2. 53. (top left) Heading into Weebubbie Cave.

some of which possess huge trunk passages which are among the largest in the world. Less than a dozen of these descend to the watertable (about nine metres above sea-level) and a handful end in spectacularly large, crystal clear lakes.

Pastoralists were among the first to explore the more obvious cave sites at the turn of the century and at places such as Weebubbie Cave water was pumped from them for stock watering. The brackish nature of the water meant that a degree of desalination was required before it could be used for domestic supply.

Dives at Weebubbie, 1961-72

Being the most accessible site, Weebubbie was the first cave to be dived in this remote area. A two-man team from Perth made a brief dive here in 1961, but was unable to proceed any great distance owing to the limitations of their equipment. They did, however, establish that the temperature was a pleasant 19-21°C and that a massive black tunnel led off into the distance. In 1972 Ian Lewis of the Cave Exploration Group of South Australia organised a large-scale expedition involving six divers and a support team of thirty cavers to give Weebubbie a thorough exploration. The ongoing passage was traversed for ninety metres into a huge, domed air-bell at the far side. Beyond this point the passage descended steeply to about twenty-seven metres' depth and the cave seemed to split into a network of very small tubes. However, on the way through the first sump, a side passage, the Railway Tunnel, was discovered and this was explored for over 243m to forty-one metres' depth.

Early Explorations of Cocklebiddy Cave, 1972-77

The most spectacular and challenging site on the Nullarbor, and, indeed, in the whole of Australia, was Cocklebiddy Cave, situated about 250 miles from Weebubbie, in western Australia. Cocklebiddy was much more isolated, and for any exploration here the divers realised that not only had they to be totally self-contained in terms of equipment and food but also had to take a large supply of drinking water. This cave too, received its first dive in 1972, when 300m of line was laid along a shallow, spacious, northward-trending passage. The team quickly recognised the potential of

this diving site and over the course of the next decade it was to assume worldwide importance.

In 1974 the pace of activities accelerated. Lewis returned with Keith Dekkers, and the other known diving sites were given a tentative examination. Inspired by what he had seen, later that year Dekkers teamed up with another determined diver from Perth, Hugh Morrison. On this trip further advances were made at both Weebubbie and Cocklebiddy.

The following year two separate expeditions were mounted to the area. The South Australians took to the field first and extended all the caves they visited. Morrison, Dekkers and friends from West Australia arrived later in the year, solely to tackle the large, inviting tunnel in Cocklebiddy. This foundered on the second day when the compressor blew up.

In May 1976 a joint South and West Australia expedition was organised, the largest to date, which involved all the previous divers together with Peter Stace and Ron Allum. Preparations were thorough, and a highly successful series of dives was made. An extract from R. Beilby's diary depicts the scene.

Today (May 17) we did a push to 2000ft. The purpose of this dive was to install three full single 72s at 2000ft into the cave. This would give us a base camp of reserve air for a later, further push. I carried my yellow single without any compensating buoyancy bag and was just about knackered when the 600 metres of line was run out. Yesterday the South Australians did a dive to 1000ft in and pitoned off [belayed the line]. We left the tanks hanging stuck to the roof with spare buoyancy vests. My tank was tied to one which was inadequate so my yellow single was additionally secured to the line by cord.

Greatest depth was thirty to thirty-five feet on the way in, averaging fifteen to twenty feet. Visibility was good at all times except where our bubbles brought down silt and flakes of rock. . . . finally returned to the main chamber one-and-a-half hours later from dive start. I had a pounding CO_2 headache from the exertion on the penetration.

This day (May 18) was the big push. Hugh Morrison and I were to carry a single in to 2000ft breathing off it and have the support divers carry it out from 2000ft. Then we two were to take two reels with a combined total of 2000ft of line and

Top right: The first sump in Weebubbie Cave.
Right: A diver at work in Weebubbie Cave below the Nullarbor Plain, Western Australia. The 1972 explorations penetrated 243m (−41m).

continue the push to the end of the line or our turnaround of two thirds air.

In the morning I felt quite nervous and was interested to see that nobody was keen to start. In fact, when everything was ready we sat around in the warm sun swapping tales and anecdotes. Finally I had to say let's get going because the dive was going to be a long one and it was already going on midday . . .

At camp 2,000 we halted and puffed up to the roof for a rest, awaiting the arrival of the three South Australians [Phil Prust, Ron Allum and Peter Stace] . . .

In the clear cavern water we hung like flies under the pale ceiling. To our right the three spare aqualungs hung under their buoyancy vests. As the three South Australians' lights came into view the water assumed a green glow, silhouetting Steve [Gard] and Hugh with their mass of paraphernalia and glinting off the silver bubbles splattered motionless under the roof. The vast size of the cavern through which we had 'flown' became apparent . . .

We continued. The tunnel stayed on the same heading, about due north, and rose and fell under arches and flat ceilings. Suddenly it took a swoop upwards into the tell-tale black nothingness of an air chamber. We broke surface and Morrison must have been whooping into his regulator before he emerged. We found two huge boulders rising to within chest height of the surface, and stood on them, nattering excitedly. Calmed down, continued.

A lake and another sump led to an even larger lake.

While I stayed put and guarded the reels Hugh removed his twinset and went exploring on a snorkel . . . It was not long before he reported (from some distance) that it ended in a rock-pile which swooped up out of torch range . . . I put my twins on the underwater rock beside Hugh's and left my helmet with its light turned on to mark the spot.

A 180m swim led to a rock-pile: 'a megalith heaving a million tons of shattered bulk up into a vast pocket of ceiling . . . Beyond lay another sump, so they had to return to collect their kit.'

Climbing the rock-pile was sheer hell. Inside my suit I felt grossly overheated. My heart was going fit to burst and so were my lungs. With frequent rests and scares and much gritting of teeth we made it to the further lake. It was bliss to let the cold cave water seep into the suit.

A ninety-metre dive followed until their line ran out:

Left: Ron Allum at Camp 2000 in Cocklebiddy Cave during a dive in 1976. Reserve cylinders were suspended in the roof of the cave at this point to support the push to the rockpile 300m further up the passage.

At the limit of our weakening torch beams an arch lay invitingly. Hugh gave me the reel and, motioning me to stay, went on. Down under the arch he went. The green glow of his light died and I was alone. It was my responsibility to retain the guideline whatever happened. My anxiety rose as the minutes ticked by and the blackness stayed complete.

Eventually Morrison returned, having made a rapid reconnaissance of about sixty to ninety metres beyond Beilby and the end of the line:

The swim out was as much of a marathon as the journey in. All torches leaked and were exhausted to the point of reducing vision to a few feet, even in the very clear water, by the time we emerged. Hugh had an accident which tore his regulator clean out of his mouth and ripped off the exhaust parts, but his presence of mind and the use of independent systems for breathing rendered the incident minor.

This was an incredible feat. Their five hours of exploration had resulted in the coverage of (what was at that time) one of the longest sumps in the world. Including the rock-pile and the additional swim beyond the end of the line the total penetration was at least 1370m/4500ft.

In 1977 the geographical separation between Perth and Sydney and the communication difficulties this presented resulted in two separate expeditions; the first by the South Australians and the second by the group from Perth.

In July that year Lewis, Allum and friends extended the cave a total of 500m into the sump beyond the rock-pile, 350m beyond the previous end of line.

Then, in August, the western Australians arrived. Considerable thought had been given to the logistics of the operation and their solution was an underwater 'floating sledge'. This was designed to transport fifteen 72 cu.ft bottles, food, lights, etc., together with a trailing telephone line, from base to the rock-pile. The incredible heavy load took three divers (Simon Jones, Steve Sinclair and Keith Dekkers) one and a half hours to push to the advance base.

At the rock-pile six cylinders, pressurised to 2500 p.s.i., were carried on to the next diving base. Using three per diver, Morrison and Jones then swam on, reached the South Australian limit and continued beyond for a further 500m, making a total distance of 2134m from the entrance. Sump 2 was now one kilometre long, and there was no end in sight. The crystal tunnel continued at between five metres' and ten metres' depth. By the time the team returned to the Entrance Lake they had been away for eleven hours, for Morrison and Jones much of it spent underwater. With a total penetration of over two kilometres, Cocklebiddy ranked foremost in the world league.

Cocklebiddy, 1979-82

The challenge presented by the cave was impossible to ignore and, while other divers around the world turned quietly green with envy, the Australians set the next round of plans in motion. In 1979 another major assault took place. In May Morrison returned with a team of nine divers and a supply of forty cylinders (72 cu.ft, pressurised to 3000 p.s.i.). After four days of intense activity the operation commenced. This time the team had brought a second sledge to transport cylinders into the sump beyond the rock-pile. In another dive lasting one and a half hours the two sledges, carrying fifteen and eight bottles respectively, were pushed to the rock-pile.

Then came the gruelling task of humping the smaller sledge, cylinders and ancillary equipment to the advance base. The rock-pile, which is twenty-four metres high and sixty metres long, proved awkward and tiring to cross, but five hours after arriving in the chamber all the necessary supplies had been moved and preparations were complete.

Pushing the sledge and breathing from three of the cylinders it supported, Simon Jones, Keith Dekkers and Hugh Morrison set off. At the previous limit of exploration, 1000m from the rock-pile, they parked the sledge and moved on into the unknown using the triple cylinders on their backs. They made a further 1000m before 'thirds' dictated their return.

The ongoing tunnel was still about fifteen metres square and visibility at the end even better than hitherto. With no green tinge to the water Dekkers described it as like looking through a vast plate glass window: '. . . to have to breathe out of a mouthpiece felt almost claustrophobic, but this could also be due to the time, because none of us had ever breathed off an aqualung for so long.'

At 2000m from the rock-pile they had made another incredible penetration. Their return trip was far from uneventful, however, as a major problem began to develop involving buoyancy.

To maintain station high in the cave passage in order to conserve air supply careful attention had to be paid to buoyancy control. The formula was complicated. It involved the normal lead-weighted belts, the varying weight of their cylinders (which became progressively more buoyant as the heavy compressed air was used up) and their buoyancy compensating bags, which were filled with air at the start to compensate for the dead weight of their load, but were steadily emptied as less buoyancy was required.

On return to the sledge these bags were nearly exhausted and it was clear that the divers would soon have difficulty in avoiding floating up to the ceiling. By the time they reached the sledge two of the three cylinders on their backs were nearly empty and therefore very buoyant, and there were three empty cylinders on the sledge (used on the way in). With insufficient air on their backs to be able to reach

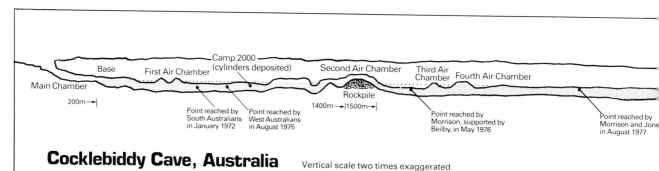

Cocklebiddy Cave, Australia   Vertical scale two times exaggerated

safety, over 900m away, plus the rapidly worsening positive buoyancy which using the last cylinder would involve, to abandon the sledge was unthinkable. This could have been a critical situation, but it was solved by cool thinking. A hole was cut in the plastic tube frame of the sledge, allowing the air to escape and stones were picked off the floor of the passage to be tied down on top of the sledge.

Above: Members of the 1979 Cocklebiddy team. Left to right: (standing) Hugh Morrison, Christine Gugiatti, Mark McKeon, Simon Jones, Bronte Heinrich and Michael Annear; (squatting) Keith Dekkers and Rex Starling.

A serious crisis was thereby averted and after four hours of constant, hard finning, the three tired explorers reached the rock-pile and a much needed rest. It then took another four hours to transport all

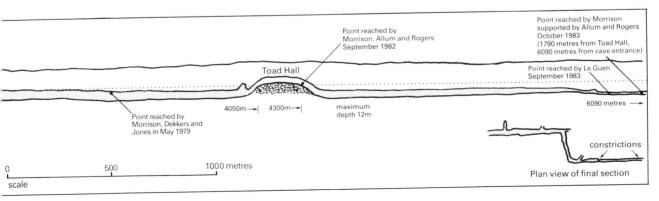

the gear back over to the far side of the pile and reassemble the two sledges for the final stage of the journey. They reached camp at 4 a.m. The entire trip had taken a total of sixteen and a half hours, of which more than seven hours had been spent below water.

The three-kilometre diving penetration at Cocklebiddy was an outstanding pioneering adventure in the epic mould. The sustained physical strain of the project, combined with its gruelling psychological aspect, invested this expedition particular significance. It is vitally important to remember that on dives of this nature things are never completely straightforward, no matter how careful the preparation, and the stress factor in particular would obviously be high. The buoyancy problem was critical and could easily have resulted in disaster. Few individuals display qualities of such extreme dedication and total self-control.

Later the same year the South Australians also made an attempt to push Cocklebiddy. Wearing five tanks apiece, the push team reached the end of the line, but were unable to progress further. This proved another marathon, four-hour continuous swim. It left all concerned with few illusions. To continue beyond this point would require a major rethink on tactics. With a terminal depth of around fourteen metres, it was also clear that decompression might soon be another problem to contend with.

In September 1982 yet another assault was organised, bringing together, for the first time, a push team consisting of Morrison, Allum and Rogers, with another large team of willing supporters. The strategy was again to use a sledge, on this occasion carrying fifteen cylinders beyond the last air-space at the rock-pile.

As they cruised quietly away from the advance base, Morrison, Allum and Rogers each had nine hours of air supply. If all went to plan, it was anticipated that they would be able to add at least 500m to the length of the cave. If they failed to surface within that time, the prospect was a gruelling six hours' continuous swimming for push and return. The dive began.

Barely had the operation got under way than a spate of remedial actions was required. The buoyancy control of the sledge proved considerably more difficult than anticipated, with the sledge and divers careering from roof to floor on more than one occasion. The trim of the sledge was by three scuba diver life-vests attached to the front, middle and rear, each being scuba-fed from tanks on the sledge. These vests were necessary to compensate for the estimated thirty kilograms of air which would be consumed during the dive. However, because air-filled life vests were present on the otherwise constant-volume sledge, depth changes during the dive from zero to fourteen metres also resulted in buoyancy changes which required constant attention.

Other excitements during the first 500m of the dive included a blown high-pressure hose on one of Morrison's regulators and an extruded O-ring from the first stage attachment on one of Roger's regulators. (These problems were subsequently attributed to the over-pressurized tanks.)

On and on they swam. At the 1800m mark Morrison indicated he had used a third of his air from the sledge, so, as arranged, the sledge was 'parked' against the roof. About 200m further on and some two and a half hours after leaving the rock-pile, they reached the end of the guideline. They were two kilometres into the dive and the long awaited thrill of breaking new ground was at hand.

As luck would have it, no sooner had they moved in to the unknown than the depth seemed to decrease. From fourteen metres' depth they reached a small air pocket at 2400m. A feeling of great optimism developed and quite suddenly, at about 2500m/8200ft from the rock-pile, a large mirror-like surface appeared above their heads – the long-sought air-chamber. They checked their decompression times and waited a few minutes. There was an incredible feeling of excitement as they surfaced. Before them lay another massive rockfall, which they soon discovered was altogether more extensive than the one they had left several hours before.

As they clambered up and over the rocks, they were extremely cautious. A broken leg or an injury of almost any kind would spell disaster. About 250m of perilously loose terrain and three and a half kilometres of diving away from the entrance chamber, they arrived at another huge lake. Before them lay yet another vast sump. Spirits were high, but even so, they were anxious not to delay too long in the new chamber for fear of worrying their friends waiting at the rock-pile.

They rested for about an hour before kitting up once more for the long swim out. The team returned uneventfully to the rock-pile after a dive of two-and-three-quarter hours and a total dive time of seven hours. The entire party finally emerged tired, but triumphant, at 6.30 a.m. to huddle around the camp fire in the cold splendour of a Nullarbor dawn. Their push had taken over fifteen hours and each diver had swum seven kilometres.

Jubilation soon turned to planning. Using the newly discovered chamber, Toad Hall, as advance base, they would tackle the next sump in twelve months' time. If sixteen divers and eighty tanks had been required to reach Toad Hall, how many more would it take to push beyond?

There were far more preparations to make for this next assault than on any of the previous ventures. Special lighting units, waterproof containers for sleeping gear, food and a multitude of other equipment had to be sought or manufactured. The method of transportation was crucial and Ron Allum put his

Below: The French base camp for their 1983 Cocklebiddy dive.

design and engineering skills to good effect. Four aluminium sledges were constructed, each capable of carrying fourteen cylinders, and equipped with special buoyancy chambers. In view of the almost catastrophic difficulties that had confronted them previously the new buoyancy compartments were capable of being progressively flooded in a controlled manner. Allum also designed special radio communication equipment which could be taken to Toad Hall to keep the surface party informed of developments ninety metres below.

The French Cocklebiddy Attempt, 1983

All was going to plan for the October 1983 expedition when the team received unexpected and shattering news. In July, completely unknown to any of the Australians, a small party of French divers arrived in Adelaide. This five-strong team was led by the two brothers Eric and Francis Le Guen, two of the most accomplished divers in Europe, together with Francis's wife Véronique*, Sylvie Goutiere and Jerome Krowicki. The French had brought with them three tons of equipment, including dry suits, high-powered Aquazepp scooters and high-pressure, composite fibre-glass tanks similar to the ones used by Bill Stone in Mexico. It had taken this group over twenty months to plan their Jules Verne adventure, the principal objective being a world record penetration at Cocklebiddy.

That a team of only five people, all complete strangers to the cave, should contemplate an objective such as Cocklebiddy seemed almost ridiculous. This, at least, was the view of the Australian divers, when news of the French project eventually reached the media, but they had failed to take account of the five people concerned.

In early September, after weeks of laborious, painstaking effort, the

* Véronique Le Guen took her own life on 18 January 1990. She was a celebrity in France following her solo, 111-day world record underground camp, which she made between 18 August and 29 November 1988 in La Grotte du Valat-Nègre in Millau in south west France. A book of her experiences, *Seule au Fond du Gouffre* was published in 1989. She was a highly accomplished caver and cave-diver and her last dive was in the Gouffre de Padirac in October 1989.

two scooters, thirty-five air and oxygen tanks, and a plethora of other equipment lay assembled on the lakeshore. In the days that followed they ferried sufficient gear to the rock-pile to mount at least two full assaults upon the distant end of the cave.

From the outset it was clear that it was logistically impossible to send two divers at a time into the third, undived sump. It was resolved, therefore, that Eric Le Guen would make the first push, supported by Francis, to the far side of Toad Hall. Despite the help of the full team to transport the heavy gear over the rock-pile it was none the less a great relief when the two brothers slid into the cool water and, with seven cylinders apiece, scootered smoothly on their way. For the next stage of the journey they had the invaluable assistance of their trusty Aquazepps and, although they were mentally keyed up, the physical demands were minimal.

The scooters were utterly indispensable on this scale of assault and, with such a small team, it was

Above: Francis and Eric Le Guen set out on (suitably christened) Aquazepps for their record Cocklebiddy dive of 1983.

calculated later that passing the second sump involved only one quarter of the air supply and half the time which would have been required if they had swum.

In Toad Hall the real difficulties began with a major porterage problem for just two men. Safety for the return was all important, and as the scooters were extremely heavy, they decided that for their first attempt they were unnecessary. Even moving sufficient equipment for one attempt on Sump 3 involved a tremendous amount of work, but many hours later the job was done and Eric Le Guen finned away into the crystal waters of the ongoing sump. With just a solitary candle for company, Francis sat back. The long wait began. After several hours a small patch of deep blue reappeared in the dark waters of Sump 3 and Francis's anxieties were over. It transpired that Eric had achieved a most impressive feat of nerve and dogged endurance in establishing, against all odds, a new world record distance dive. Finally halted at a constriction, he had traversed an incredible 1450m/4757ft of shallow virgin passage, in itself one of the longest unassisted dives ever achieved.

The brothers slowly retraced their steps and started on the long tiring journey back to the cave entrance. Over thirty-five hours later they were finally able to unwind, eat, drink and take a well-earned sleep.

But Cocklebiddy had not come to an absolute dead end. Beyond the constriction, the tunnel, although smaller than hitherto, continued. Now it was Francis's turn. Once again the filling of bottles and the ferrying of equipment began. The immensity of the task ahead was almost overwhelming. To push on further everything had to go perfectly. Any damage to equipment would spell certain failure.

The day of the push arrived. Véronique Le Guen and Sylvie Goutiere preceded the pair to the rock-pile and again set about the arduous transport of gear to Sump 2. After an approach time of twenty-four hours, the lead pair reached Toad Hall and, after a hasty meal, settled down to try and get some rest. Lying on their dry suits between two space blankets the temperature was a comfortable 25°C. But there was simply too much to think about for Francis to sleep. The scooters, with a duration of several hours, were performing well. There was plenty of air at their disposal. But everything was being conserved to the utmost. Their lights, for example, were powered by batteries and, instead of lead weights, the pair had spare batteries distributed about their bodies for ballast. During the approach dives, only the lead diver had his light switched on, while the other followed close behind in darkness.

They had a few hours well-deserved rest, then commenced the arduous task of carrying the kit forward. Five hours later all the gear had been safely ferried across Toad Hall to Sump 3. Francis Le Guen prepared himself for the big dive, equipped with a quite incredible array of cylinders. His diary relates:

The final details of my harnessing are checked. On my chest, four relay fibreglass tanks look like an accordion. [His main supply was contained in five back-mounted cylinders] It is my turn to try a solitary dive. I have enough air and guide line to stay more than five hours underwater . . .

Everything is ready. However I am afraid. But no more excuses can delay my departure. I gulp greedily at one of the regulators and, after a last wave goodbye, sink into the lake. The cold water chills my face for a second, there is a brief shiver in the small of my back and, suddenly, I feel fine. The lake, which is rather small, opens into a sumptuous flooded gallery.

When it was down to half pressure, his first-stage bottle was dropped at 400m, his second at 800m. It was a long tiring swim, the final 300m down a passage becoming progressively smaller.

At the end of the guide line, my heart begins to beat faster. Here begins the unknown . . .

A curiously shaped rock divides the passage. I choose to swim over. My tanks scrape a little and I cannot go farther – too narrow. I try to take the relay twin-set off my chest, but I still cannot move to do it. Something must have hooked on the ceiling above. Some disorganised pushing and pulling just help me become more jammed and I give up for a while in despair. This uncomfortable position increases my heartbeat and I begin to sweat in my mask.

I recover quietly with the simple realisation that I have enough air supply to get off, whatever time it takes. Some sediment falling from the ceiling begins to block my view. With my free hand, I throw the roll of the guide line in front of me and push the line aside so it is not in my way. I succeed in taking off one of the fittings that hold the twin tanks. A short slip to the left and the vice has loosened. I can now take the other strap off and let the tanks slip aside. Then I push them in front of me. A short back and forth movement and I am free. I have passed!

Looking back at the stony jaws, I can see where the red paint on my tanks left bloody tracks . . . Slowly advancing, I discover ninety metres more and penetrate into a pipe that is not wider than sixty centimetres. With my stomach pressed to the floor, my back tanks scrape again . . . Three metres ahead the passage pinches more . . . The sump is finished.

On the way back, all the side leads were explored, but all closed down within a short distance. Three and a half hours later the brothers were reunited. They had achieved everything they had set out to do. Desperately tired, the long return journey commenced:

We meet Jerome who came to help us in the first air chamber [the rock-pile], where fatigue and hallucinations begin to overwhelm us. Convinced that I lost a light, I begin digging up a large rock before I find it on my arm. Eric complains that his lamp has a bad connection and I see him holding onto a burnt out candle.

We dive again, setting our submarine scooters on maximum

Above: Francis and Eric Le Guen signal in triumph on their return from a record 6000m penetration into Cocklebiddy cave. The distance was later extended to 6090m by the Australian team operating without the aid of scooters.

speed. Risking an underwater collision, we'll take only seven minutes to cover the last aquatic lock separating us from the surface.

Some forty-seven hours after entry, Eric and Francis Le Guen regained the surface. Over the two major explorations, two of the most outstanding feats of human endurance, they had pushed the longest cave dive in the world to a phenomenal new record. The limit of penetration was now of the order of six kilometres from the entrance. On 15 September 1983 their dream was realized. The end of Cocklebiddy had finally been reached . . . Or had it?

The Australian Cocklebiddy Attempt, 1983

As news of this incredible feat reached the Australian team, they were devastated. However, back in Adelaide,

detailed discussions between Ron Allum and the French served to bring about a change of attitude.

At 1550m into Sump 3 the end of Cocklebiddy may have been small, but it had not been totally blocked. Francis Le Guen had been wearing five back-mounted cylinders when he reached his limit. Being optimistic, therefore, it was feasible that a more streamlined diver might be able to proceed further. The Australian trip was all prepared. Early in October a strong team of fourteen experienced cave divers converged on the cave to try and push exploration even further.

Three compressors were put into operation, eighty-six tanks were topped up and the four sledges were loaded. Four days after arriving six divers, each wearing triple back-mounted sets, left Rockpile Chamber pushing three heavily laden sledges. Each sledge carried fourteen tanks, from which the divers breathed, plus food, drink and sleeping gear. All went smoothly. With two divers per sledge it was another long hard swim. Two and a half hours later they arrived in Toad Hall. Although the sledges were unloaded that evening, none of the equipment was carried through to the far side of the chamber because of the necessity to avoid strenuous activity after a decompression dive. Communication was achieved with the surface party and, after a hot meal, the team curled up to sleep.

Shortly after noon the following day Morrison, Allum and Peter Rogers set off into Sump 3, pushing a single sledge carrying fourteen tanks. Simon Jones, Graham Morrison and Philip Prust settled down for a long wait.

At the 1300m mark in Sump 3 the sledge proved too massive for the narrowing passage and it was parked. The three continued, breathing from the triple 90s they were wearing. Morrison also carried a single set under his arm to explore the smaller leads. At 1460m, at the limit of the first French push, Morrison dumped his triples and continued using the single set. His companions wriggled through the narrow section and all three divers moved forward to the 'end'.

The terminal constriction was very tight, but determined to push to the absolute limit, Morrison removed his single bottle from his back. Pushing it in front of him he wriggled through. For Allum and Rogers there followed a worrying wait of over twenty-two minutes. Morrison continued up the tunnel:

The tunnel was very tight and I had to keep the cylinder in front of me as I went. I was so pleased to have got past the tight entrance and the French [terminal point] that the full impact of what I was doing didn't hit me at first . . .

After about five minutes I began to dwell on the single regulator, cylinder and torch . . . My heart was going twenty to the dozen. The tunnel was like the inside of a Swiss cheese and vivid white. Bits of the roof projected in all directions and several times I used the base of the cylinder to break off some of the sharp projections which obstructed the way.

After 250m I had used approximately one third of the cylinder . . . By now the thought of equipment failure was playing heavily on my mind . . . I wound the cord around a projecting tongue of rock and cut the line.

The return was a blur of honeycombed rock and falling silt. When I arrived back at the entrance to the new tunnel my breathing rate was almost uncontrollable and it took several minutes to return to normal and for me to relax.

Four hours and twenty minutes after starting out the trio returned to Toad Hall. They had emptied fourteen of their twenty-three air tanks. After spending a second night in the cave all the equipment was gathered together, and the following morning the final retreat began. Approximately fifty-five hours after entry the push team finally arrived back on the surface. Within a space of seven days the expedition was over.

Morrison had made another epic advance, proving conclusively that Cocklebiddy did close down. Eleven years of exploration had lead the team to a new world record and the effective 'end' of the cave. Cocklebiddy had been penetrated for 6090m/19980ft, to terminate 1790m/5872ft from air in Sump 3.

Explorations in Pannikin Plain Cave, 1980-88

If the Nullarbor contained a cave such as Cocklebiddy it was reasonable to assume that other sites might present Australian explorers with a similar challenge. This proved to be the case at another site dived as early as 1974 and which came into the limelight during later years, namely Pannikin Plain Cave.

It was not until 1980 that Pannikin Plain Cave was visited again, when Peter Rogers discovered a huge Cocklebiddy-type tunnel a short distance from diving base. The roof of this lay at a depth of twenty-seven metres. Rogers and Allum commenced the exploration of the system which in Australia today ranks second only to Cocklebiddy.

The cave has, to the time of writing, been explored underwater for about two and a half kilometres and includes several large air-chambers. One of these, Concorde Landing – named after a huge rock which resembles a wing of the supersonic jet – is the largest and most spectacular chamber found beneath the Nullarbor.

All the advanced techniques developed over the years to tackle Cocklebiddy have been adopted at this site. At the end of 1987, for example, scooters were used in conjunction with a sledge and, with this assistance, a successful camp was made at Concorde Landing. From this point Rogers and Chris Brown were able to progress 470m into the final sump, from which point the huge tunnel still continued tantalisingly into the distance.

In December 1988 a massive expedition was undertaken, with the objective not only of pushing the cave

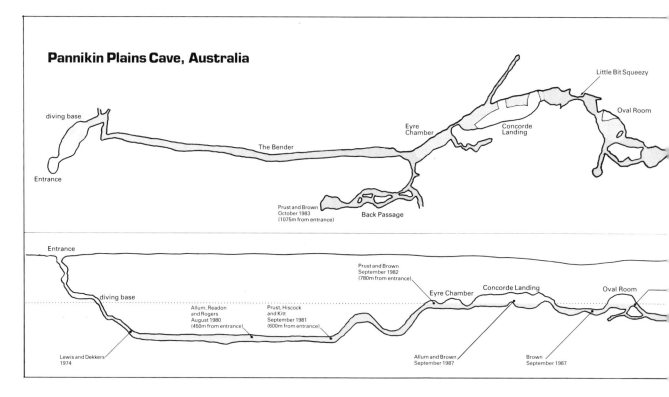

Pannikin Plains Cave, Australia

diving base

Entrance

The Bender

Eyre Chamber

Concorde Landing

Little Bit Squeezy

Oval Room

Prust and Brown
October 1983
(1075m from entrance)

Back Passage

Entrance

diving base

Prust and Brown
September 1982
(780m from entrance)

Allum, Readon
and Rogers
August 1980
(450m from entrance)

Prust, Hiscock
and Kitt
September 1981
(600m from entrance)

Eyre Chamber

Concorde Landing

Oval Room

Lewis and Dekkers
1974

Allum and Brown
September 1987

Brown
September 1987

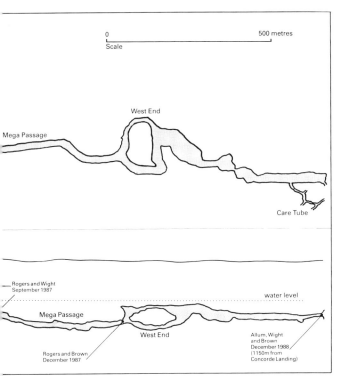

as far as possible but also of recording the exploit on film. The venture was an international event with invited participants such as the leading American diver Wes Skiles and Rob Palmer from Britain. With a full complement of equipment and experienced personnel, the cave was extended to its present limit of 2150m. Here a boulder blockage was encountered, an obstacle which may conceivably yield to a stream-lined diver.

The expedition was a major success, but undoubtedly the most exciting event took place during the final retreat from the cave. It was 4.30 p.m. in the afternoon when virtually the full team assembled on the subterranean lakeside and started unloading the equipment which had just arrived from the depths of the system. On the surface a freak cyclone hit the area, destroying the camp and, within a period of twenty-five minutes, depositing more than twice the

Right: The team assemble at the entrance lake of Pannikin Plains Cave for the 1988 explorations. Left: The huge cavern at Concorde Landing.

area's annual rainfall. Before those underground became aware of the magnitude of the event a torrent of water poured into the vertical shaft, causing a massive landslide and collapse. Miraculously, despite a hail of boulders crashing into the chamber at the bottom, no one was injured. The exit route was completely blocked and thirteen of the team were effectively entombed. With an air of calm resignation, they set about organising themselves for survival for an unknown length of time.

Fortunately radio communication was established within hours of the disaster. An escape route through the chaos of boulders was pioneered the next day, and all arrived safely on the surface by 8 p.m. on Saturday. Their equipment, valued at over Australian $200,000, had to be left where it lay, to await retrieval after a suitable period of natural stabilisation.

Above: Large Aquazepps were used to tow the sledge.

Accidents at Mount Gambier

The isolation of the Nullarbor has meant that only a few of the more experienced divers have ventured underground, with the result that there have been, fortunately, few incidents – that at Pannikin Plains Cave being a freak event – and no fatalities to date.

The picture is rather different in other regions. The Mount Gambier area of South Australia, 200 miles south-east of Adelaide, is comparatively popular as a diving area. Here there are a considerable number of deep surface potholes filled with water. Tragically many deaths have occurred at these sites, including eleven in the five years between 1969 and 1974. Three of these fatalities took place in one incident at Death Cave in 1973, when the divers, who had not used a line, became disorientated just a short distance from the surface on their outward journey. Another incident the following year saw the death of four divers, for essentially the same reasons, though here narcosis was probably an additional factor, as the dive went to a depth of sixty metres.

Predictably, the response by public and press to these incidents was one of alarm. With the fear of legal

Above: Ron Allum using a special communication system to speak to surface supporters – the device played a crucial role in the subsequent rescue.

liability and other general responsibilities landowners (both private and government) seriously contemplated the closure of all the holes to divers. The onus on the sporting fraternity was such that rather than loose access to some of the finest inland sites in the world, the Cave Divers Association of Australia (CDAA) was formed in September 1973. In defence of the sport a united voice was presented to landowners and public alike. A Category Rating System was proposed, listing the varying difficulties of the sites, and backed up by an educational programme involving training and assessment. Today, therefore, both diving sites and

Left: Scenes during the Pannikin Plains explorations: Using the sledge on an aerial runway to ferry equipment into the cave (top left); the loaded sledge in the entrance lake (top right); heavily loaded divers guide the sledge through Sump 1 to Concorde Landing.

the divers themselves are categorised and the CDAA has made a tremendous impact on both safety standards and the sport in general.

Cave Diving in Tasmania

Apart from the Nullarbor and Mt Gambier areas, a brief mention must be made of Tasmania, which has the longest and deepest caves in Australia. Tremendous potential exists not only for diving but also for normal caving exploration of the passages which exist beyond the sumps. The Mole Creek area witnessed the first major diving connection in 1978, when a South Australian team finally linked the long resurgence sump (496m) of Kubla Khan through two further sumps of 117m and 38m respectively to reach the spectacular main cave beyond. Although shallow throughout its 651m length, conditions here are far from favourable and can best be equated with typical upland sites in Britain with poor visibility, silting problems and an average water temperature of 6°C.

The Florentine Valley in southern Tasmania has seen deeper and more technical diving operations. Junee Cave is perhaps the most exciting prospect in the area, holding not only the lure of a major extension beyond the second upstream sump but also the long-term possibility of a connection with the extensive Growling Swallet system nine kilometres away. For Tasmania as a whole it is clear that the scope for discoveries is vast.

NEW ZEALAND

Cave diving in New Zealand has been carried out by a small group of enthusiasts rather than by any organisation. This has led to little continuity of people or techniques. It also means that there is no rescue organisation, although the national speleological organisation holds a small amount of rescue gear.

Diving has been carried out in three major caving areas, which can be characterised by their rock types and the kind of diving that results.

In the central North Island, around the well-known Waitomo Caves, systems are generally small in section, although often reasonably long. When the native forests were felled for farming many years ago,

there was a spate of erosion, making these caves notoriously muddy, so that limited exploration has been conducted. Nevertheless, there is considerable potential for significant finds in this area.

On the west coast of South Island there has been some diving activity, but the muddy limestone and lack of major horizontal development has meant that little success has been achieved to date.

By far the most fruitful area has been the northern end of South Island. Here, about fifty kilometres from Nelson, the hard marble rock has resulted in clear water, and both longer and deeper dives have been undertaken, even though the mountainous terrain creates access difficulties and water temperatures are low. These, together with constraints on finance (and hence equipment), have meant that the deepest dive so far has been to fifty-four metres' depth in the Pearse River resurgence. This lies near Nettlebed Cave, the country's deepest at 889m/2917ft.

In the same area, but slightly further north, lies Takaka Hill. From the point of view of cavers and cave divers, explorations here have met with the greatest degree of success. The major caving discovery in this area has been Greenlink Cave, which was explored downstream to a fine, clear water sump at a depth of 287m in the late 1970s. Keith Dekkers subsequently passed this six-metre dive and another of similar length in January 1978. Beyond, the cave continued to a depth of 372m/1220ft, at the time the deepest in the country. A dye trace from this cave (which also provided the cave's name) was to prove a connection with the major Riwaka Resurgence several kilometres away.

Riwaka Resurgence itself has been the focus of considerable interest from divers and has proved the most successful in terms of discoveries to date. Exploration has reached Sump 3, situated over one and a half kilometres from the entrance. This has been penetrated for a distance of 150m from diving base to a point approximately two kilometres from Greenlink Cave. The overall depth potential of this system is 670m/2198ft.

As in all other caving areas, there are many challenging projects waiting to be undertaken in New Zealand. Despite the isolation of the areas involved and the relative shortage of experienced activists, places such as the Riwaka Resurgence will keep cave divers busy for many years to come.

SOUTHERN AFRICA

Sinoia Caves, Zimbabwe, 1959-69

As previously mentioned, deep cave dives were made early in the sport most notably in France, where, in Vaucluse, seventy-five metres' depth was achieved in 1955. Soon after this, two remarkable diving operations were made at the Sinoia Caves in Zimbabwe (or Southern Rhodesia as it then was).

In 1959 a depth of ninety metres was achieved at the Sleeping Pool. This proved to be the practical limit on pure compressed air; but the sump continued. The chief problems encountered in the course of the dive were nitrogen narcosis (all three divers were severely affected) and negative buoyancy, which increased with depth. However, below thirty metres

the suits had little compression left, so the effect was not too drastic. The insulation of the suits was poor for a dive of any duration, but, as the water temperature was 22°C the cold did not present too great a problem.

In 1969 Rolly Nyman, Ian Robertson and brothers Johnny and Danny van der Walt performed a mixed gas dive to a depth of 102m. The gas ratio was 40% helium, 48% nitrogen and 12% oxygen, which provided, in theory, a maximum depth potential of 152m. Breathing pure oxygen would induce oxygen poisoning at ten metres' depth, while a normal air mixture containing 20% oxygen would induce the same symptoms below ninety metres. To overcome this barrier, the percentage of oxygen has to be reduced to below normal, owing to acute complications brought about by the increased partial pressure (toxicity) of the gas at depth.

At Sinoia, in 1969, the oxygen content was reduced to 12% by the addition of helium, allowing diving to 152m and giving the added bonus of decreasing

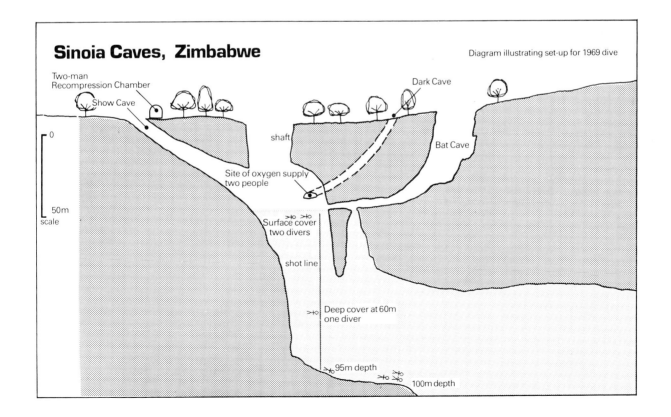

Sinoia Caves, Zimbabwe   Diagram illustrating set-up for 1969 dive

Two-man Recompression Chamber
Show Cave
Dark Cave
0
shaft
Bat Cave
Site of oxygen supply two people
50m scale
Surface cover two divers
shot line
Deep cover at 60m one diver
95m depth
100m depth

the effects of nitrogen narcosis. At a depth of ninety metres the level of narcosis was calculated to be the same as at about fifty metres on ordinary compressed air. In the event, the maximum depth attained was 102m.

One point which should be emphasised is that the gas mixture used on the deep dive would not have supported normal active life on the surface, but functioned adequately below the six metre mark, that is, three seconds after the start of the dive.

Twin 70 cu.ft cylinders were adopted, as before, and slightly over-charged to give each diver 150 cu.ft of mixture. Spare bottles of ordinary air were fixed to the line at about thirty-three metres for decompression use (it being essential to get the helium out of the system as soon as possible), and for the final decompression stage the divers breathed a supply of pure oxygen, thereby cutting decompression times by a half.

The dive failed to reach any conclusion and the operation was curtailed, leaving a huge tunnel gradually dipping away into the distance. Even so the exploration was certainly a major international achievement and the dive was to constitute an African record for nearly twenty years.

Cango and Efflux Caves, 1973

Apart from the obvious challenge and enjoyment presented by diving sites such as Sinoia, there were many localised, shallow cave sumps also awaiting exploration. One of the first noteworthy attempts was in June 1973 at the famous Cango Caves, Cape Province, South Africa. Here the principal caving organisation of the area, the South African Speleological Society (SASA), assisted diver Charles Maxwell of the Atlantic Underwater Club, based in Cape Town, to dive the terminal upstream sump. A very shallow penetration of twenty metres was finally achieved, leading to a constricted flowstone blockage. The indications were clear: if the water level could be lowered, there was every possibility of a dry extension. This was subsequently undertaken and many hundreds of metres of the most spectacular and beautifully decorated cave in South Africa were discovered. Maxwell and his friend Dick Howell scored another

early success at Efflux Cave just twenty kilometres from Cango. Here the pair traversed another short sump to discover over 1000 metres of virgin cave.

The Verhulsel Tragedy, Sterkfontein

Despite a beneficial exchange of ideas between divers and cavers, it was to be the impressive, crystal clear lakes in Southern Africa which were to capture the cave divers' imagination. Apart from Sinoia, there are others such as Wetsgat and the Sterkfontein Tourist Cave, occupying surface areas of 875 and 610 square metres respectively.

Diving at such easily accessible places slowly gained in popularity, and most undertakings were, indeed still are, conducted by non-caving members of local diving clubs. Johannesburg lies approximately 600 kilometres from the coast and sporting divers in search of inland training have understandably been enticed by large, crystal-clear cave diving sites in preference to dried up rivers or muddy dams. Unfortunately, a lack of appreciation of natural caving hazards has led to a number of fatalities among members of these clubs.

Perhaps the most tragic instance occurred at the Sterkfontein Tourist Caves in the Transvaal close to Johannesburg. Sterkfontein's immense underground lake possesses numerous flooded passageways leading off into the darkness. It was here that twenty-nine-year-old post-graduate student Peter Verhulsel disappeared during a dive on 29 September 1984. Verhulsel had been introduced to caving in the early 1970s, when for a few years he was a member of the South African Speleological Society. In the mid-1970s his interest in the sport waned, subsequently to be replaced by diving. Consequently, when he joined his friends Nuno Gomes, chairman of the Witwatersrand University Diving Club, and Malcolm Keeping for a dive at Sterkfontein, Peter Verhulsel felt confident that it was an undertaking well within his ability.

Gomes and Keeping had visited the cave previously but for Verhulsel this was to be his first experience of the vast, but largely shallow, complex. The objectives were not overly ambitious and, in view of the fact that a substantial air-space exists over the water's surface, it was not thought unduly rash that Verhulsel should

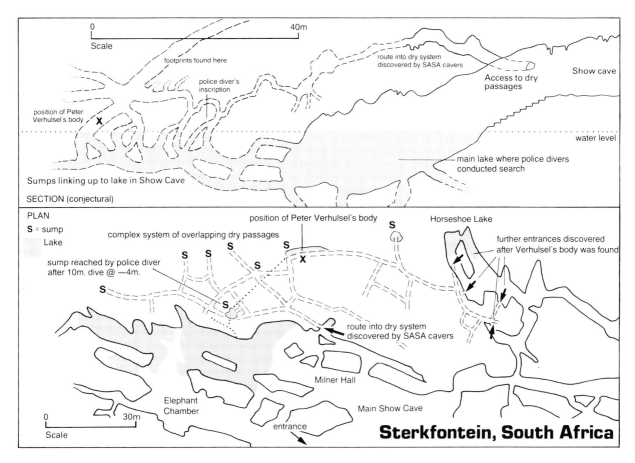

0   40m
Scale

footprints found here

route into dry system
discovered by SASA cavers

Access to dry
passages

Show cave

police diver's
inscription

position of Peter
Verhulsel's body   X

water level

main lake where police divers
conducted search

Sumps linking up to lake in Show Cave

SECTION (conjectural)

PLAN

S = sump
Lake

complex system of overlapping dry passages

position of Peter Verhulsel's body   S

Horseshoe Lake

further entrances discovered
after Verhulsel's body was found

sump reached by police diver
after 10m. dive @ −4m.

S   S   S   S
S   S   X

route into dry system
discovered by SASA cavers

Milner Hall

0   30m
Scale

Elephant
Chamber

Main Show Cave

entrance

Sterkfontein, South Africa

be equipped with just a single aqualung and a single, hand-held light. The team was well acquainted with cave diving procedures, and, while Gomes led off, Verhulsel brought up the rear. As the least experienced of the three, and despite knowledge of the fundamental rules of cave diving practice, Verhulsel soon chose to disconnect himself from the guide-line. Twice his companions found him off-line examining tunnels to the side. Verhulsel was confident in the environment, but it was this very familiarity which was to cost him his life.

A little later Gomes and Keeping noticed Verhulsel was missing yet again. They turned about and swam back along the line, along a tunnel now partially obscured by silt. On this occasion, though, Verhulsel had completely disappeared. The pair were fully aware of the gravity of the situation and spent a harrowing three hours searching the known parts of

the cave without success.

The police were notified and accordingly assumed full responsibility for the subsequent search, but the operation was shortly shrouded in controversy, when they ignored the advice of caving experts in favour of ill-judged actions of their own.

From the outset the 'official' police rescuers had it firmly fixed in their heads that Verhulsel had drowned. For those inexperienced in matters of cave rescue, particularly one of this nature, this was the most likely conclusion. However, in the absence of a body and in view of the three-dimensional, complex nature of the cave system, the cavers realised that there was a chance that Verhulsel had emerged into an unknown section of passage and was waiting to be rescued.

The events that unfolded later were to prove a catalogue of disaster. The police were totally untrained for such an operation and, when underwater visibility

Above: Peter Verhulsel, who died in tragic circumstances in Sterkfontein Cave, South Africa, 1984.

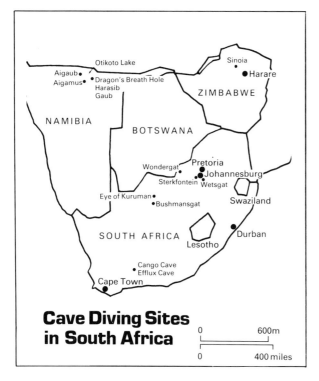

**Cave Diving Sites
in South Africa**

0   600m

0   400 miles

reduced to nearly zero, the controllers withdrew their team. The search was postponed until such time as conditions improved. To the dismay of the family and expert cavers, experienced cave divers accustomed to conditions of extreme silting, were forbidden entry.

The police remained stubbornly unreceptive to advice, and suggestions of pumping the lake out and using a chemical flocculent* were rejected out of hand.

Equally disturbing was the fact that several local cavers, from whom the police did take advice, appear to have been equally short-sighted. They assured the experienced SASA cavers that the Tourist Cave had been thoroughly checked for possible side tunnels and that there was no possibility of finding any route off in the direction where Verhulsel had disappeared. As a consequence of this the SASA rescue volunteers were deterred from mounting their own search of the cave and instead implemented an independent excavational operation in a neighbouring system.

The police evidently did not want to risk the possibility of another civilian incurring the same fate they presumed Verhulsel had met. They continually ignored civilian pleas which pointed out that in Britain, for example, the police took overall control of rescue situations such as this, while at the same time allowing civilian experts to undertake the work.

As the weeks passed all hope was ruled out. Even if he had found an unknown dry passage or air-space he would by this time have died from exposure and starvation.

After a total of six days spent searching the lake, spread over almost as many weeks, the police finally withdrew. The official operation was concluded. To their credit, the SASA cavers had steadfastly continued their 'dry' search. On the fifth week the cavers switched their operations to the Tourist Cave and were rewarded almost immediately by the discovery of a strongly draughting hole very close to the lake.

A dig was soon passed and an extensive series of passages and sumps was revealed. Within a short distance of the breakthrough choke they found an

---

* A flocculent is a chemical which when added to water forms a fluffy snow-like precipitate. As this settles other particles, such as mud and silt, adhere to it and are also carried to the bottom, leaving the water clear. Aluminium Sulphate is one of the most common flocculents and is often used for purification of drinking water and to clarify swimming pools.

inscription on the wall adjacent to a small lake. This had been made by one of the police divers, who, it later transpired had only swum ten metres at a maximum depth of four metres to reach the point.

To the police diver the small cave passage leading off directly above the water was of little significance. The cavers continued along this dry upper route and suddenly they found footprints. Six weeks to the day after Verhulsel had gone missing the cavers stooped along a short section of tunnel to find his body, lying alongside his diving gear at the edge of the sump pool.

Indented marks along the walls indicated that Verhulsel had attempted to draw the attention of rescuers to his position, and, before his diving light had finally expired, he left a brief message to his family. But the real tragedy, the terrible irony of the incident lay in the very condition of the emaciated body. The post-mortem revealed that Peter Verhulsel had three weeks' growth of beard; stranded in blackness and despair he had lost 20kg in body weight. Peter Verhulsel had been alive for three whole weeks . . . and might well have been rescued alive had both expert cavers and cave divers been allowed to participate in the search from the outset.

Clearly Peter Verhulsel had violated the basic rules of cave diving and he had paid for it dearly. For all concerned the lessons were clear: such a tragedy must never be repeated.

Explorations in Namibia

Normal explorations were resumed in a comparatively new area: the barren wastes of Namibia. At the heart of this arid terrain water is extremely scarce. Yet deep underground lie vast caverns and some of the largest subterranean lakes in the world.

In 1966 SASA surveyed a little-frequented site named Harasib, finding its crystal lake to be even larger than Sinoia. It was 1974 before any diving took place here, and again Charles Maxwell, Dick Howell and their team were successful. Having overcome an arduous 150m descent to the water they promptly swam down to seventy metres' depth. Maxwell's diary relates:

Strange blind barbel swam between the formations, as if time had stood still for thousands of years . . . with eyes reflecting amazement and narcosis, we looked up at the hole in the roof

Above: South African cave diving pioneer, Charles Maxwell.

clearly silhouetted far above us, sparkling like a blue jewel with long lines of bubbles racing towards the surface.

They could go no deeper. According to the Cross* correlation method of altitude adjustment their dive, at an altitude of 1500 metres above sea-level, was equivalent to an eighty-five metre dive in the ocean.

* High altitude decompression tables designed by E.R. Cross in 1970

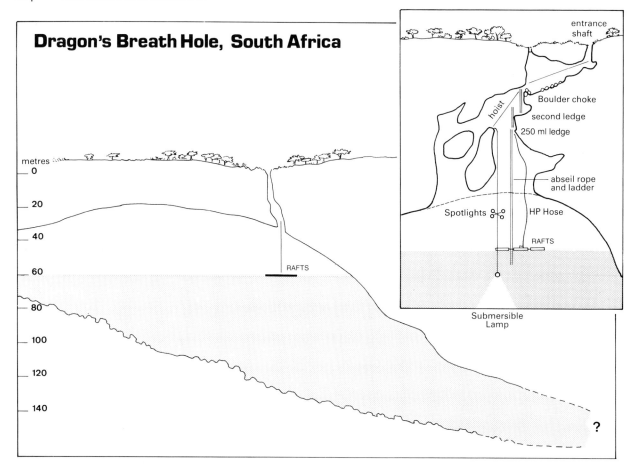

Dragon's Breath Hole, South Africa

Dragon's Breath Hole, 1986

Harasib was evidently a proposition for the future, but twelve years later and just five kilometres away an equally incredible site was discovered.

During the winter of 1986 careful analysis of aerial photographs led a team of cavers to a small opening from which a strong updraught emerged. The cave was named 'Drachenhauchloch' or Dragon's Breath Hole. After descending several pitches to a depth of sixty metres, Adam Duffy reached the silent waters of an immense lake. It was an eerie feeling. His torch was powerless in such a spooky cavern and this first exploration failed to reveal any walls or indeed a floor.

It was soon apparent that the lake at the bottom of Dragon's Breath was bigger than anything so far recorded in the world. The following year the cave was the scene of a major expedition and again it was

Charles Maxwell who organised the thirty-strong team of divers and cavers. Swiss speleologist Gerald Favre was to document the exploration on film, and eventually three tons of equipment, including inflatable boats, generators, compressors and a decompression chamber found its way to the cave entrance.

Diving rafts, telephones, oxygen resuscitators, and countless sets of diving equipment were soon ferried into the cave. Bottles were filled on the diving platform by means of a 150m length of high pressure hose, which ran from the compressor stationed above the entrance. The entire cave was then lit by two powerful surface lights and a submersible mercury vapour light. A magnificent sight was revealed: an awesome cavern of Gothic cathedral proportions, generating a profound feeling of isolation and tranquillity, the silence broken only by the gentle lapping of water on the cave walls.

After nine days of preparation the diving commenced. The water was a very pleasant 24°C and wonderfully clear. It was tremendously reassuring for the divers to be able to orientate themselves using the mercury vapour light, which was plainly visible through the water at a distance of 250m. Stalactites were noted to a depth of fifteen metres, giving at least one valuable insight to the past history of the cave. A systematic survey was duly accomplished, leading the explorers ever deeper into a huge passage beneath the northern overhang.

In view of the isolation of the site and the fact that it was impossible to transport the decompression chamber into the cave it was necessary to take careful precautions against mishap. Strenuous exertion immediately following a deep dive has been known to bring on the 'bends'. Before embarking upon the hot, sweaty, sixty-metre climb back to the surface, an hour's rest was taken after the majority of dives. In the event of an accident or the omission of a decompression stop, the team was prepared to mount immediate remedial action. The diver would be sent straight down to nine-metres' depth, where he would breath pure oxygen, possibly for up to an hour. Depending upon the severity of the case, he would then be brought up very slowly, at a rate of twelve minutes per metre, as prescribed in Carl Edmonds's Australian 'wet therapeutic' oxygen tables.

Two members of the Swiss team, Alain Vuagniaux and Christian Rufi, performed the deepest dive of the expedition, to a depth of ninety metres. Carefully calculated mixtures of helium, oxygen and nitrogen were adopted. Each diver wore four, huge, eighteen-litre cylinders on his back, a total weight of 120kg. The dive was to prove a great spectacle as even at maximum depth they could be seen 'looking like diminutive ants crawling upon the bottom'.

With the survey complete and the cave explored to such extreme depth, the expedition drew to a successful conclusion. Dragon's Breath had presented the team with a subterranean lake of just over two hectares. Its status as the largest expanse of cave water in the world was officially confirmed.* For the present, here

* According to the *Guiness Book of Records* the largest such lake had previously been the Lost Lake of Tennessee with a surface area of 1.8 hectares.

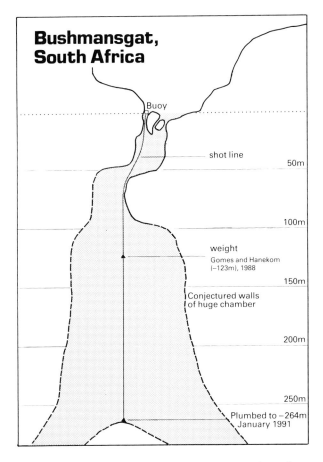

Bushmansgat, South Africa

Buoy

shot line — 50m

100m

weight
Gomes and Hanekom (–123m), 1988

150m

Conjectured walls of huge chamber

200m

250m

Plumbed to –264m January 1991

the story ends, but far beneath the placid surface of Drachenhauchloch a huge ongoing tunnel leads mysteriously into the distance.

Depth Records at Bushmansgat amd Guinas Lake
Exploration in southern Africa is now proceeding at a rapid pace. The lure of such marvellous diving is obvious, and the problems of extreme depth certainly pose the major difficulty at the present time, though several very deep dives have been achieved. Early in 1988, for example, Nuno Gomes and Dian Hanekom established a new record when they made a 123m deep penetration in Bushmansgat, northern Cape Province. More recently, Boetie Scheun and Eben Benade have bettered this with a descent to 132m in Guinas Lake, Namibia. With a multitude of sites still awaiting investigation, the future offers tremendous prospects in this area.

CHAPTER TWELVE

FUTURE POSSIBILITIES

Cave diving is one of the most exciting pioneering sports of our times with immense potential for development. Much new exploration will be hard won, but there will always be determined individuals prepared to accept the challenge.

New cave systems will be explored, each with sumps to dive. Many of these will be far easier to vanquish than those which have offered years of resistance in well-established caves. In recent years, for example, fabulous new caving areas have been discovered in countries such as Malaya and China. In 1984 and 1985 I was fortunate enough to have the opportunity of making the first dive in the impressive Clearwater Cave in Sarawak, and also at sites in southern China. In both instances relatively easy sumps were passed, and in Clearwater at least, access was gained to an extremely impressive major extension.

In this general outline of diving activities in various corners of the globe little mention has been made of South America or the vast land mass of southern Asia. Dive explorations have been made in both areas, but to date these have been minor in comparison to activity in Europe and America. Tremendous scope exists, especially in Asia, where major discoveries are to be expected.

With advances in caving technique, both long and deep dives are now being made at the end of some of the world's most challenging and logistically difficult caves. Lightweight equipment has proved essential for such ventures including the use of high-pressure aluminium-fibreglass composite cylinders (as used on the Huautla project). In view of their high pressure such cylinders have to be handled with greater care, but their use will undoubtedly help chances at remote underground sites. At present these cylinders, as far as sport divers are concerned, are still in the 'experimental' category.

The most exciting advances in terms of the development of cave diving as a sport will be in longer and deeper dives. In Britain, in 1970, the longest dives were about 300m but by the end of the decade they were over 1000m. In areas such as Florida 'staging' and the utilisation of DPVs have today taken penetrations beyond 2000m. In continental Europe the Swiss GLPS divers have resorted to the use of huge twenty-litre steel cylinders organised into back-mounted, four- and five-cylinder configurations to allow dives of prodigious lengths.

Depth, with its associated limitations and dangers, is no longer the overruling deterrent that it once was. Jochen Hasenmayer and Sheck Exley have pioneered the way. The barriers have been broken. Greater technical expertise is now more readily available. For example, computer-generated decompression formulae like that devised by Dr Bill Hamilton in the United States have proved of immense value, and indeed every branch of the diving support industry is making constant improvements to its products.

Lengthy decompression stops may constitute a high price to pay for a long, deep exploration, but, with careful forethought and planning, even the discomfort of this irksome experience can be lessened. The introduction of 'habitats' in the 1980s made a big contribution to explorations in Florida, significantly alleviating discomfort and also providing divers with a greater margin of safety. Later sophistications, like Dr Bill Stone's variable-depth structure for use at Wakulla, shows that innovation will invariably improve on a good original idea. With its surface-fed gas supply and variable depth features this unique habitat could well prove the forerunner of a more permanent underwater base, from which divers could make much longer forays.

The November 1987 Wakulla project was a major

landmark in the history of cave diving. Not only did it serve to define the limits of contemporary open-circuit aqualung equipment in deep diving, but it also provided a fascinating insight into the long-term future of such exploration. Stone's Cis-Lunar MK-1 Rebreather received its first major field test and demonstrated the likely course of development in the next few years. This highly sophisticated piece of apparatus offers the diver a potential underwater duration of two or more days.

Several companies are now in the process of developing rebreathers. The Carmellan Rebreather was used on the 1987 Andros project. This proved a useful piece of apparatus, but sadly as far as cave diving is concerned, the unit must be used in conjunction with an independent bail-out system, namely a set of open circuit apparatus. For long distance work the Cis-Lunar MK-2 would appear to be the optimum choice at the present time. Used in conjunction with a similarly reliable, long-distance, high-powered scooter, one can imagine some absolutely incredible penetrations being undertaken. Indeed, Olivier Isler's outstanding success using semi-closed circuit breathing apparatus at the Emergence du Ressel in August 1990, demonstrates that rebreathers are on the verge of becoming a significant factor in cave exploration. However, with the greater range and depth they permit will come a corresponding extension in decompression times.

At this point it is worth considering some of the deep sea diving techniques and equipment which might be employed to counteract this growing decompression problem. One possible tactic, suitable for sites like Wakulla, would be the adoption of a 'one-atmosphere' diving system and vehicle. Here the diver is encased in a crush-proof suit, comparable to a medieval suit of armour, though more bulky. Inside this a sea-level (one-atmosphere) pressure is maintained throughout the dive. Several of these 'tin-man' suits are presently used for commercial diving operations, including models known by the acronyms JIM, WASP and NEWT. Unfortunately none of these would be suitable for the untethered operations of cave exploration. Nevertheless, research is continuing

and a lightweight, composite-shell, one-atmosphere suit with greater flexibility may be the outcome. This could be applicable to cave-diving, especially if used in conjunction with an advanced form of DPV.

Another possibility is the use of one-man submarines. One such unit, Deep Rover, produced by Deep Ocean Engineering Inc., has already demonstrated its effectiveness in diving to depths of 1000m remaining underwater for over four days. The current range of this vehicle appears to be up to fifteen kilometres, which in a large tunnel with clear visibility presents interesting possibilities. As continual advances are being made in this field, and as Wakulla and some other sites may well offer long-distance exploration potential, it is clear that even submarines may have a caving function.

The use of such craft would obviously pose certain safety problems. Existing submarines are not able to lay line, so, if visibility was lost, the exit route might be difficult to locate. Another obvious hazard would be the possibility of the submarine becoming wedged or being unable to turn in a constricted dead-end tunnel. Such equipment ideas may seem futuristic, but technology is advancing rapidly and its application to cave diving is a growing possibility. This, in turn, will prompt another question: would greater reliance on sophisticated equipment mean a departure from the spirit of the sport? Even if it does, it is well to remember that sites such as Wakulla are few; the majority of explorations, while still highly dependent upon technological advance, will be conducted using lightweight equipment.

Whether heavyweight or lightweight, the cost of such equipment will be considerable, especially to explorers essentially of amateur status. The benefits of group organisation, with the sharing and maintenance of expensive apparatus, will become an increasing factor in the planning of expensive expeditions.

As ever, the real pioneers will be few in number, and to mount some of their undertakings it is inevitable that considerable financial support and sponsorship will be required. This will be accompanied by demands from publicity agents and the media. As a result, extra pressure may be placed on divers as they try to honour their commitments. It will be essential to take steps to manage these extra factors, and this may involve, for example, resisting pressures to dive at set times (e.g. for television crews or assembled pressmen) when conditions or the diver's psychological state are unfavourable.

Close on the heels of the pioneers, there will be many others keen to emulate and enjoy for themselves the wonders of such a unique and remote environment. This tendency is readily apparent in Florida with the adoption of stage diving techniques and the use of scooters. In Britain, too, as equipment and techniques are proven safe, more and more cavers are adopting diving apparatus in order to explore distant dry extensions.

International co-operation and exchange of ideas have also aided the development of the sport. The British have proven expertise in the smaller cave systems with low visibility; the Americans, French and Swiss are masters of the longer and deeper penetrations, and the exchange of information has been greatly improved thanks to the efforts of organisations such as the UIS (Union Internationale de Speleologie) Commission for Cave Diving.

Equally important in the development of the sport is the steady improvement in the quality and variety of diving equipment. With more critical assessments by independent bodies and widespread reporting on performance and deficiencies, the manufacturers quickly seek to modify and upgrade their products. All these factors help, in psychological and practical terms, to allow explorations to be conducted more safely. Another factor which should be noted is safety education by the various diving organisations, which is particularly useful in training novices. The days of ignorance and horrific statistics now seem to be in the past. However, there is no room for complacency. Cave diving will always be an objectively dangerous sport, but providing it is approached in a mature, responsible manner, then the future prospects can be as equally exciting as, though perhaps less hazardous than, those of the past.

Future Possibilities in Britain and Ireland

Where will exploration take place? In Britain the Yorkshire Dales will continue to reveal spectacular discoveries, especially in the major and ever growing Three Counties System, stretching between Aygill (Cumbria) in the west, through the systems of Leck Fell (Lancashire) to Kingsdale (Yorkshire) in the east. The many classic caves associated with the Leck Beck hydrological network are on the verge of a major link-up and once achieved, the overall length will exceed sixty-five kilometres. Keld Head will assuredly constitute a further part of this fine system at some stage, and given the recent (June 1991) connection of Keld Head to King Pot on the east side of Kingsdale it is interesting to speculate upon an eventual extension of this incredible complex to Chapel Le Dale. By this stage the total passage length will be well in excess of eighty kilometres.

Again in Ribblesdale there is considerable mystery regarding the Penyghent drainage system, the outlets for which are Douk Gill and Brant's Gill. Another rising at Dub Cote may be associated with this system and it is certainly worthy of note that beyond the long series of sumps here, there lies a two-and-a-half-kilometre dry extension, which extends to within 800m of Magnetometer Pot.

In Wharfedale an even larger system, behind the major rising of Black Keld, awaits exploration. This takes water from those two classic systems Mossdale and Langcliffe Pot. Further east lies another inviting challenge, the conquest of the Nidd Head System. Nearly two kilometres of passage are so far unaccounted for, a diving traverse which, when finally achieved, will be in excess of two and a half kilometres.

In Derbyshire P8 (Jackpot) and the mysteries of the Peak-Speedwell complex will not be easy to solve.

Wales, in both northern and southern caving regions, presents considerable potential. In the south the Pwll y Cwm project – an underwater excavation to provide access to Wales's own 'Keld Head' – will quite probably yield the final key to the mysteries of

Top right: Aquazepps in use in Jackson Blue Spring, Florida. Near right: Clark Pitcairn wearing an experimental five-cylinder rig at Wakulla, 1987. The small bottle of nitrogen is used to inflate the drysuit. The rig proved impractical as its sheer bulk made it unstable when riding an Aquazepp. Far right: Bill Stone testing the MK-2r rebreather in Jackson Blue Spring, 1989.

Above: Examining archeological relics discovered in Grotte de Han Sur Lesse, Belgium, in the early 1950s.

Llangattock Mountain. In addition, Llygad Llwchwr, Schwyllt and Wellhead are all major resurgences awaiting a consistent, determined assault.

Beneath the Mendip Hills the origins of Wookey Hole will keep explorers occupied for many years, but the most stimulating developments, certainly in the 1990s, are to be expected at the Cheddar River Cave.

Ireland has many of the greatest challenges. The Green Holes off the west coast of County Clare, the major waterways beneath the lowlands of County Galway, the incredible subterranean flow from Lough Mask to Cong in County Mayo, and the equally staggering traverse between Aille River Cave and Polltoomary Rising all offer exciting possibilities, which collectively constitute the ultimate challenge in western Europe.

Future Possibilities in Europe

In France, indeed right across Europe, there are countless thrilling projects waiting to be tackled. The

mysteries of the great Fontaine de Vaucluse are no nearer a solution; likewise, that other early diving site, the Fontaine de St George and its associated feeder system, the eighteen-kilometre Gouffre de Padirac, will keep determined activists occupied for many years. In Italy there has been little progress with regard to the penetration of the giant Timavo Spring, a complex of about eighteen resurgences at San Giovanni di Duino, known to take water from a distance of at least forty kilometres at Skocjanske Jama in Yugoslavia. These are just a few of the many possibilities.

Practical Uses in Archaeology

For those who doubt the value of such dangerous pursuits and who may argue that there is little point in the activity, I include a few lines. In the fields of archaeology and palaeontology the contributions made by cave divers have been immense. As early as 1922 Norbert Casteret discovered the oldest known statues beyond the sumps in Montespan. In the late 1950s diver Marc Jasinski and his friends uncovered a wealth of material dating back to the Bronze Age in the underwater sections of the Grotte de Han Sur Lesse in Belgium. Mayan artifacts are being discovered deep inside the clear waters of the Yucatan caves. Invaluable fossil remains have been retrieved from the depths of Wakulla. In 1959 human brain tissue over 10,000 years old was discovered at an archaeological site deep in Warm Mineral Spring, Florida.

Practical Uses:
Biological, Geomorphological, Hydrological

In the biological field discoveries have been equally exciting: blind troglodic cave fish such as Lucifuga Speleotes have been found in the Bahamas, while in 1979 Dr Jill Yager discovered a completely new class of primitive crustacean – the Remipedia – in Lucayan Caverns, Grand Bahama.

Complex dating techniques have been adopted on calcite structures which have been retrieved from the depths in places such as the Blue Holes of the Bahamas, and these have shed invaluable light on the fluctuating levels of the ocean during the Ice Ages. Other advanced techniques in, for example, uranium isotope sampling have proved extremely advantageous in water tracing in areas where conventional techniques would be ineffective.

It is especially in the field of applied science that cave divers have so much to offer. At the most basic level, divers' surveys provide invaluable information concerning the location and extent of groundwater reserves, and may indicate suitable points from which a supply may be tapped. Such projects have come to fruition in places such as the South of France, where the city of Montpellier has long drawn a supply from the Source de Lez. In more recent times divers have penetrated the sump for over 518m/1700ft to a terminal depth of 75m/246ft. At this terminal point the passage continuation takes the form of a seemingly bottomless shaft and presents an ideal location from which to pump the necessary water. A $6 million project has been initiated to extract water from this source, a fraction of the cost of treating the water from nearby rivers. The utilisation and harnessing of its water resources have also proved a priority of the Chinese, and a project which has aroused considerable interest in the south of the country has been the charting of the course of the River Tisu. This massive river, which has a flow varying from 4 cumecs in the dry season to 390 cumecs between May and August, flows underground for over fifty kilometres before it resurges on the north bank of the Hungshui River. Unfortunately, despite the location of 'windows' into an exceptionally deep and seemingly totally flooded subterranean conduit, divers have yet to make any significant penetration of this extensive hydrological network. In such a mountainous region the difficulties of extraction are immense. The problem of effective water utilisation exists in many, if not all, arid limestone areas of the world.

Practical Uses in Pollution Monitoring

In Florida the demands of expanding cities such as Tallahassee present even more complex problems. Not only is pressure on the available resources growing but there is also a far more serious threat from groundwater pollution, caused by, among other things, ignorance or disregard of the permeable characteristics of limestone rock. Disposal of sewage effluent is a case in point. Instead of being treated at purpose built plants, in several instances this is being disposed of by 'deep injection' – pumping it thousands of metres into the aquifer – the presumption being that it will disperse harmlessly at such depth. The possibilities are quite horrific and leading divers such as Wes Skiles are presently involved in monitoring water quality far into the caves. Another major expedition is planned to Wakulla in 1992, and on this an extremely elaborate series of dye tests is planned. In so doing hydrologists will be able to trace a particular area to a particular tunnel, not just to the Wakulla main entrance.

Sporting Considerations

For the sporting fraternity cave diving needs no justification. It is a completely natural expression of human curiosity – as valid a pursuit and as technically demanding as the challenge of outer space. Wes Skiles described this succinctly:

> Pushing out, exploring and mapping; I find all this extremely stimulating; . . . it's your choice; all I want to do is think about how to stay alive and maximise the enjoyment of what I do while I'm down there.

In more general terms we could do no better than recall Norbert Casteret's simple justification:

> I know and love caverns, abysses, and subterranean rivers. Studying and exploring them has been my passion for years. Where can one find such excitment, see such strange sights, enjoy such intellectual satisfactions as in exploration below ground?

Cave diving always has been and probably still is the most dangerous sport and also one of the most exciting as Casteret so splendidly demonstrated in his Montespan explorations nearly seventy years ago. However, there is no disguising the fact that the technique is extreme, having dissuaded many potential explorers in the past and this undoubtedly will temper the enthusiasm of many in the years to come. Common sense and caution have been the hallmark of the pioneers up to now, but, having said that, one can look forward to an extremely exciting age of progress. Individual qualities will count for everything, and successful explorers will require exceptional determination. We await their feats with keen interest.

APPENDICES

APPENDIX I: DECOMPRESSION

Decompression sickness, better known as the 'bends' can be an extremely traumatic and crippling disorder. It is essential that careful consideration and preventative measures are made at the planning stage of any 'deep' dive. The very worst place to succumb to the bends is in a cave. The following is a very brief summary of the subject, but divers should refer to the fuller explanations found in the various up-to-date manuals.

Decompression sickness normally occurs if a diver ascends too rapidly after a prolonged period at depth. Its onset is related to an excessive quantity of inert gas (a gas such as nitrogen or helium) which is present in the body tissues, accompanied by a lowering of ambient pressure. The simple view is that it is due to the formation of bubbles of nitrogen in the blood, bubbles which block small blood vessels and so cause the death of tissue supplied by those vessels. Shortage of blood to nervous tissue can result in fits, paralysis, coma and death.

The occurrence, or otherwise, of decompression sickness depends largely upon a diver's length of stay at depth, any recent diving, and the speed of his subsequent ascent. If a diver remains at depth for an extended period, his body tissues absorb nitrogen; when he ascends, if all goes correctly, the nitrogen comes out of solution in the tissues, to be dissolved in the blood. It is then returned to the lungs and voided harmlessly. This process of 'gas exchange' takes time. The theoretical side of this is quite complicated, involving the rules of 'partial pressure'. Very simply, each component of air (nitrogen, oxygen, trace elements, etc.) independently effects a pressure balance with the corresponding pressure of that particular gas in the respiratory system. If the diver ascends too rapidly there is insufficient time for the circulation to be able to keep pace with the partial-pressure gradient. If the body cannot shed the excess nitrogen fast enough the gas will come out of solution into the blood or tissues and form bubbles.

Bubble formation occurs when the partial pressure of nitrogen within the body cells becomes approximately twice that of the ambient partial pressure. The disorder reveals itself in the small fatty deposits associated with the restricted areas of circulation for example the joints – hence the term 'bends' – and in the tiny fat deposits associated with the nervous system. Evidence suggests that long, shallow dives tend to create problems in the joints, while short, deep exposures seem to affect the nervous

system more directly. Quite apart from the immediate problems that are occasioned by decompression sickness there are other long term effects which may not manifest themselves for many years: damage to brain cells and bone tissue (aseptic bone necrosis) fall into this category.

Early recognition and treatment of decompression sickness is essential. In approximately 85% of cases symptoms occur within one hour of surfacing. Only one per-cent occur more than six hours later. This time factor is a major aid in diagnosis but the disorder can be confused with muscle strain and joint sprain. If there are signs of problems to the central nervous system, or if there is serious doubt as to the nature of the pain, remedial measures must be implemented as soon as possible. No medication should be taken, as this may confuse the subsequent treatment.

If the disorder is suspected the only safe recourse is for him to undergo a rapid recompression (driving the nitrogen back into solution in the body), followed by a slow decompression; this is usually undertaken in a special chamber, under close medical supervision. Oxygen should be administered during evacuation and the individual should be rushed to the re-compression chamber with all urgency – possibly by low-flying helicopter if necessary. Recompression of a stricken diver in the water should not normally be attempted unless – due to extreme isolation, or in the depths of a cave – there is no other option. This is an altogether more complicated and risky operation.

The important factor in avoiding decompression sickness lies in making an accurate assessment of the amount of nitrogen that has been absorbed into the body during a dive. Basically, the deeper and more prolonged the dive, the greater will be the amount of nitrogen absorbed. Shallow dives of less than ten metres, involve little risk in this respect, but at thirty metres depth, a twenty-minute dive is all that one can safely undertake before the need arises to take special care with decompression procedures. If one exceeds this time, a decompression 'stop' must be made during the ascent, for example a five minute stop at five metres' depth.

Special tables have been published – in Britain, the United States and elsewhere detailing the necessary decompression time needed (no stop and stop) in relation to various times and depths of dive. The term 'no stop' indicates the greatest period of time that can be spent in diving to, and remaining at, a specific depth, without the need for a decompression stop on the ascent. Deep dives should always be thoroughly planned in advance; if complications associated with decompression are anticipated, preparations should be made accordingly. No diver with a limited supply of air should accidentally run the risk of exceeding his 'no stop' times. Decompression stops, according to British tables, are normally made by interrupting the ascent for the required length of time at a depth of ten metres and later at five metres. American tables differ slightly in that depths are quoted in feet, and that the majority of decompression is conducted at depths of twenty and ten feet.

To conduct a safe decompression it is necessary to carry an accurate depth gauge, or to install a line from the surface clearly marked with the required decompression depths. Decompression meters, which automatically determine decompression time, are rapidly gaining popularity with divers. These must be used with caution, and in several instances have been proved unreliable. There is no substitute for a basic, first-hand knowledge of this subject used in conjunction with a set of submersible decompression tables. These should be regarded as an essential item on any deep dive and divers must know how to use them.

Planned decompression often involves the use of an extra cylinder of compressed air (or oxygen), already valved, which is tied securely to the line at the required depth during the descent, ready for the decompression stop on the return.

Another important factor to note in decompression calculations is that repeated dives during a twenty-four hour period have a cumulative effect and if this is necessary specially prepared 'repetitive tables' must be followed.

There are many other factors that impinge on this complex problem. A diver, for example, who is excessively chilled or overheated has a greater susceptibility to decompression problems and therefore, in extreme conditions extra care must be taken. The altitude at which diving takes place must also be taken into account. Normal procedures can be adopted to a water surface height of 152m but above this point an adjustment must be made to the tables. The diver's physical condition can cause complications: the diver who is unfit, over-weight, exhausted, dehydrated, depressed or dependent upon drugs (or alcohol) is at greater risk. Exertion, either on the dive itself or afterwards, should be avoided. There are also some indications that women are more susceptible to decompression sickness. If there are any factors present that might make individuals more prone to decompression problems extra caution is essential.

In general the following procedures are recommended:
- At the planning stage make sure of the locations of the nearest decompression facilities and of their availability. Telephone numbers are essential; likewise knowledge of the quickest evacuation route.
- The actual point in the cave where decompression is proposed must be suitable and known to each member of the dive team, taking due note of the layout of the cave and other difficulties such as currents, or bad visibility.
- Extra supplies of air or oxygen must be installed at the point of decompression with an allowance for possible equipment failure.
- Monitoring of dive time and air supply should be rigidly followed by each member of the team.
- Exertion should be avoided at every stage of the dive and preferably for an hour or more afterwards. Dive assistants should be made fully aware of this problem.

All cave divers should treat decompression with ultra-conservatism. They must be thoroughly familiar with the many inter-related facets of the problem and act accordingly. Read the manual carefully.

To give an idea of the limited time that can be spent underwater without decompression I include a list of times and respective depths based on the U.S. Navy Decompression Table.

No-decompression Limits for No-decompression Air Dives			
Depth (feet)	Time Limit (minutes)	Depth (feet)	Time Limit (minutes)
20		90	30
25		100	25
30		110	20
35	310	120	15
40	200	130	10
50	100	140	10
60	60	150	5
70	50	160	5
80	40		

APPENDIX II: USEFUL ADDRESSES

Cave Diving Association of Australia:
P.O. Box 290, North Adelaide 5006

Cave Diving Group of Great Britain:
Secretary: Clive Westlake, 25 Cross Street, Kettlebrook, Tamworth, Staffs B77 2AS

Commission Plongée Souterraine
President: C. Locatelli, 94 rue Michelet, 01 100 Oyonnax

Federation Française De Speleologie
130, rue Saint – Maur, Paris – XIe.

National Speleological Society
Cave Avenue, Huntsville, Alabama, 35810, U.S.A.

Aflo   A hand-held device incorporating equipment for underwater lighting, navigation (compass) and line-laying. Its use was abandoned in the late 1950s.

Alkali   A substance having strong basic properties (i.e. anti-acid). Strong alkalis are caustic (burning) and absorb carbon dioxide.

Amphibian   See Oxygen Rebreathing.

Anoxia   Acute lack of oxygen, leading to death.

Aqualung   An open-circuit breathing apparatus which in normal use is fed with compressed air. For deep diving mixed gas may be used. The supply to the diver is controlled by a demand valve which only releases gas when the diver inhales. Each exhaled breath is blown to waste in the water.

Aven   A localised vertical development in a cave passage.

Belay   A fixed object, such as a large rock or boulder, to which the line is attached.

'Bends'(Caisson's Disease)   A condition which seriously affects divers who are subjected to a sudden decrease in pressure. It is due to the formation of nitrogen bubbles in the bloodstream. This occurs when the gas comes rapidly out of solution as the pressure drops. The bubbles then travel in the blood to lodge in the arm or leg joints or, more seriously, in the vital organs.

Bottom walking   Walking along the bottom of an underwater passage. The diver normally wears lead-weighted boots to maintain contact with the floor. This technique was abandoned by the early 1960s.

Breathing drill   A technique associated with closed-circuit apparatus, whereby the diver expels nitrogen from his breathing bag and lungs before the start of a dive.

Caplamp   A miner's lamp fixed to a helmet. It takes its power from a rechargeable battery worn at the back of the waist.

Carbide   The substance, usually in solid form, used as fuel in a carbide lamp. It reacts with a regulated water supply to produce acetylene gas. This is inflammable and produces light.

Caustic solution   A substance that exerts a corroding or burning action on skin and flesh; a strong alkali.

Cave Rescue Organisation   A body of people dedicated to the rescue of those in distress underground.

Closed-Circuit   See Oxygen Rebreathing.

Cocktail   Incursion of caustic solution into the respiratory system with extremely damaging results.

Controller   A member of the support party who monitors the movements of the divers.

Cylinder   A tubular container capable of withstanding the very high pressure of a diver's breathing supply. Normally made of steel.

Decompression   The gradual reduction of pressure on returning to the surface (normal atmospheric pressure) from depth. This causes dissolved gases (mainly nitrogen in the case of a compressed air dive) to be released from the blood.

Demand Valve   A precision instrument which releases gas from the breathing supply only when the diver inhales through his mouthpiece.

Depth   In a caving context this refers to the overall depth reached below the level of the cave entrance; in a cave diving context it is the depth reached below the water's surface. q.v. Depth Gauge.

Depth Gauge   An instrument designed to register the diver's depth at any given time.

Diver's Log   A personal record of a dive, giving for example, equipment used, time spent underwater and results.

Doline   A collapse into an underground cave.

Dry Suit   A waterproof diving dress. It is usually underlaid with warm clothing to provide thermal insulation.

D.S.E.A.   See Oxygen Rebreathing.

Duck   A cave passage almost filled with water but with an airspace of several centimetres remaining.

Duration   The length of time spent below water.

Elbow   The lowest point in a sump.

Embolism   In diving technology this means the rupture of the lung tissue caused by failure to exhale a sufficient volume of gas consistent with one's speed of ascent.

Fins   Flat, ribbed sheets of moulded rubber, similar to a fish's fins. They are attached to the diver's feet and are used to aid propulsion.

Free-diving   Passing a sump without the aid of breathing apparatus.

Hooter   A mechanical device, similar to a car horn, used to attract another diver's attention under water.

Hyper-ventilation   A technique whereby one takes a series of deep breaths in rapid succession, thereby flushing carbon dioxide out of the respiratory system.

Hypoxia   Shortage of oxygen.

Lead weight   A piece of moulded lead, normally fashioned for threading on to a belt. It is used to counteract the diver's natural buoyancy.

Lightweight diving equipment   Equipment specially designed for ease of carriage through difficult caves.

Line   A thin rope or wire which the diver lays as a route marker.

Line reel   A simple spool or spindle used to lay out and (in later models) retrieve diving line.

Lip   The edge of a precipice.

Mask   A plate of glass or perspex set into a rubber housing and fixed by rubber straps to the face. The layer of air trapped between the face and the front plate gives the diver greatly improved visibility.

Mixture   A combination of gases forming the diver's breathing supply.

Narcosis   Drowsiness or euphoria induced by diving to depths in excess of 30 metres. Individuals have varying tolerance.

Nitrogen   An inert gas comprising 80% of the air which we breathe.

Open Circuit   A breathing apparatus normally fed with compressed air (for deeper dives mixed gas is used), in which each exhaled breath is blown to waste in the water.

Oxygen poisoning   This is induced when a diver breathing pure oxygen (in early forms of rebreathing apparatus) descends below 10 metres depth. It often takes the form of sudden blackout, the individual being completely unaware of any warning symptoms. The hazard may also be induced with open circuit compressed-air apparatus below a depth of 90 metres. Oxygen poisoning takes effect when the partial pressure of the gas exceeds two atmospheres.

Oxygen rebreathing   A form of breathing apparatus in which exhaled gases are returned to the apparatus for re-use. Several forms of ex-War Department equipment were modified for use in caves after 1945, the principal ones being:

A.T.E.A.	Amphibian Tank Escape Apparatus
D.S.E.A.	Davis Submerged Escape Apparatus
P. Party	Port party long duration closed-circuit apparatus
Salvus	A dual purpose, fire-fighting and diving apparatus
S.E.B.A.	Submarine Escape Breathing Apparatus
S.G.A. Mk.2	Siebe Gorman Amphibian Mark 2
U.B.A.	Universal Breathing Apparatus

This apparatus was rendered obsolete by the early 1960s.

A new generation of rebreathers has appeared in recent years:
The Speleo-Twin Rebreather designed and constructed by Jochen Hasenmayer in 1980.
The Carmellan Rebreather, first used for cave exploration in 1987.
The Cis-Lunar Rebreather designed and constructed by Dr. Bill Stone, which received its first field test at Wakulla in 1987.
The RI 2000 semi-closed rebreather designed and constructed by Alain Ronjat and Olivier Isler. This went into operational use in 1990.

Pit/Pitch   A vertical section of cave, normally passed with the use of a ladder or rope.

Pressure gauge   An instrument designed to register the pressure in a diving cylinder, and therefore the approximate duration of the gas supply.

Resurgence   The point at which an underground stream or river reappears on the surface.

Rising   See Resurgence.

Sediment   The natural product of erosion. It can take the form of fine mud, silt, gravel or stones.

Self-contained diving apparatus   Equipment which allows the diver complete freedom of movement, without any restraints from his diving base.

Shallow water black-out   A hazard associated with closed-circuit apparatus. Apparently incorporating a psychological basis, the black-out can strike without warning.

Sherpa   A person who lends assistance with the transport of diving equipment, to and from the underground diving base.

Single Rope Technique   A technique whereby one descends and later ascends a shaft using specialist equipment in conjunction with a single rope.

Soda Lime   A chemical substance (calcium oxide – sodium hydroxide), used as a carbon dioxide absorbent.

Standard Equipment   An early form of diving apparatus involving the continuous supply of air from the surface. The diver himself was normally equipped with a dry suit, brass helmet and lead-weighted boots. He regulated the supply of air to his helmet by means of a pressure-release valve.

Streamway   A cave passage occupied by a flowing stream.

Sump   A cave passage completely filled with water, leaving no air space.

Siphon   A sump.

Third Rule   A prudent procedure whereby a diver begins his return to base after one third of his air supply has been used, thus leaving a wide margin of extra supply to set against any unexpected developments.

Traverse   Movement along a cave passage, normally in a horizontal plane, some distance above the floor.

U.B.A.   See Oxygen Rebreathing.

Uni-suit   A sophisticated form of dry suit, composed of neoprene. It is usually worn with a single layer of underclothes.

Valve   Part of the diver's breathing apparatus for regulating the flow of gas.

Wet suit   A skin-tight suit of foam neoprene rubber which provides thermal insulation but does not keep the diver dry.

continued from page 277

PETER VERHULSEL   Sterkfontein Cave, S. Africa, 1984
Open-water diver and sometime caver. During a modest dive he left line and got lost and reached an unexplored dry passage. Died at least three weeks later of starvation etc. as a result of serious errors in rescue strategy.

BILL McFADEN   Little Dismal Cave, Florida, USA, 1988
Experienced cave diver. Ran out of air after a sequence of stressful incidents. An accident that nearly took three lives.

ROBERTA SWICEGOOD
Arch Cave Spring, Pennsylvania, USA, 1988
Experienced cave diver. Ran out of air after severe line entanglement and (possibly) subsequent disorientation.

APPENDIX IV: ACCIDENT ANALYSIS

Fatalities involving British cave divers since 1934 plus other fatalities described in this book.

GORDON MARRIOTT Wookey Hole, Mendips, 1949
Experienced open-water diver but no cave diving experience. Died of anoxia while returning through known sump. He made some unexplained error, ran out of oxygen and then dropped his reserve cylinder which was not effectively attached to his equipment. *Result* Cave Diving Group updated its safety rules and issued directives concerning the use of reserve cylinders.

JACK WADDON Minneries Pool, Mendips, 1962
Experienced cave diver. Died of anoxia while training with experimental equipment. He made an error in adjusting his regulator and this led to oxygen starvation. No line-connection to the surface. *Result* The transition from closed-circuit equipment to open-circuit equipment was hastened.

ALAN CLEGG Lancaster Hole, Pennines, 1964
Experienced cave diver. While exploring new sump he lost his mouthpiece (which was not supported by a neckstrap) in a constricted space. *Result* Recommendations were made against the use of the twin-hose valve, which was considered too fragile, being easily severed and generally unsuitable for cave diving conditions.

ALAN ERITH Keld Head, Pennines, 1970
Inexperienced cave diver. Drowned while training in a complex, semi-explored resurgence. He appears to have lost direction and headed upstream, away from the entrance. No reserve system carried.

PAUL ESSER Porth yr Ogof, South Wales, 1971
Open-water diver with limited cave diving experience. Drowned while training and collecting line in known cave system. He mistakenly followed line up a partially explored passage, became over committed and had insufficient air left for a retreat.

ROGER SOLARI Agen Allwedd, South Wales, 1974
Experienced cave diver. Drowned while making a rapid return from a bold exploratory push. It appears that Solari became entangled in the line, possibly while changing to his reserve air supply. An accident that underlined the importance of 'Third Rule', neutral buoyancy and optimum physical fitness.

JOHN SMITH Merlin's Pipe, Derbyshire, 1974
Cave diver with limited experience. Ran out of air while returning through muddy constricted passage.

DEREK TRINGHAM Cueva de Vegalonga, Spain, 1976
Experienced cave diver. Disappeared while exploring a downstream sump. Line reel (not fully run out) discovered after extensive searches, but no sign of the diver.

MIKE NELSON Ilam Rising, Derbyshire, 1977
Cave diver with limited experience. Drowned while exploring a new sump. He appears to have lost his line in poor visibility and then run out of air very quickly, probably as a result of mounting stress.

IAN PLANT Bull Pot of the Witches, Cumbria, 1980
Experienced cave diver. Lost line in poor visibility and ran out of air.

MARK WOODHOUSE Keld Head, Pennines, 1980
Novice cave diver. Became severely disoriented, temporarily lost line and panicked. Drowned within a few metres of the 100 metre air bell.

DAVID WOODS Pollnacrom, N. Ireland, 1981
Experienced cave diver. Suffered an acute "valve failure" (grit caused free flow) in an extremely constricted, silty sump. Victim drowned less than two metres from air.

KEITH POTTER Wookey Hole, Mendips, 1981
Cave diver with limited experience. Apparently lost mouthpiece and drowned just a few metres from the airsurface in Chamber 20.

DEREK CROSSLAND Hurtle Pot, Pennines, 1985
Experienced cave diver. During solo dive to test gear, died in mysterious circumstances just a short distance from the surface.

NICK WHAITE Unnamed Cave, Barbondale, Cumbria, 1988
Novice cave diver. Lost sense of direction and drowned while exploring an extremely constricted sump without a line. Body discovered 10 metres from the surface.

A comprehensive listing of overseas accidents would be both exhausting and repetitive. Those incidents that are recorded in the book are listed, however, as having some cautionary element that might be instructive.

HENRI LOMBARD Lirou Cave, Montpellier, France, 1950
Experienced cave diver. Died while returning through a short sump, possibly as a result of chilling.

RANDY HYLTON Florida, USA, 1965
Experienced cave diver. Believed to have suffered a heart attack while trying to extricate himself from a line entanglement at a depth of forty-seven metres.

ADOLF HOLDER Blautopf, Blaubeuren, Germany, 1966
Club member miscalculated his air supply – his main cylinder developed a fault and his back up bottle was empty.

JOHN CARCELLE Benjamin's Blue Hole, Bahamas, 1971
Inexperienced diver. Panicked at a depth of fifty-five metres. Acted irrationally and used up air.

FRANK MARTZ Benjamin's Blue Hole, Bahamas, 1971
Experienced cave diver. Disappeared at −90m while conducting a deep diving exploration.

ARCHIE FORFAR & ANNE GUNDERSON
 Stafford Creek, Bahamas, 1971
Experienced open-water divers. Despite precautions both died attempting an open-water depth record. Became unconscious as a result of oxygen poisoning and sank. Exley, supporting, also blacked out but recovered.

UNKNOWN Uncle Charlie's Blue Hole, Bahamas, c.1979
Ill-equipped open-water diver. Appears to have become disorientated (no line or reserve air supply) and ran out of air while trying to find an escape route. *continued at foot of page 276*

APPENDIX V: THE LONGEST AND THE DEEPEST CAVES

Note: Although caves are listed in length order, this has reduced significance as conditions and techniques greatly effect diving difficulties.

LONGEST CAVE DIVES (assessed as total underwater distance from base)

cave	country	length/depth	sumps	continues?	diver(s) (*scooter assisted)
Cocklebiddy Cave	Australia	5290m (−30m)	3	continues/tight	H. Morrison, R. Allum, P. Rogers 1983
Cathedral Canyon	USA	3334m (−60m)	1	continues	* S. Exley, 1990
Chip's Hole Cave	USA	3183m (−41m)	1	continues	S. Exley, 1989
La Doux de Coly	France	3100m (−57m)	1	continues	* O. Isler & GLPS, 1984
La Source du Bestouan	France	2665m (−32m)	1	continues	* M. Douchet, 1990
Trou Madame	France	2510m (−18m)	9	blocked	F. Le Guen & Speleo Club of Paris, 1978
NoHoch Nah Chich	Mexico	2438m (−14m)	2	continues	M. Madden, S. Gerrard, J.J. Tucat, 1987
Friedman Sink (Manatee Springs)	USA	2342m (−30m)	1	blocked	B. Main, B. Gavin, 1987†
Cogol dei Veci	Italy	2340m (−54m)	1	continues	* O. Isler & Swiss/Italian team, 1990
Emergence de Bourne	France	2250m (−43m)	7	continues	* O. Isler & GLPS, 1982
Pannikin Plains Cave	Australia	2150m (−32m)	4	semi blocked	* A. Wight, C. Brown, R. Allum, 1988
Hornsby Sink	USA	2055m (−58m)	1	continues	* S. Exley, C. Pitcairn, 1982
Emergence du Ressel	France	1860m (−70m)	1	continues	* O. Isler, 1990
Sullivan Sink (upstream)	US	1828m (−40m)	1	continues	B. Main, B. Gavin, 1987
Big Dismal Sink	USA	1782m (−48m)	1	continues	S. Exley, C. Pitcairn, M. Eckhoff, 1981
Source de la Loue	France	1720m (−48m)	1	blocked	* O. Isler & GLPS, 1985
Creux Jannin	France	1720m (−20m)	1	continues/tight	* F. Le Guen, 1987
Font del Truffe	France	1710m (−30m)	11	continues	P. Penez, F. Vergier, 1983
Fraits Puits	France	1690m (−33m)	1	continues	F. Le Guen, 1989
Port Miou	France	1670m (−80m)	1	continues	B. Leger, 1982-83
Jameos del Agua (Atlantida Tunnel)	Canaries	1618m (−64m)	1	blocked	* O. Isler & GLPS, 1986
Grotte de Pacques	France	1570m (−30m)	4	blocked	B. Leger, 1980
Buwe Marino	Sardinia	1550m (−50m)	8	continues	J. Hasenmayer, 1977
Blue Springs (Jackson Co.)	USA	1545m (−38m)	1	ends	S. Exley, P. DeLoach, 1979
Fontaine de St. George	France	1520m (−76m)	2	continues	C. Brandt & GLPS, 1987‡
Madison Blue	USA	1497m (−37m)	1	ends	S. Exley, P. DeLoach, 1980
Indian Springs	USA	1387m (−91m)	1	continues	S. Exley, J. Stone, 1982
Hole in the Wall Spring	USA	1328m (−30m)	1	blocked	S. Exley, D. Sweet, 1978
Grotte de Mescla	France	1275m (−80m)	3	continues	* F. Le Guen, 1988
Fontaine de Nimes	France	1275m (−40m)	1	continues	B. Leger, 1980
Wakulla Springs	USA	1273m (−98m)	1	continues	* W. Skiles, T. Morris, P. Heinerth, 1987
Blautopf	Germany	1250m (−45m)	1	continues	J. Hasenmayer, 1985
Source de Landenouze	France	1240m (−88m)	1	continues	J. Hasenmayer, 1981
Devil's Eye Spring	USA	1219m (−30m)	1	continues	W. Skiles, T. Morris, W. Jasper, 1986
Emergence de la Finou	France	1190m (−33m)	5	continues	F. Le Guen, 1989

† *This final advance, 5m more than Exley's and Pitcairn's 1981 limit, was made up a minor side passage.*   ‡ *Later explored 400m further along a dry passage by F. Le Guen.*

DEEPEST KNOWN CAVE DIVES

Nacimiento del Rio Mante	Mexico	−267m		S. Exley, 1989
Fontaine de Vaucluse	France	−205m	Modexa −315m	J. Hasenmayer, 1983
Touvre D'Angouleme	France	−148m		O. Isler, 1990
Goul du Pont	France	−140m		J. Schneider, 1986
Emergence de la Chaudanne	Switzerland	−140m	608m from base	C. Brandt, 1988
Fontaine des Chartreux	France	−137m		C. Touloumdjian, 1989
Guinas Lake	Namibia	−132m		B. Scheun, E. Benade, 1988
Cenote Xkolac	Mexico	−128m	plumbed to −130m	P. DeLoach, S. Exley, 1990
Bushmansgat	South Africa	−123m	plumbed to −264m	N. Gomes, D. Hanekom, 1988
Lighthouse Reef Blue Hole	Belize	−125m		* Falco & Laban (in mini sub)
Sorgente del Elephante Bianco	Italy	−122m		J. J. Bolanz, 1987
Gorgazzo	Italy	−119m		J. J. Bolanz, 1987
Font D'Estramar	France	−115m		C. Touloumdjian, 1988
Goul de la Tannerie	France	−113m	−125m observation	B. Leger, 1982
Wakulla Springs	USA	−111m	c.900m from base	* W. Skiles, T. Morris, P. Heinerth, 1987
Hranicka Abiss	Czechoslovakia	−110m	−254m echo sounded	L. Benyesek, F. Travenek

Cenote Ucil	Mexico	−110m		S. Exley, 1989
Die Polder 2	USA	−110m		D. Sweet, 1980 (mixed gas); S. Exley (comp. air)
Mystery Sink	USA	−109m	−119m echo sounded	H. Watts, 1970
Boiling Hole	Bahamas	−103m		S. Exley, 1977
Grotte de Môtiers	Switzerland	−102m		J. J. Bolanz, 1985
Notre Dame des Anges	France	−102m		C. Touloumdjian, 1986
Sinoia Caves	Zimbabwe	−102m		R. Nyman, I. Robertson, J. & D. van der Walt, 1969
Olhos de Agua do Aliviela	Portugal	−101m		P. Jolivet, 1989
Great North Road	Bahamas	−100m		S. Clough, R. Palmer, 1989

Other deep caves with measured depths include: Crveno Jezero, Yugoslavia (plumbed to −249m); Red Snapper Sink (echo sounded to −183m and dived to 93m)

LONGEST UNDERWATER TRAVERSES *(in America and Britain)*

Sullivan – Cheryl Sink	USA	2591m (−73m)	* B. Main, P. Turner, L. English, B. Gavin, 1988
King Pot – Keld Head	GB	3100m (−30m)	G. Crossley, G. Yeadon, 1991 (August)

Most Extensive Underwater Cave Systems: Cathedral Canyon (USA) 10668m; **Lucayan Caverns** (Bahamas) 10058m; **Sullivan Sink** (USA) 9754m; **Naharon/Mayan** (Mexico) 8000m; **Peacock Springs** (USA) 7100m; **Cueva Quebrada** (Mexico) 5000m; **Manatee Springs** (USA) 3978m; **Wakulla Springs** (USA) 3310m.

APPENDIX VI: SELECTED BIBLIOGRAPHY

Entries marked with an asterisk are books. Other entries are articles, reports etc.

* F.G. Balcombe, P. Powell and others *The Log of the Wookey Hole Exploration Expedition* Published privately (limited edition). 1935
F.G. Balcombe *Swildon's Hole* British Caver No. 1. 1937
F.G. Balcombe *C.D.G. Report on Operations in Keld Head, Alum Pot, Goydon Pot* British Caver XIV. 1946
F.G. Balcombe *C.D.G. Operation Prehistory, Wookey Hole* Br. Caver XV. 1946
F.G. Balcombe *Swildon's III* Journal of Wessex Cave Club, No. 47. 1954
* E. Bauer *The Mysterious World of Caves* Collins, London. 1971
G.J. Benjamin *Diving into the Blue Holes of the Bahamas* National Geographic, Vol. 138, No. 3. 1970
J.M. Boon *Cave Diving on Air* C.D.G. Technical Review No. 1. 1966
* J.M. Boon *Down to a Sunless Sea* Stalactite Press, Edmonton, Alberta. 1977
* Robert F. Burgess *The Cave Divers* Dodd Mead & Co., New York. 1976.
* Norbert Casteret *Ten Years Under The Earth* Dent, London. 1939
* Norbert Casteret *My Caves* Dent, London. 1947
* Norbert Casteret *More Years Under The Earth* Spearman, London. 1962
Caves & Caving Bulletin of the British Cave Research Association
Caving International Magazine Nos. 1-14, Edmonton, Alberta
D.A. Coase *Stoke Lane II* British Caver XVI. 1947
* J. Cordingley *The Peak Cavern System – A Caver's Guide* Vitagraph Ltd.
* J.Y Cousteau with Frederic Dumas *The Silent World* Hamish Hamilton, London 1953, Harper, New York. 1953
* Roger Cowles *The Making of the Severn Valley Railway Tunnel* Alan Sutton, Gloucester. 1989 (describes Alexander Lambert's dives of the 1880s)
* C.D. Cullingford *British Caving* Routledge & Keegan Paul, London. 1953
* P. Davies *A Pictorial History of Swildon's Hole* Wessex Cave Club. 1975
R.E. Davies *Black Keld* Cave Science II, No. 13. 1950
R.E. Davies *Water at a Depth of −5 feet, Discovered by Diving in Peak Cavern* Nature CLXVI. 1950
R.E. Davies *Diving in the New Part of Peak Cavern* British Caver XXIII. 1952
R.E. Davies *Discovery of Wookey 13* Wessex Cave Club Journal, No. 54. 1956
* Sir R.H. Davies *Deep Diving and Submarine Operations* De Montfort Press. 1935
Descent Magazine, Ambit Publishing, Gloucester
Leo Dickinson *Anything is Possible* Jonathan Cape, London. 1989
R. Ellis, J. Martini & M. Sefton *A Report on the Events Surrounding the Search for Mr. P. Verhulsel at Sterkfontein Tourist Cave* South African Spelaeological Association
S. Exley *Basic Cave Diving – A Blueprint for Survival* Cave Diving Section of the National Speleological Society, Jacksonville, Florida
* S. Exley & India Young *N.S.S. Cave Diving Manual* The Cave Diving Section of the National Speleological Society, Jacksonville, Florida. 1982
* Martyn Farr *The Darkness Beckons* Diadem Books, London. 1980
* Martyn Farr *The Great Caving Adventure* Oxford Illustrated Press, Yeovil. 1984
M. Gascoyne *Uranium – Series Ages of Speleothems from Bahamian Blue Holes* Cave Science, 11 (1). 1984
J.C. Gilbert *Peak Cavern, Buxton and Speedwell Waters* Cave Science II. 1949
W.R. Halliday *Depths of the Earth* Harper & Row, New York. 1976
M. Jasinski *Plongées Sous la Terre* Flammarion, Paris, 1965 (deals mainly with cave diving in Belgium and France)
Francis Le Guen *Down-Down-Under* Australian Geo. Mag, No. 5. 1985
* Guy de Lavaur *Caves and Cave Diving* Robert Hale, London. 1956
* I. Lewis and Peter Stace *Cave Diving in Australia* Published privately (I. Lewis)
O.C. Lloyd *A Cave Diver's Training Manual* C.D.G. Tech. Review No. 2. 1975
* Jim Lovelock *Life and Death Underground* Bell, London. 1963
Magazine (1) UIS Cave Diving Commission Ed. Alessio Fabbricatore, Via Fatebenefratelli 26, 34170 Gorizia, Italy
C. Maxwell *Cave Diving in South Africa* Maxwell, Cape Town. 1988
* J. Middleton & Tony Waltham *The Underground Atlas* Robert Hale, London
* Tom Mount *Safe Cave Diving* National Association for Cave Diving, U.S.A.
Newsletter Cave Diving Group of Great Britain
Newsletter Info Plongées Federation Francaise De Speleologie, Paris
Newsletter NACD News Gainsville, Florida
Newsletter The South Wales Caving Club
Newsletter Underwater Speleology Cave Diving Section of the N.S.S. Florida
* Rob Palmer *The Blue Holes of the Bahamas* Jonathan Cape, London. 1985
* Rob Palmer *Deep into Blue Holes* Unwin Hyman, London. 1989
* Rob Palmer and others *Cave Diving: The Cave Diving Group Manual* Mendip Publishing (Castle Carey Press). 1990
P. Raynes *Shallow Diving in Cave Exploration* British Caver, XV. 1946
* P. Rias *−1455 Metres et Apres?* Aventures Extraordinaires, France 1981
* D.I. Smith *Limestones and Caves of the Mendip Hills* David & Charles, Newton Abbott. 1975
* Dr. W. Stone *Wakulla Springs Project* National Speleological Society, Huntsville, Alabama. 1988
J.P. Thiry *Techniques de la Plongée Souterraine* Union de Speleologie Commission de Plongée, France. 1985
* Alan Thomas (editor) *The Last Adventure* Ina Books, Wells, Somerset. 1989
* T.A. Walker *The Severn Tunnel – Its Construction and Difficulties* Kingsmead Reprints, Bristol
* T.J. Waldron, J. Gleeson *The Frogmen* Pan Books, London. 1950
* A.C. Waltham *Caves* Macmillan, London. 1974
* A.C. Waltham *The World of Caves* Orbis Publishing Ltd. London. 1976
O.C. Wells *Deep Diving at Wookey* R.N. Diving Magazine, VI, No. 3. 1958
O.C. Wells *New Ground at Wookey Hole* Wessex Cave Club Journal, No. 68. 1958
O.C. Wells *Swildon's Five and Six* Wessex Cave Club Journal, No. 72. 1958
T.G. Yeadon *Line Laying and Following* Technical Review 3, Cave Diving Gr. 1981

INDEX